PRIMITIVE Boyfriend

3

art by

KO KITAFUKU

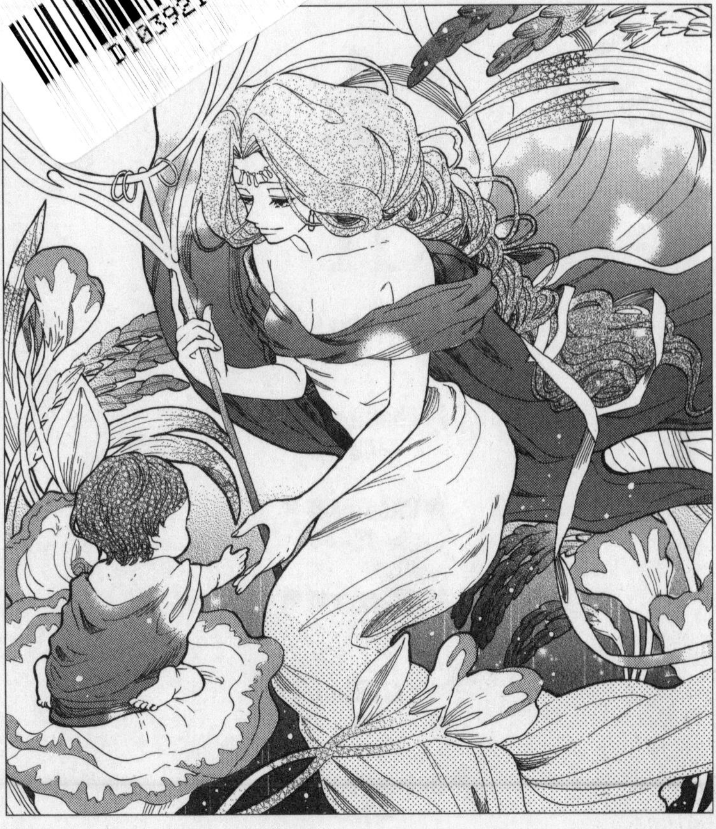

PRIMITIVE BOYFRIEND 3 CONTENTS

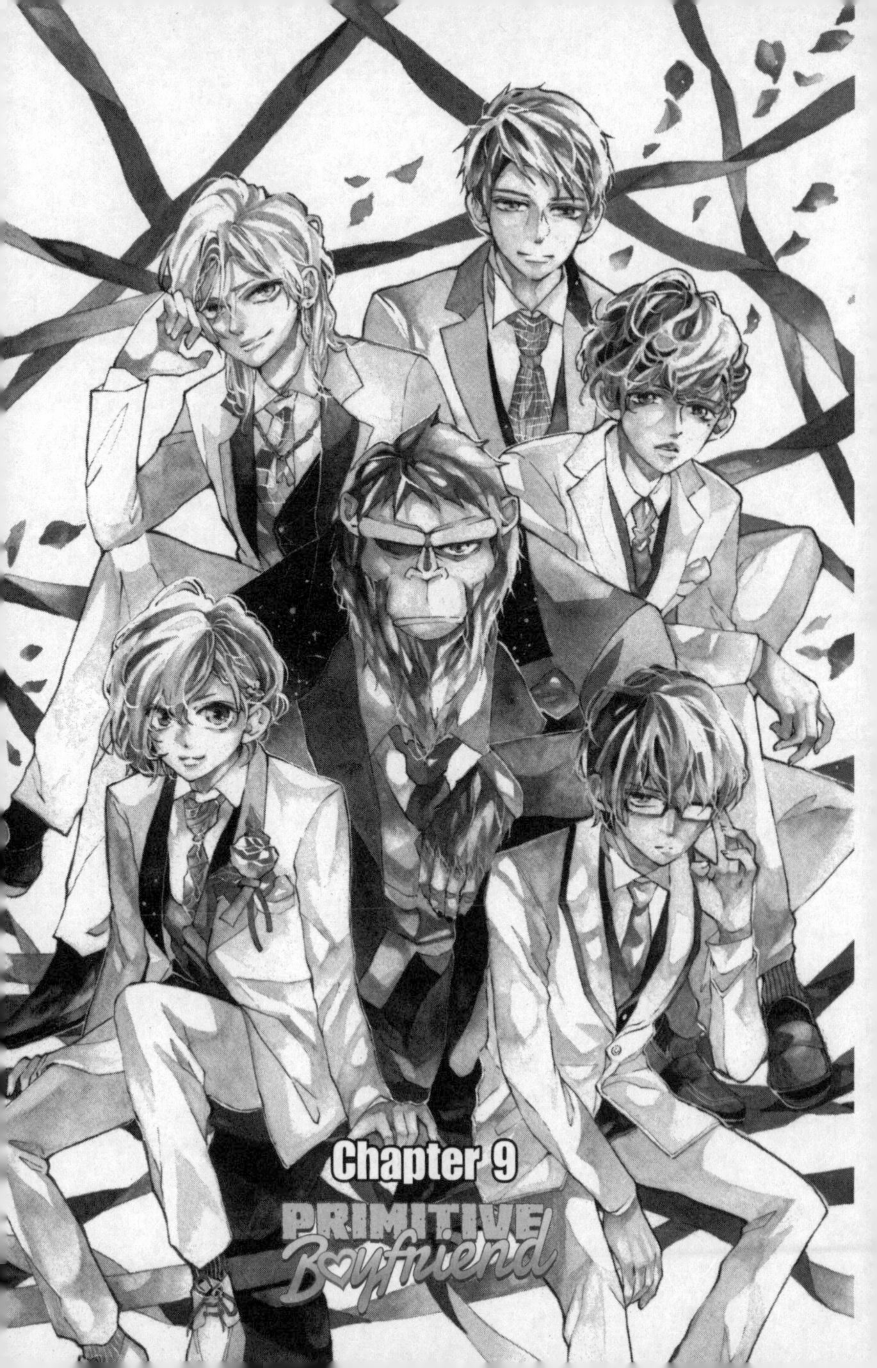
Chapter 9
PRIMITIVE
Boyfriend

PRIMITIVE BOYFRIEND by Yoshineko Kitafuku PRIMITIVE BOYFRIEND

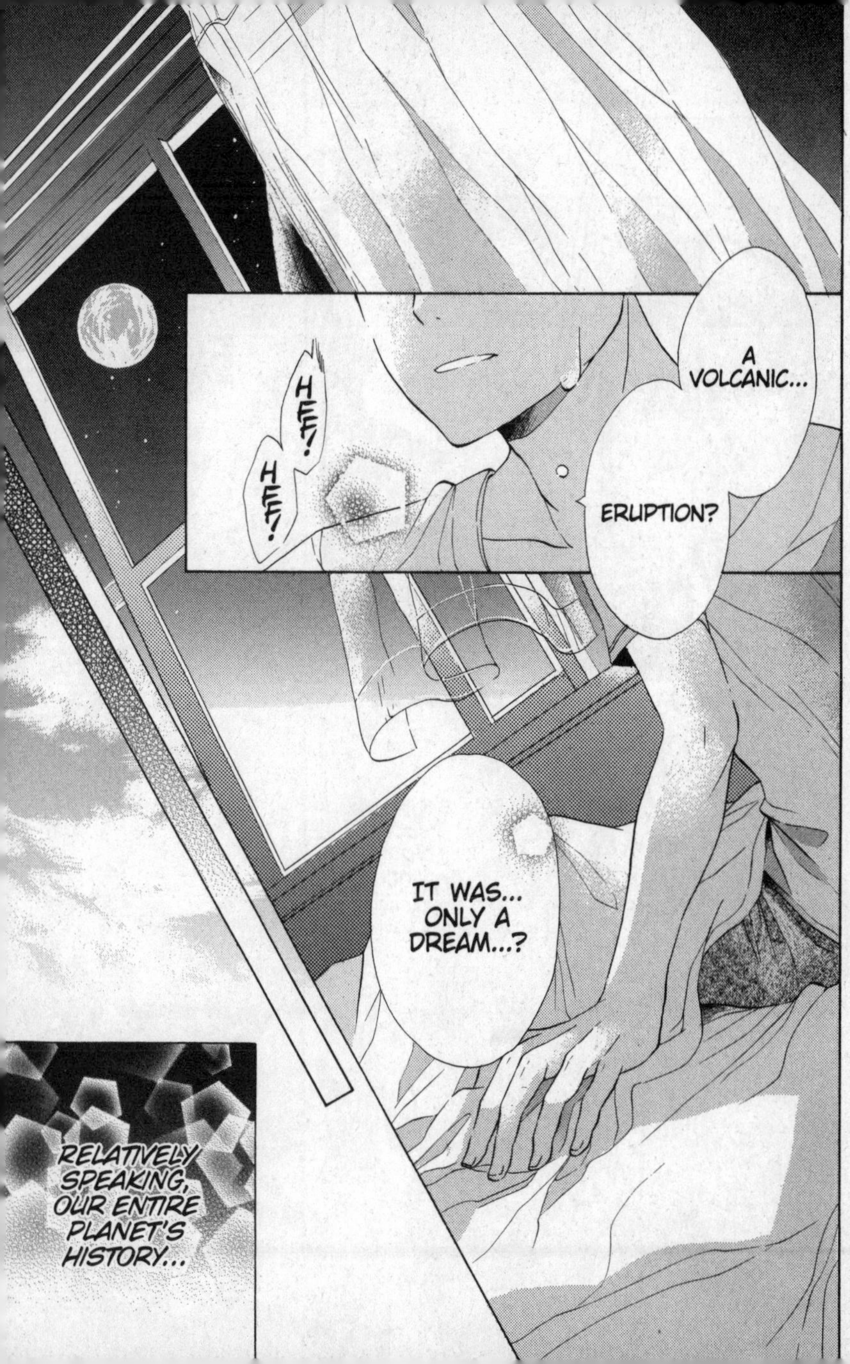
A VOLCANIC...
ERUPTION?
HEF! HEF!
IT WAS... ONLY A DREAM...?
RELATIVELY SPEAKING, OUR ENTIRE PLANET'S HISTORY...

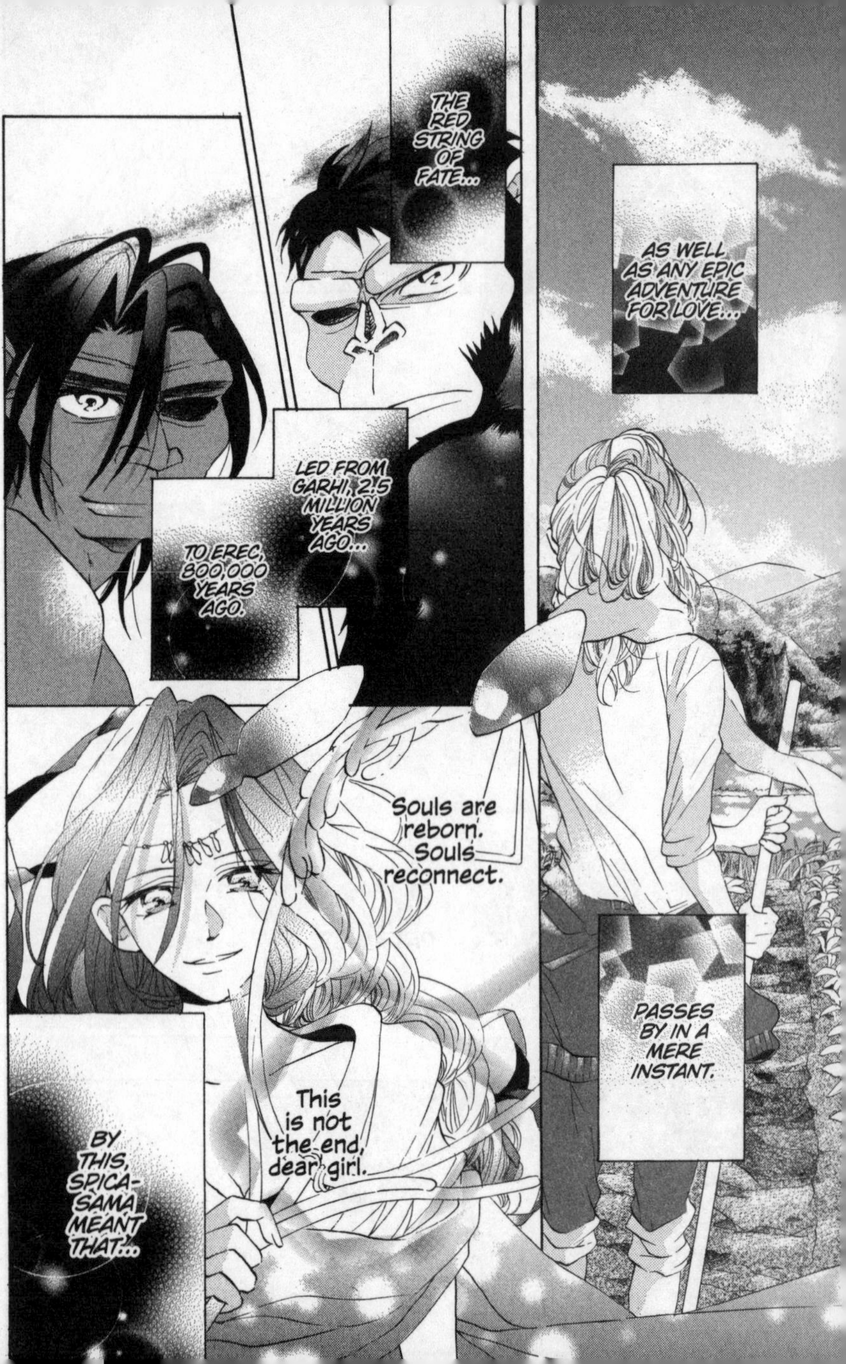
THE RED STRING OF FATE...
LED FROM GARHI, 2.5 MILLION YEARS AGO...
TO EREC, 800,000 YEARS AGO.
AS WELL AS ANY EPIC ADVENTURE FOR LOVE...
PASSES BY IN A MERE INSTANT.
Souls are reborn. Souls reconnect.
This is not the end, dear girl.
BY THIS, SPICA-SAMA MEANT THAT...

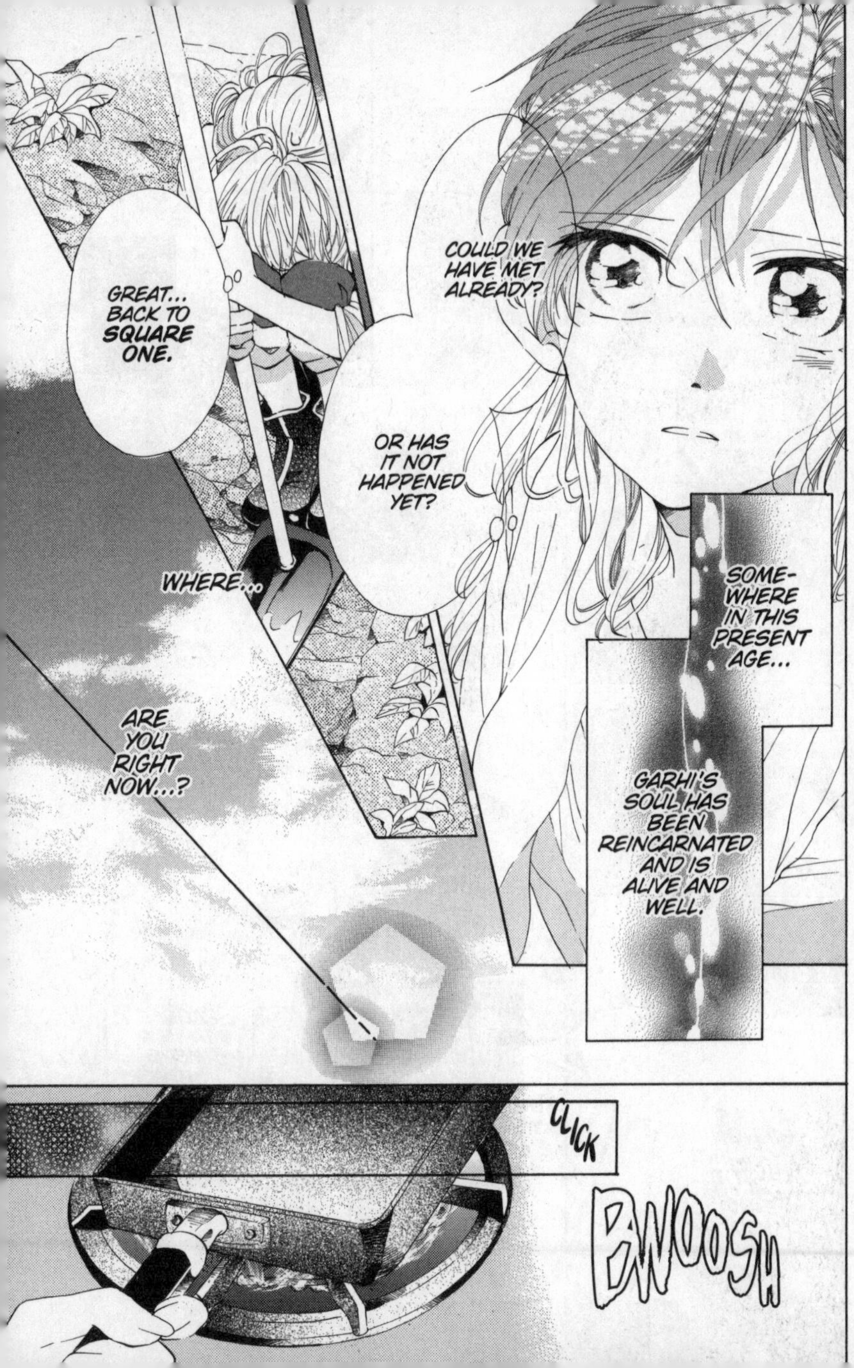
COULD WE HAVE MET ALREADY?
OR HAS IT NOT HAPPENED YET?
SOME-WHERE IN THIS PRESENT AGE...
GARHI'S SOUL HAS BEEN REINCARNATED AND IS ALIVE AND WELL.
GREAT... BACK TO SQUARE ONE.
WHERE...
ARE YOU RIGHT NOW...?
CLICK
BWOOSH

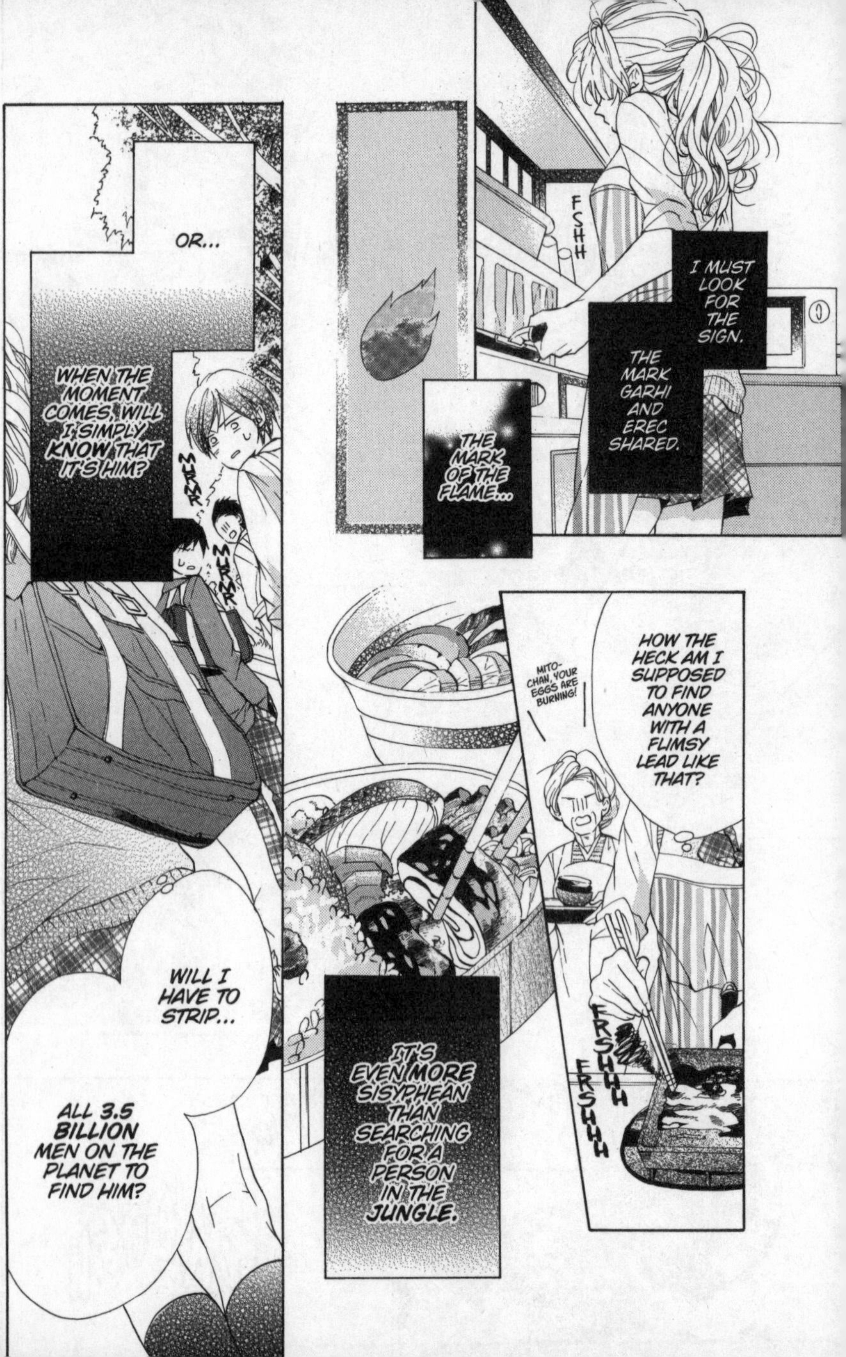
FSHH
I MUST LOOK FOR THE SIGN.
THE MARK GARHI AND EREC SHARED.
THE MARK OF THE FLAME...
HOW THE HECK AM I SUPPOSED TO FIND ANYONE WITH A FLIMSY LEAD LIKE THAT?
MITO-CHAN, YOUR EGGS ARE BURNING!
FRSHHH
FRSHHH
IT'S EVEN MORE SISYPHEAN THAN SEARCHING FOR A PERSON IN THE JUNGLE.
OR...
WHEN THE MOMENT COMES, WILL I SIMPLY KNOW THAT IT'S HIM?
MURMR
MURMR
WILL I HAVE TO STRIP...
ALL 3.5 BILLION MEN ON THE PLANET TO FIND HIM?

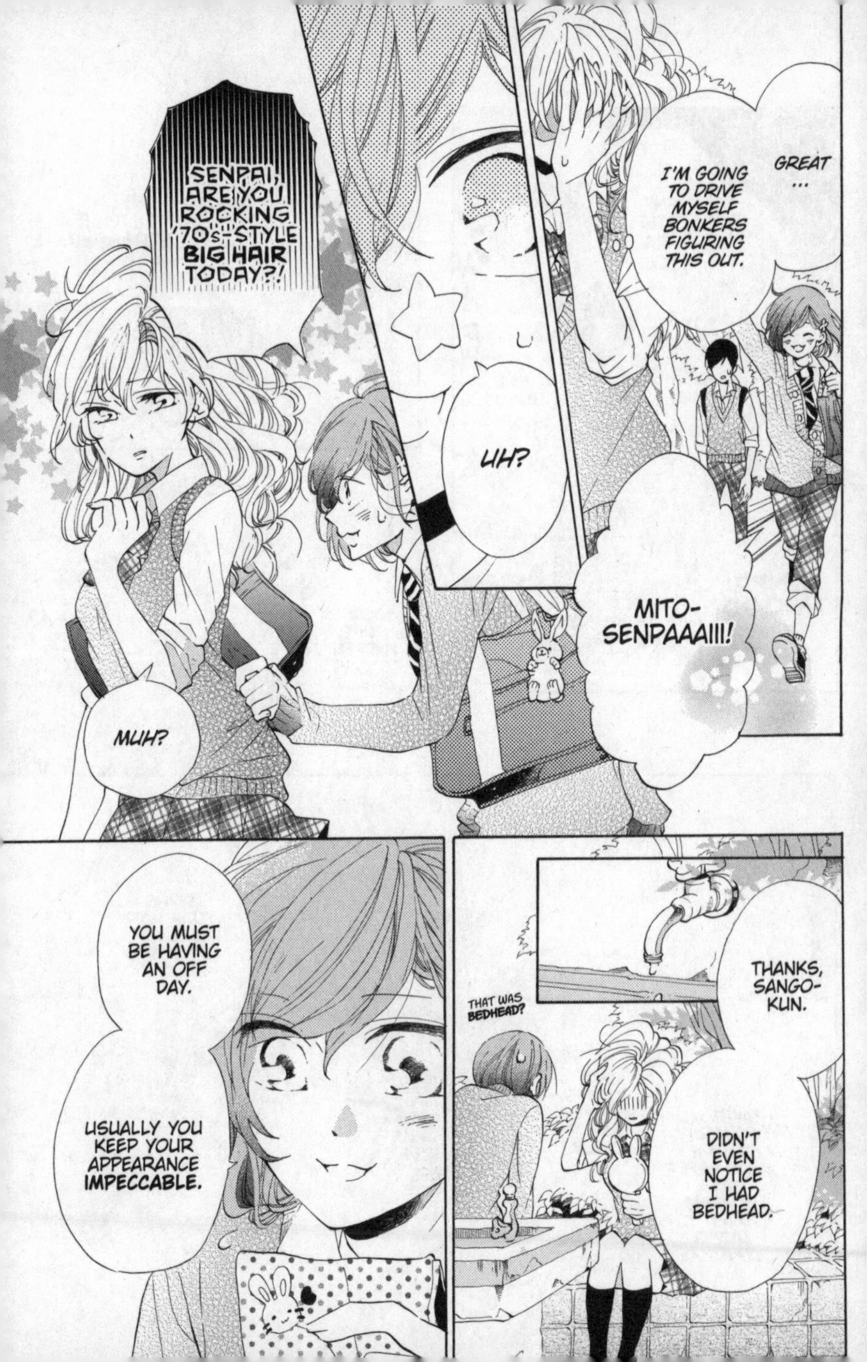
GREAT ...
I'M GOING TO DRIVE MYSELF BONKERS FIGURING THIS OUT.
MITO-SENPAAAIII!
UH?
SENPAI, ARE YOU ROCKING '70s-STYLE BIG HAIR TODAY?!
MUH?
THANKS, SANGO-KUN.
DIDN'T EVEN NOTICE I HAD BEDHEAD.
THAT WAS BEDHEAD?
YOU MUST BE HAVING AN OFF DAY.
USUALLY YOU KEEP YOUR APPEARANCE IMPECCABLE.

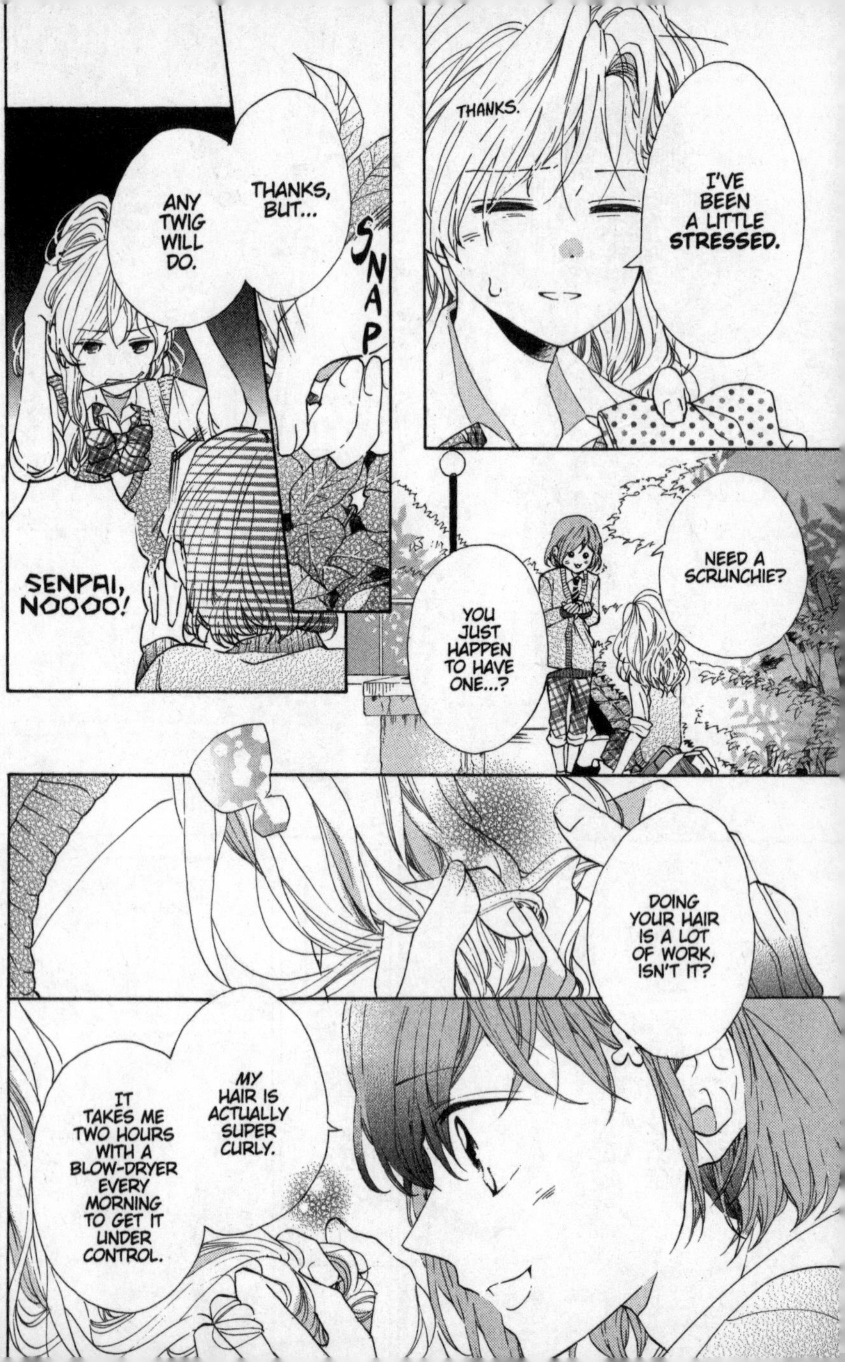
I'VE BEEN A LITTLE STRESSED.
THANKS.
NEED A SCRUNCHIE?
YOU JUST HAPPEN TO HAVE ONE...?
THANKS, BUT...
ANY TWIG WILL DO.
SNAP
SENPAI, NOOOO!
DOING YOUR HAIR IS A LOT OF WORK, ISN'T IT?
MY HAIR IS ACTUALLY SUPER CURLY.
IT TAKES ME TWO HOURS WITH A BLOW-DRYER EVERY MORNING TO GET IT UNDER CONTROL.

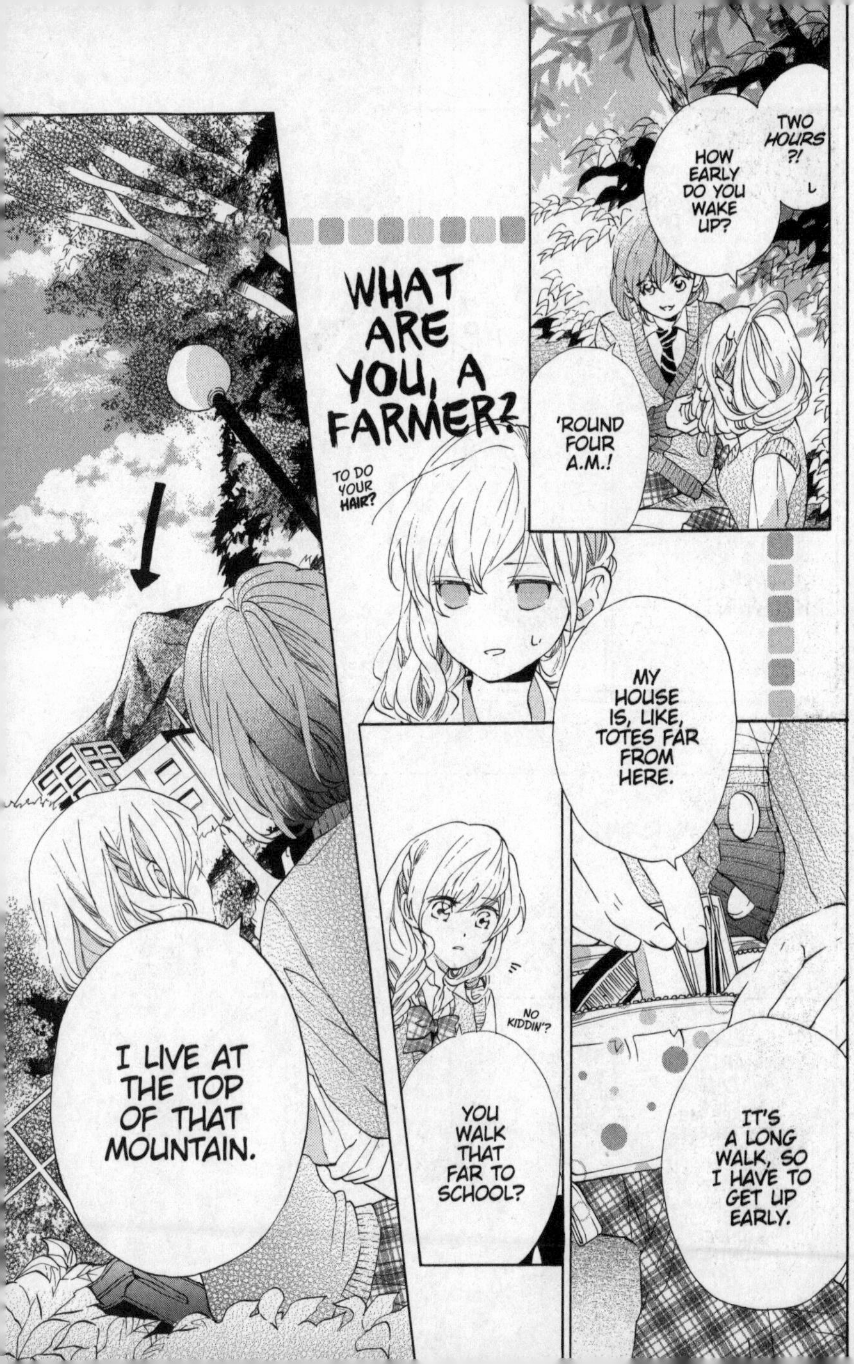
HOW EARLY DO YOU WAKE UP?
'ROUND FOUR A.M.!
TWO HOURS ?!
TO DO YOUR HAIR?
WHAT ARE YOU, A FARMER?
MY HOUSE IS, LIKE, TOTES FAR FROM HERE.
IT'S A LONG WALK, SO I HAVE TO GET UP EARLY.
NO KIDDIN'?
YOU WALK THAT FAR TO SCHOOL?
I LIVE AT THE TOP OF THAT MOUNTAIN.

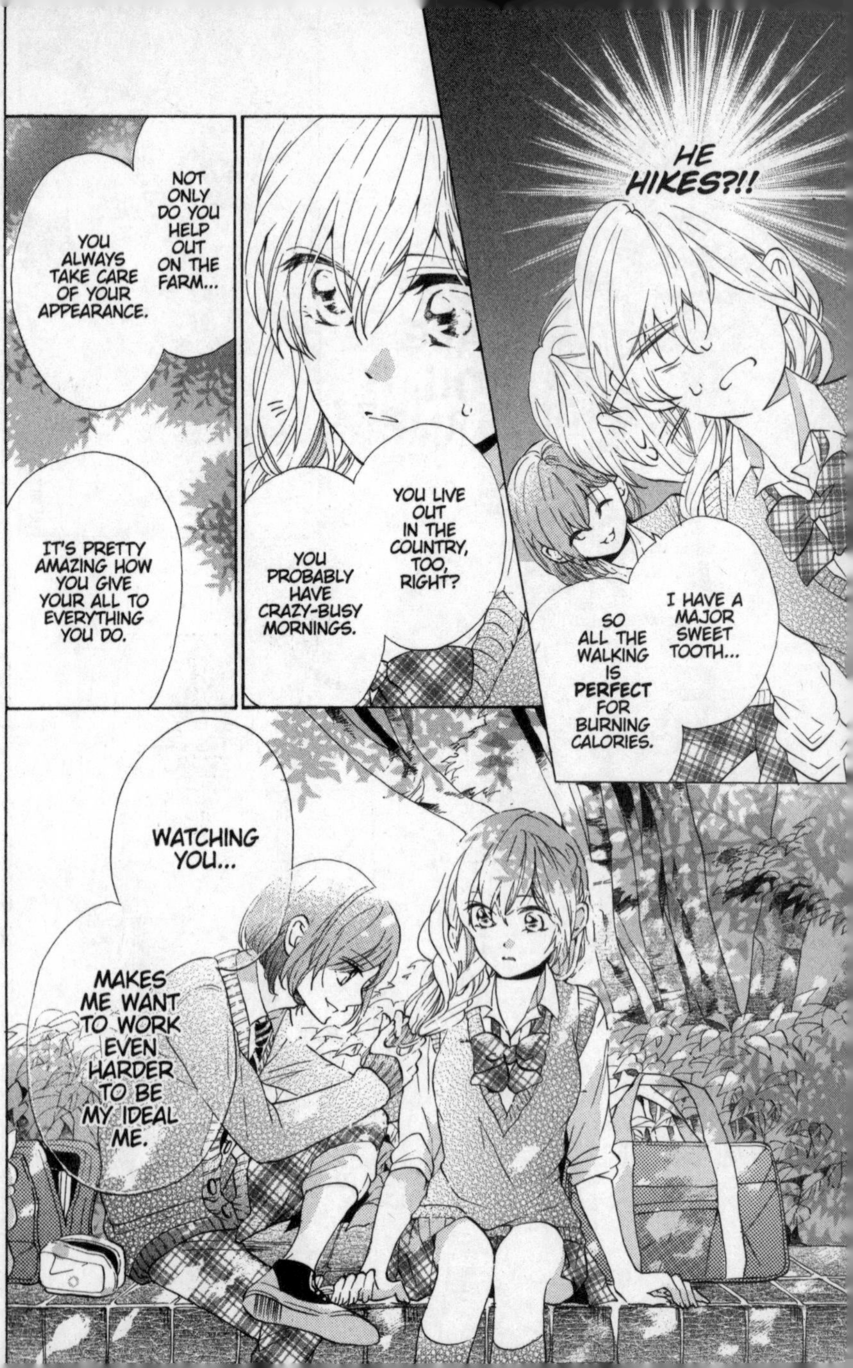
HE HIKES?!!
I HAVE A MAJOR SWEET TOOTH...
SO ALL THE WALKING IS PERFECT FOR BURNING CALORIES.
YOU LIVE OUT IN THE COUNTRY, TOO, RIGHT?
YOU PROBABLY HAVE CRAZY-BUSY MORNINGS.
NOT ONLY DO YOU HELP OUT ON THE FARM...
YOU ALWAYS TAKE CARE OF YOUR APPEARANCE.
IT'S PRETTY AMAZING HOW YOU GIVE YOUR ALL TO EVERYTHING YOU DO.
WATCHING YOU...
MAKES ME WANT TO WORK EVEN HARDER TO BE MY IDEAL ME.

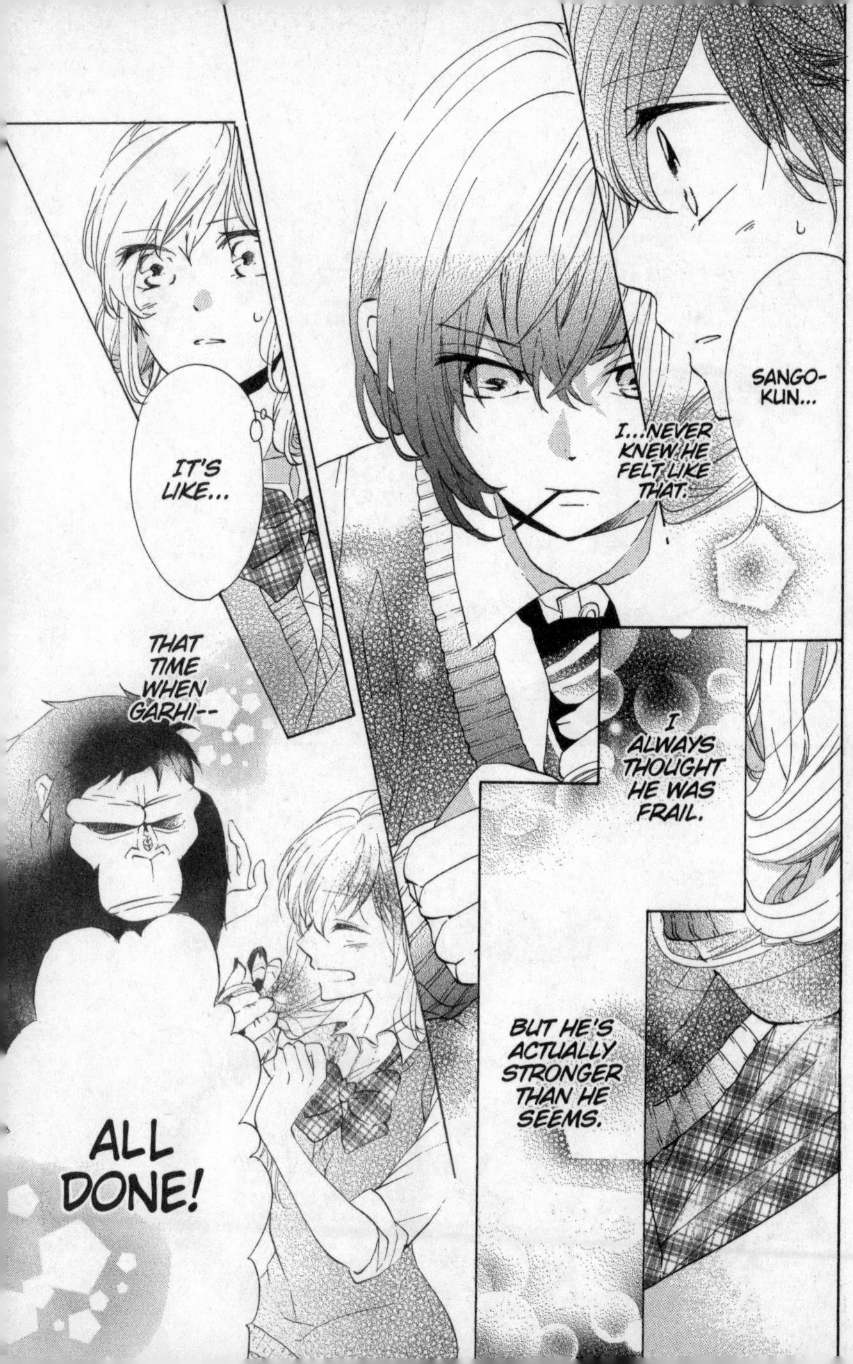
SANGO-KUN...
I...NEVER KNEW HE FELT LIKE THAT.
IT'S LIKE...
I ALWAYS THOUGHT HE WAS FRAIL.
BUT HE'S ACTUALLY STRONGER THAN HE SEEMS.
THAT TIME WHEN GARHI--
ALL DONE!

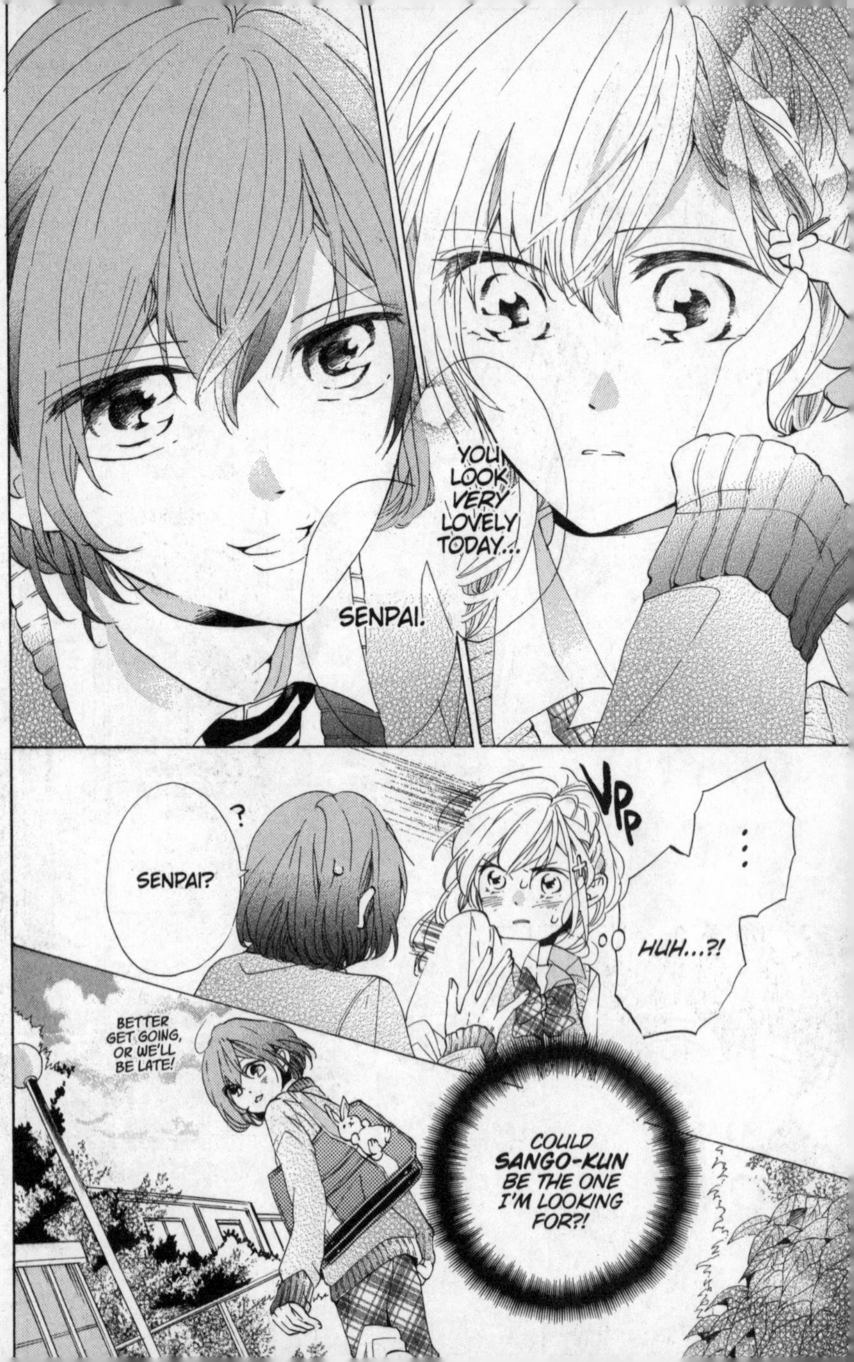

YOU LOOK VERY LOVELY TODAY...
SENPAI!
VPP
...
HUH...?!
?
SENPAI?
COULD SANGO-KUN BE THE ONE I'M LOOKING FOR?!
BETTER GET GOING, OR WE'LL BE LATE!

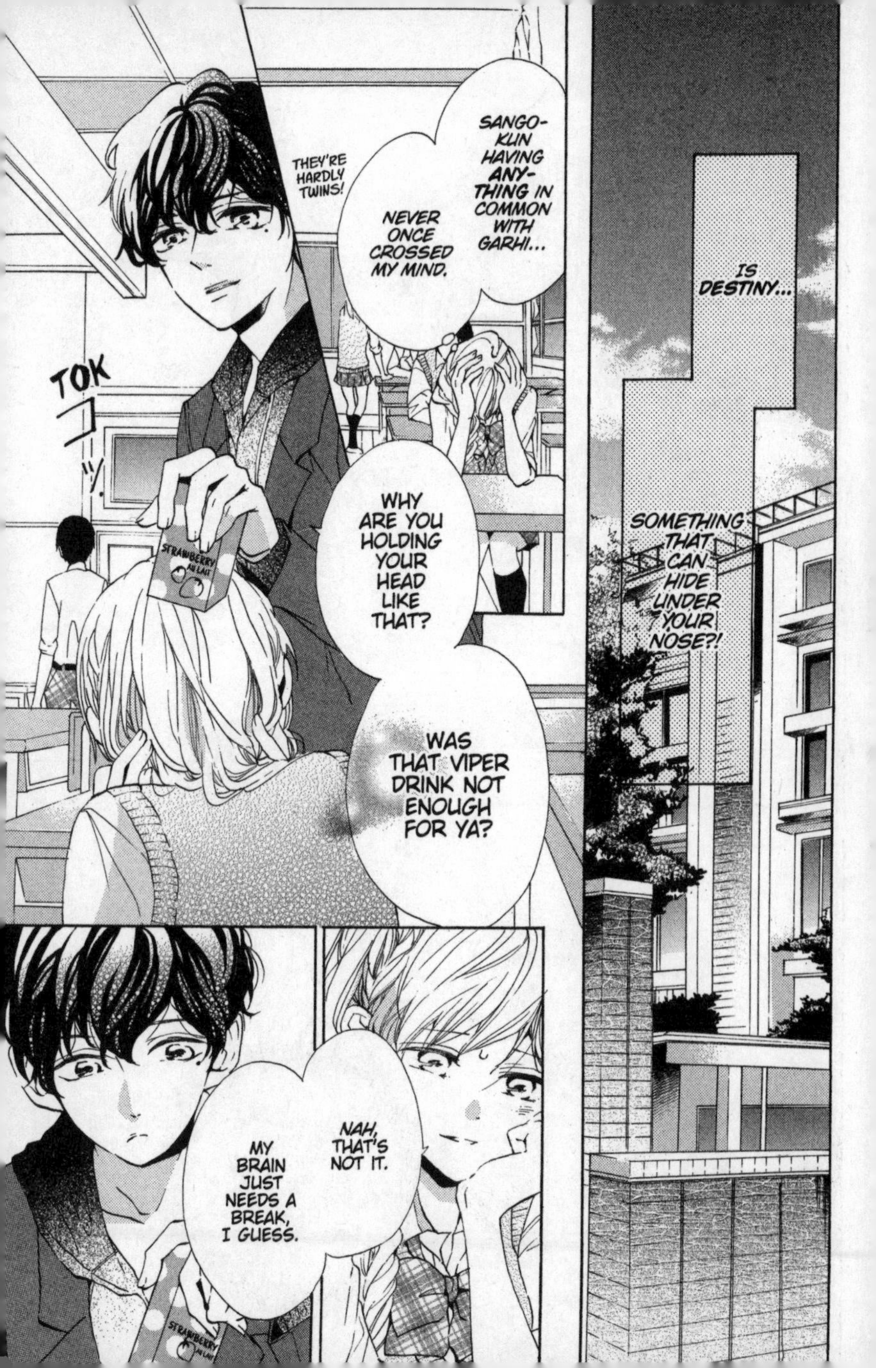
IS DESTINY...
SOMETHING THAT CAN HIDE UNDER YOUR NOSE?!
SANGO-KUN HAVING ANYTHING IN COMMON WITH GARHI...
NEVER ONCE CROSSED MY MIND.
THEY'RE HARDLY TWINS!
TOK
STRAWBERRY AU LAIT
WHY ARE YOU HOLDING YOUR HEAD LIKE THAT?
WAS THAT VIPER DRINK NOT ENOUGH FOR YA?
NAH, THAT'S NOT IT.
MY BRAIN JUST NEEDS A BREAK, I GUESS.
STRAWBERRY AU LAIT

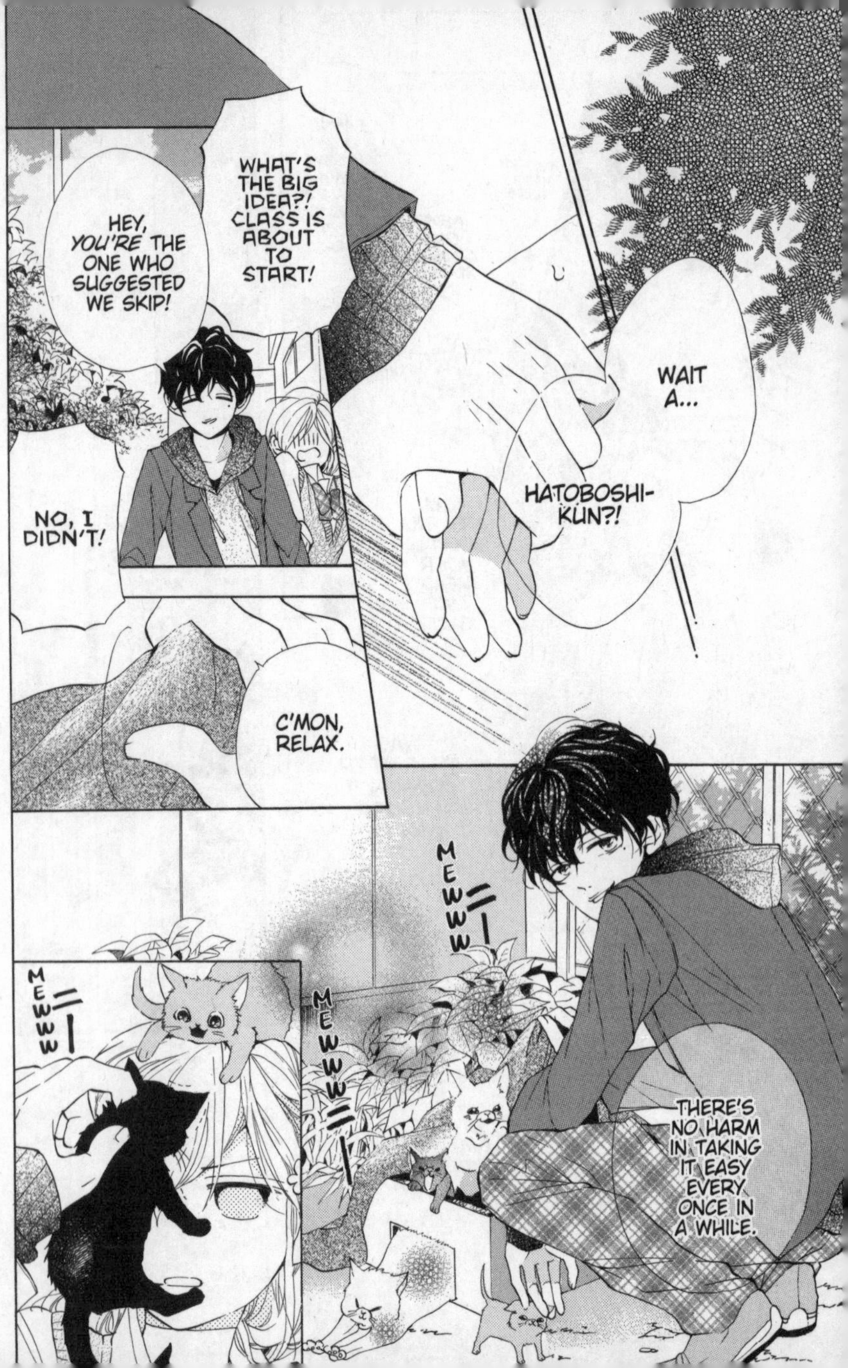

WAIT A...
HATOBOSHI-KUN?!
WHAT'S THE BIG IDEA?! CLASS IS ABOUT TO START!
HEY, *YOU'RE* THE ONE WHO SUGGESTED WE SKIP!
NO, I DIDN'T!
C'MON, RELAX.
THERE'S NO HARM IN TAKING IT EASY EVERY ONCE IN A WHILE.
MEWWW=!
MEWWWW=!
MEWWW=!

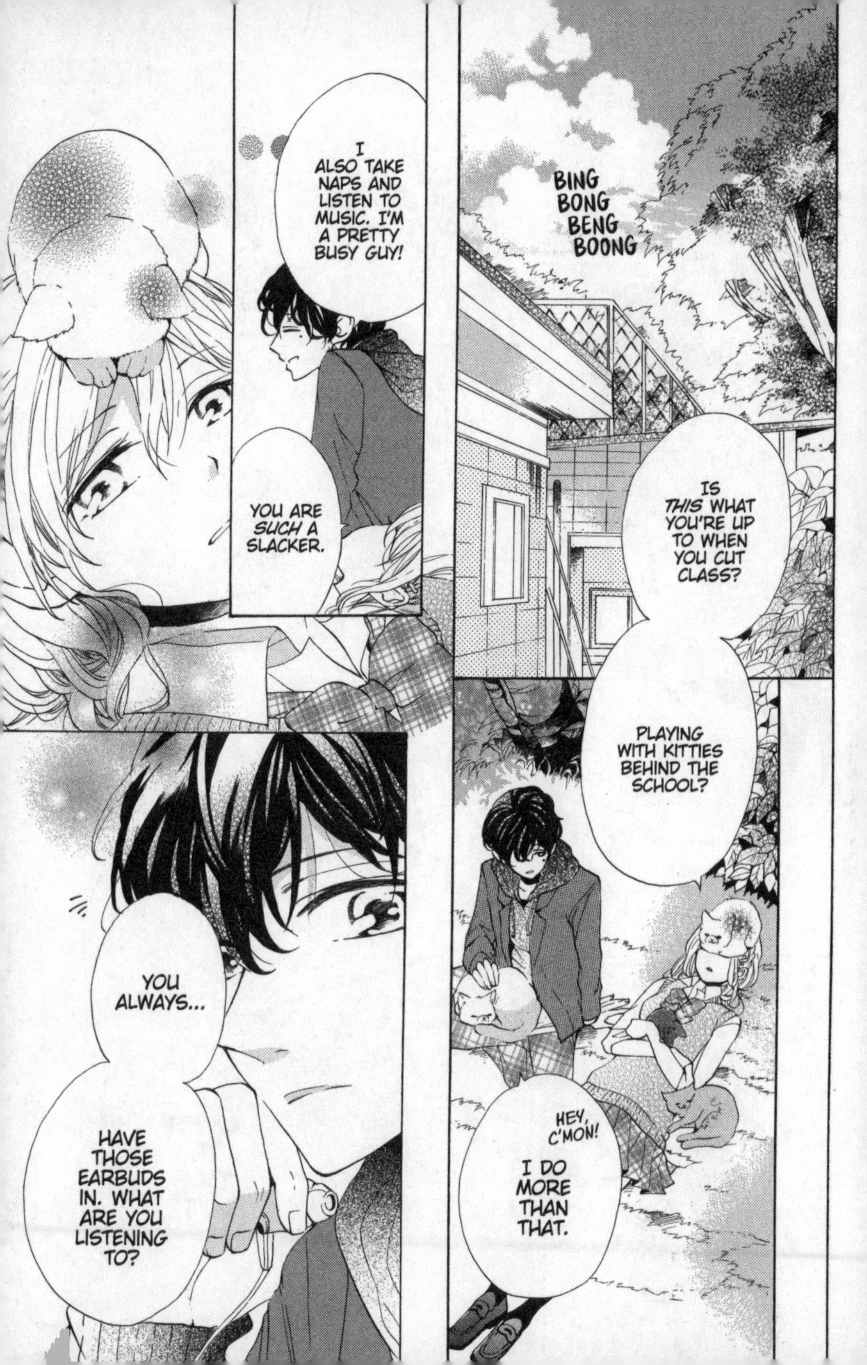
BING BONG BENG BOONG
IS THIS WHAT YOU'RE UP TO WHEN YOU CUT CLASS?
PLAYING WITH KITTIES BEHIND THE SCHOOL?
HEY, C'MON!
I DO MORE THAN THAT.
I ALSO TAKE NAPS AND LISTEN TO MUSIC. I'M A PRETTY BUSY GUY!
YOU ARE SUCH A SLACKER.
YOU ALWAYS...
HAVE THOSE EARBUDS IN. WHAT ARE YOU LISTENING TO?

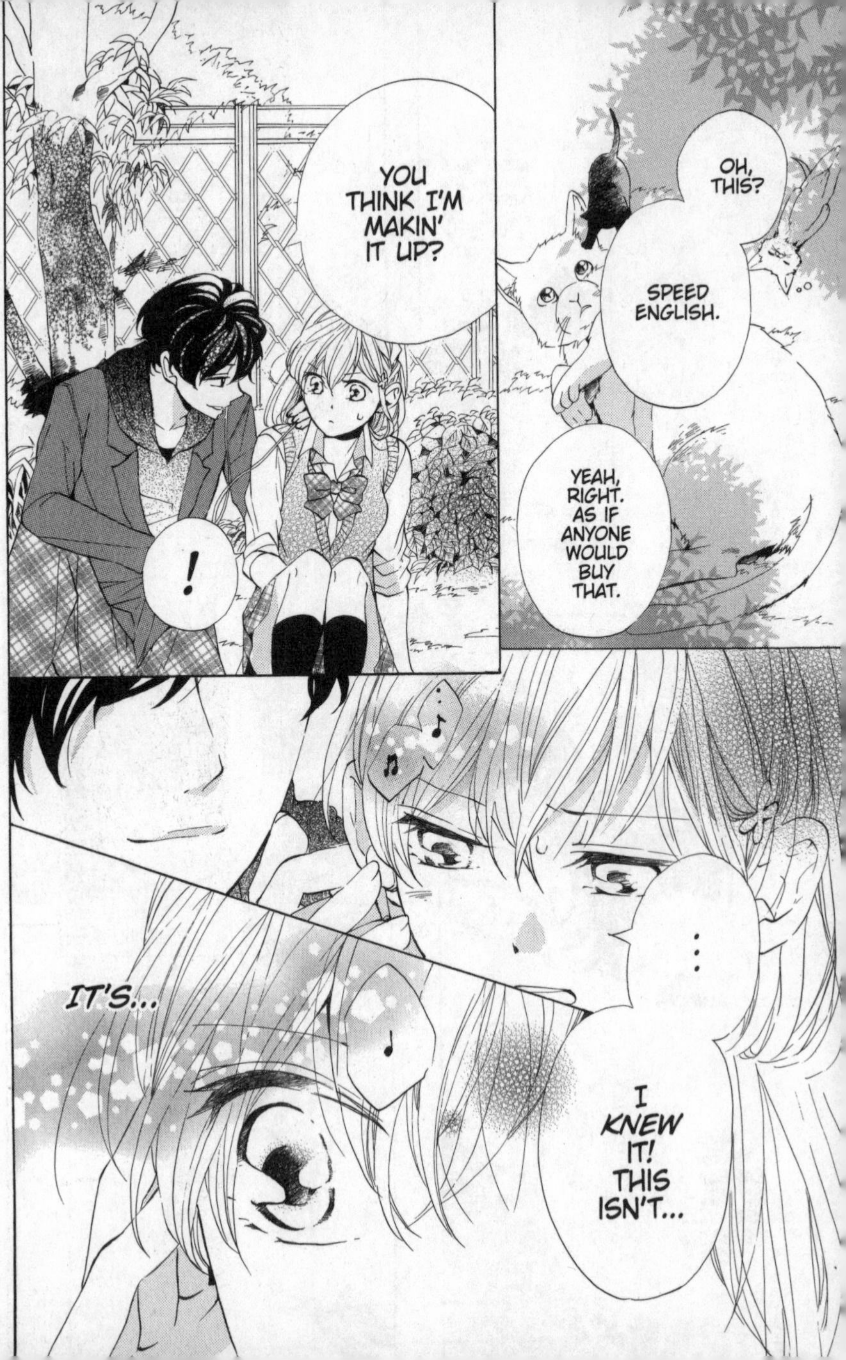
OH, THIS?
SPEED ENGLISH.
YEAH, RIGHT. AS IF ANYONE WOULD BUY THAT.
YOU THINK I'M MAKIN' IT UP?
!
...
I *KNEW* IT! THIS ISN'T...
IT'S...

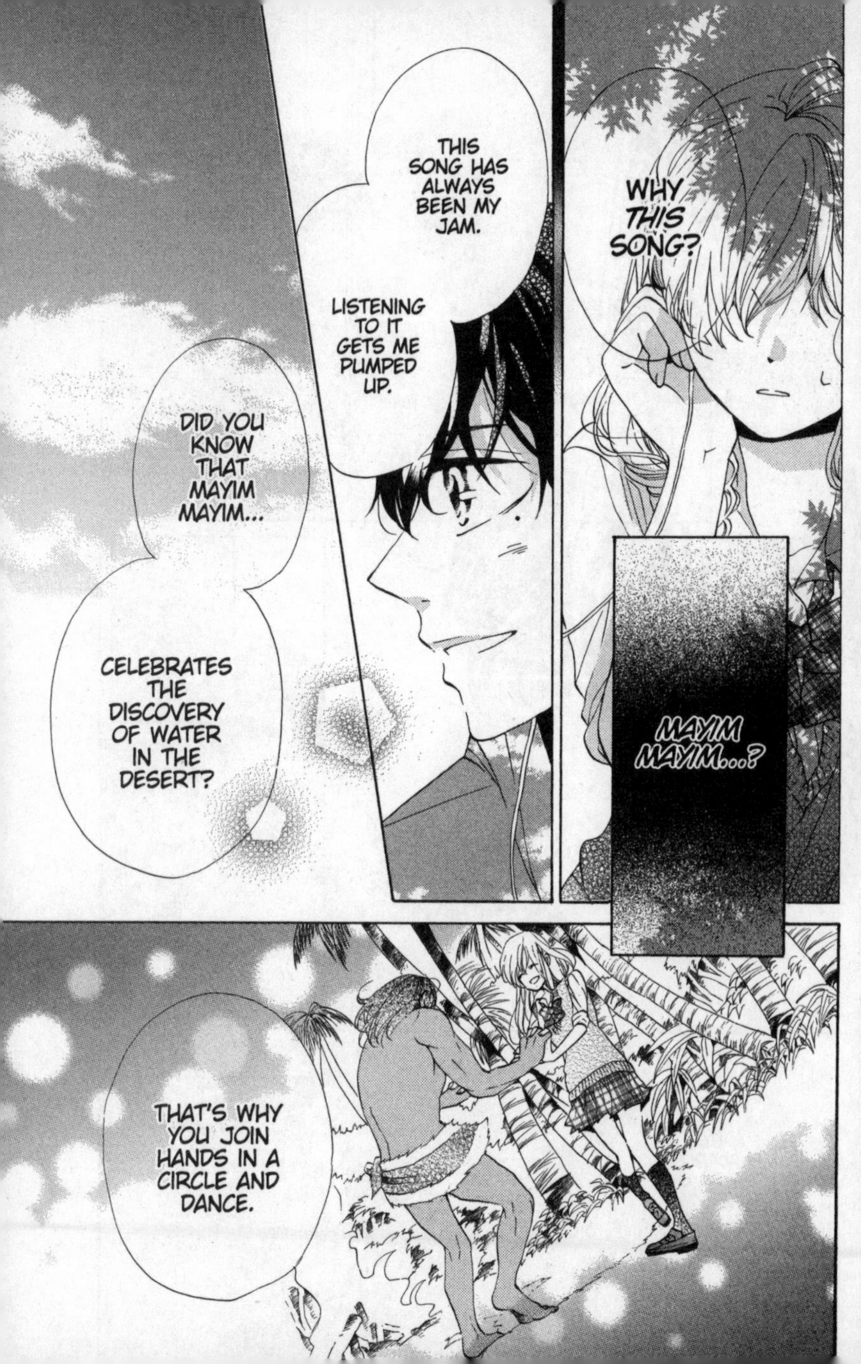
WHY THIS SONG?
MAYIM MAYIM...?
THIS SONG HAS ALWAYS BEEN MY JAM.
LISTENING TO IT GETS ME PUMPED UP.
DID YOU KNOW THAT MAYIM MAYIM...
CELEBRATES THE DISCOVERY OF WATER IN THE DESERT?
THAT'S WHY YOU JOIN HANDS IN A CIRCLE AND DANCE.

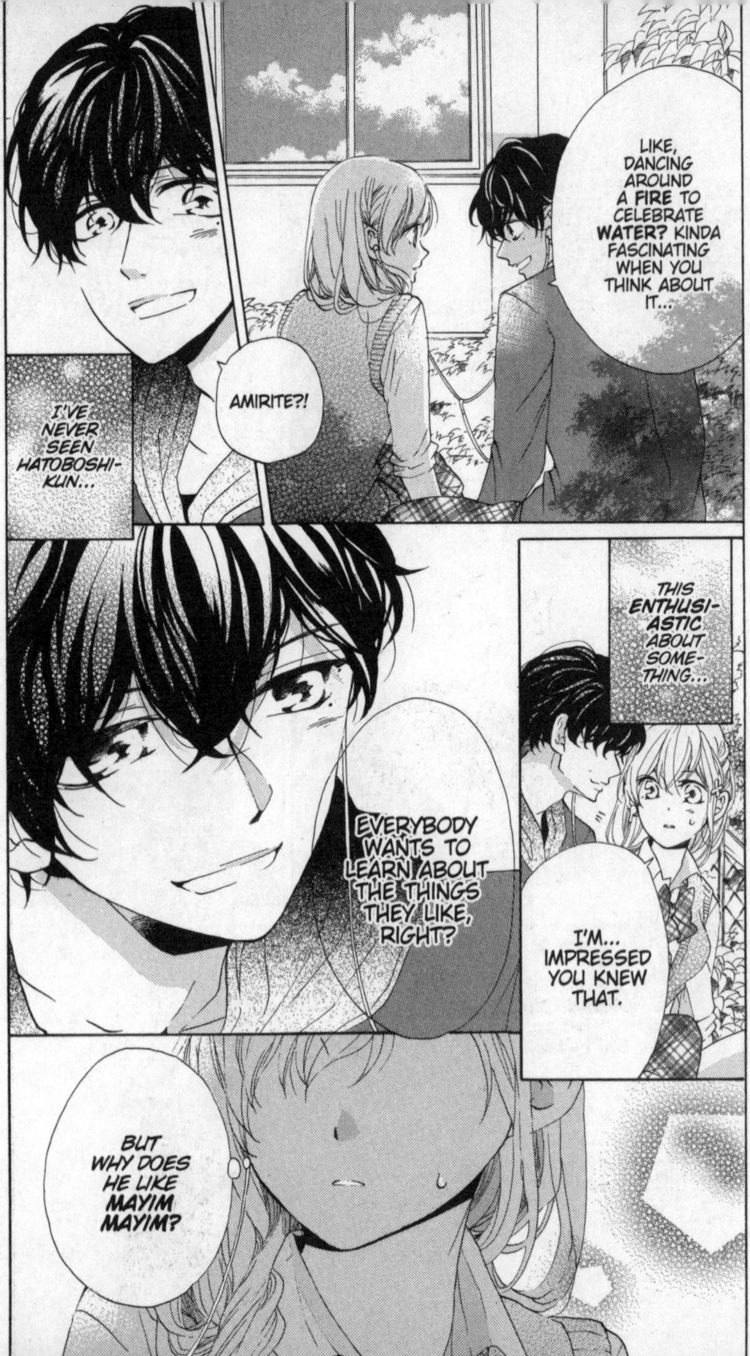
LIKE, DANCING AROUND A FIRE TO CELEBRATE WATER? KINDA FASCINATING WHEN YOU THINK ABOUT IT...
AMIRITE?!
I'VE NEVER SEEN HATOBOSHI-KUN...
THIS ENTHUSI-ASTIC ABOUT SOME-THING...
I'M... IMPRESSED YOU KNEW THAT.
EVERYBODY WANTS TO LEARN ABOUT THE THINGS THEY LIKE, RIGHT?
BUT WHY DOES HE LIKE MAYIM MAYIM?

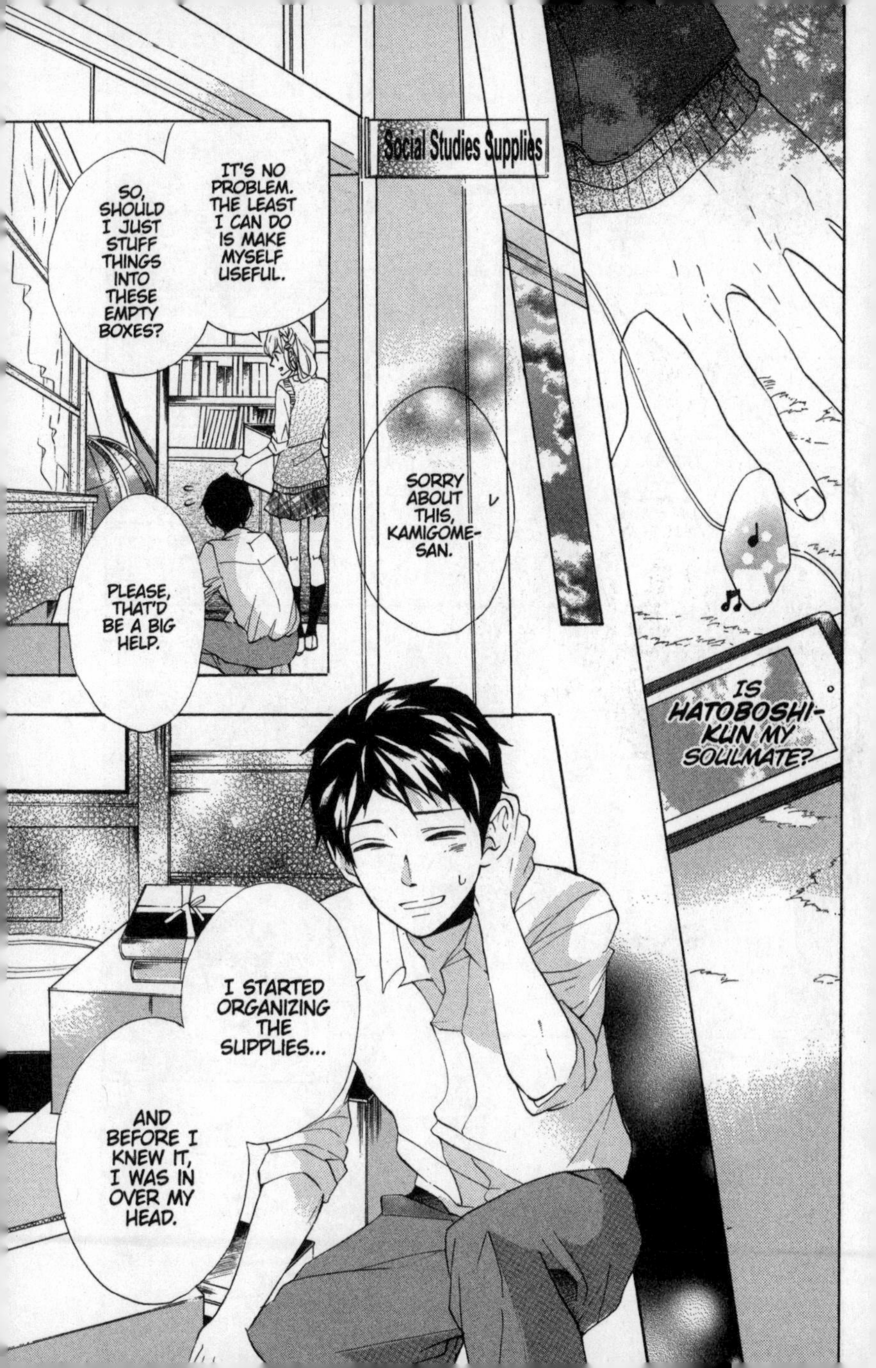
IS HATOBOSHI-KUN MY SOULMATE?
IT'S NO PROBLEM. THE LEAST I CAN DO IS MAKE MYSELF USEFUL.
SO, SHOULD I JUST STUFF THINGS INTO THESE EMPTY BOXES?
PLEASE, THAT'D BE A BIG HELP.
Social Studies Supplies
SORRY ABOUT THIS, KAMIGOME-SAN.
I STARTED ORGANIZING THE SUPPLIES...
AND BEFORE I KNEW IT, I WAS IN OVER MY HEAD.

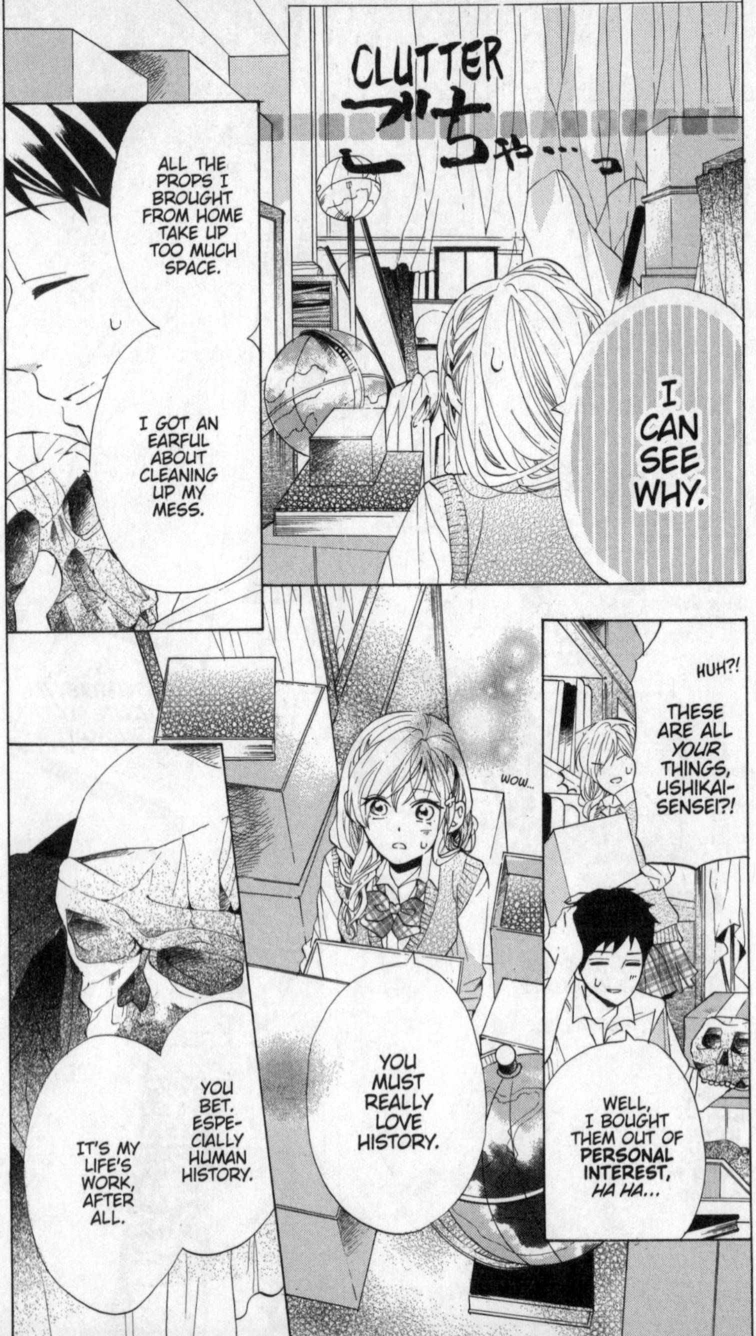
CLUTTER
ごちゃ…っ
I CAN SEE WHY.
ALL THE PROPS I BROUGHT FROM HOME TAKE UP TOO MUCH SPACE.
I GOT AN EARFUL ABOUT CLEANING UP MY MESS.
HUH?!
THESE ARE ALL *YOUR* THINGS, USHIKAI-SENSEI?!
WELL, I BOUGHT THEM OUT OF PERSONAL INTEREST, *HA HA...*
WOW...
YOU MUST REALLY LOVE HISTORY.
YOU BET. ESPECIALLY HUMAN HISTORY.
IT'S MY LIFE'S WORK, AFTER ALL.

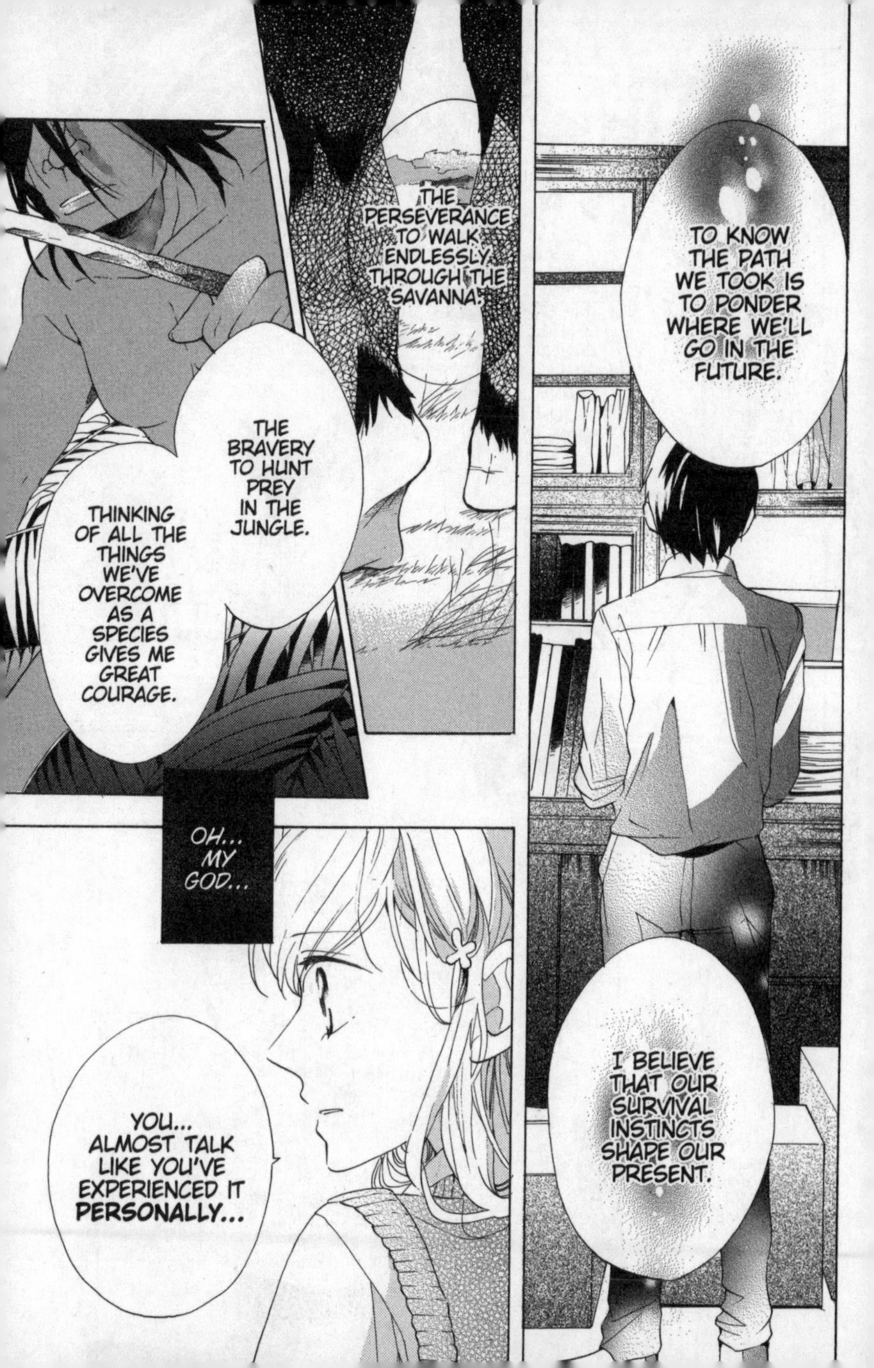
TO KNOW THE PATH WE TOOK IS TO PONDER WHERE WE'LL GO IN THE FUTURE.
I BELIEVE THAT OUR SURVIVAL INSTINCTS SHAPE OUR PRESENT.
THE PERSEVERANCE TO WALK ENDLESSLY THROUGH THE SAVANNA.
THE BRAVERY TO HUNT PREY IN THE JUNGLE.
THINKING OF ALL THE THINGS WE'VE OVERCOME AS A SPECIES GIVES ME GREAT COURAGE.
OH... MY GOD...
YOU... ALMOST TALK LIKE YOU'VE EXPERIENCED IT **PERSONALLY...**

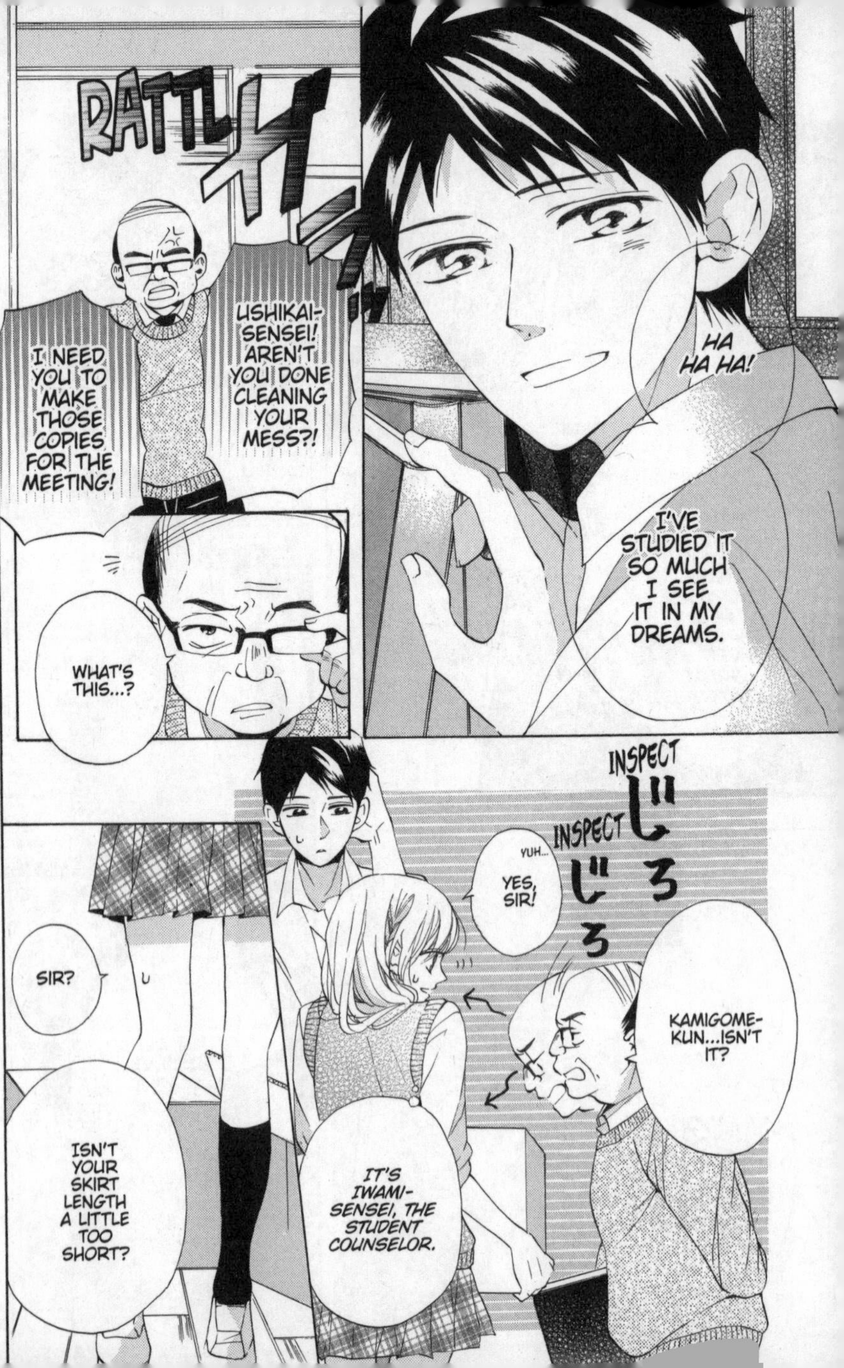
HA HA HA!
I'VE STUDIED IT SO MUCH I SEE IT IN MY DREAMS.
RATTL
USHIKAI-SENSEI! AREN'T YOU DONE CLEANING YOUR MESS?!
I NEED YOU TO MAKE THOSE COPIES FOR THE MEETING!
WHAT'S THIS...?
INSPECT じろ
INSPECT じろ
KAMIGOME-KUN...ISN'T IT?
YUH... YES, SIR!
IT'S IWAMI-SENSEI, THE STUDENT COUNSELOR.
SIR?
ISN'T YOUR SKIRT LENGTH A LITTLE TOO SHORT?

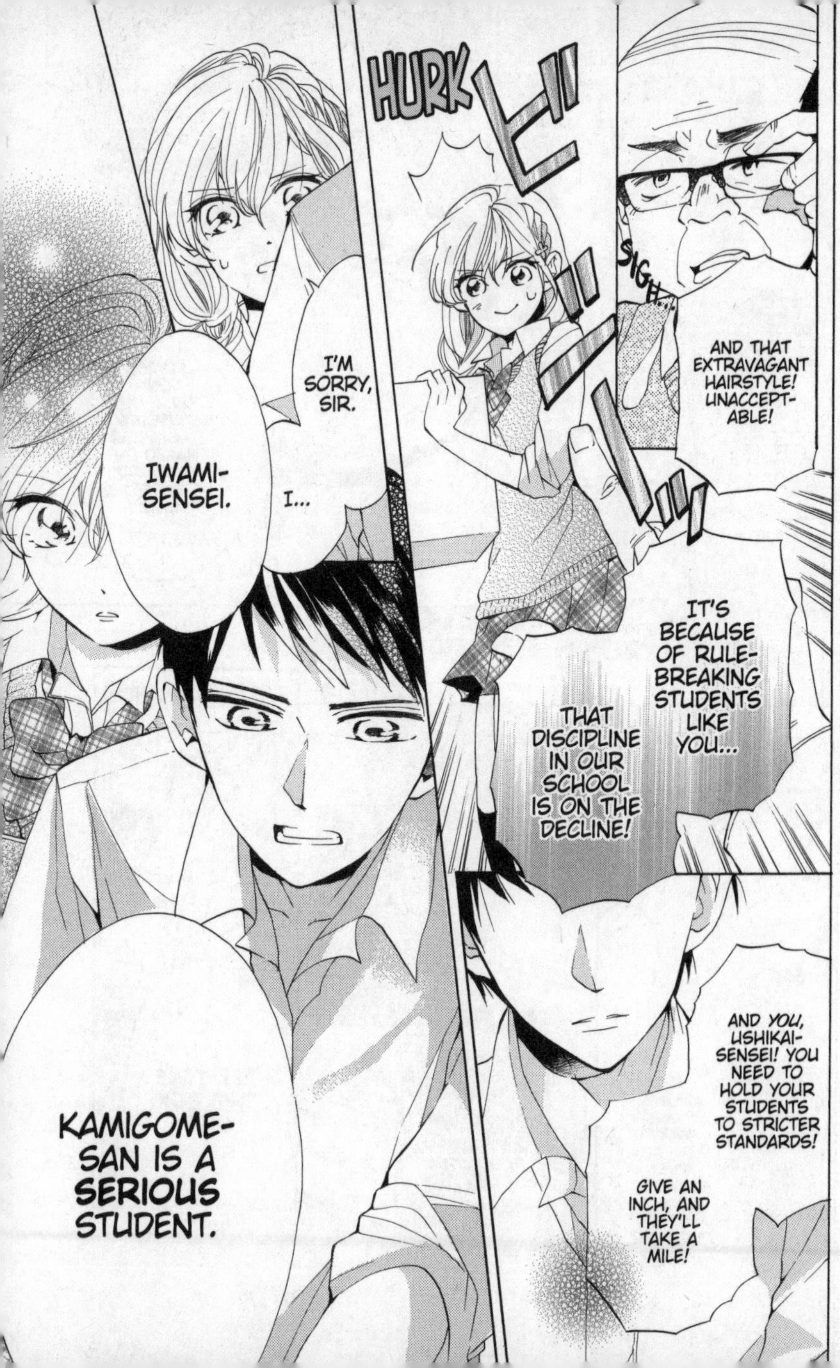
SIGH...
AND THAT EXTRAVAGANT HAIRSTYLE! UNACCEPTABLE!
HURK
IT'S BECAUSE OF RULE-BREAKING STUDENTS LIKE YOU...
THAT DISCIPLINE IN OUR SCHOOL IS ON THE DECLINE!
I'M SORRY, SIR.
I...
AND YOU, USHIKAI-SENSEI! YOU NEED TO HOLD YOUR STUDENTS TO STRICTER STANDARDS!
GIVE AN INCH, AND THEY'LL TAKE A MILE!
IWAMI-SENSEI.
KAMIGOME-SAN IS A SERIOUS STUDENT.

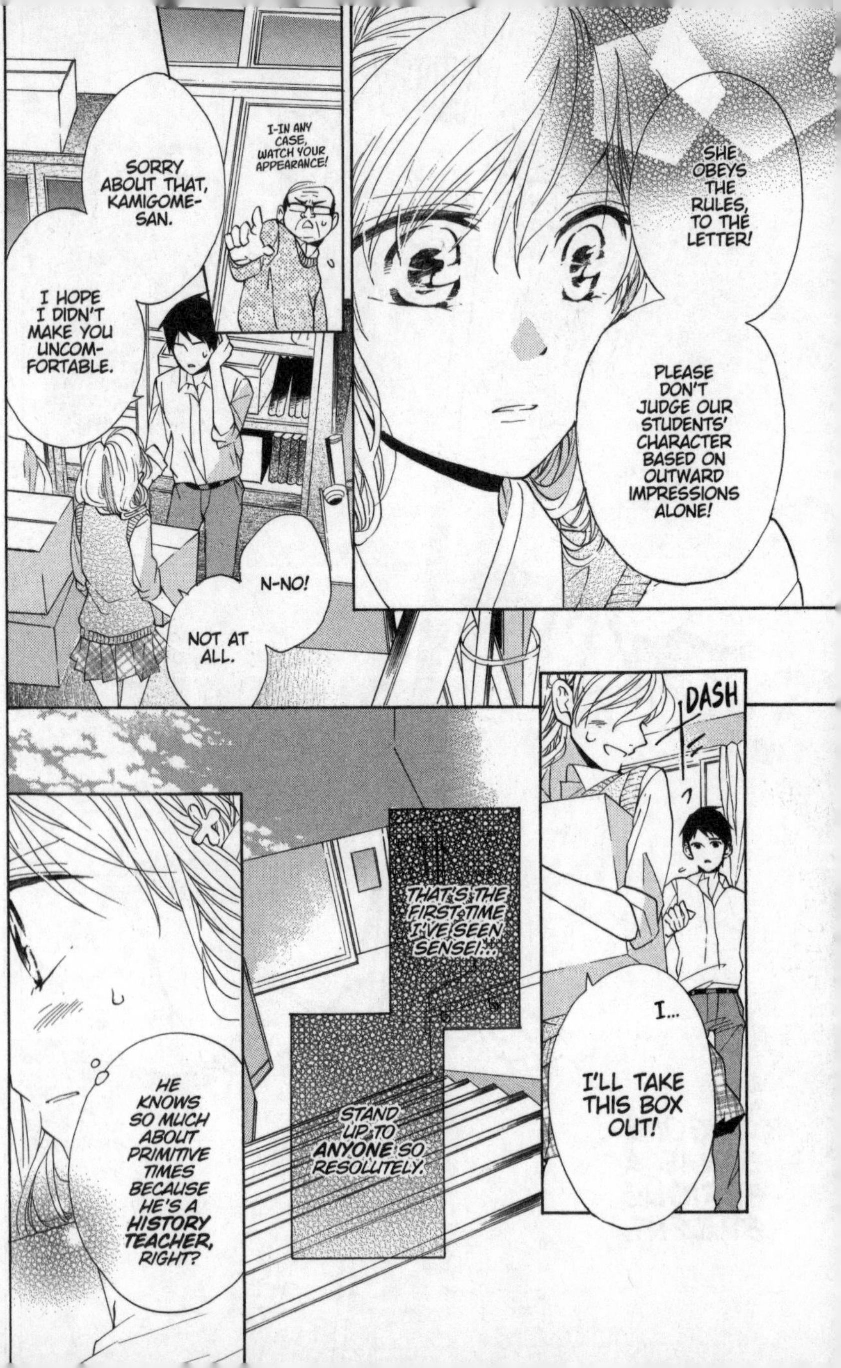
SHE OBEYS THE RULES, TO THE LETTER!
PLEASE DON'T JUDGE OUR STUDENTS' CHARACTER BASED ON OUTWARD IMPRESSIONS ALONE!
I-IN ANY CASE, WATCH YOUR APPEARANCE!
SORRY ABOUT THAT, KAMIGOME-SAN.
I HOPE I DIDN'T MAKE YOU UNCOM-FORTABLE.
N-NO!
NOT AT ALL.
DASH
I...
I'LL TAKE THIS BOX OUT!
THAT'S THE FIRST TIME I'VE SEEN SENSEI...
STAND UP TO ANYONE SO RESOLUTELY.
HE KNOWS SO MUCH ABOUT PRIMITIVE TIMES BECAUSE HE'S A HISTORY TEACHER, RIGHT?

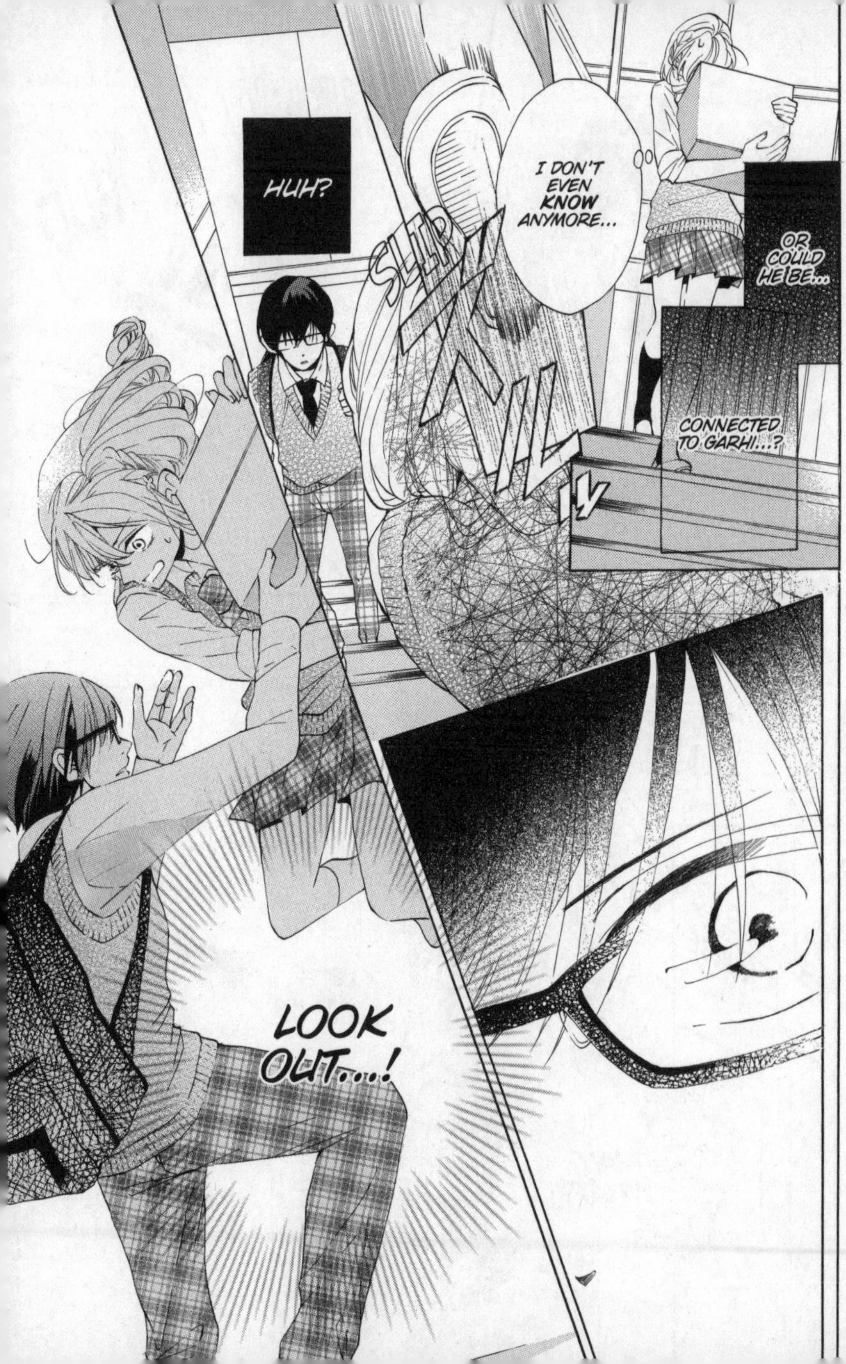
OR COULD HE BE...
CONNECTED TO GARHI...?
I DON'T EVEN KNOW ANYMORE...
SLIP
HUH?
LOOK OUT...!

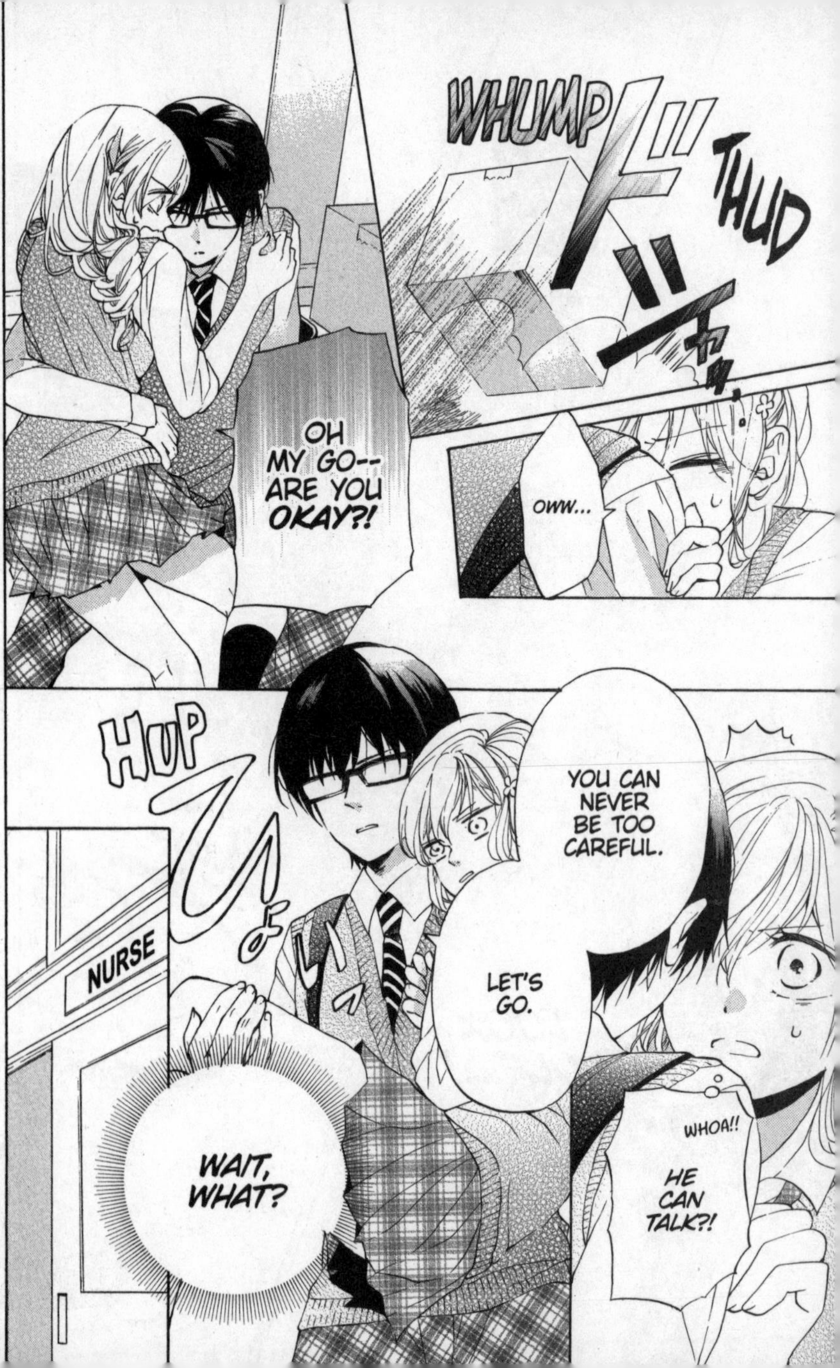
WHUMP
THUD
OWW...
OH MY GO-- ARE YOU OKAY?!
YOU CAN NEVER BE TOO CAREFUL.
HUP
LET'S GO.
WHOA!!
HE CAN TALK?!
NURSE
WAIT, WHAT?

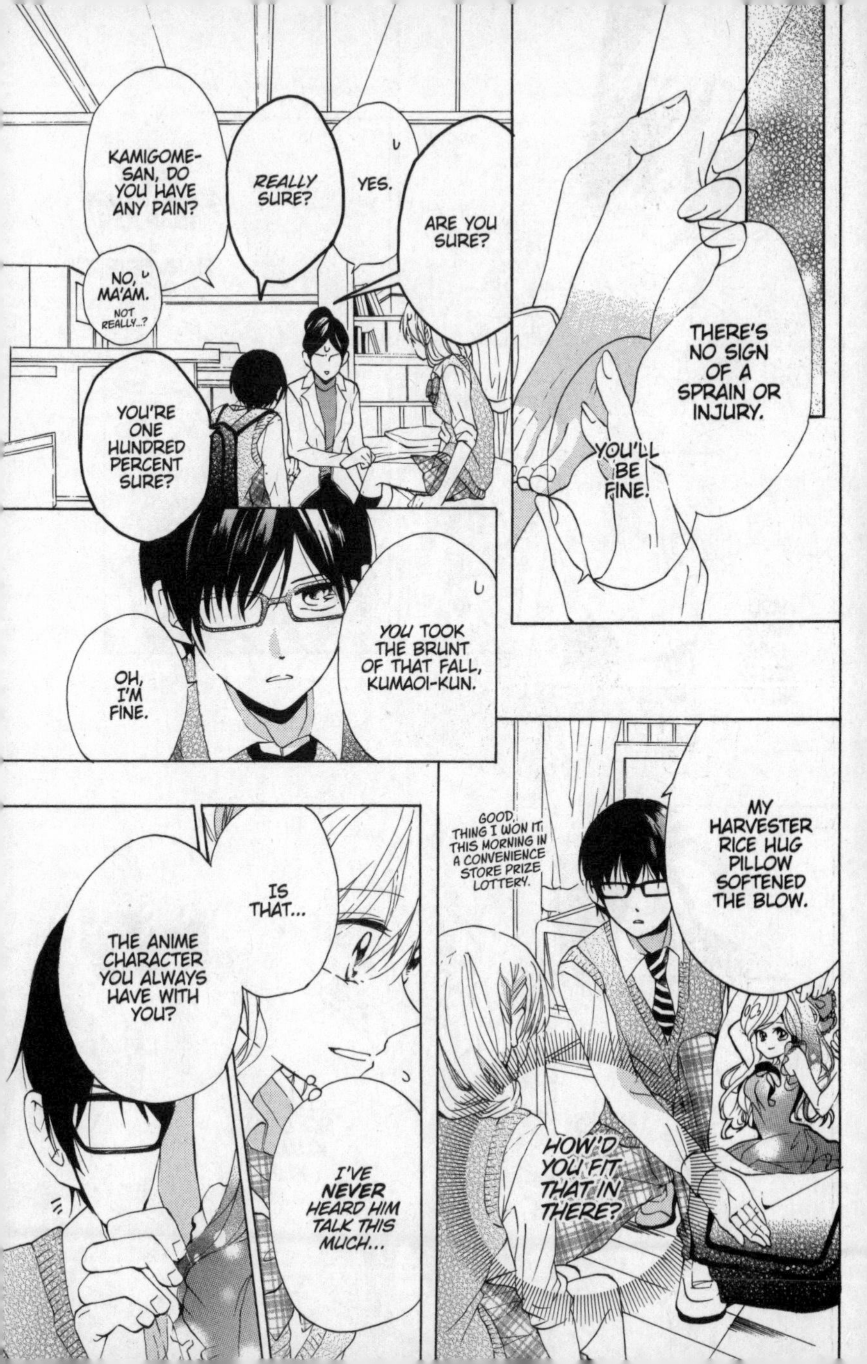
THERE'S NO SIGN OF A SPRAIN OR INJURY.
YOU'LL BE FINE.
ARE YOU SURE?
YES.
REALLY SURE?
KAMIGOME-SAN, DO YOU HAVE ANY PAIN?
NO, MA'AM.
NOT REALLY...?
YOU'RE ONE HUNDRED PERCENT SURE?
YOU TOOK THE BRUNT OF THAT FALL, KUMAOI-KUN.
OH, I'M FINE.
MY HARVESTER RICE HUG PILLOW SOFTENED THE BLOW.
GOOD THING I WON IT THIS MORNING IN A CONVENIENCE STORE PRIZE LOTTERY.
HOW'D YOU FIT THAT IN THERE?
IS THAT...
THE ANIME CHARACTER YOU ALWAYS HAVE WITH YOU?
I'VE NEVER HEARD HIM TALK THIS MUCH...

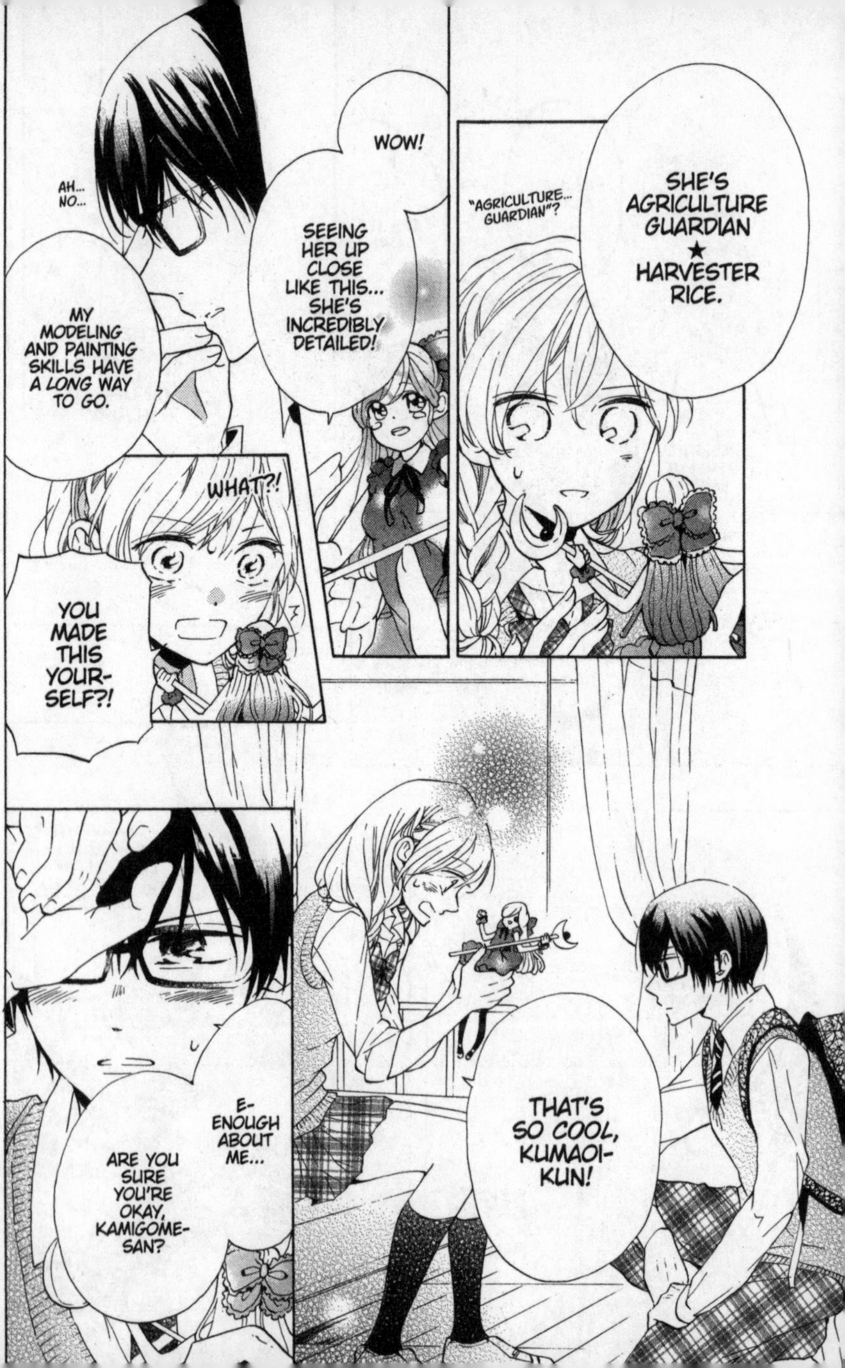
SHE'S AGRICULTURE GUARDIAN ★ HARVESTER RICE.
"AGRICULTURE... GUARDIAN"?
WOW!
SEEING HER UP CLOSE LIKE THIS... SHE'S INCREDIBLY DETAILED!
AH... NO...
MY MODELING AND PAINTING SKILLS HAVE A LONG WAY TO GO.
WHAT?!
YOU MADE THIS YOUR-SELF?!
THAT'S SO COOL, KUMAOI-KUN!
E-ENOUGH ABOUT ME...
ARE YOU SURE YOU'RE OKAY, KAMIGOME-SAN?

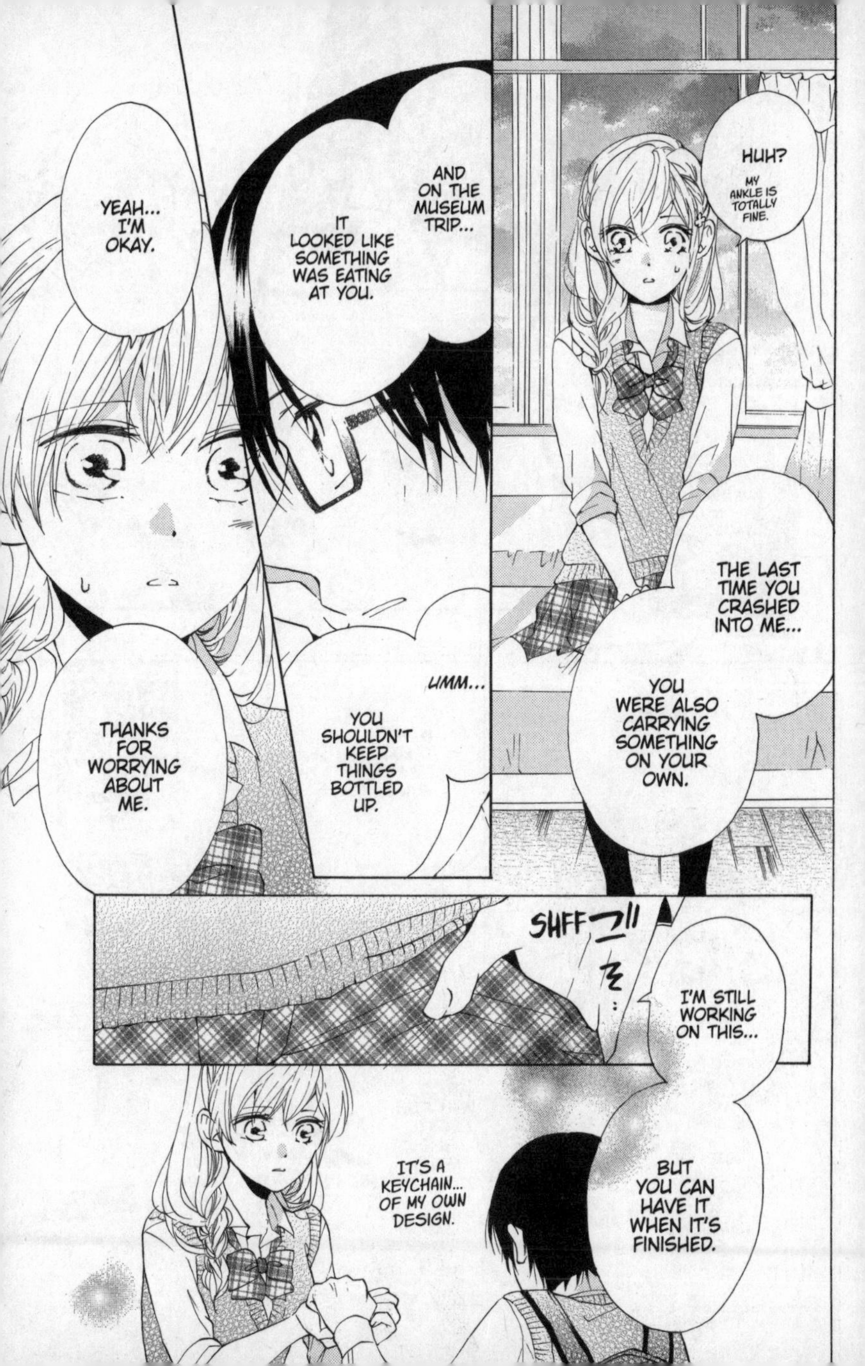
HUH?
MY ANKLE IS TOTALLY FINE.
THE LAST TIME YOU CRASHED INTO ME...
YOU WERE ALSO CARRYING SOMETHING ON YOUR OWN.
AND ON THE MUSEUM TRIP...
IT LOOKED LIKE SOMETHING WAS EATING AT YOU.
UMM...
YOU SHOULDN'T KEEP THINGS BOTTLED UP.
YEAH... I'M OKAY.
THANKS FOR WORRYING ABOUT ME.
SHFF
I'M STILL WORKING ON THIS...
BUT YOU CAN HAVE IT WHEN IT'S FINISHED.
IT'S A KEYCHAIN... OF MY OWN DESIGN.

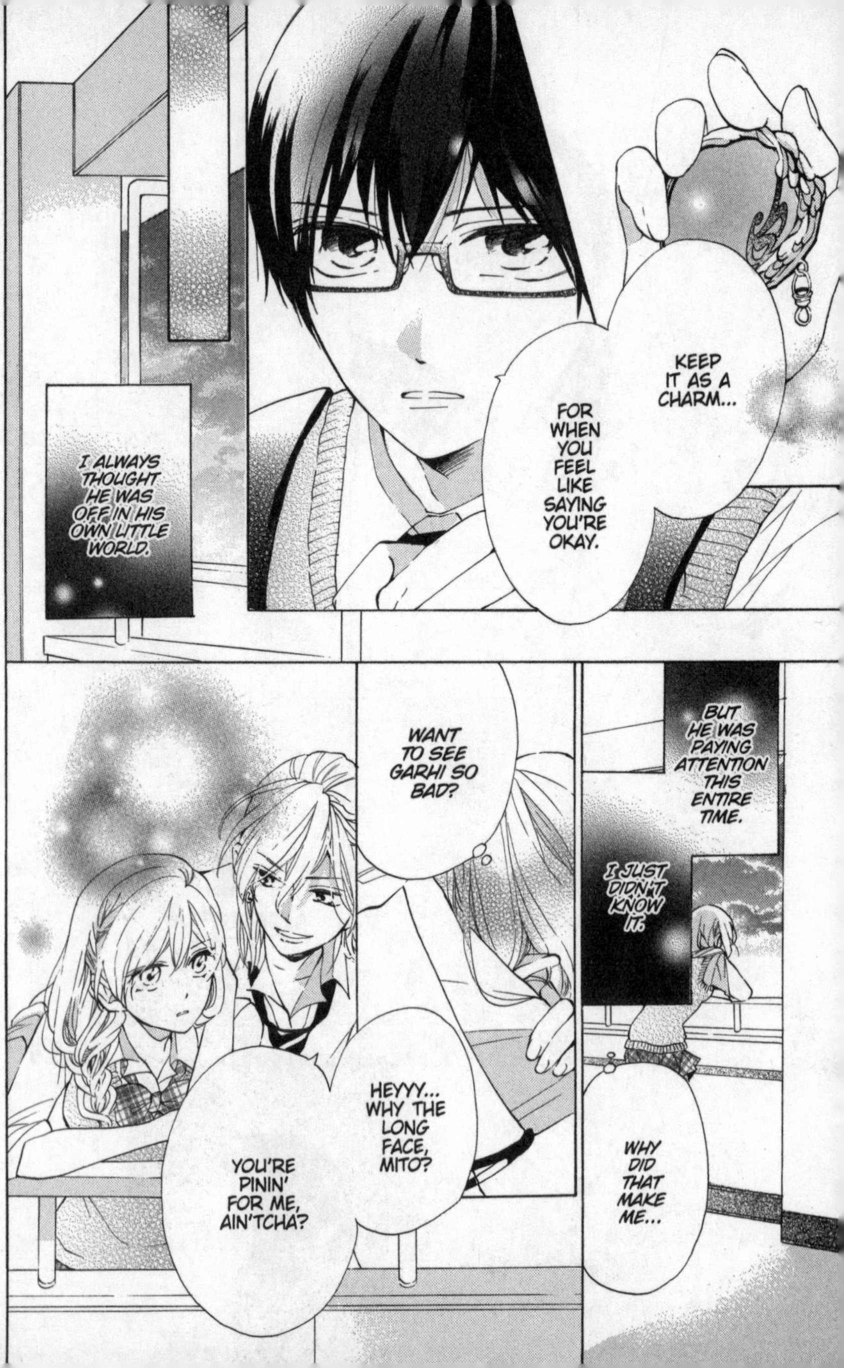
KEEP IT AS A CHARM...
FOR WHEN YOU FEEL LIKE SAYING YOU'RE OKAY.
I ALWAYS THOUGHT HE WAS OFF IN HIS OWN LITTLE WORLD.
BUT HE WAS PAYING ATTENTION THIS ENTIRE TIME.
I JUST DIDN'T KNOW IT.
WHY DID THAT MAKE ME...
WANT TO SEE GARHI SO BAD?
HEYYY... WHY THE LONG FACE, MITO?
YOU'RE PININ' FOR ME, AIN'TCHA?

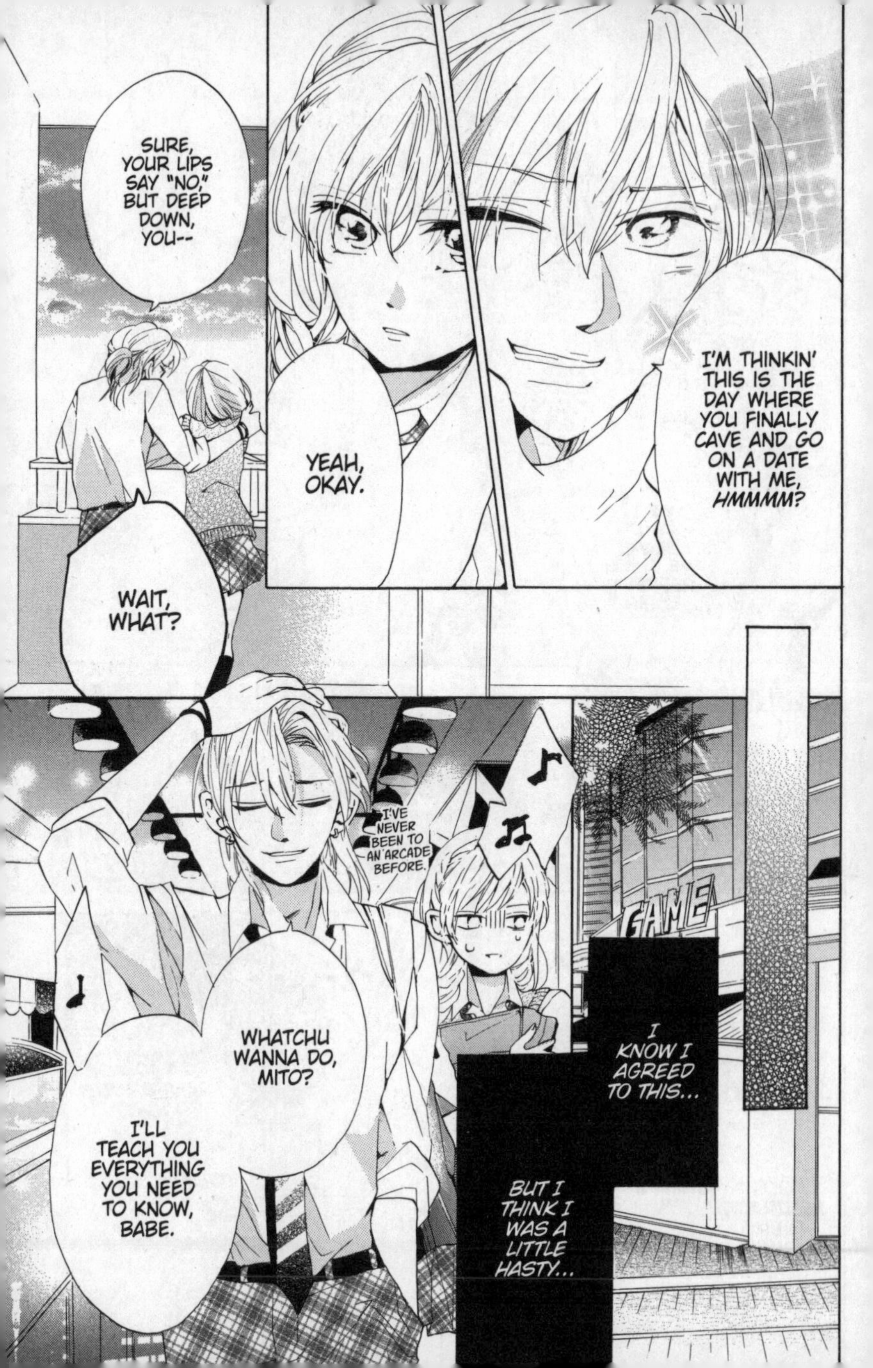
I'M THINKIN' THIS IS THE DAY WHERE YOU FINALLY CAVE AND GO ON A DATE WITH ME, *HMMMM?*
YEAH, OKAY.
SURE, YOUR LIPS SAY "NO," BUT DEEP DOWN, YOU--
WAIT, WHAT?
GAME
I'VE NEVER BEEN TO AN ARCADE BEFORE.
WHATCHU WANNA DO, MITO?
I'LL TEACH YOU EVERYTHING YOU NEED TO KNOW, BABE.
I KNOW I AGREED TO THIS...
BUT I THINK I WAS A LITTLE HASTY...

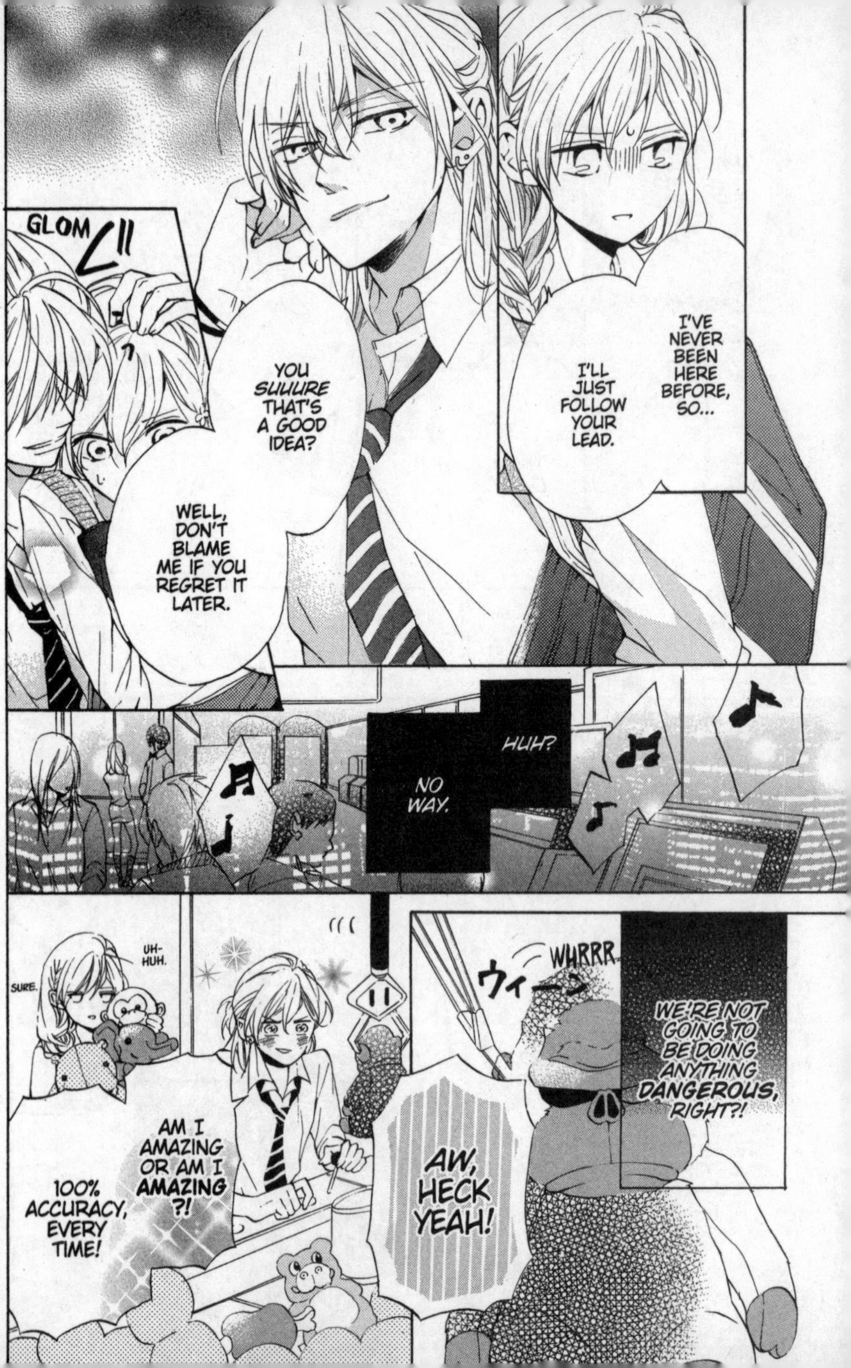
I'VE NEVER BEEN HERE BEFORE, SO...
I'LL JUST FOLLOW YOUR LEAD.
GLOM
YOU SUUURE THAT'S A GOOD IDEA?
WELL, DON'T BLAME ME IF YOU REGRET IT LATER.
HUH?
NO WAY.
WHURRR
ウィーン
WE'RE NOT GOING TO BE DOING ANYTHING DANGEROUS, RIGHT?!
AW, HECK YEAH!
UH-HUH.
SURE.
AM I AMAZING OR AM I AMAZING?!
100% ACCURACY, EVERY TIME!

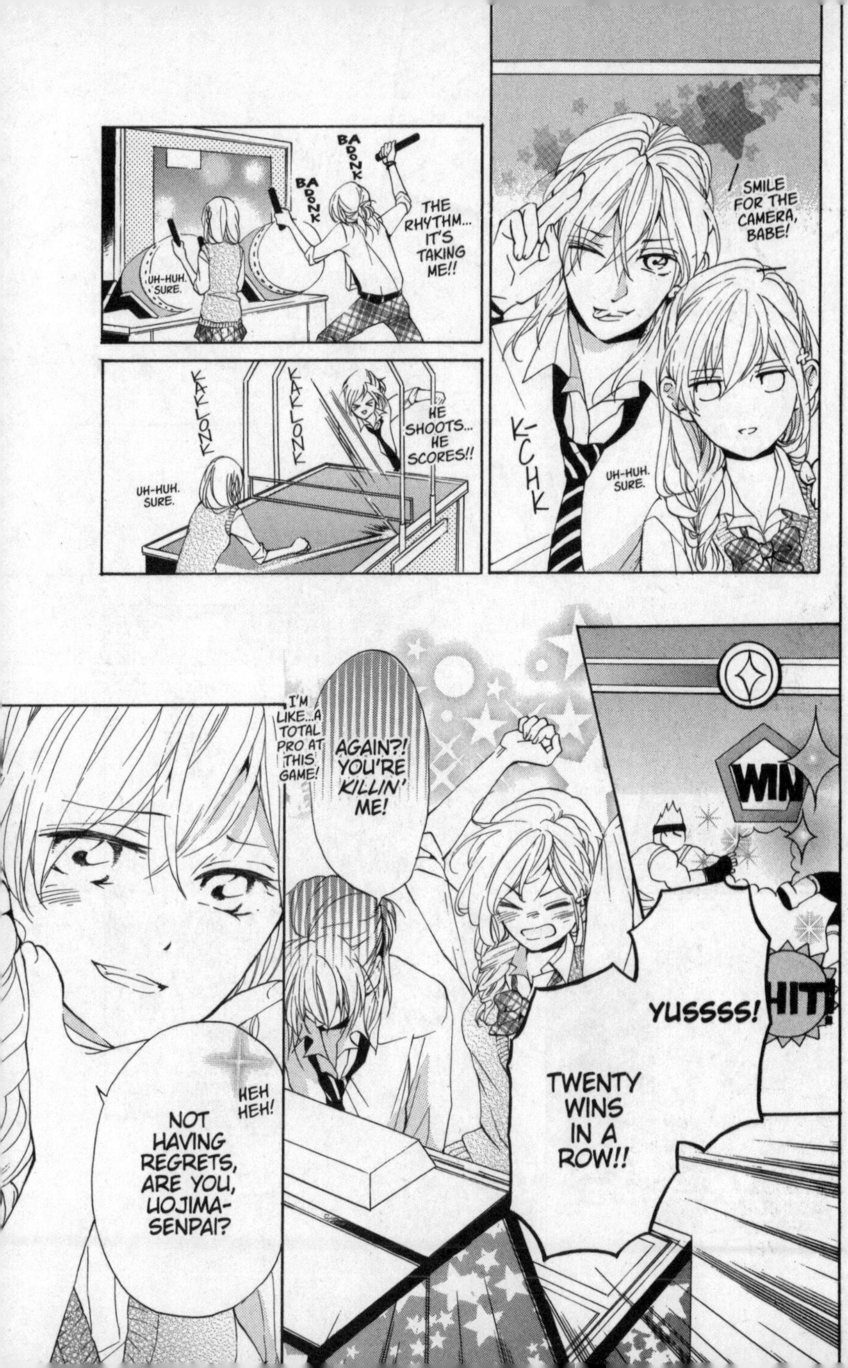
SMILE FOR THE CAMERA, BABE!
K-CHK
UH-HUH. SURE.
BADONK
BADONK
THE RHYTHM... IT'S TAKING ME!!
UH-HUH. SURE.
KAKLONK
KAKLONK
HE SHOOTS... HE SCORES!!
UH-HUH. SURE.
WIN
I'M LIKE...A TOTAL PRO AT THIS GAME!
AGAIN?! YOU'RE KILLIN' ME!
HIT!
YUSSSS!
TWENTY WINS IN A ROW!!
HEH HEH!
NOT HAVING REGRETS, ARE YOU, UOJIMA-SENPAI?

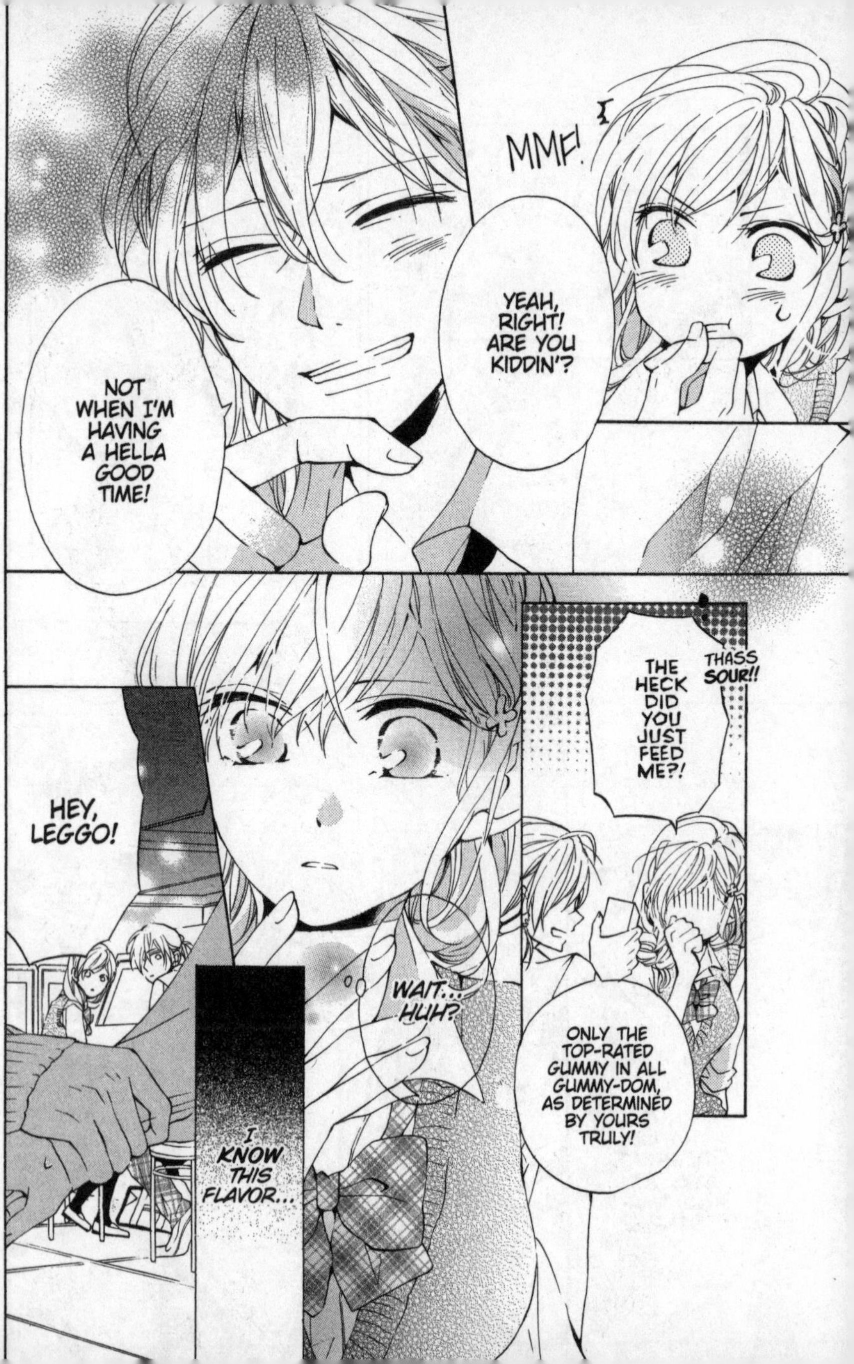
MMF!
YEAH, RIGHT! ARE YOU KIDDIN'?
NOT WHEN I'M HAVING A HELLA GOOD TIME!
THASS SOUR!!
THE HECK DID YOU JUST FEED ME?!
ONLY THE TOP-RATED GUMMY IN ALL GUMMY-DOM, AS DETERMINED BY YOURS TRULY!
WAIT... HUH?
I KNOW THIS FLAVOR...
HEY, LEGGO!

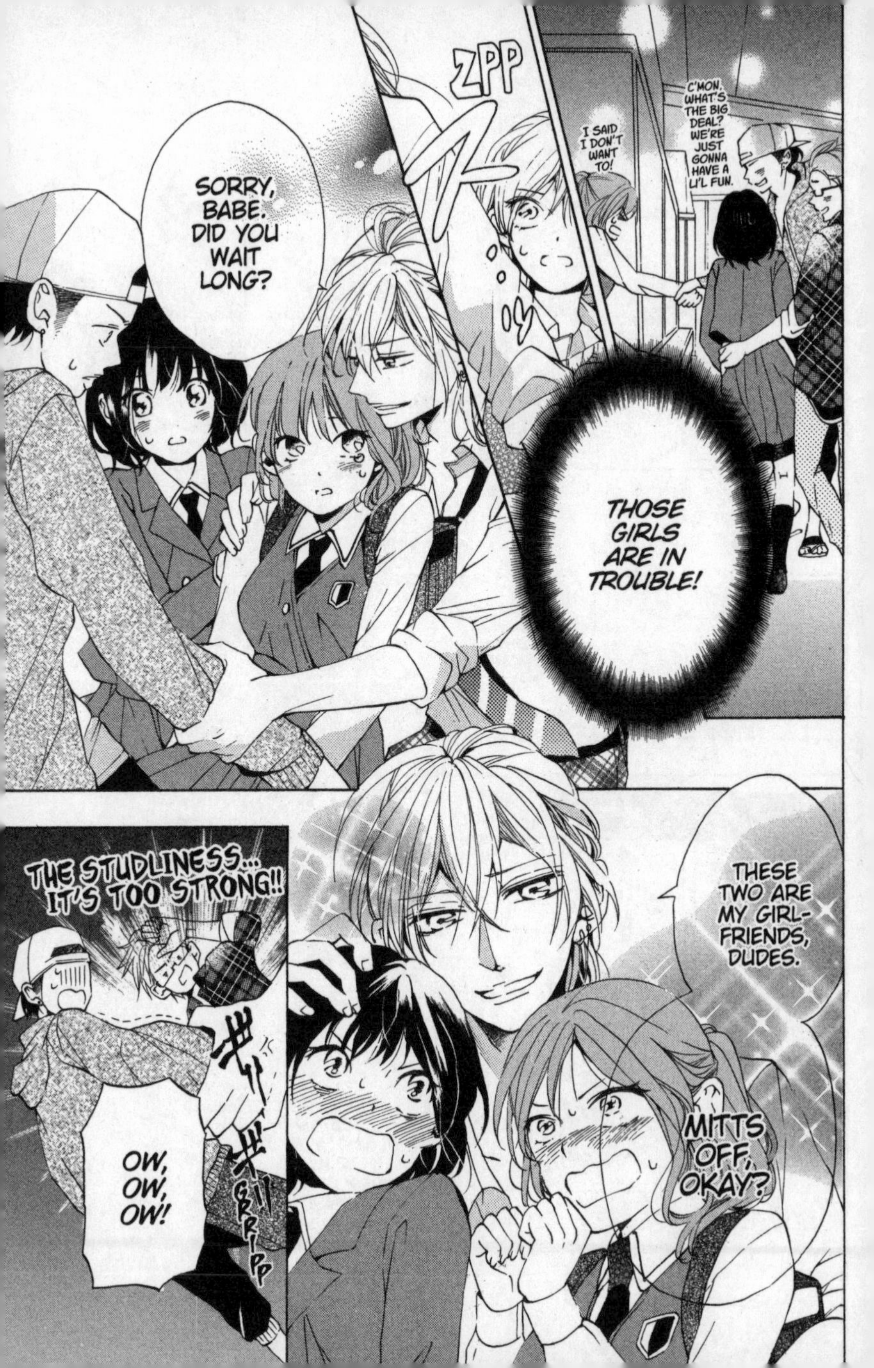
C'MON, WHAT'S THE BIG DEAL? WE'RE JUST GONNA HAVE A LI'L FUN.
I SAID I DON'T WANT TO!
THOSE GIRLS ARE IN TROUBLE!
ZPP
SORRY, BABE. DID YOU WAIT LONG?
THESE TWO ARE MY GIRL-FRIENDS, DUDES.
MITTS OFF, OKAY?
THE STUDLINESS... IT'S TOO STRONG!!
OW, OW, OW!
GRIPP

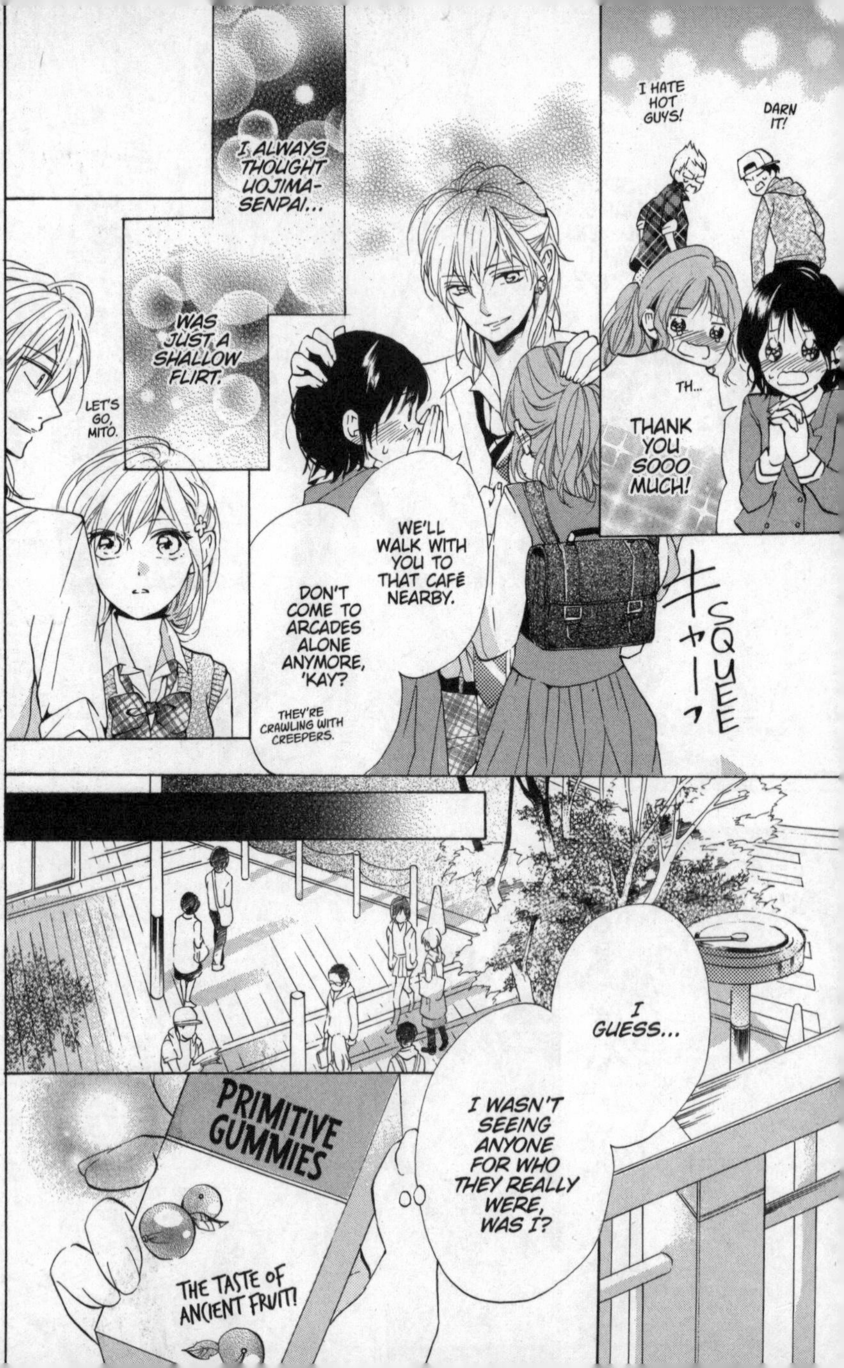
DARN IT!
I HATE HOT GUYS!
TH...
THANK YOU SOOO MUCH!
I ALWAYS THOUGHT UOJIMA-SENPAI...
WAS JUST A SHALLOW FLIRT.
SQUEE
WE'LL WALK WITH YOU TO THAT CAFÉ NEARBY.
DON'T COME TO ARCADES ALONE ANYMORE, 'KAY?
THEY'RE CRAWLING WITH CREEPERS.
LET'S GO, MITO.
I GUESS...
I WASN'T SEEING ANYONE FOR WHO THEY REALLY WERE, WAS I?
PRIMITIVE GUMMIES
THE TASTE OF ANCIENT FRUIT!

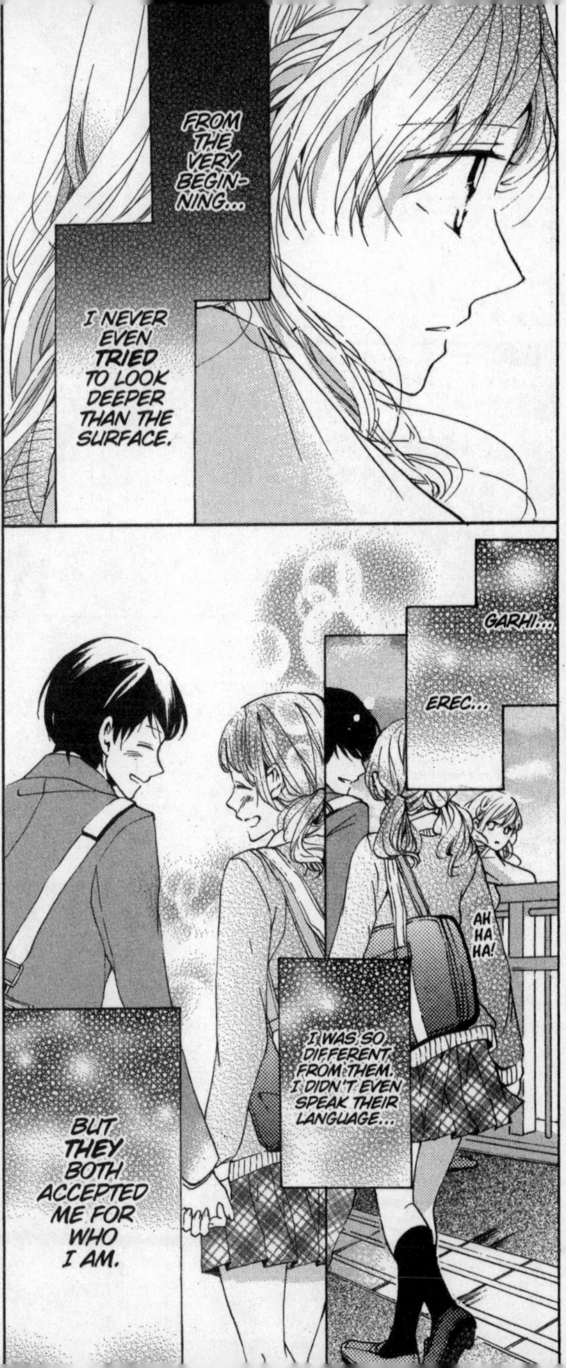
FROM THE VERY BEGINNING...
I NEVER EVEN TRIED TO LOOK DEEPER THAN THE SURFACE.
GARHI...
EREC...
AH HA HA!
I WAS SO DIFFERENT FROM THEM. I DIDN'T EVEN SPEAK THEIR LANGUAGE...
BUT THEY BOTH ACCEPTED ME FOR WHO I AM.

1

HI THERE! IT'S ME, YOSHINEKO KITAFUKU.

THANK YOU SO MUCH FOR PICKING UP PRIMITIVE BOYFRIEND, VOLUME 3!

IT'S THE FINAL VOLUME!

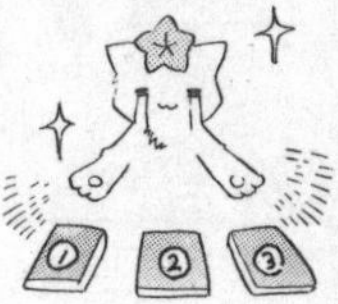

I'M ETERNALLY GRATEFUL TO HAVE BEEN ALLOWED THE OPPORTUNITY TO DRAW THREE WHOLE VOLUMES.

TO THOSE OF YOU WHO'VE BEEN READING SINCE VOLUME 1, AND THOSE OF YOU WHO JUST STARTED, I'D BE GRATEFUL IF YOU FOLLOWED THE FATE OF MITO'S EPIC HUSBAND HUNT.

I HOPE YOU ENJOY IT!

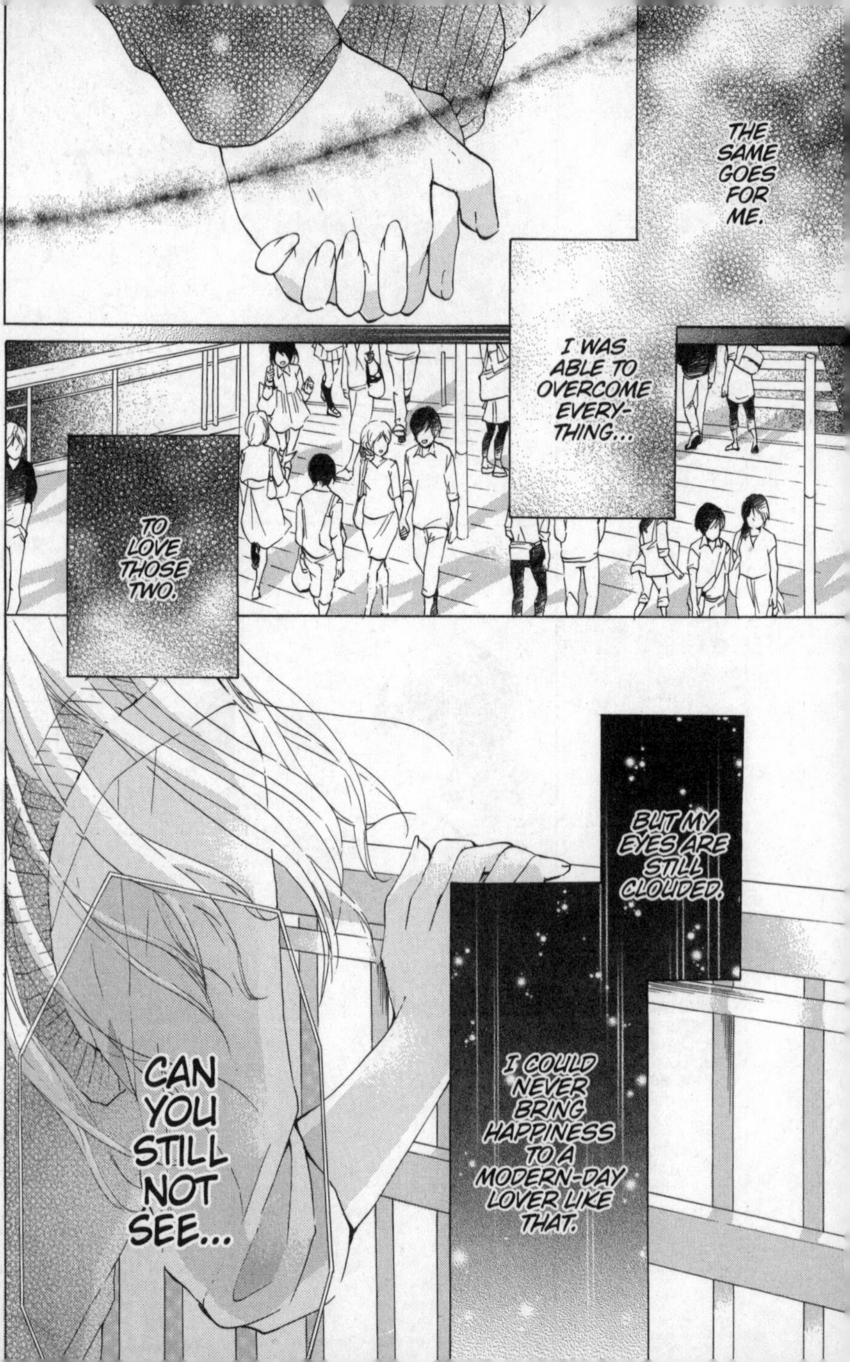
THE SAME GOES FOR ME.
I WAS ABLE TO OVERCOME EVERY-THING...
TO LOVE THOSE TWO.
BUT MY EYES ARE STILL CLOUDED.
I COULD NEVER BRING HAPPINESS TO A MODERN-DAY LOVER LIKE THAT.
CAN YOU STILL NOT SEE...

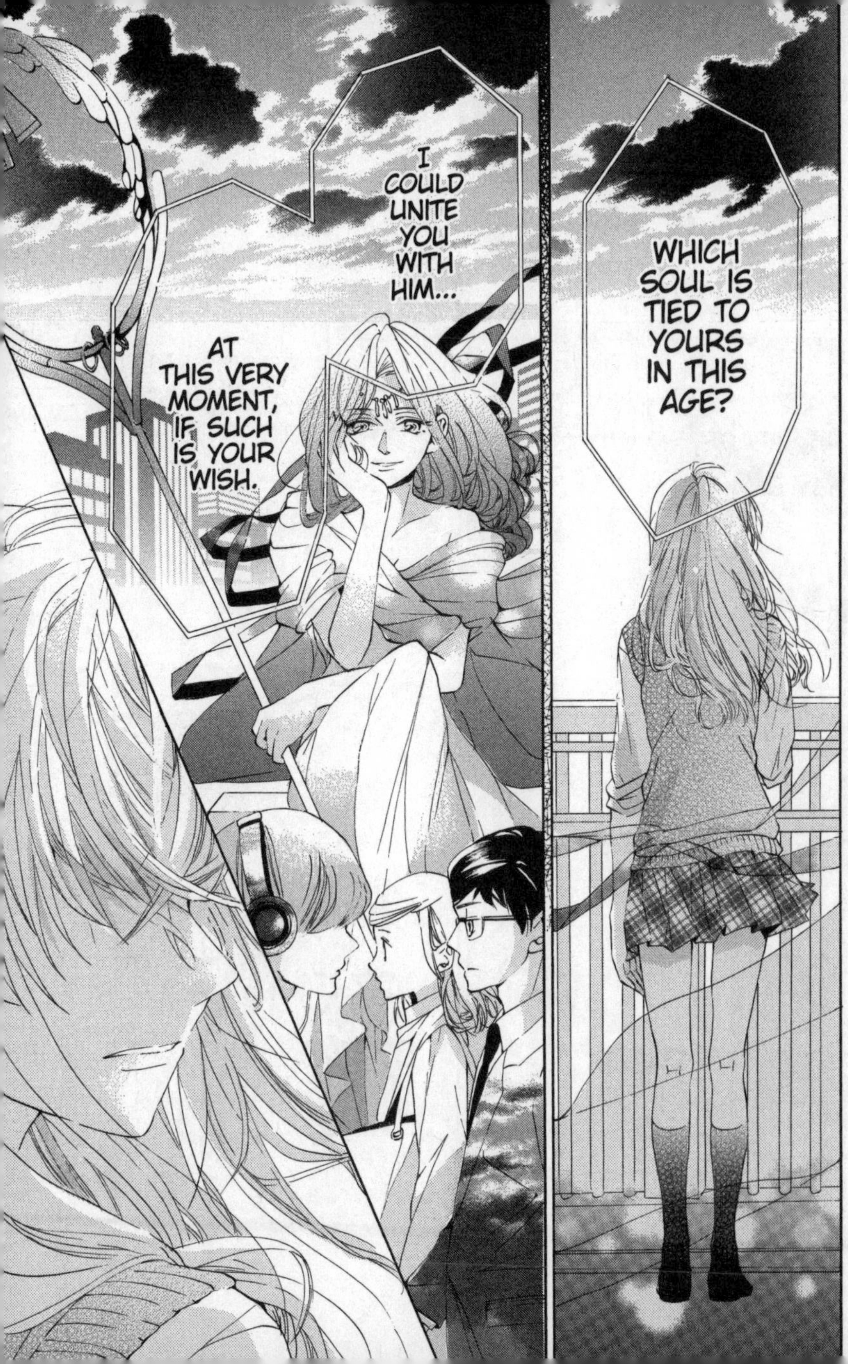
WHICH SOUL IS TIED TO YOURS IN THIS AGE?
I COULD UNITE YOU WITH HIM...
AT THIS VERY MOMENT, IF SUCH IS YOUR WISH.

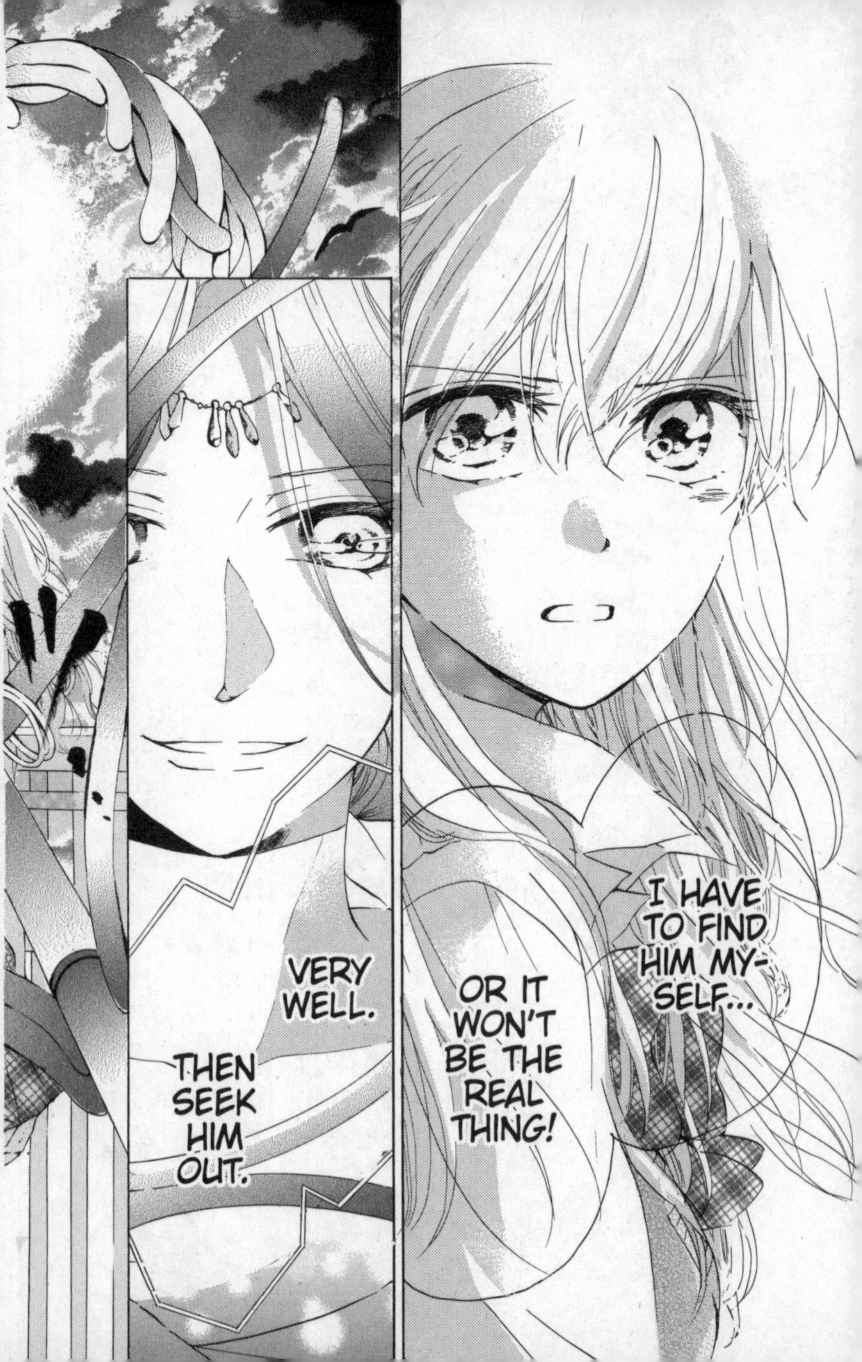
I HAVE TO FIND HIM MY-SELF...
OR IT WON'T BE THE REAL THING!
VERY WELL.
THEN SEEK HIM OUT.

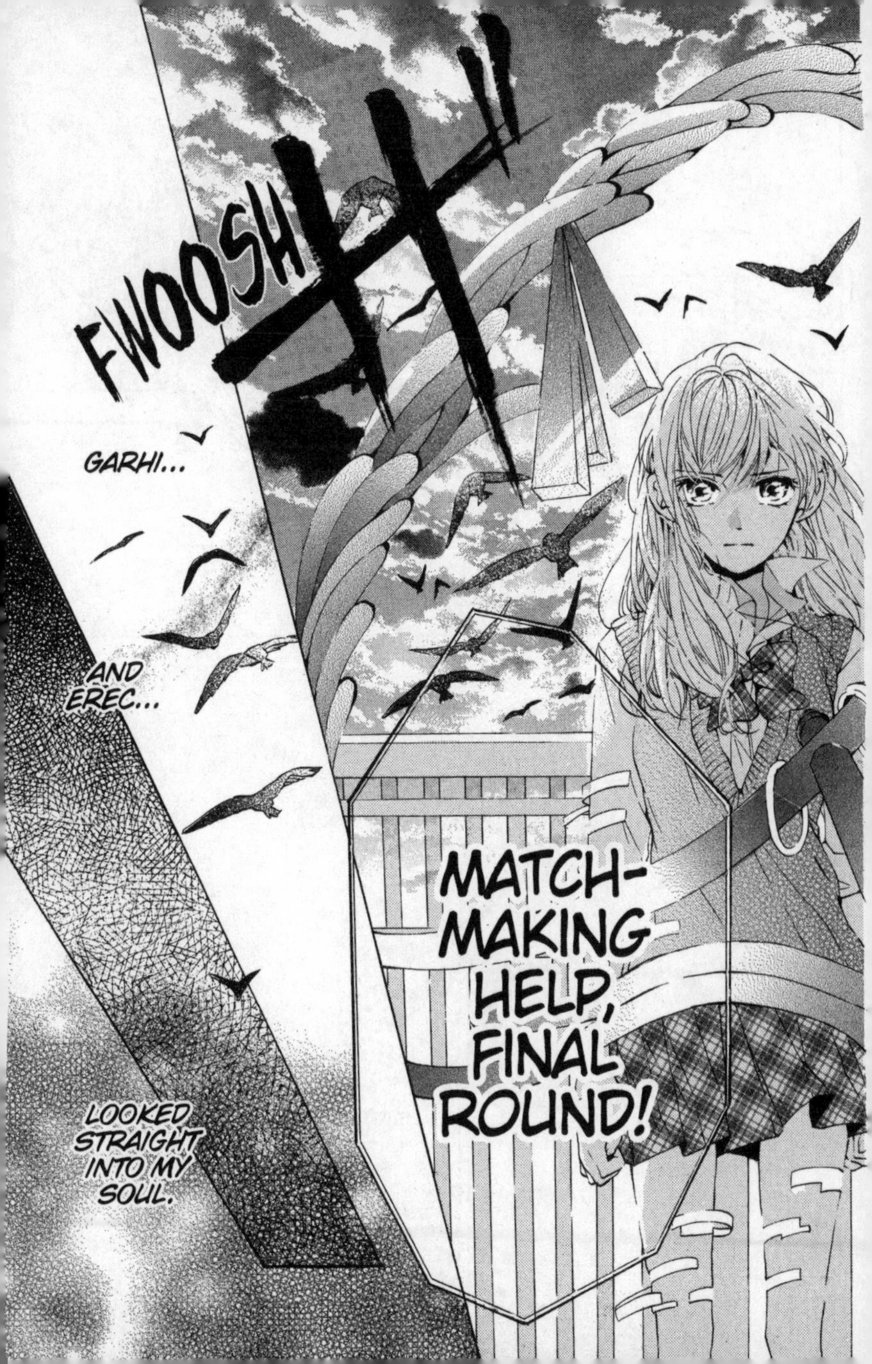
FWOOSH!!
MATCH-MAKING HELP, FINAL ROUND!
GARHI...
AND EREC...
LOOKED STRAIGHT INTO MY SOUL.

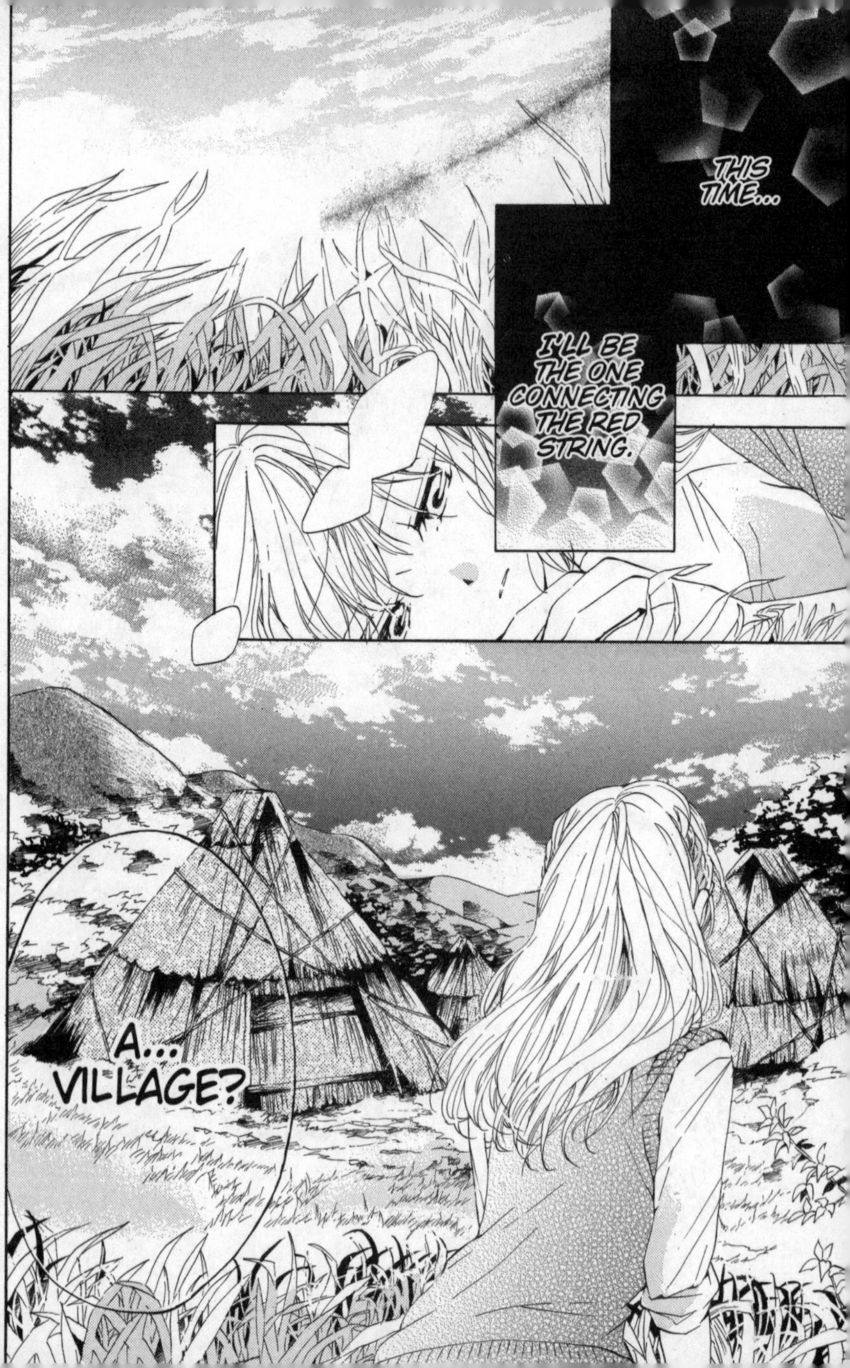
THIS TIME...
I'LL BE THE ONE CONNECTING THE RED STRING.
A... VILLAGE?

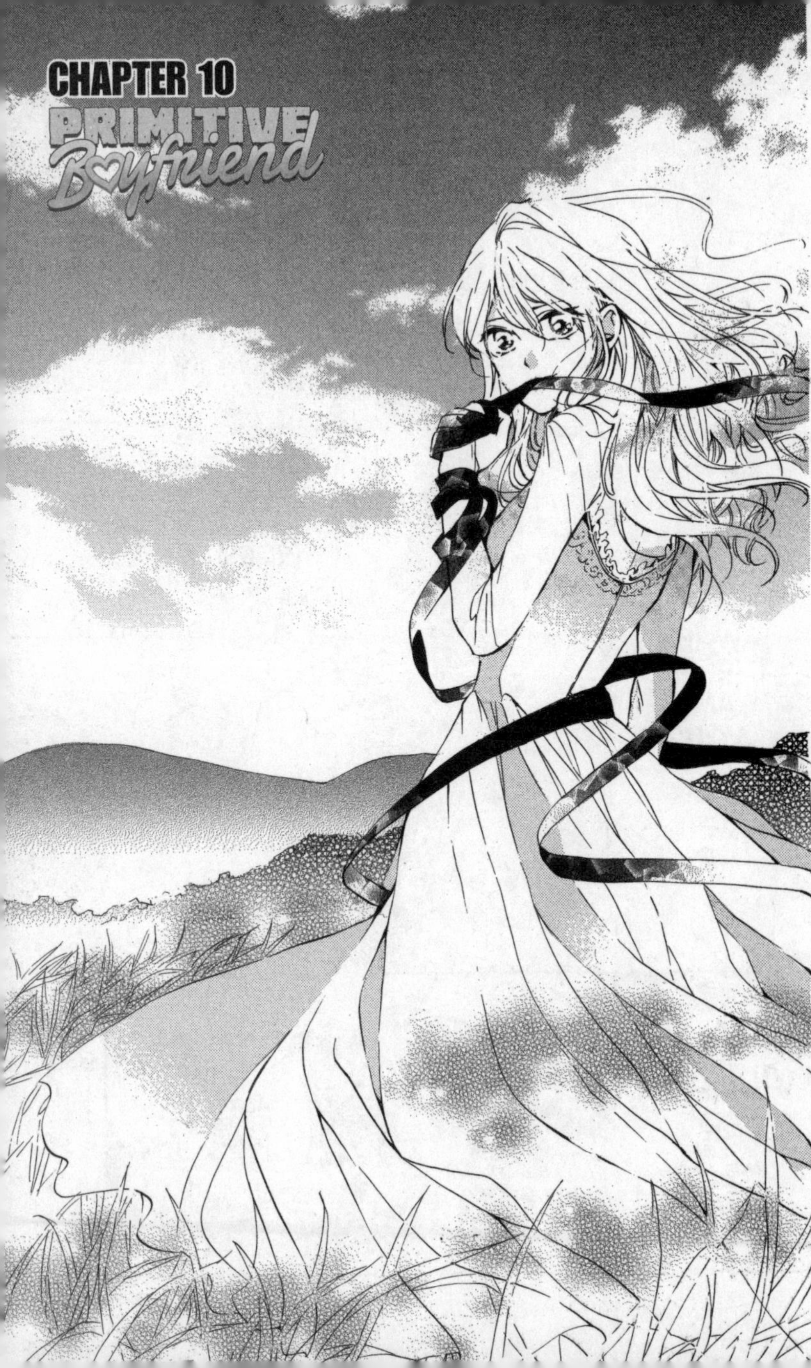
CHAPTER 10
PRIMITIVE
Boyfriend

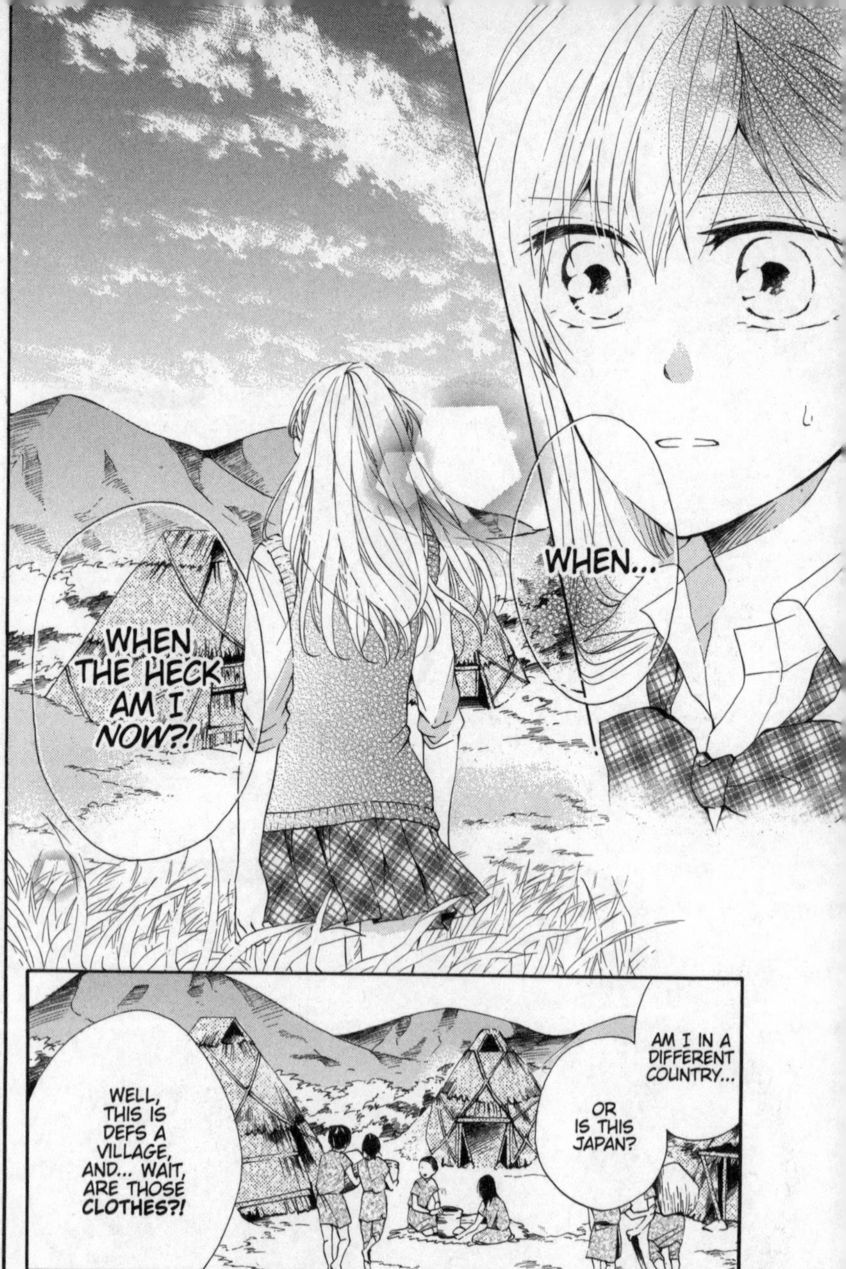
WHEN...
WHEN THE HECK AM I NOW?!
AM I IN A DIFFERENT COUNTRY...
OR IS THIS JAPAN?
WELL, THIS IS DEFS A VILLAGE, AND... WAIT, ARE THOSE CLOTHES?!

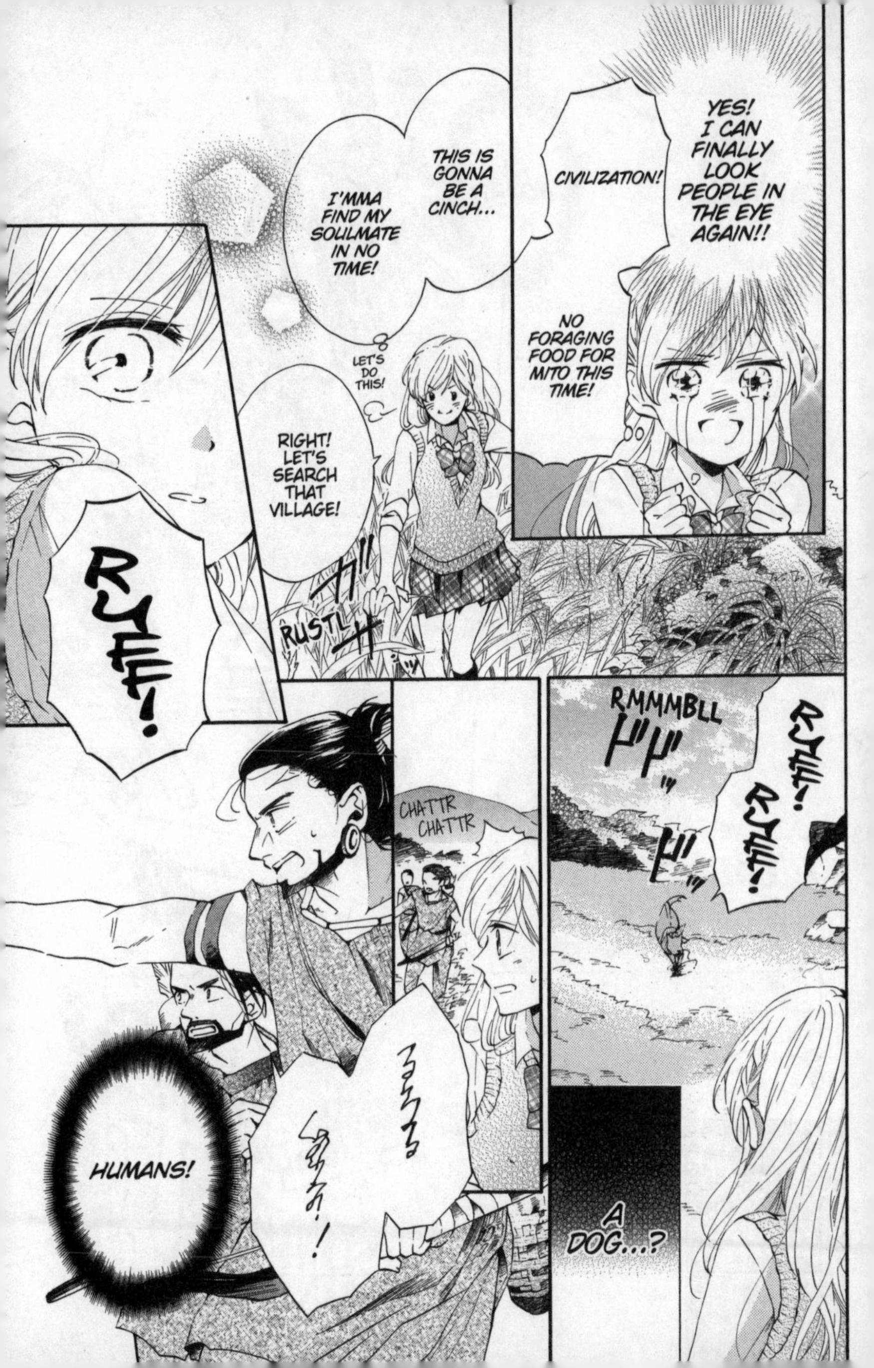
YES! I CAN FINALLY LOOK PEOPLE IN THE EYE AGAIN!!
CIVILIZATION!
NO FORAGING FOOD FOR MITO THIS TIME!
THIS IS GONNA BE A CINCH...
I'MMA FIND MY SOULMATE IN NO TIME!
LET'S DO THIS!
RIGHT! LET'S SEARCH THAT VILLAGE!
RUSTL
RUFF!
RMMMBLL
RUFF! RUFF!
A DOG...?
CHATTR CHATTR
HUMANS!

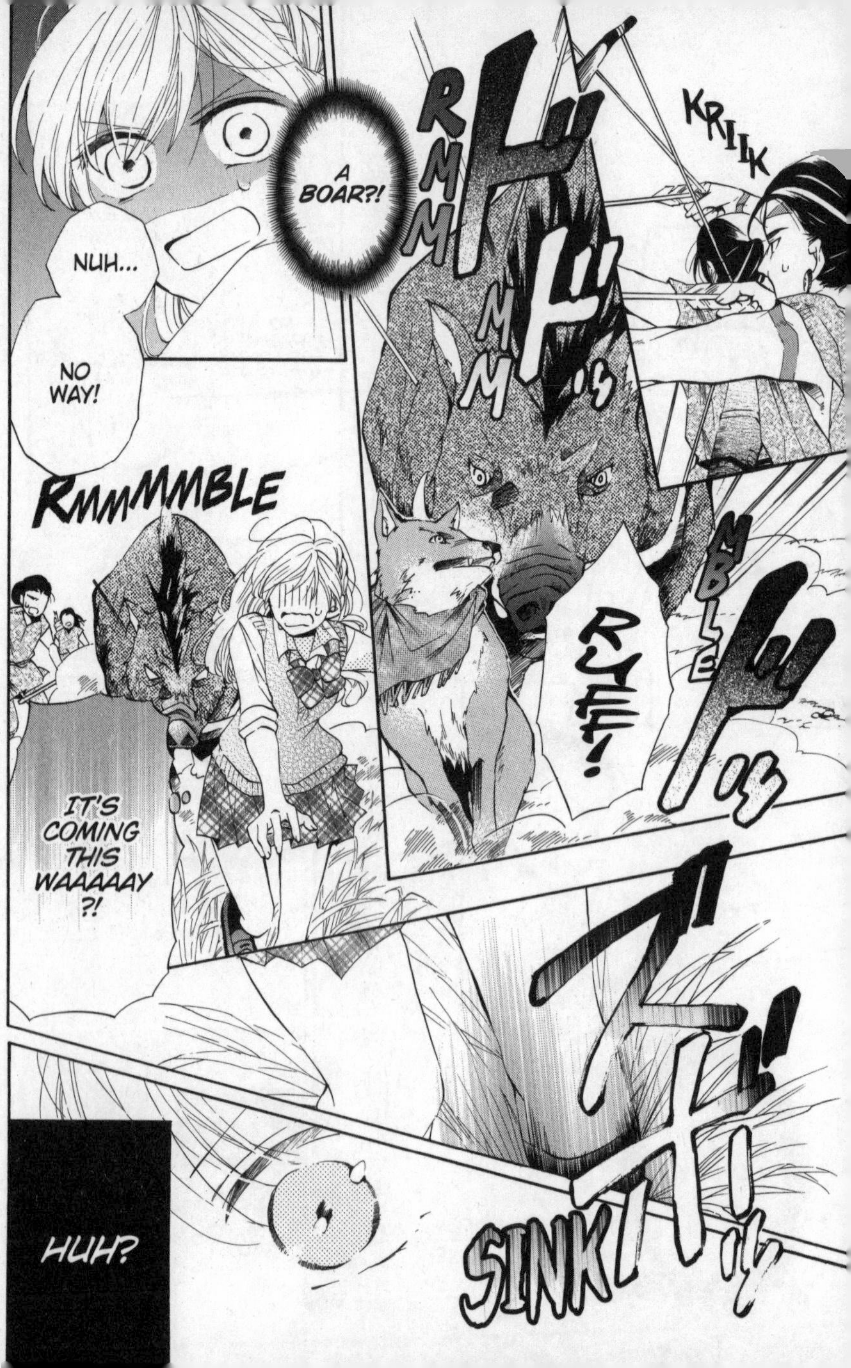

KRIIK
RMMM
MMM
A BOAR?!
NUH...
NO WAY!
MBLE
RUFF!
RMMMMBLE
IT'S COMING THIS WAAAAAY?!
SINK!
HUH?

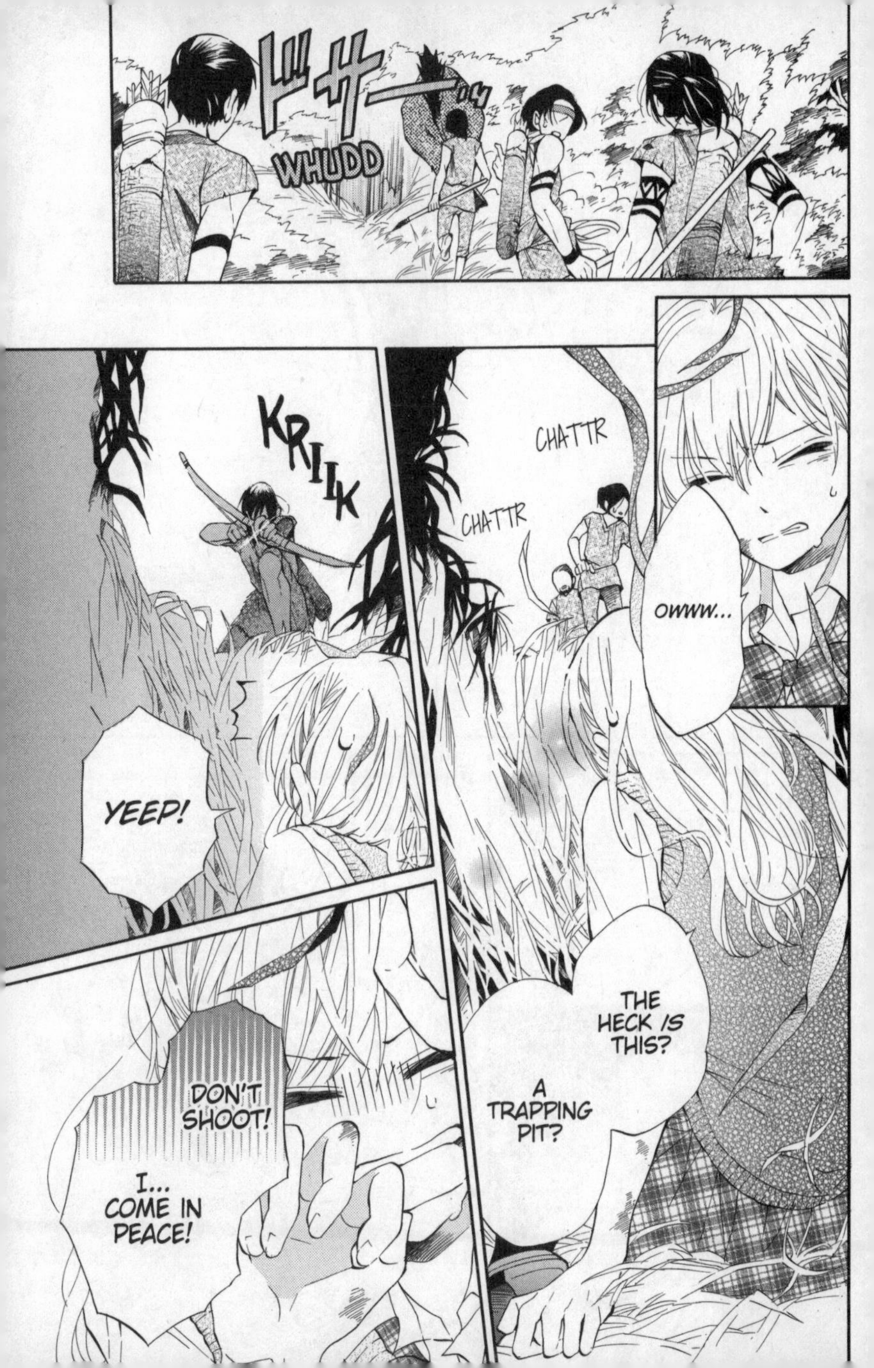
ドサーッ
WHUDD
OWWW...
CHATTR
CHATTR
THE HECK IS THIS?
A TRAPPING PIT?
KRIIIK
YEEP!
DON'T SHOOT!
I... COME IN PEACE!

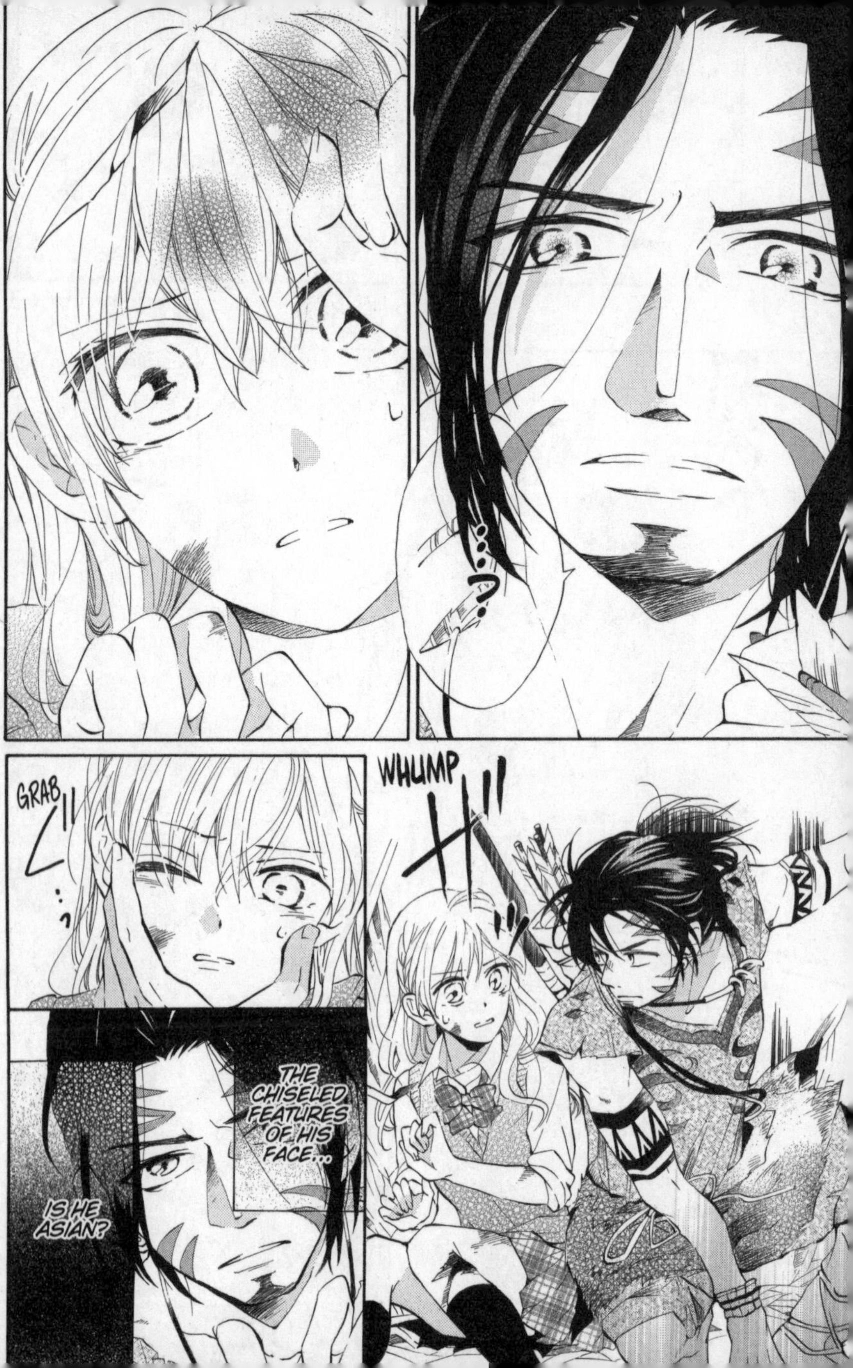
WHUMP
GRAB
THE CHISELED FEATURES OF HIS FACE...
IS HE ASIAN?

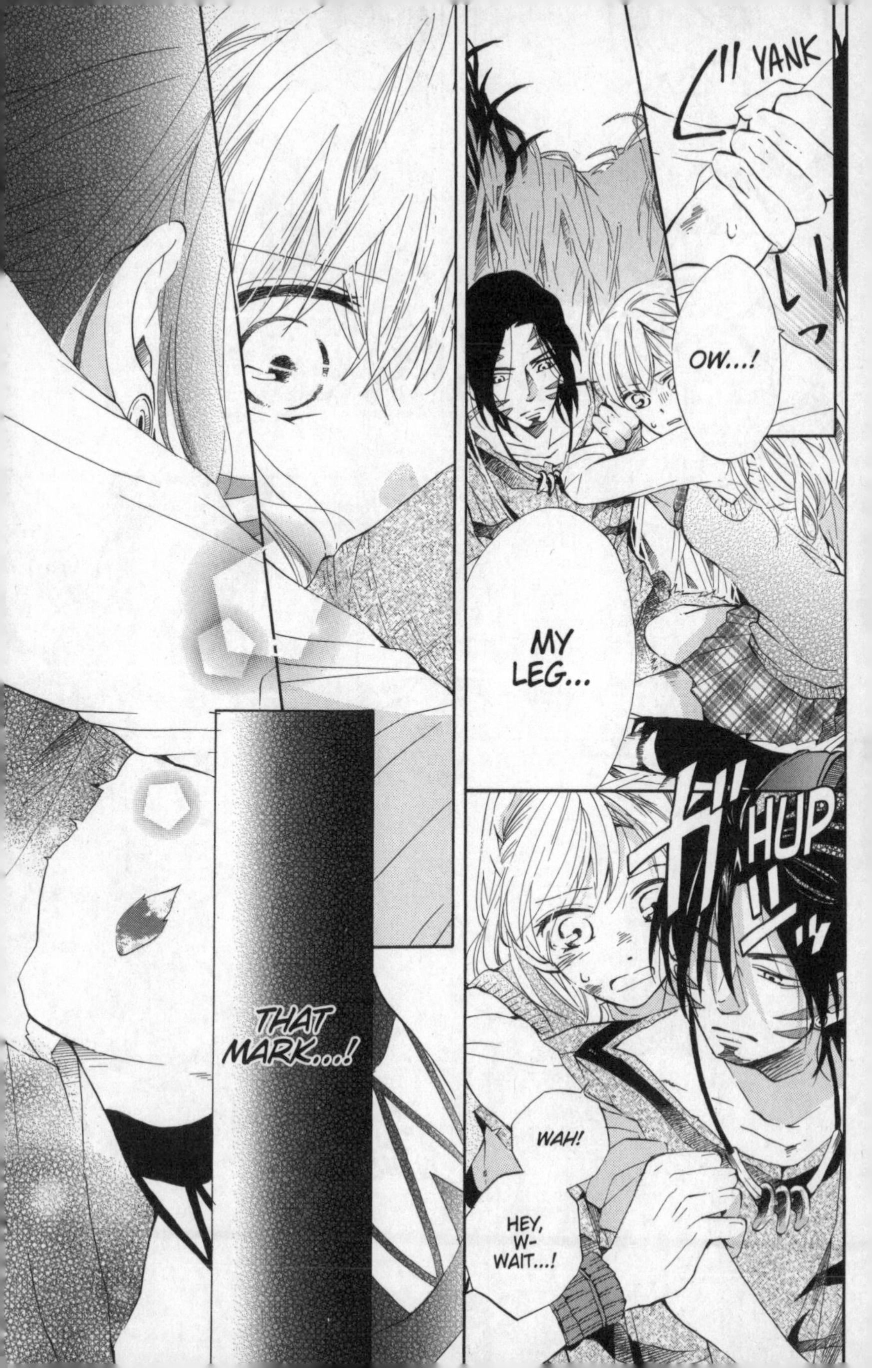
YANK
OW...!
MY LEG...
HUP
WAH!
HEY, W-WAIT...!
THAT MARK...!

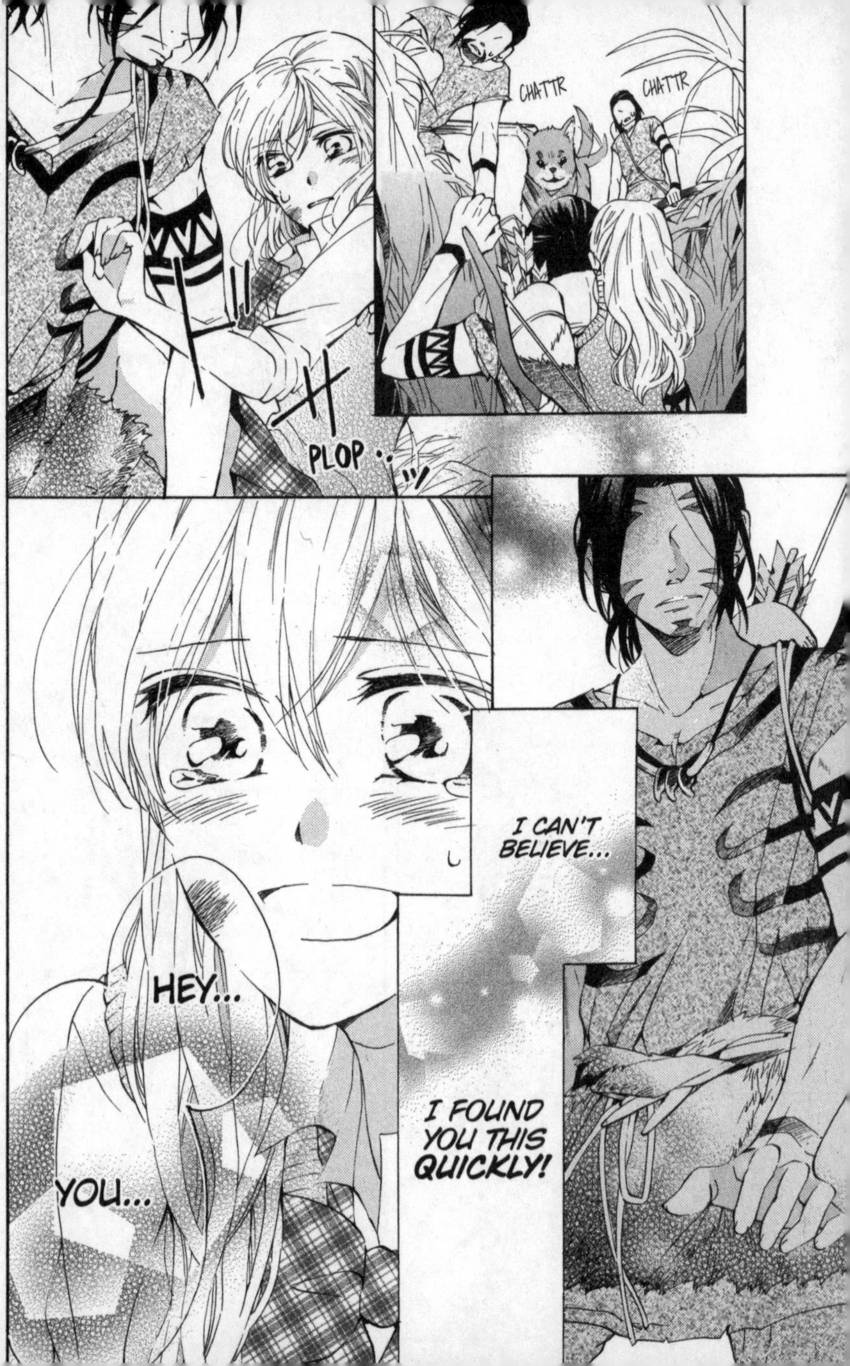
CHATTR
CHATTR
PLOP..
I CAN'T BELIEVE...
I FOUND YOU THIS QUICKLY!
HEY...
YOU...

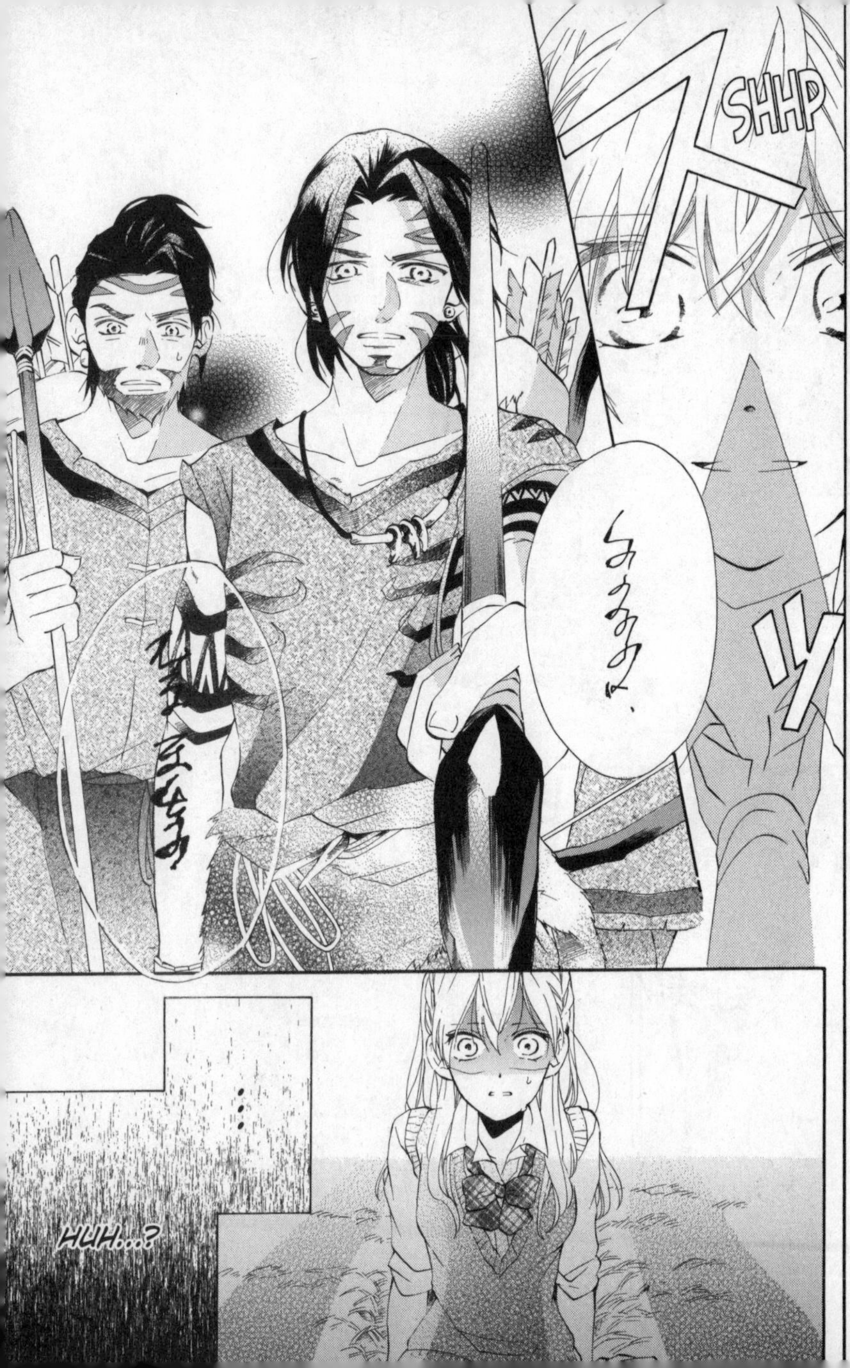
SHHP
...
HUH...?

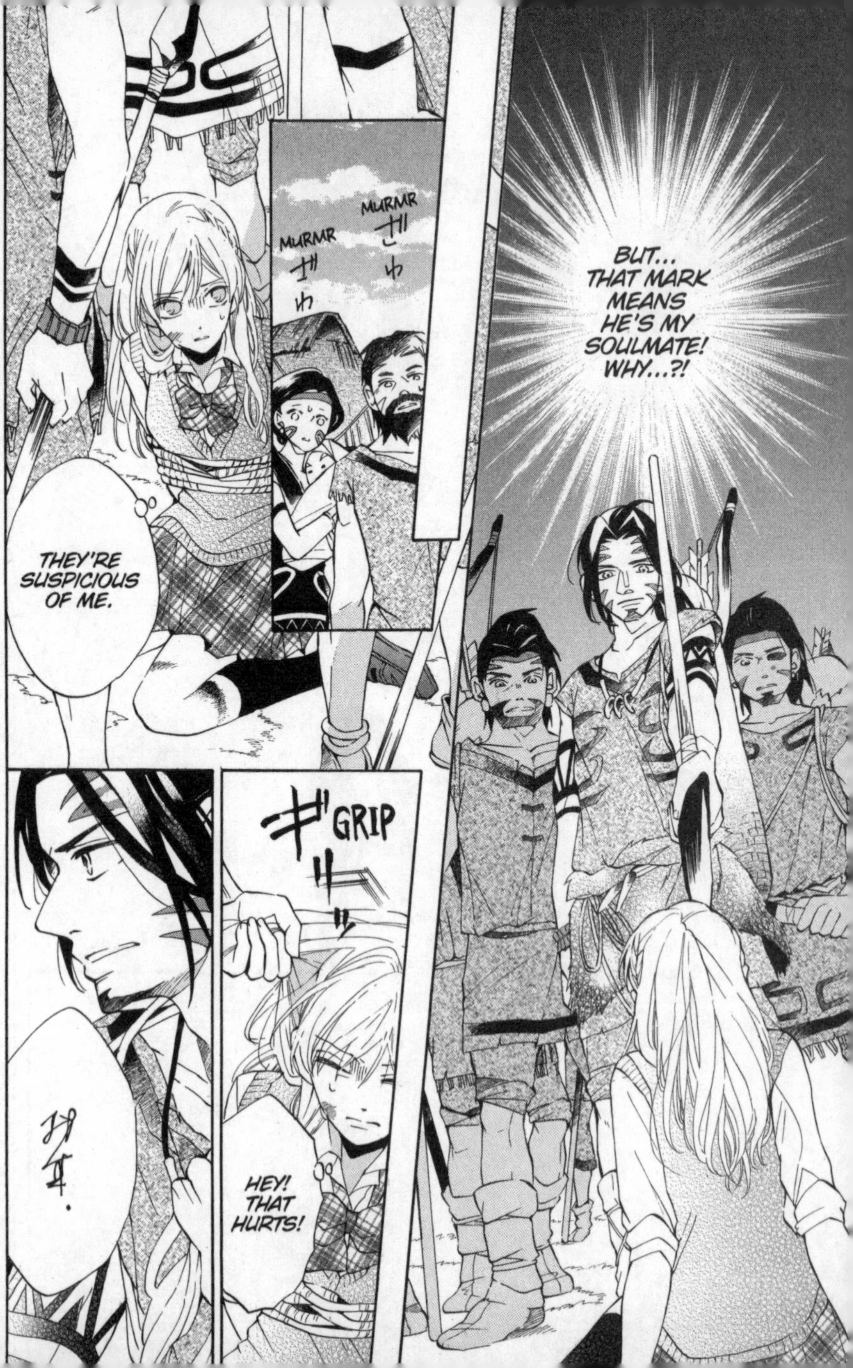
BUT... THAT MARK MEANS HE'S MY SOULMATE! WHY...?!
MURMR
ざわ
MURMR
ざわ
THEY'RE SUSPICIOUS OF ME.
GRIP
HEY! THAT HURTS!

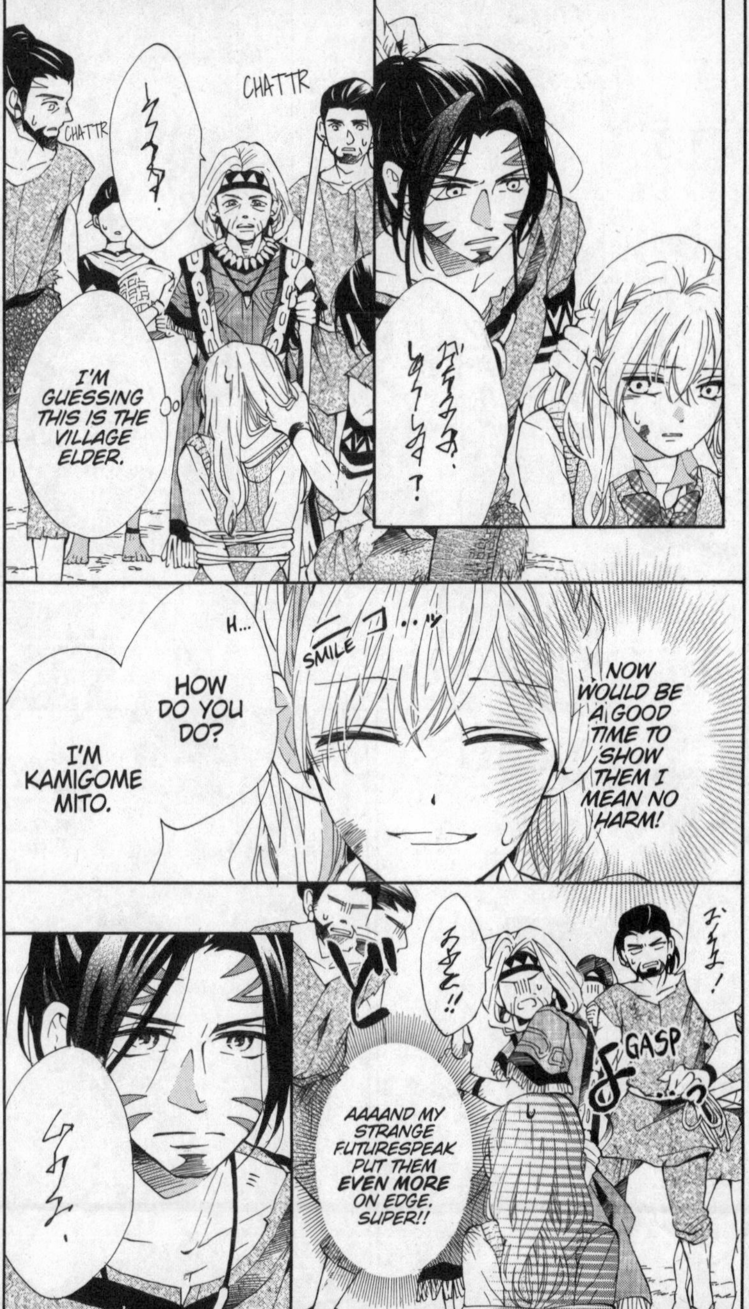
CHATTR
CHATTR
I'M GUESSING THIS IS THE VILLAGE ELDER.
NOW WOULD BE A GOOD TIME TO SHOW THEM I MEAN NO HARM!
SMILE
H...
HOW DO YOU DO?
I'M KAMIGOME MITO.
GASP
AAAAND MY STRANGE FUTURESPEAK PUT THEM EVEN MORE ON EDGE. SUPER!!

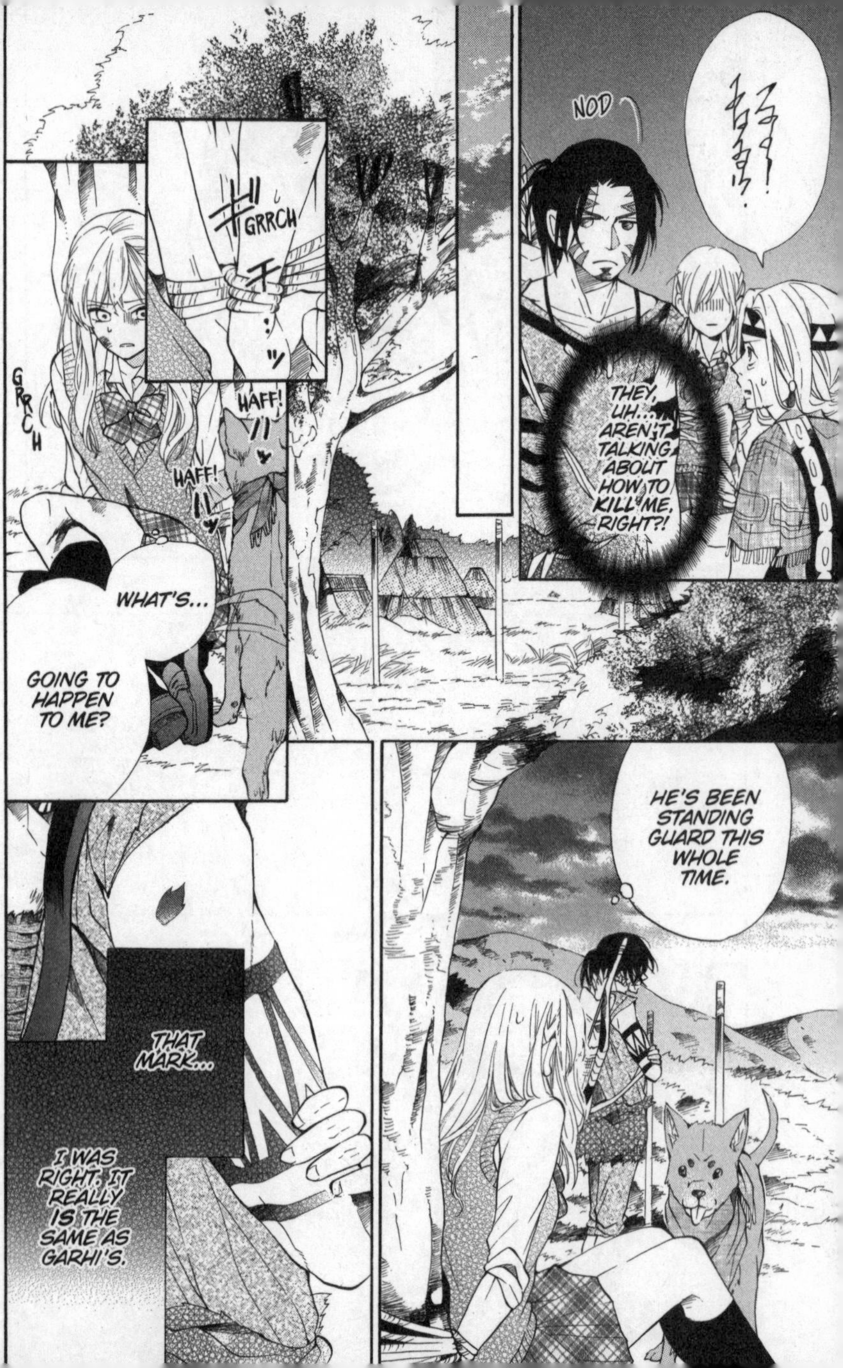
NOD
THEY, UH... AREN'T TALKING ABOUT HOW TO KILL ME, RIGHT?!
GRRCH
GRRCH
HAFF!
HAFF!
WHAT'S...
GOING TO HAPPEN TO ME?
HE'S BEEN STANDING GUARD THIS WHOLE TIME.
THAT MARK...
I WAS RIGHT. IT REALLY IS THE SAME AS GARHI'S.

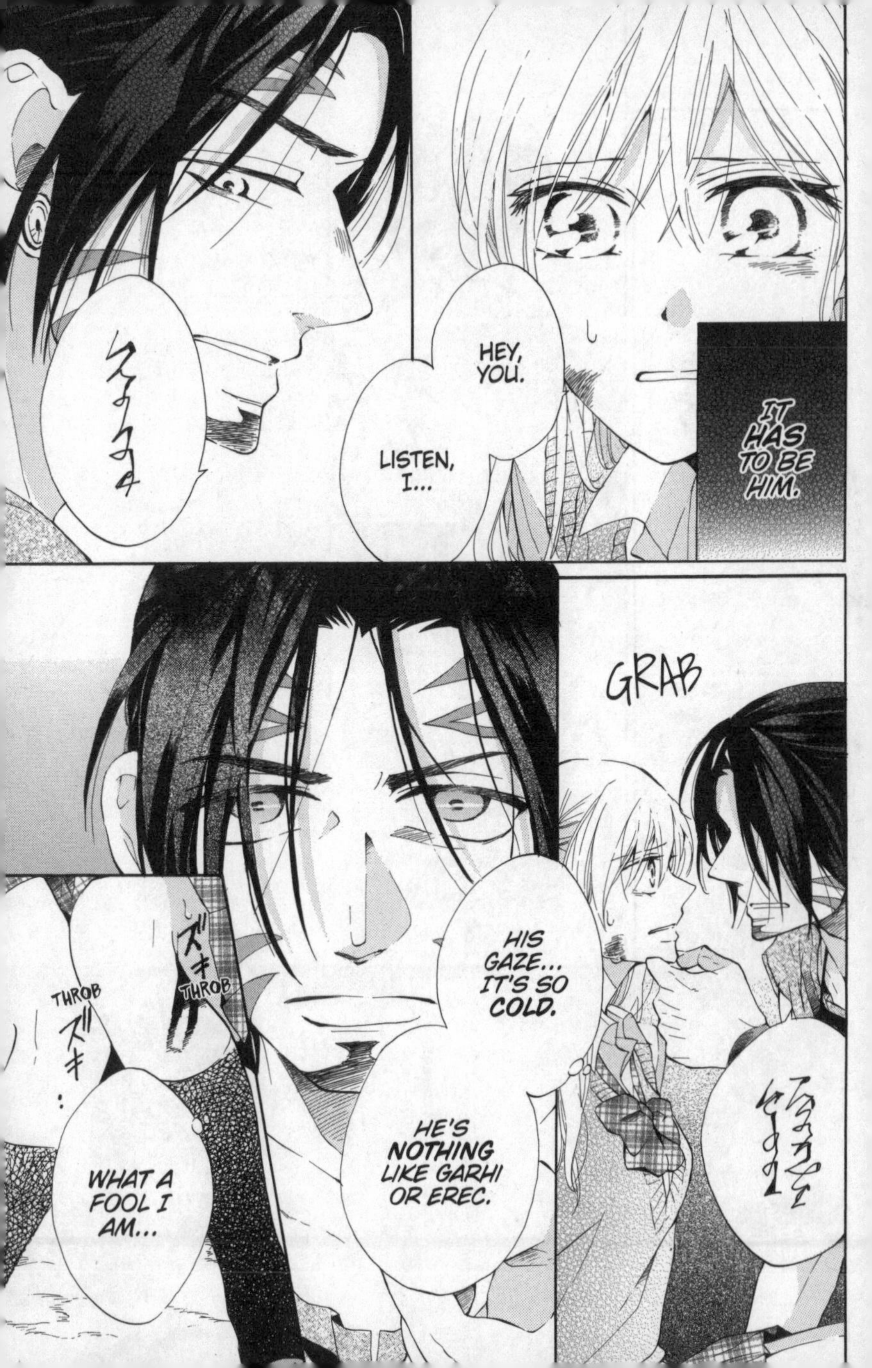
IT HAS TO BE HIM.
HEY, YOU.
LISTEN, I...
GRAB
HIS GAZE... IT'S SO COLD.
HE'S NOTHING LIKE GARHI OR EREC.
THROB
THROB
WHAT A FOOL I AM...

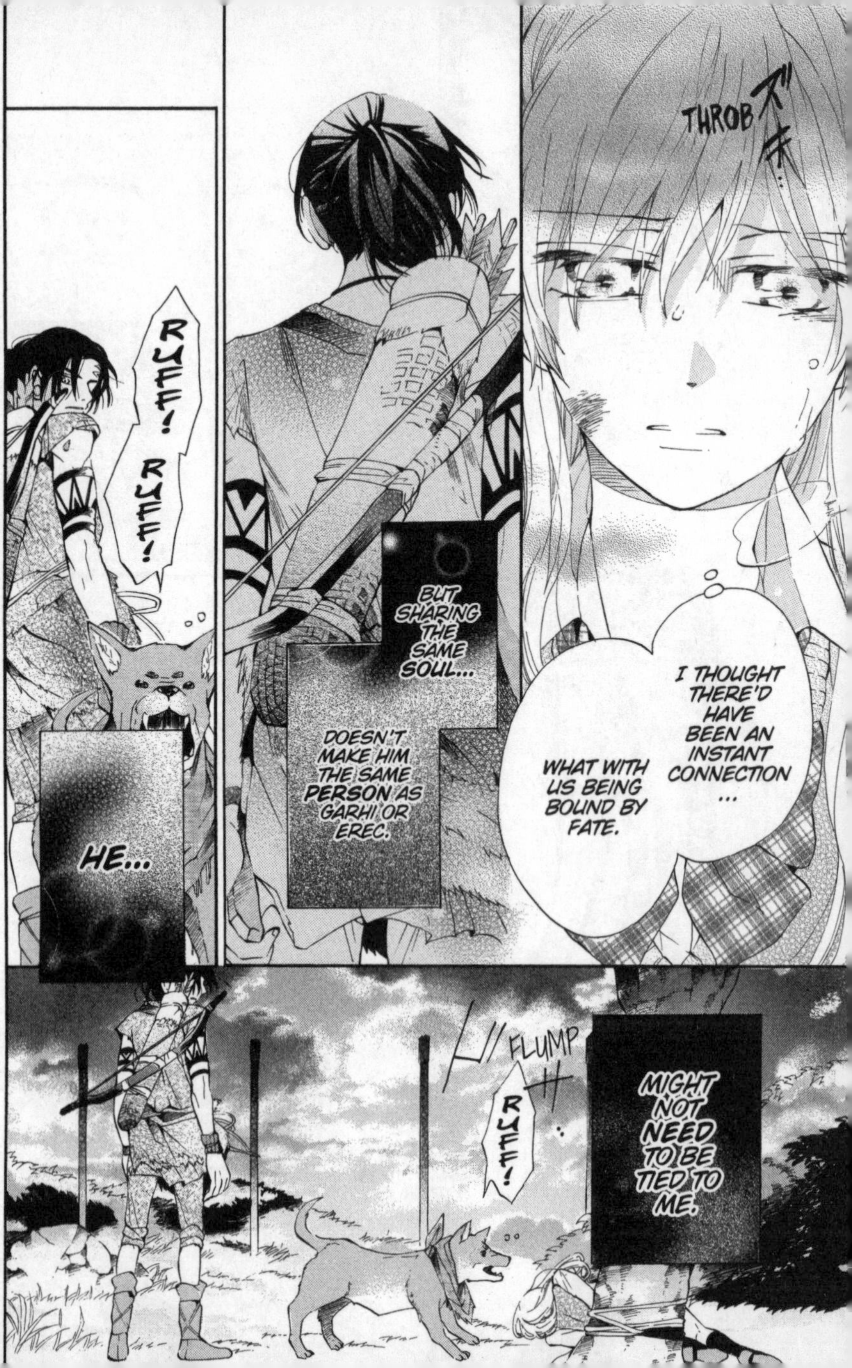
THROB
I THOUGHT THERE'D HAVE BEEN AN INSTANT CONNECTION...
WHAT WITH US BEING BOUND BY FATE.
BUT SHARING THE SAME SOUL...
DOESN'T MAKE HIM THE SAME PERSON AS GARHI OR EREC.
RUFF! RUFF!
HE...
MIGHT NOT NEED TO BE TIED TO ME.
FLUMP
RUFF!

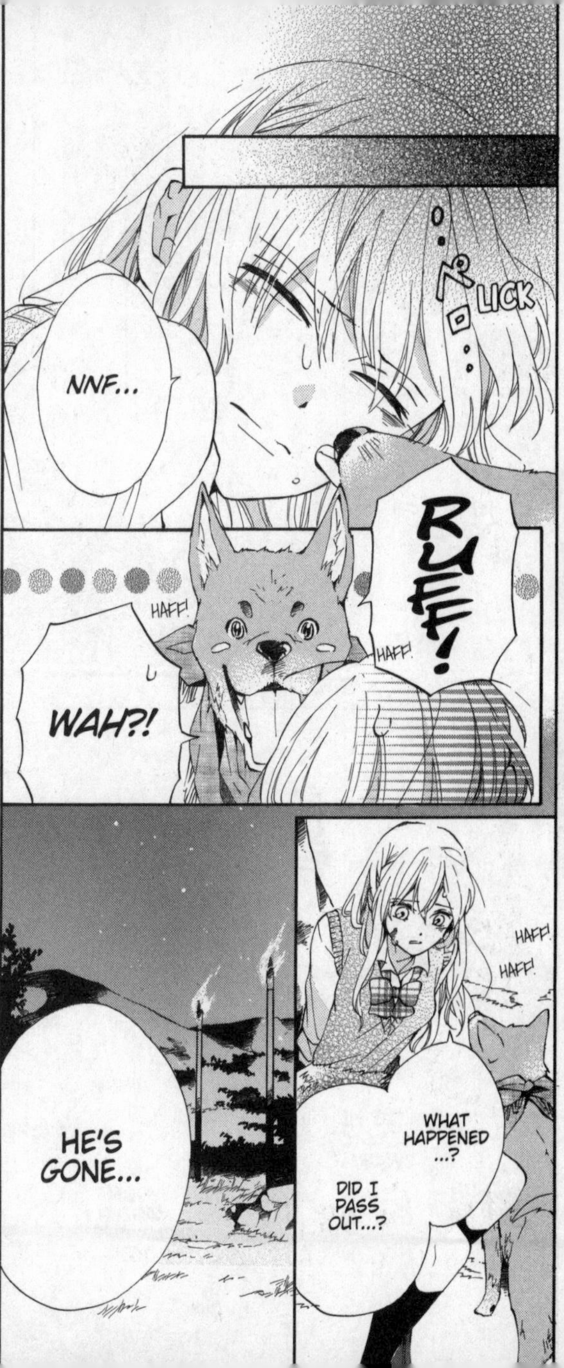
LICK
NNF...
RUFF!
HAFF!
HAFF!
WAH?!
HAFF!
HAFF!
WHAT HAPPENED ...?
DID I PASS OUT...?
HE'S GONE...

2

WELL, I HAD PLANNED ON PUTTING SOME MAKING-OF STORIES IN HERE, BUT ALL I CAN REMEMBER NOW IS HOW CHAOTIC IT ALL WAS... NOW WHAT...? OH!

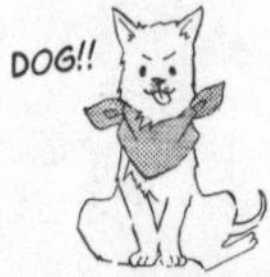
DOG!!

I GOT AN UNUSUAL NUMBER OF COMPLIMENTS FROM MY EDITOR AND FAMILY ON THE BOAR AND DOG IN THIS CHAPTER, AND IT MADE MY CHEST SWELL.

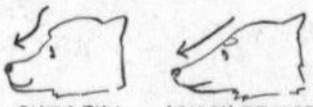

SHIBA INU   JOMON PERIOD DOG

THE SLANT OF THE SNOUT WAS DIFFICULT TO GET RIGHT.

THIS DOGGY'S NAME, KUU, COMES FROM THE AINU WORD FOR "BOW."

HE MUST BE LIKE HIS MASTER'S BOW.

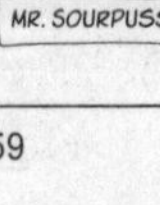

MR. SOURPUSS

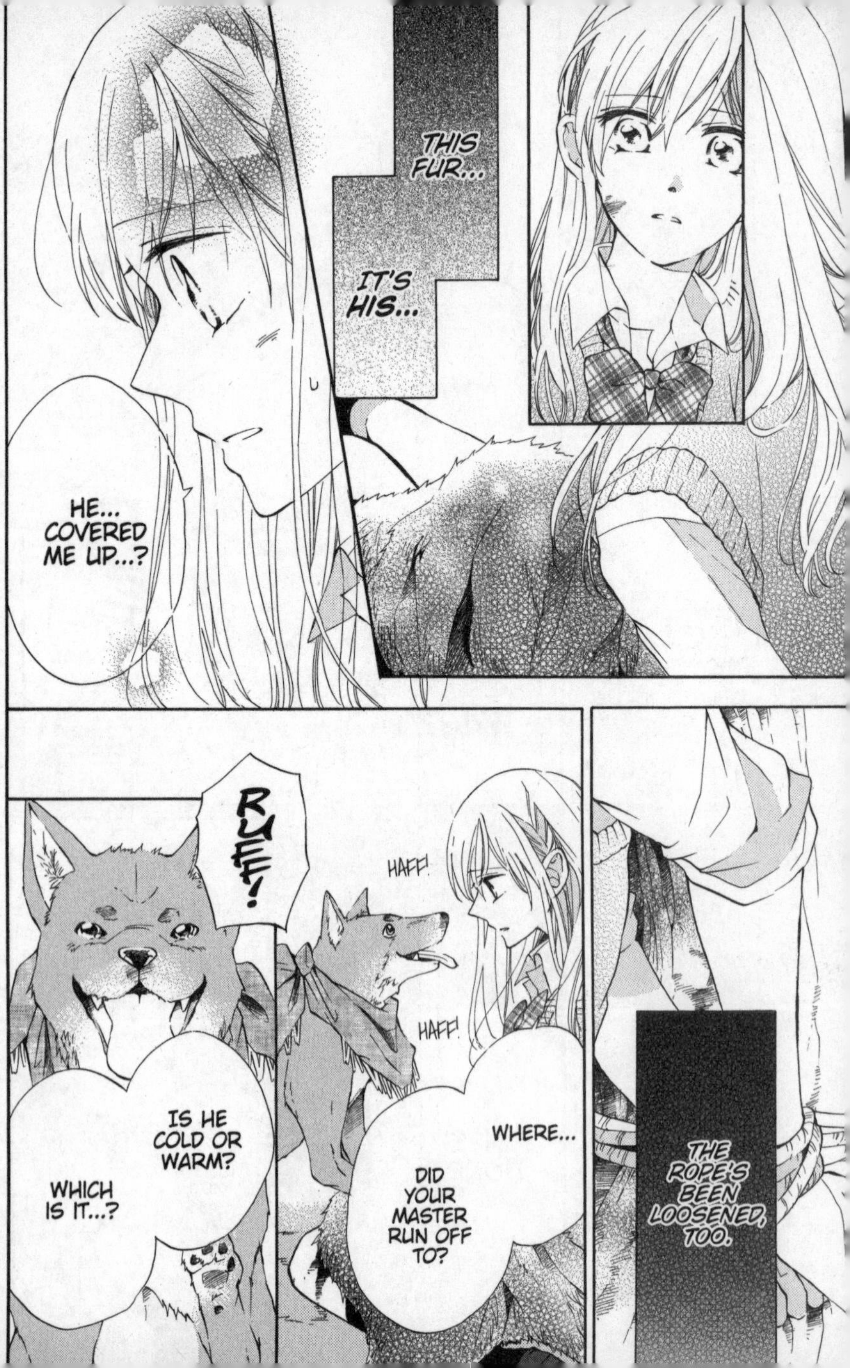
THIS FUR...
IT'S HIS...
HE... COVERED ME UP...?
THE ROPE'S BEEN LOOSENED, TOO.
HAFF!
RUFF!
HAFF!
WHERE...
DID YOUR MASTER RUN OFF TO?
IS HE COLD OR WARM?
WHICH IS IT...?

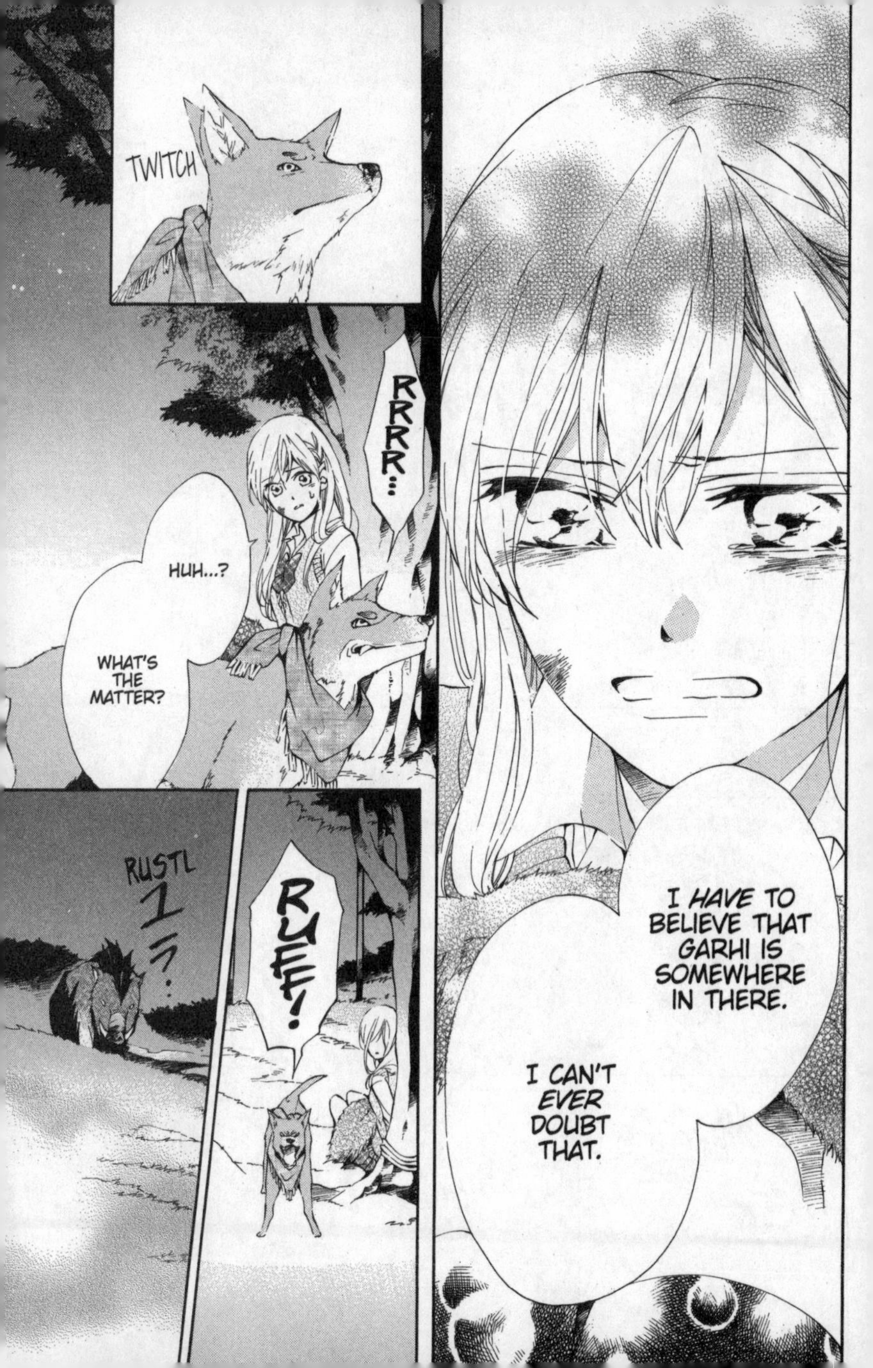
I HAVE TO BELIEVE THAT GARHI IS SOMEWHERE IN THERE.
I CAN'T EVER DOUBT THAT.
TWITCH
RRRR..
HUH...?
WHAT'S THE MATTER?
RUFF!
RUSTL

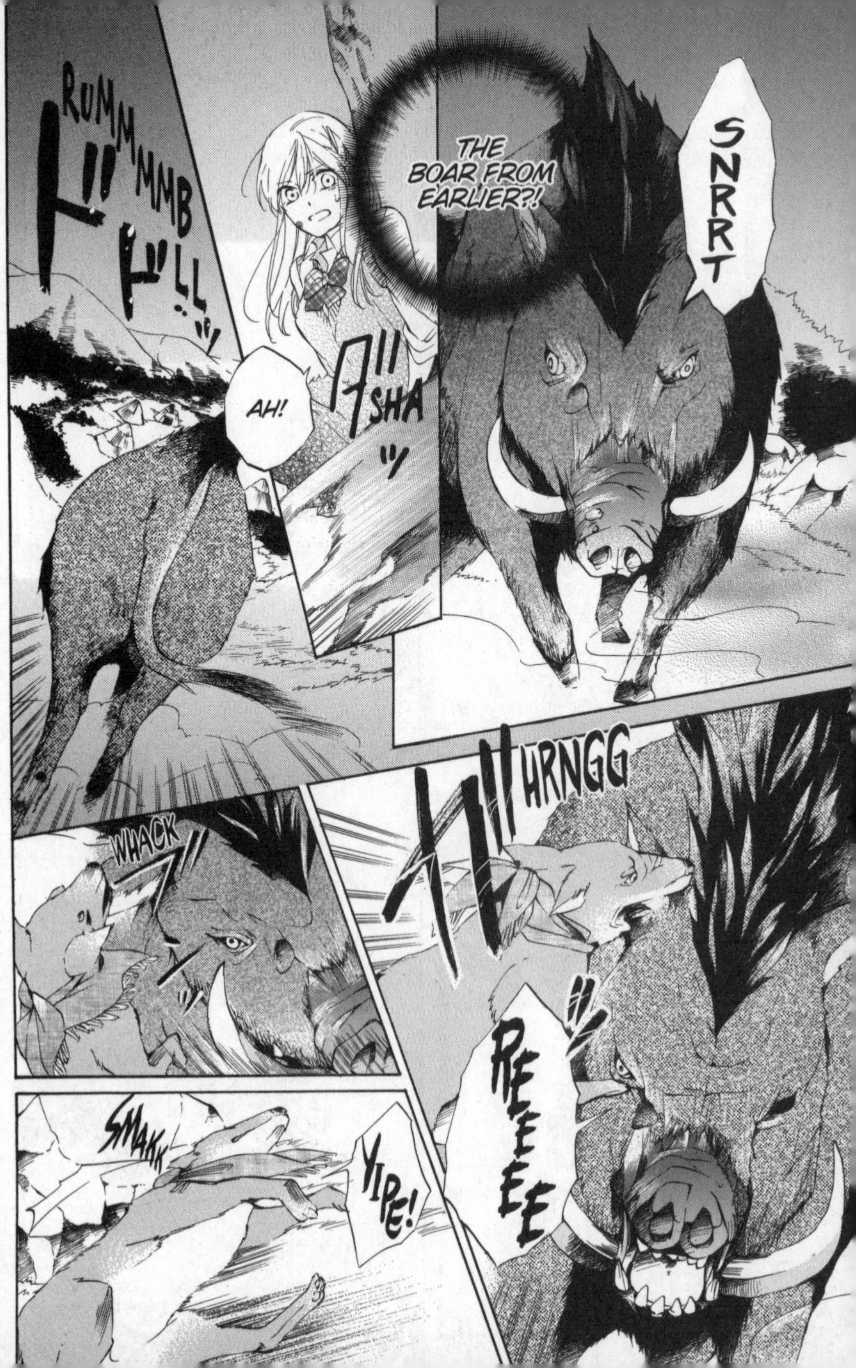
SNRRT
THE BOAR FROM EARLIER?!
SHA
AH!
RUMMMMB
LLL
HRNGG
REEEEEE
WHACK
YIPE!
SMAKK

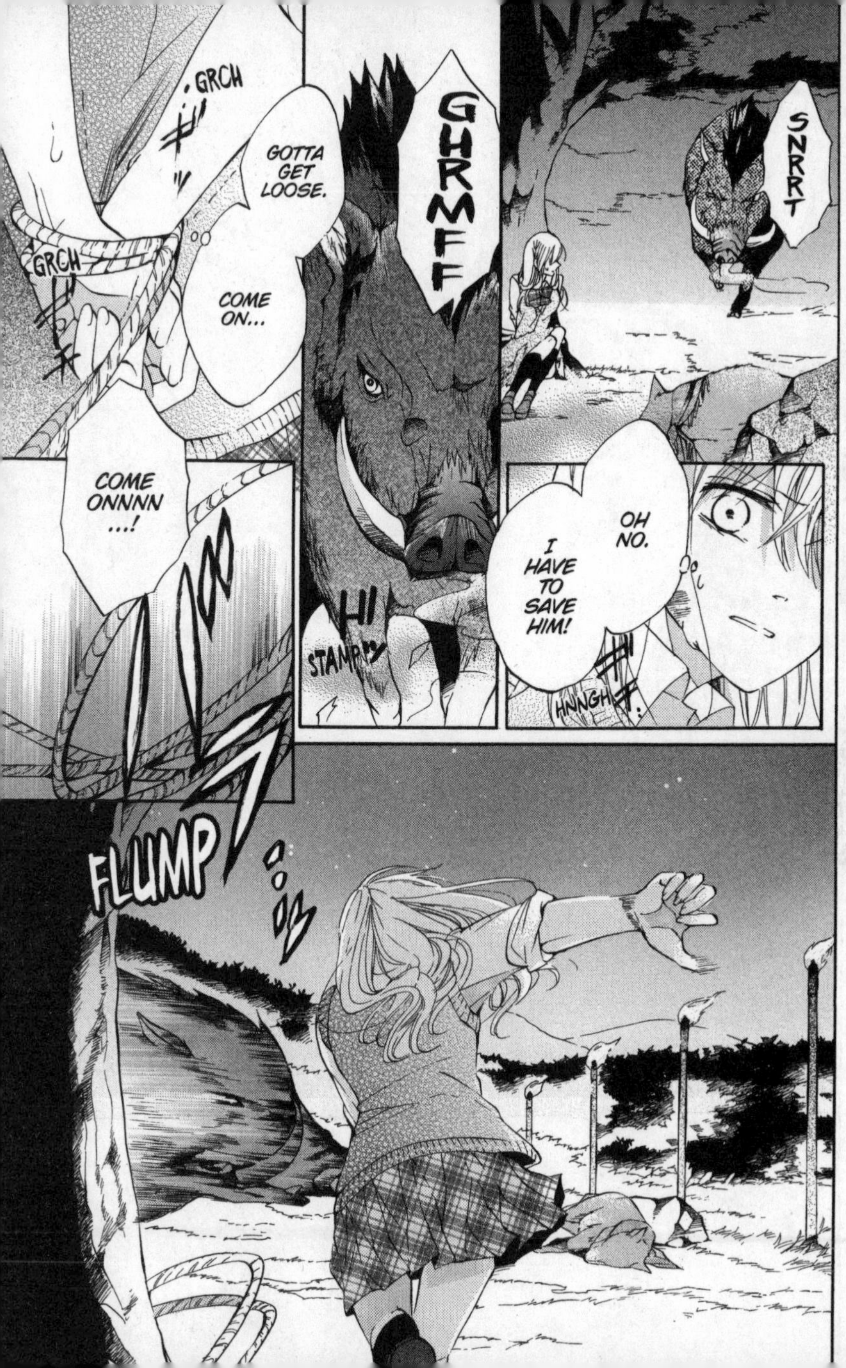
SNRRT
OH NO.
I HAVE TO SAVE HIM!
HNNGH
GHRMFF
HI
STAMP
GRCH
GOTTA GET LOOSE.
GRCH
COME ON...
COME ONNNN ...!
FLUMP

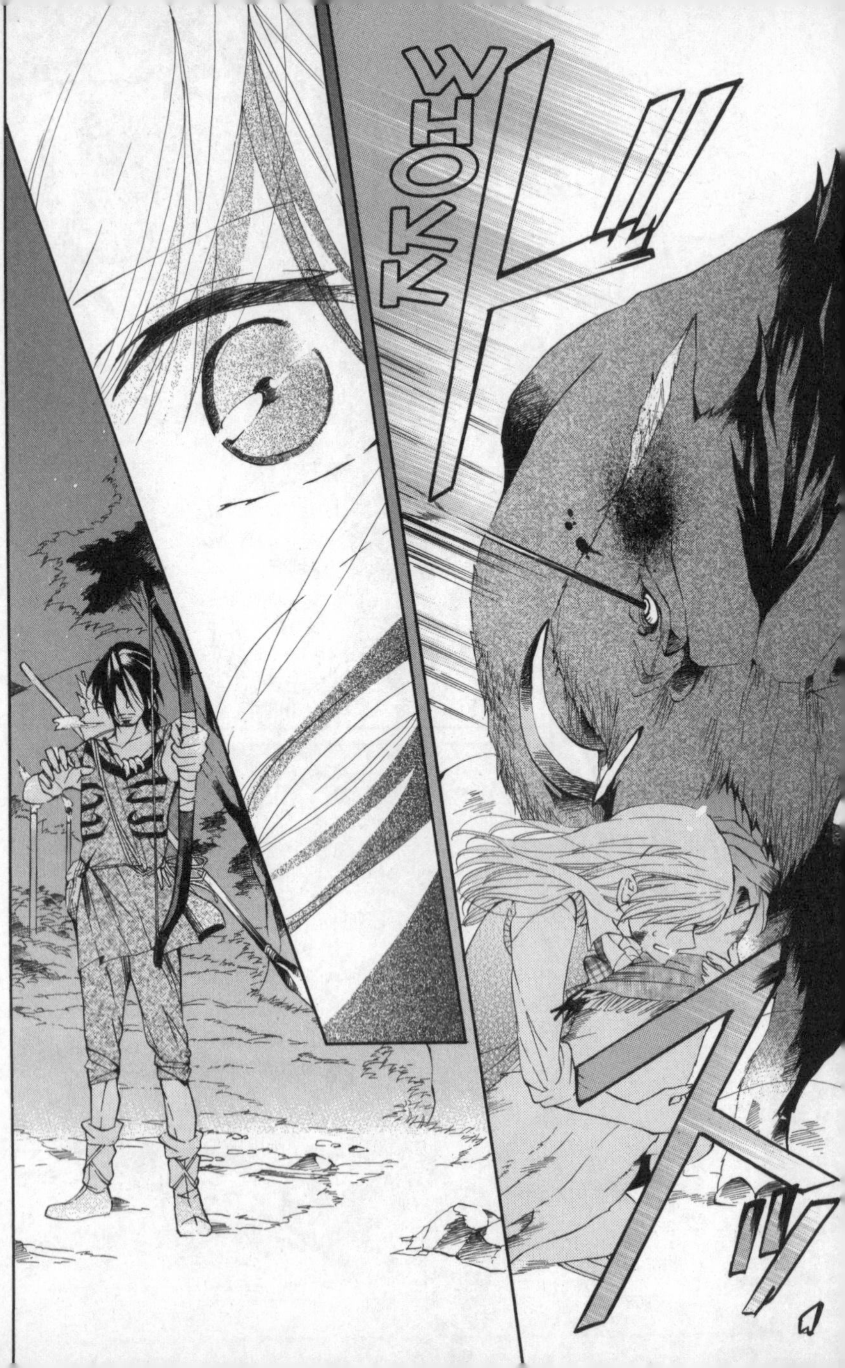
WHOKK

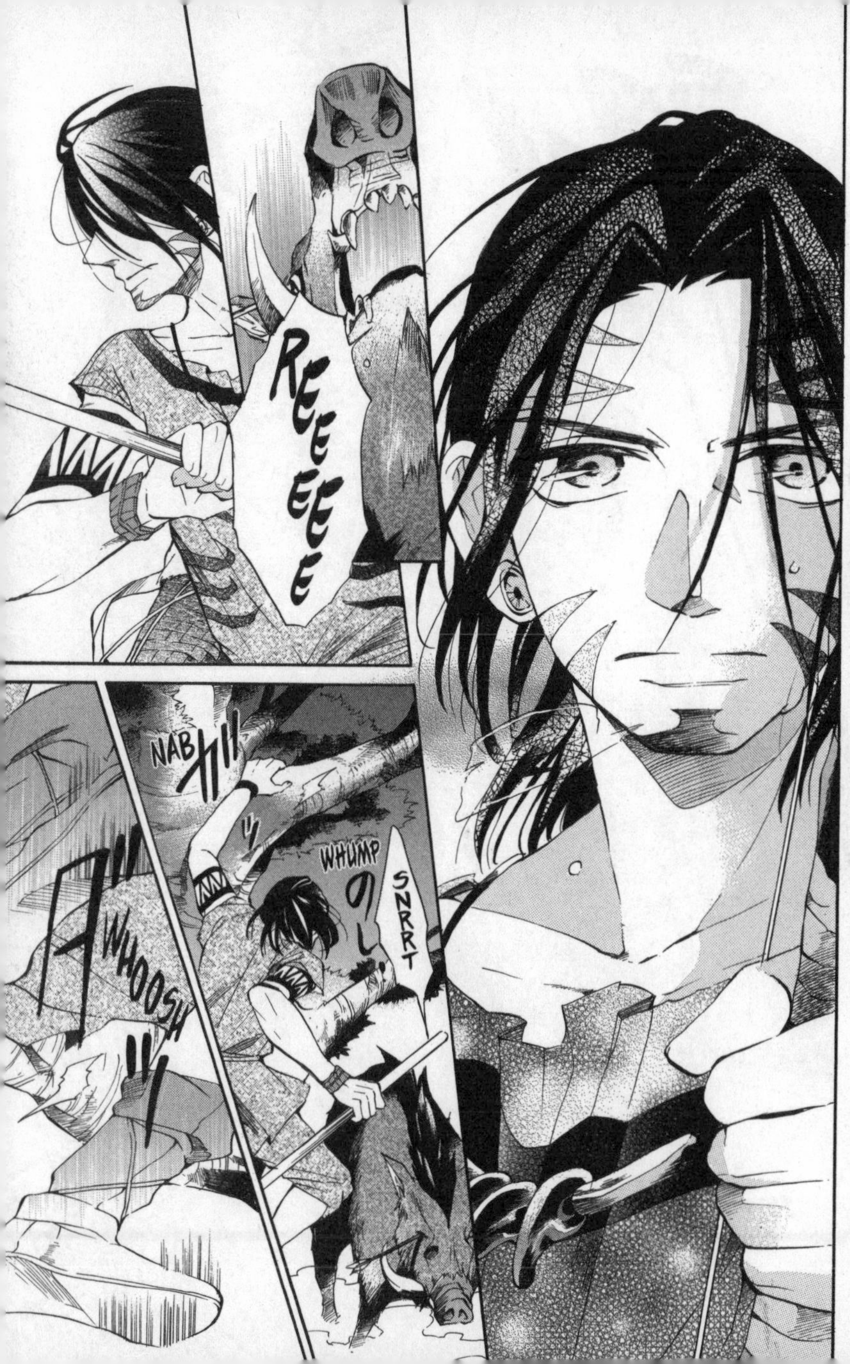
REEEEEE
NAB
WHUMP
SNRRT
WHOOSH

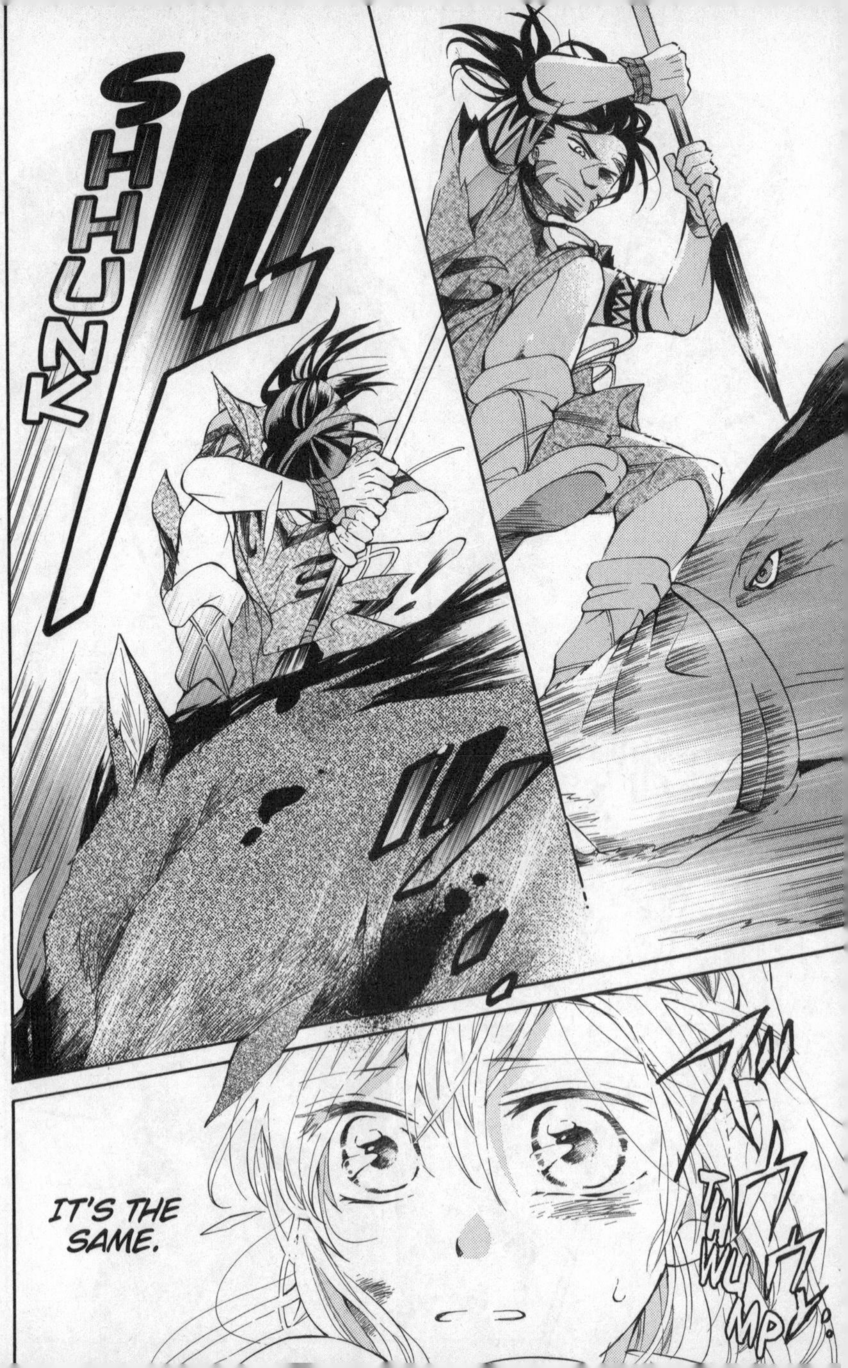
SHHUNK
THWUMP
IT'S THE SAME.

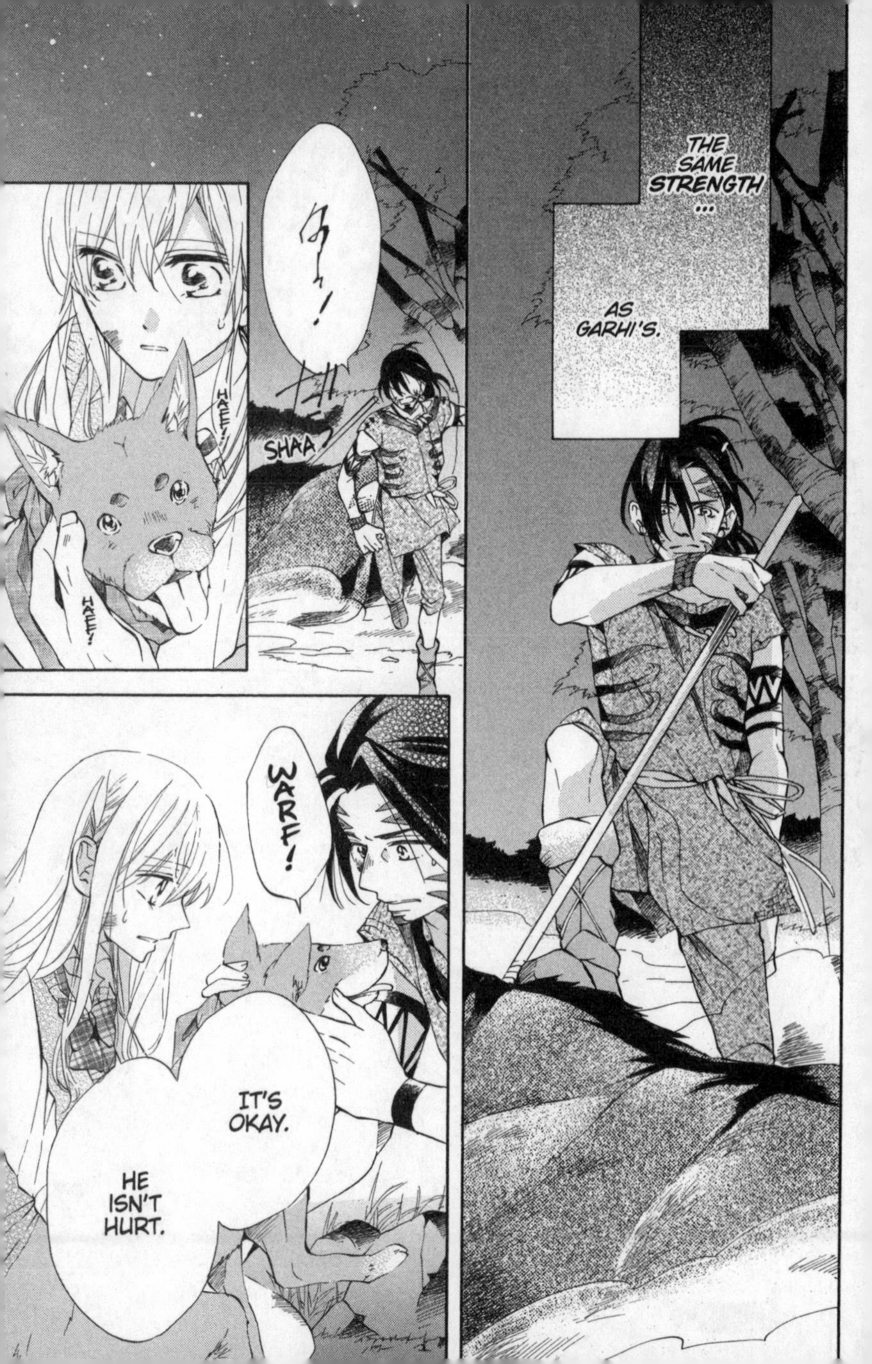
THE SAME STRENGTH...
AS GARHI'S.
SHAA
HAFF!
HAFF!
WARF!
IT'S OKAY.
HE ISN'T HURT.

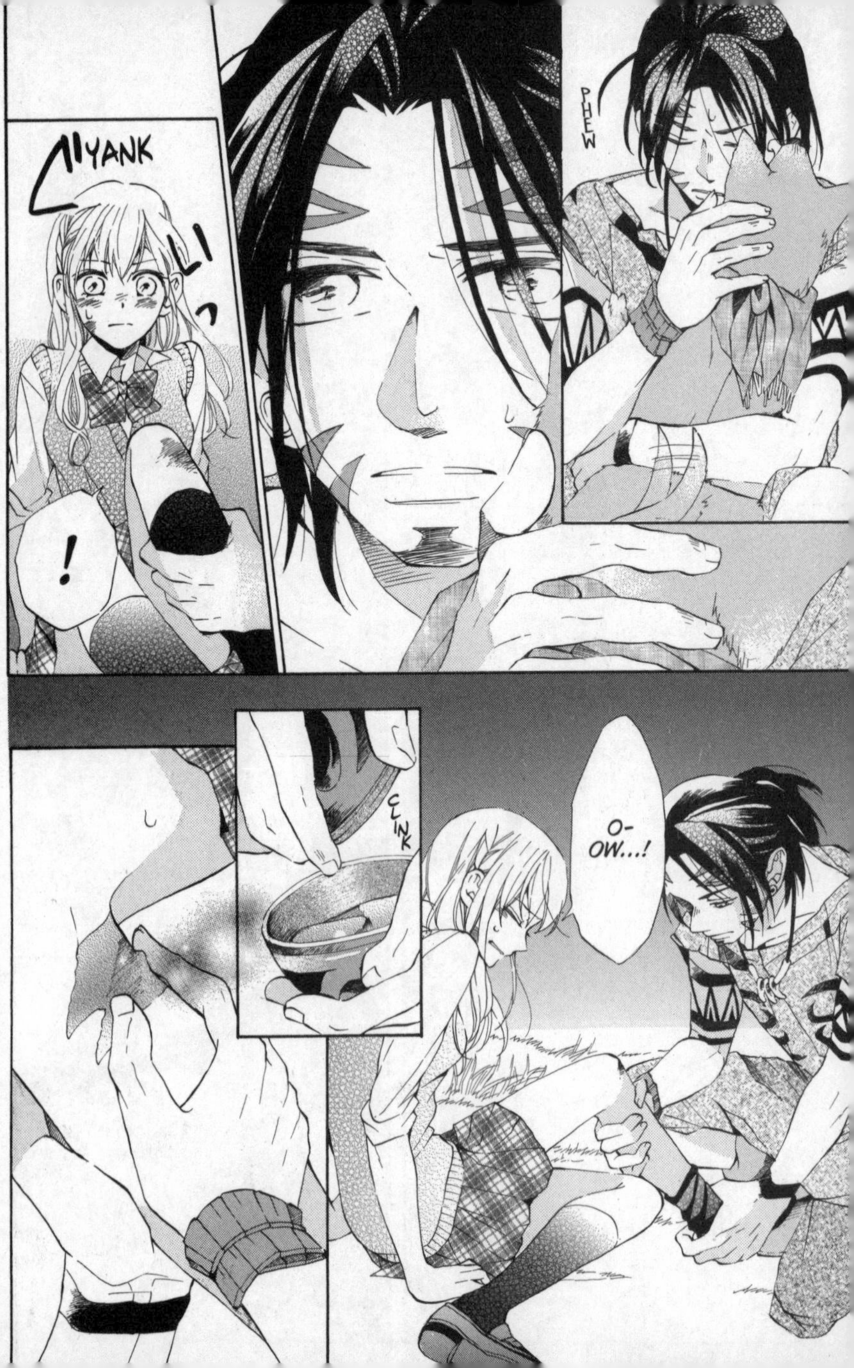
PHEW
YANK
!
O-OW...!
CLINK

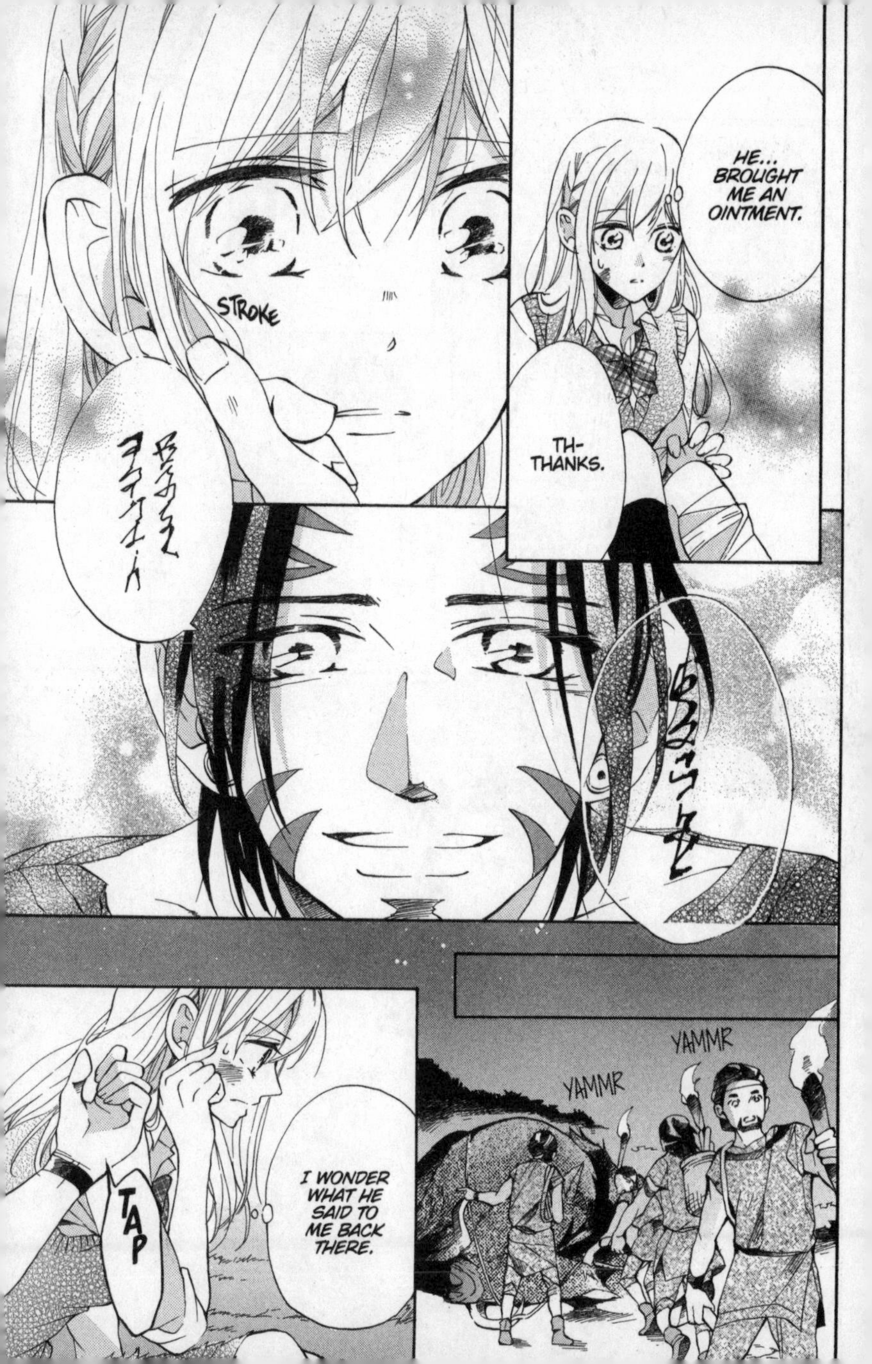
HE... BROUGHT ME AN OINTMENT.
TH- THANKS.
STROKE
YAMMR
YAMMR
TAP
I WONDER WHAT HE SAID TO ME BACK THERE.

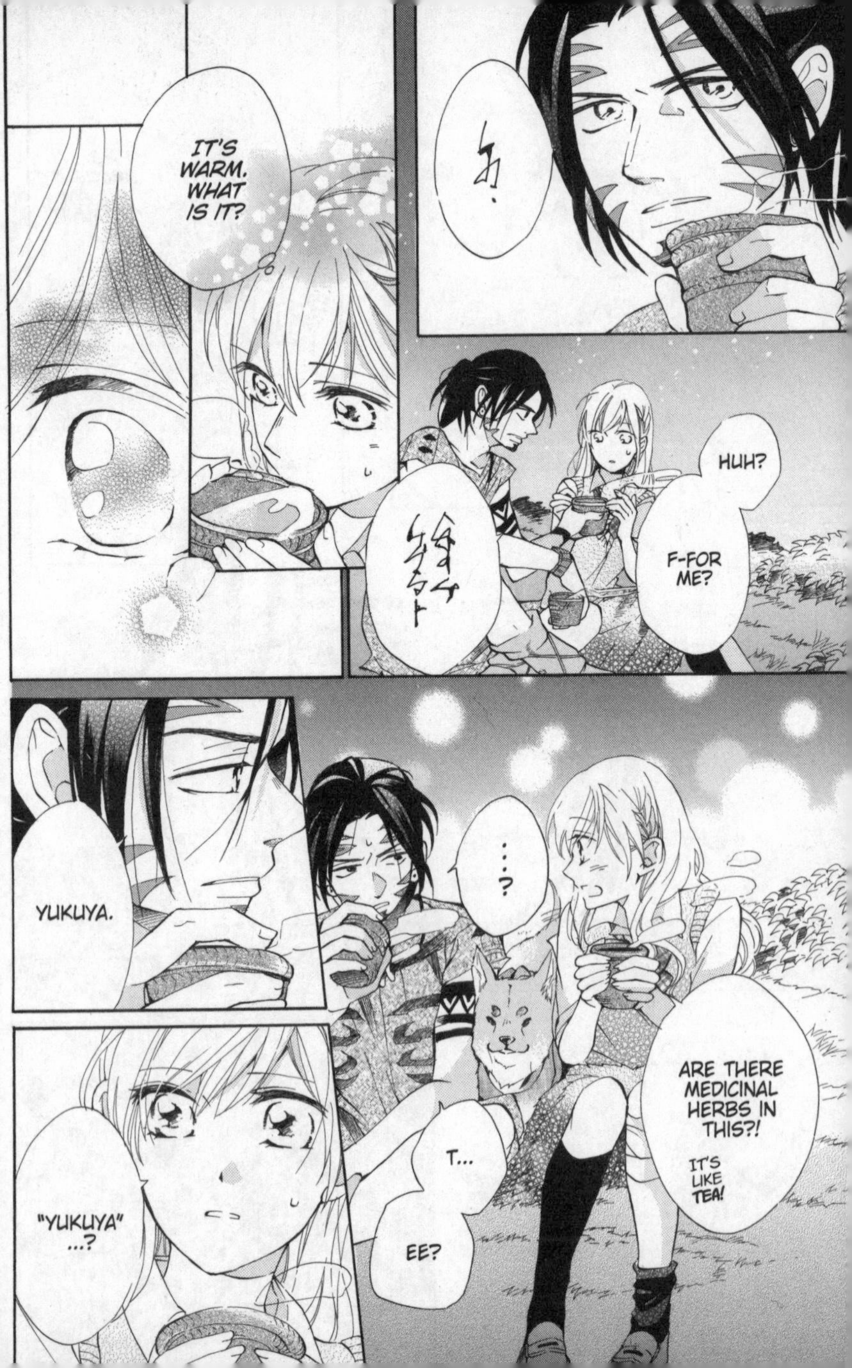
あ.
HUH?
F-FOR ME?
IT'S WARM. WHAT IS IT?
ARE THERE MEDICINAL HERBS IN THIS?!
IT'S LIKE TEA!
...?
YUKUYA.
T...
EE?
"YUKUYA" ...?

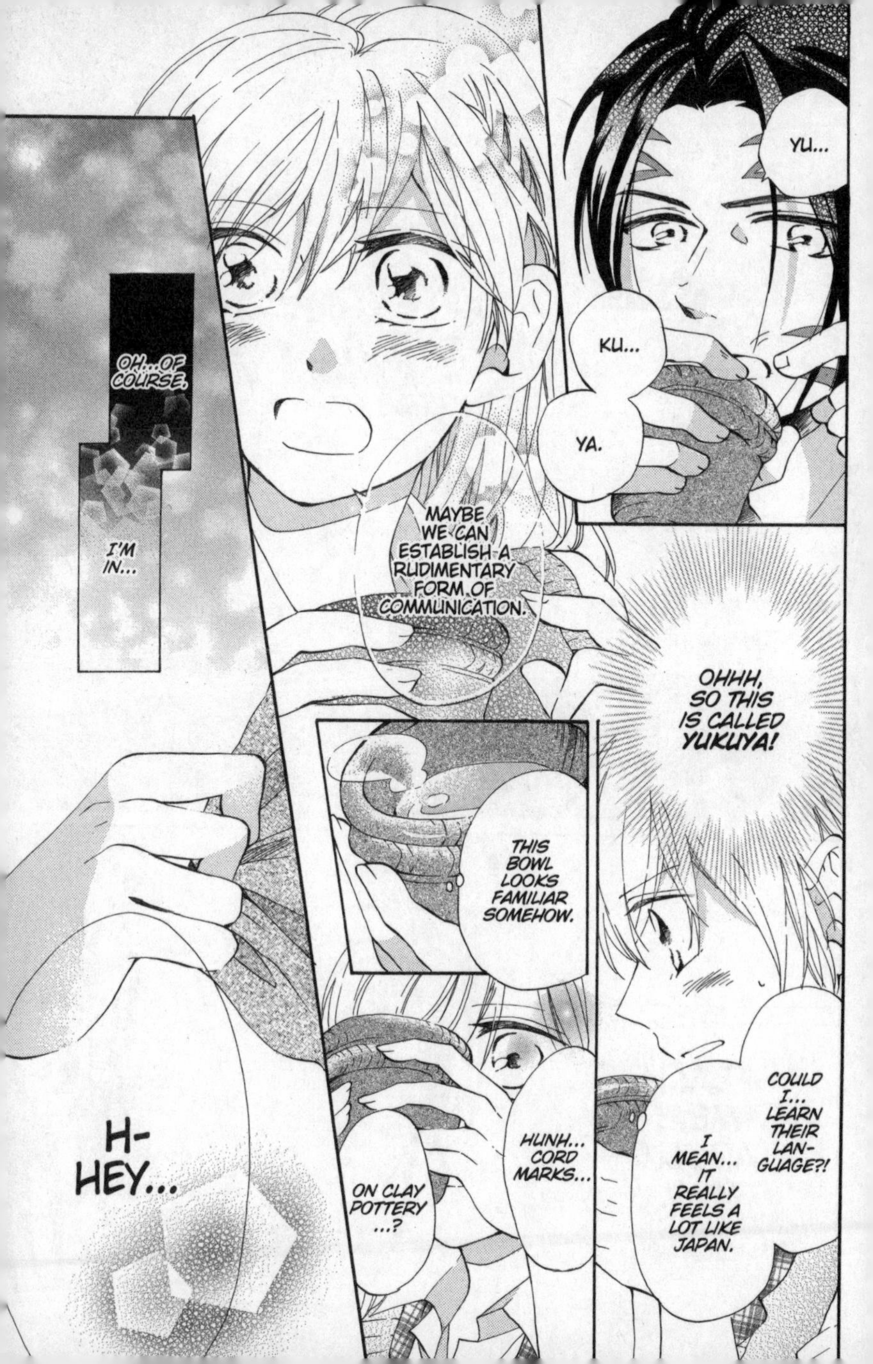
YU...
KU...
YA.
MAYBE WE CAN ESTABLISH A RUDIMENTARY FORM OF COMMUNICATION.
OH...OF COURSE.
I'M IN...
OHHH, SO THIS IS CALLED YUKUYA!
COULD I... LEARN THEIR LAN-GUAGE?!
I MEAN... IT REALLY FEELS A LOT LIKE JAPAN.
THIS BOWL LOOKS FAMILIAR SOMEHOW.
HUNH... CORD MARKS...
ON CLAY POTTERY ...?
H-HEY...

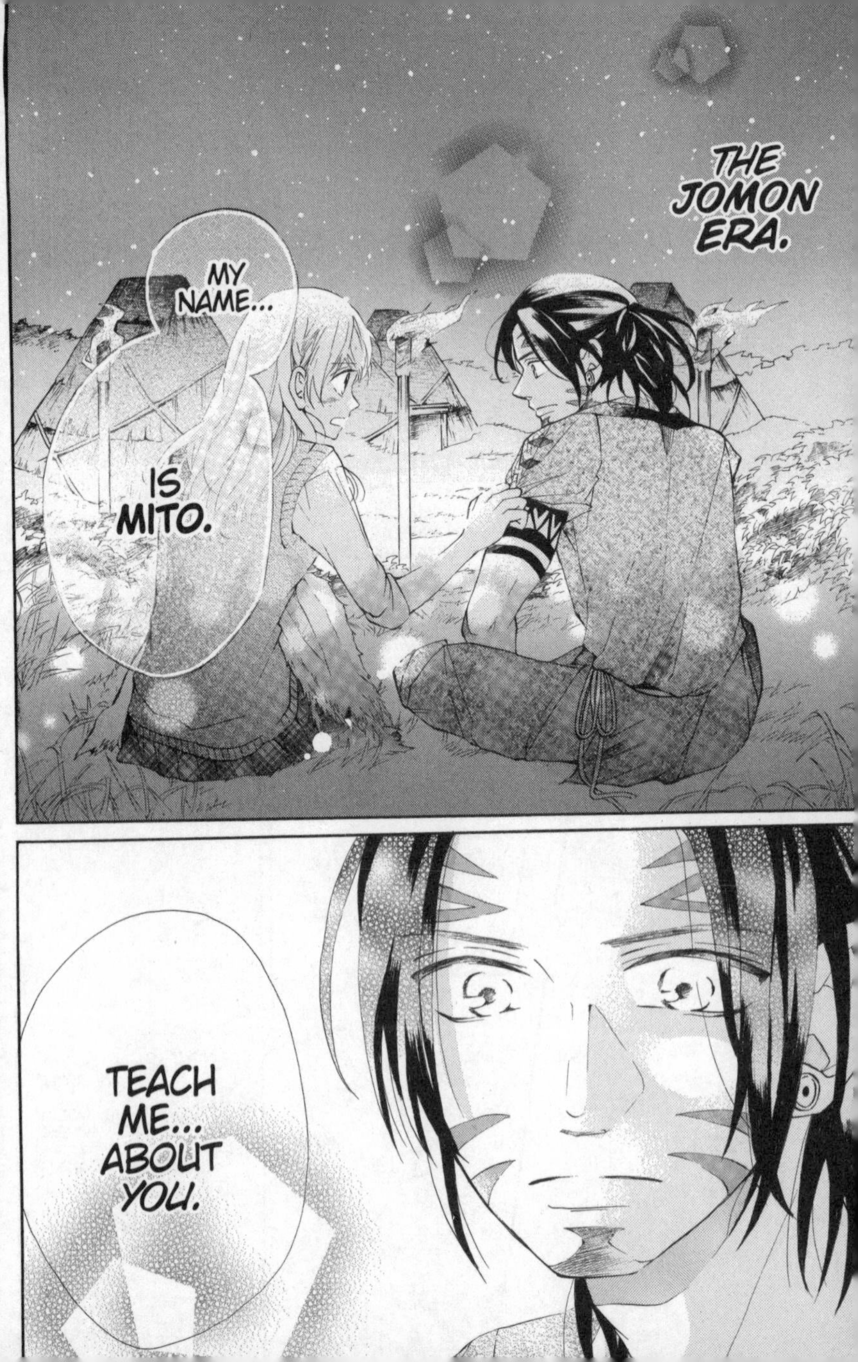
THE JOMON ERA.
MY NAME... IS MITO.
TEACH ME... ABOUT YOU.

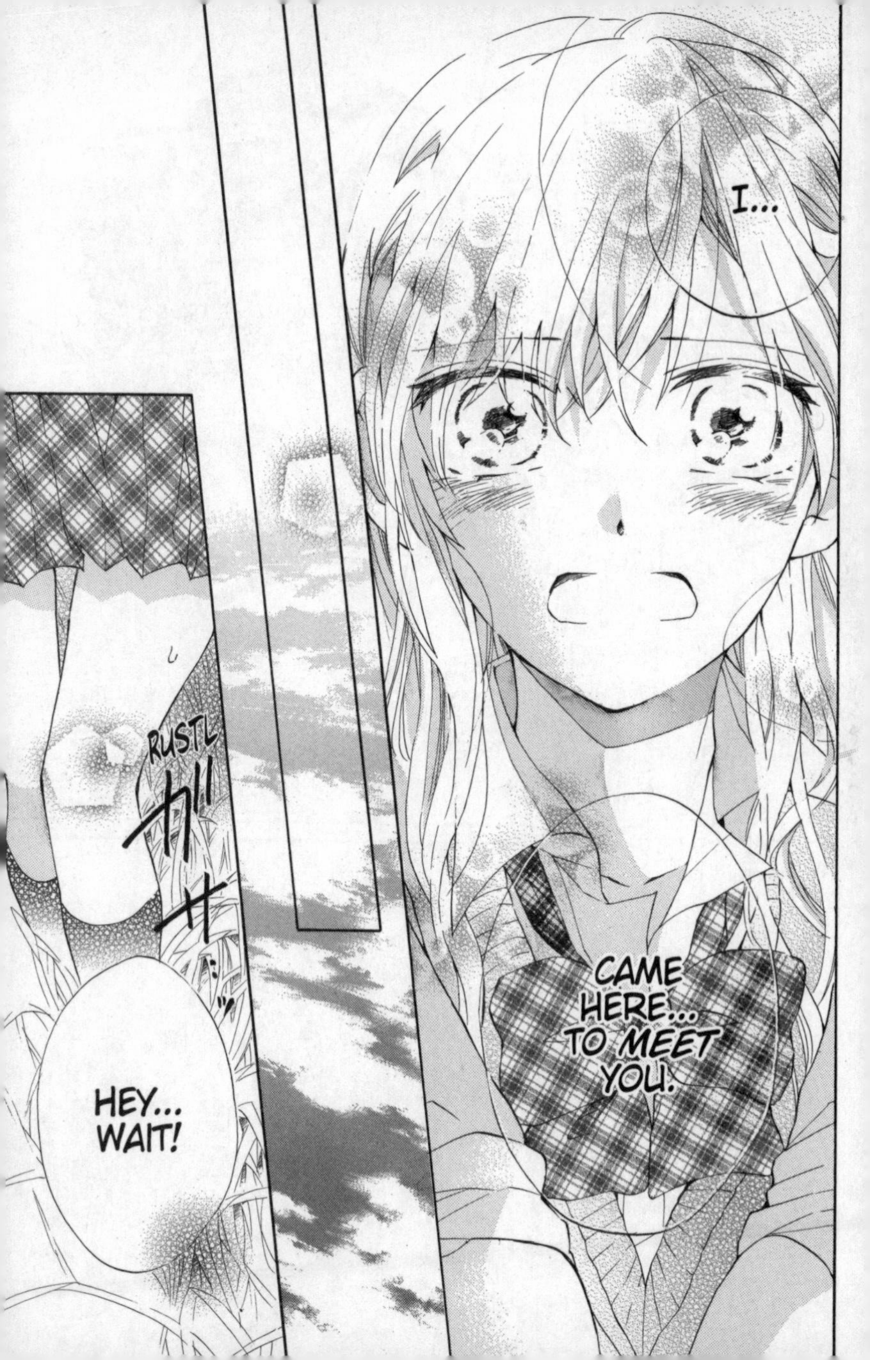
I...
CAME HERE... TO MEET YOU.
RUSTL
HEY... WAIT!

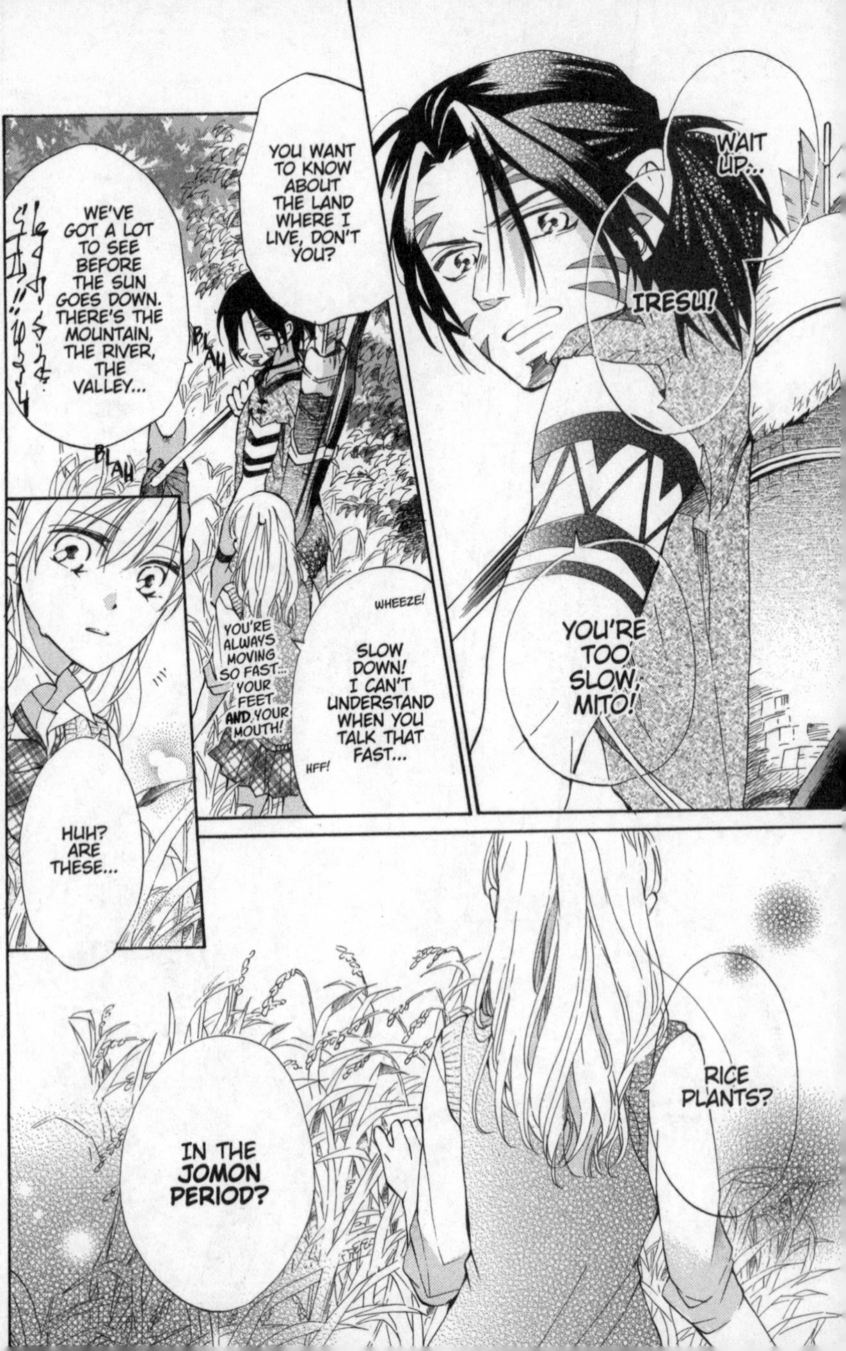
WAIT UP...
IRESU!
YOU'RE TOO SLOW, MITO!
YOU WANT TO KNOW ABOUT THE LAND WHERE I LIVE, DON'T YOU?
WE'VE GOT A LOT TO SEE BEFORE THE SUN GOES DOWN. THERE'S THE MOUNTAIN, THE RIVER, THE VALLEY...
BLAH
BLAH
WHEEZE!
SLOW DOWN! I CAN'T UNDERSTAND WHEN YOU TALK THAT FAST...
HFF!
YOU'RE ALWAYS MOVING SO FAST... YOUR FEET AND YOUR MOUTH!
HUH? ARE THESE...
RICE PLANTS?
IN THE JOMON PERIOD?

CHAPTER 11

PRIMITIVE Boyfriend

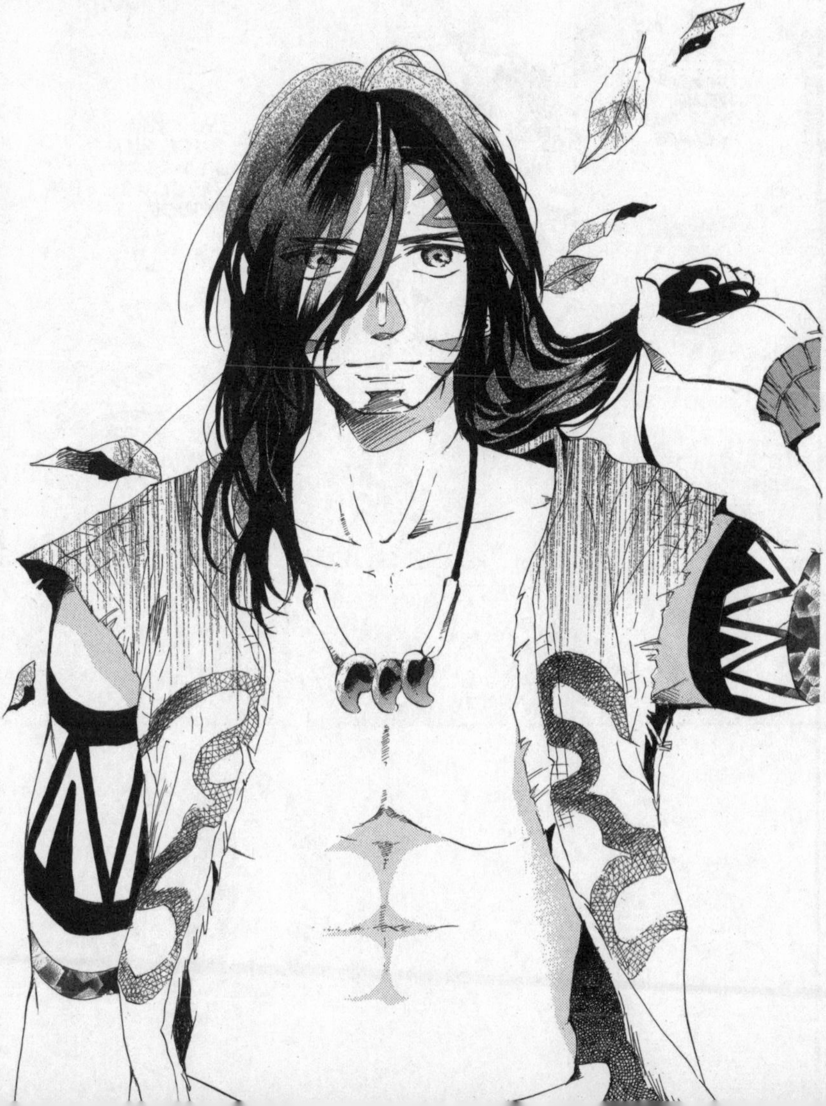

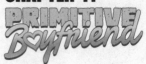

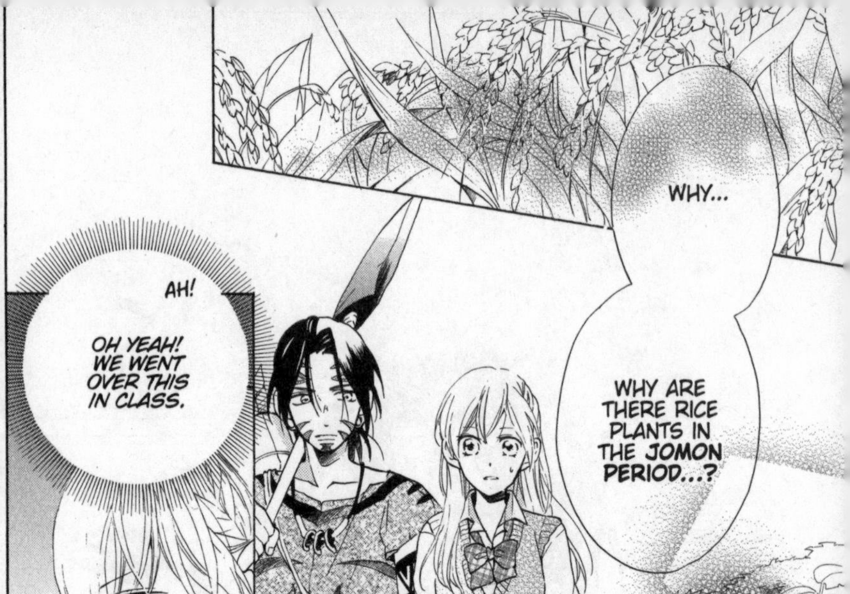
WHY...
WHY ARE THERE RICE PLANTS IN THE JOMON PERIOD...?
AH!
OH YEAH! WE WENT OVER THIS IN CLASS.
We used to think rice farming began in the Yayoi period. How-ever...

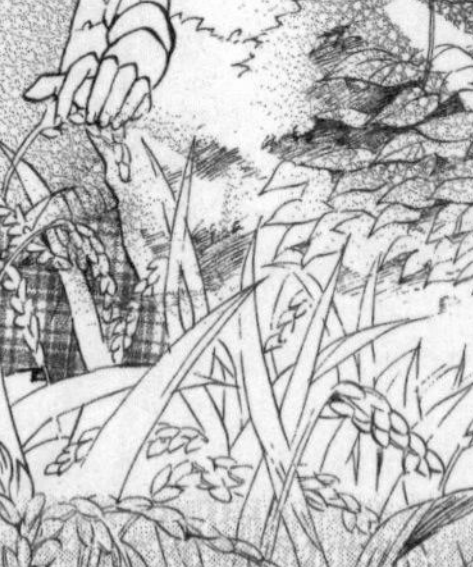
PRIMITIVE BOYFRIEND by Yoshineko Kitafuku PRIMITIVE BOYFRIEND

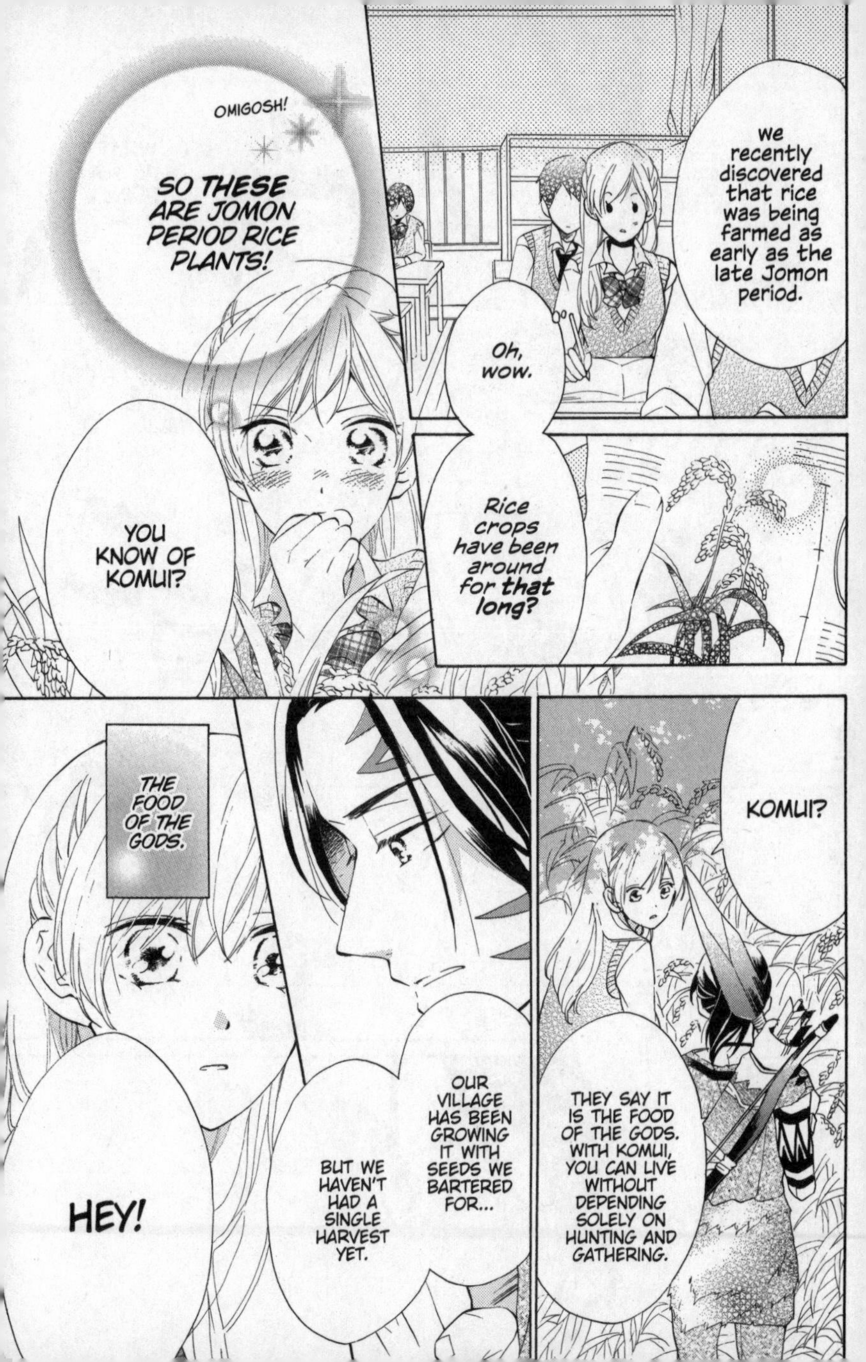
we recently discovered that rice was being farmed as early as the late Jomon period.
Oh, wow.
Rice crops have been around for **that** long?
OMIGOSH!
SO THESE ARE JOMON PERIOD RICE PLANTS!
YOU KNOW OF KOMUI?
KOMUI?
THEY SAY IT IS THE FOOD OF THE GODS. WITH KOMUI, YOU CAN LIVE WITHOUT DEPENDING SOLELY ON HUNTING AND GATHERING.
OUR VILLAGE HAS BEEN GROWING IT WITH SEEDS WE BARTERED FOR...
BUT WE HAVEN'T HAD A SINGLE HARVEST YET.
THE FOOD OF THE GODS.
HEY!

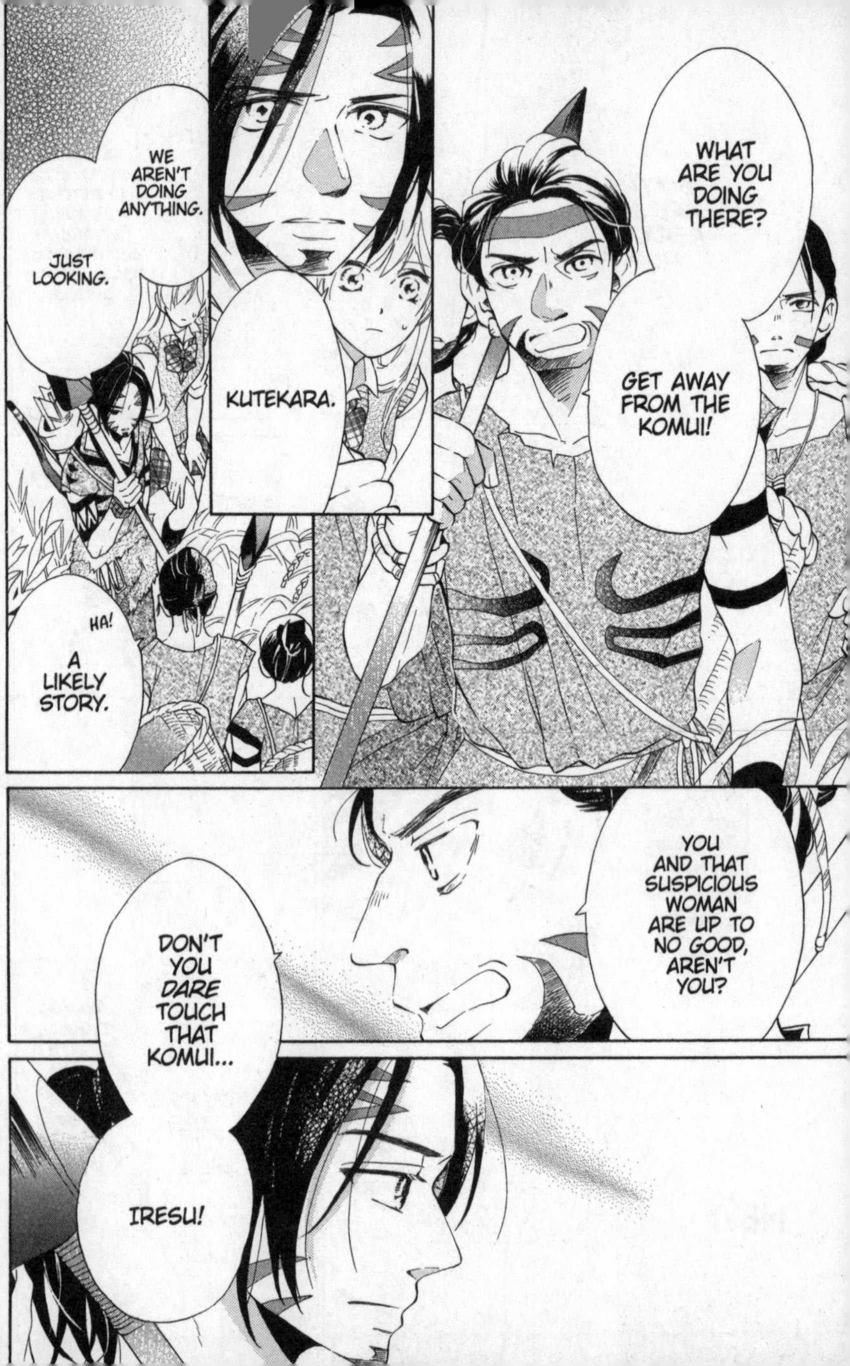
WHAT ARE YOU DOING THERE?
GET AWAY FROM THE KOMUI!
KUTEKARA.
WE AREN'T DOING ANYTHING.
JUST LOOKING.
HA!
A LIKELY STORY.
YOU AND THAT SUSPICIOUS WOMAN ARE UP TO NO GOOD, AREN'T YOU?
DON'T YOU *DARE* TOUCH THAT KOMUI...
IRESU!

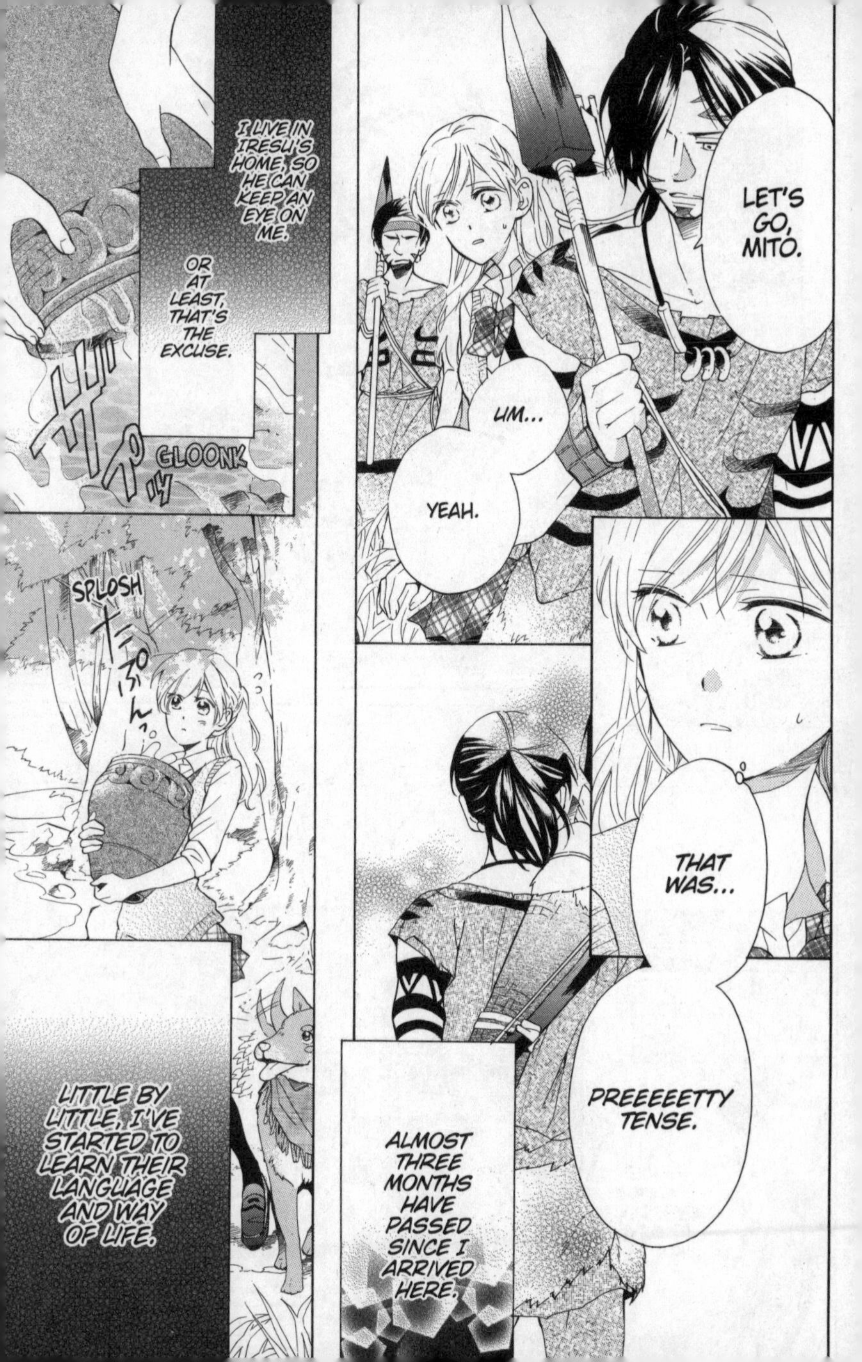
LET'S GO, MITO.
UM...
YEAH.
THAT WAS...
PREEEEETTY TENSE.
ALMOST THREE MONTHS HAVE PASSED SINCE I ARRIVED HERE.
I LIVE IN IRESU'S HOME, SO HE CAN KEEP AN EYE ON ME.
OR AT LEAST, THAT'S THE EXCUSE.
GLOONK
SPLOSH
LITTLE BY LITTLE, I'VE STARTED TO LEARN THEIR LANGUAGE AND WAY OF LIFE.

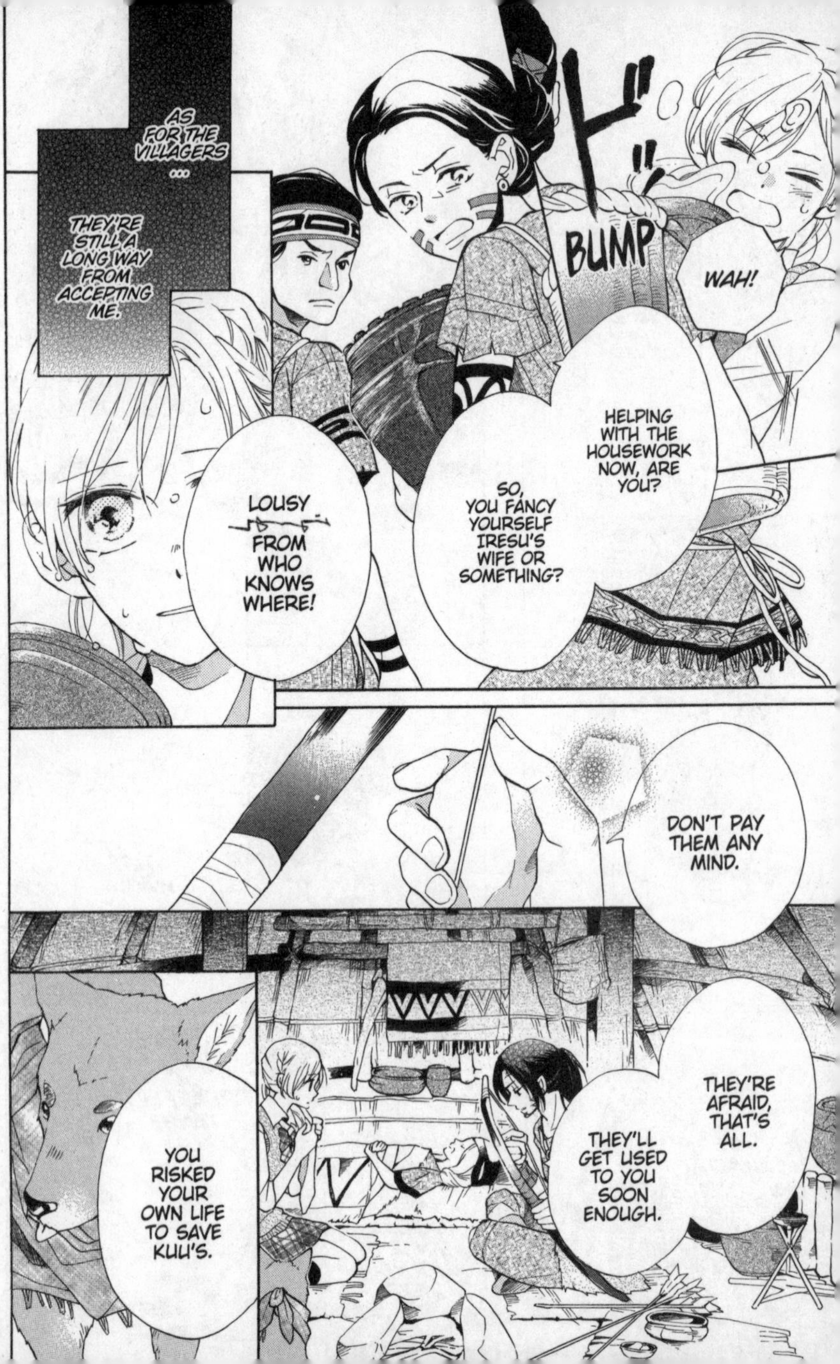
BUMP
WAH!
HELPING WITH THE HOUSEWORK NOW, ARE YOU?
SO, YOU FANCY YOURSELF IRESU'S WIFE OR SOMETHING?
LOUSY FROM WHO KNOWS WHERE!
AS FOR THE VILLAGERS...
THEY'RE STILL A LONG WAY FROM ACCEPTING ME.
DON'T PAY THEM ANY MIND.
THEY'RE AFRAID, THAT'S ALL.
THEY'LL GET USED TO YOU SOON ENOUGH.
YOU RISKED YOUR OWN LIFE TO SAVE KUU'S.

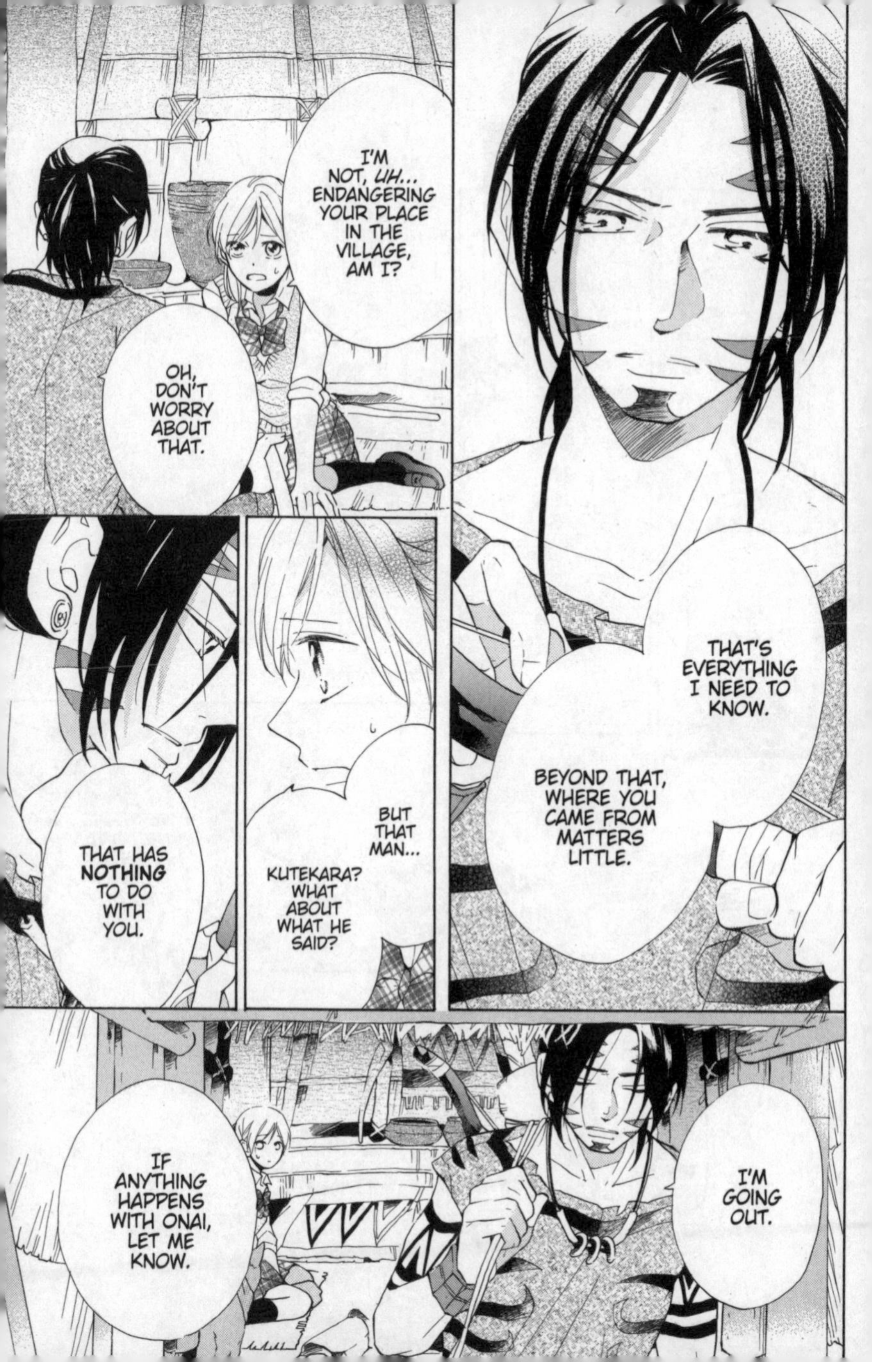

I'M NOT, *UH*... ENDANGERING YOUR PLACE IN THE VILLAGE, AM I?
OH, DON'T WORRY ABOUT THAT.
THAT'S EVERYTHING I NEED TO KNOW.
BEYOND THAT, WHERE YOU CAME FROM MATTERS LITTLE.
BUT THAT MAN...
KUTEKARA? WHAT ABOUT WHAT HE SAID?
THAT HAS **NOTHING** TO DO WITH YOU.
I'M GOING OUT.
IF ANYTHING HAPPENS WITH ONAI, LET ME KNOW.

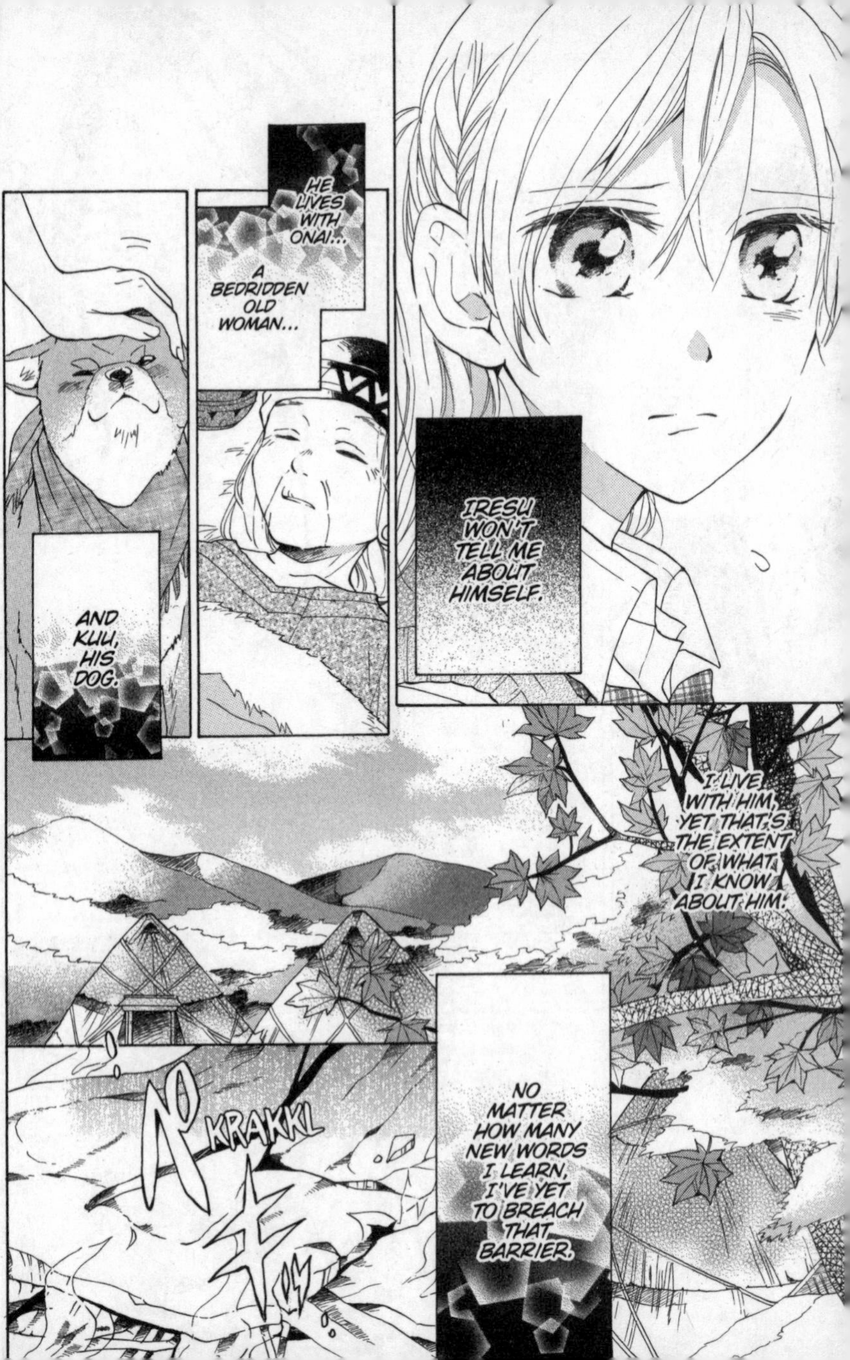
IRESU WON'T TELL ME ABOUT HIMSELF.
HE LIVES WITH ONAI...
A BEDRIDDEN OLD WOMAN...
AND KUU, HIS DOG.
I LIVE WITH HIM, YET THAT'S THE EXTENT OF WHAT I KNOW ABOUT HIM.
NO MATTER HOW MANY NEW WORDS I LEARN, I'VE YET TO BREACH THAT BARRIER.
KRAKKL

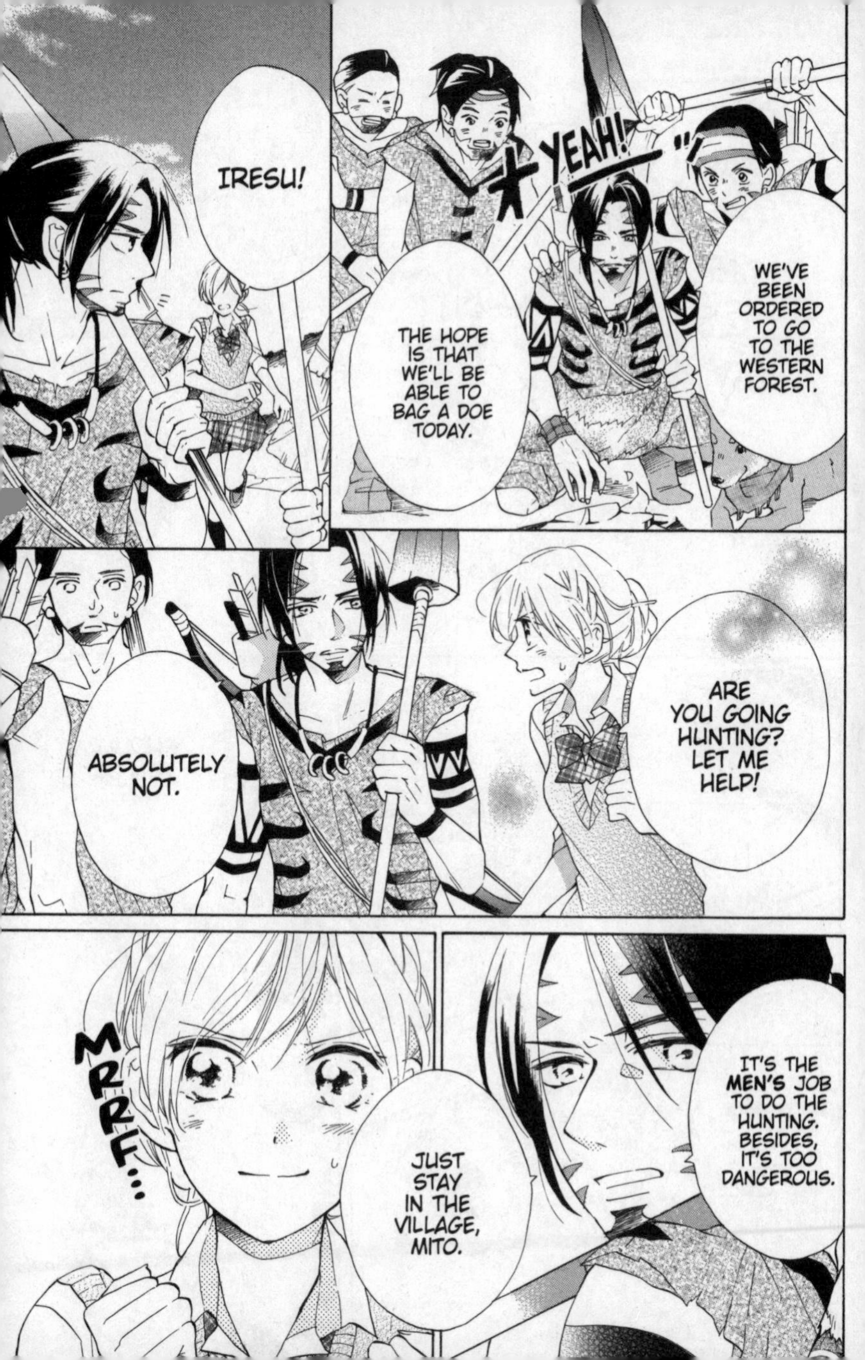
YEAH!
WE'VE BEEN ORDERED TO GO TO THE WESTERN FOREST.
THE HOPE IS THAT WE'LL BE ABLE TO BAG A DOE TODAY.
IRESU!
ARE YOU GOING HUNTING? LET ME HELP!
ABSOLUTELY NOT.
IT'S THE MEN'S JOB TO DO THE HUNTING. BESIDES, IT'S TOO DANGEROUS.
JUST STAY IN THE VILLAGE, MITO.
MRRF...

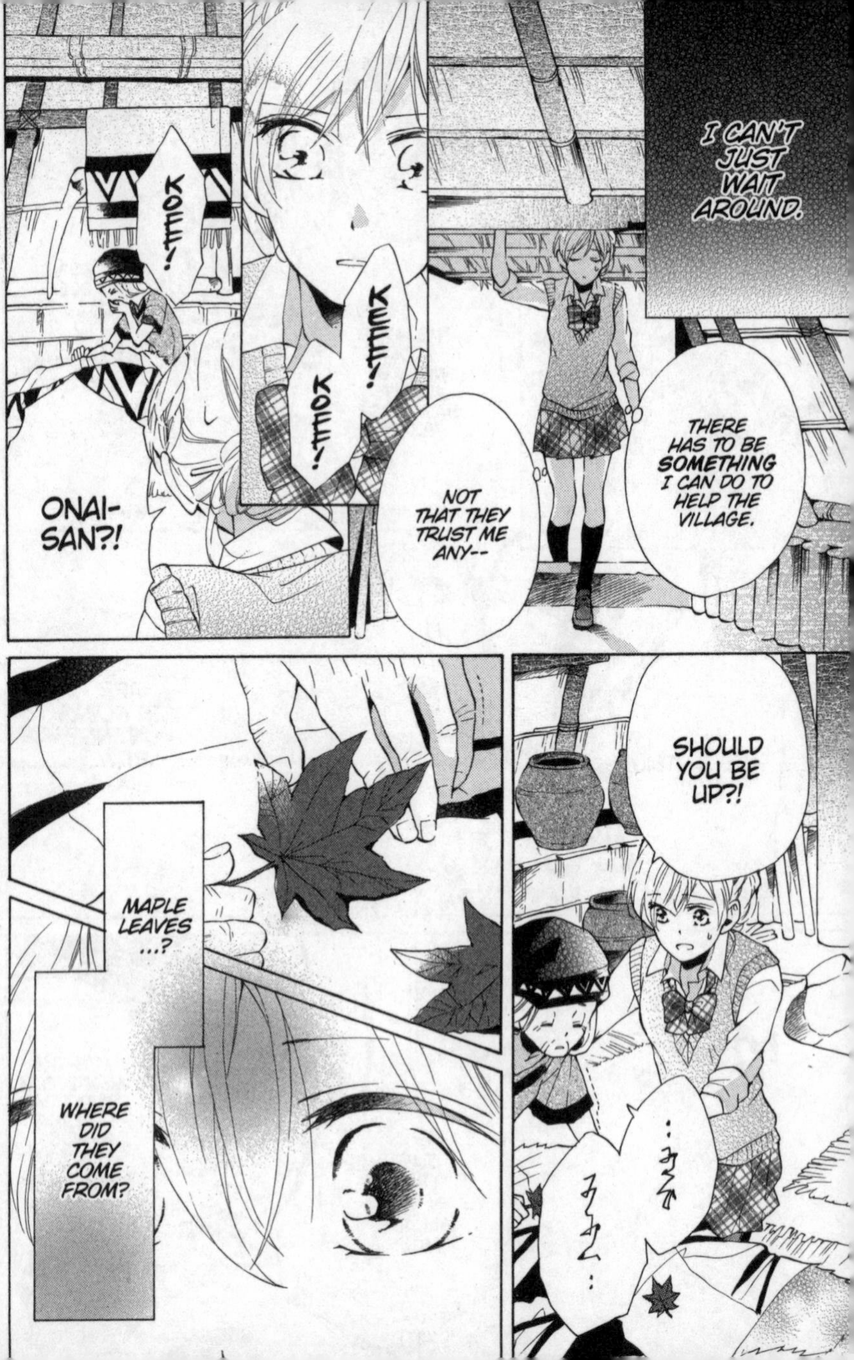
I CAN'T JUST WAIT AROUND.
THERE HAS TO BE SOMETHING I CAN DO TO HELP THE VILLAGE.
NOT THAT THEY TRUST ME ANY--
KEFF!
KOFF!
KOFF!
ONAI-SAN?!
SHOULD YOU BE UP?!
MAPLE LEAVES ...?
WHERE DID THEY COME FROM?

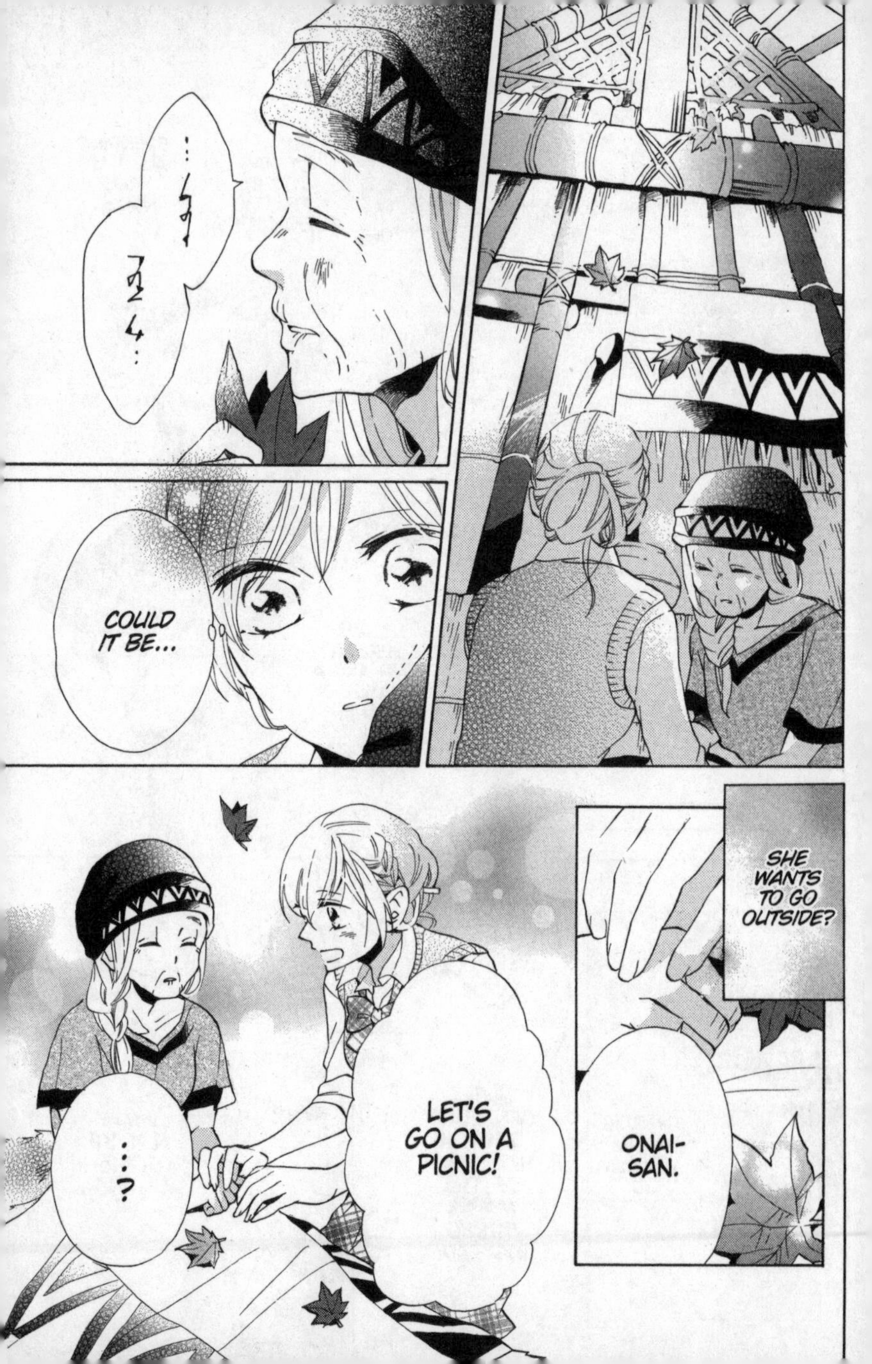
COULD IT BE...
SHE WANTS TO GO OUTSIDE?
ONAI-SAN.
LET'S GO ON A PICNIC!
...?

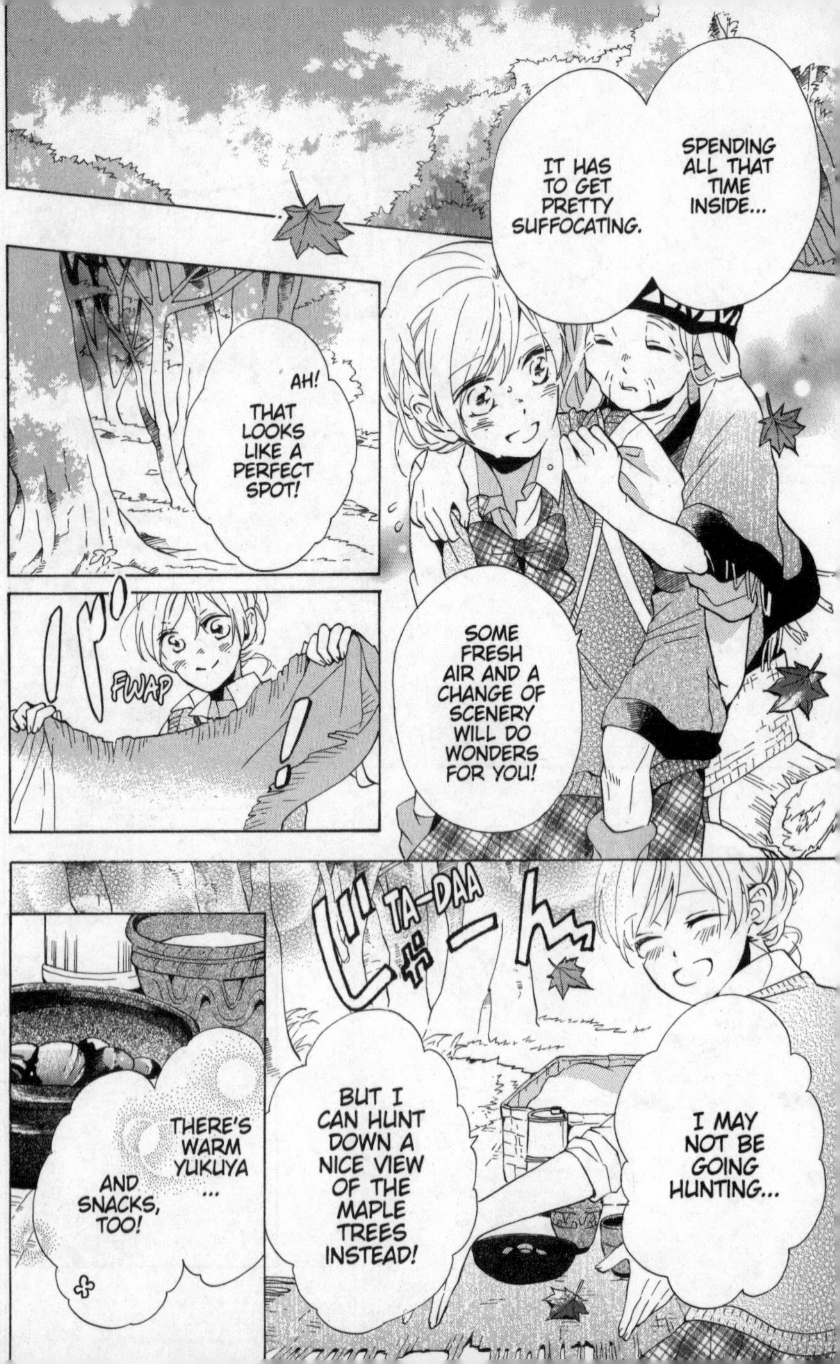
SPENDING ALL THAT TIME INSIDE...
IT HAS TO GET PRETTY SUFFOCATING.
SOME FRESH AIR AND A CHANGE OF SCENERY WILL DO WONDERS FOR YOU!
AH!
THAT LOOKS LIKE A PERFECT SPOT!
FWAP
TA-DAA
I MAY NOT BE GOING HUNTING...
BUT I CAN HUNT DOWN A NICE VIEW OF THE MAPLE TREES INSTEAD!
THERE'S WARM YUKUYA ...
AND SNACKS, TOO!

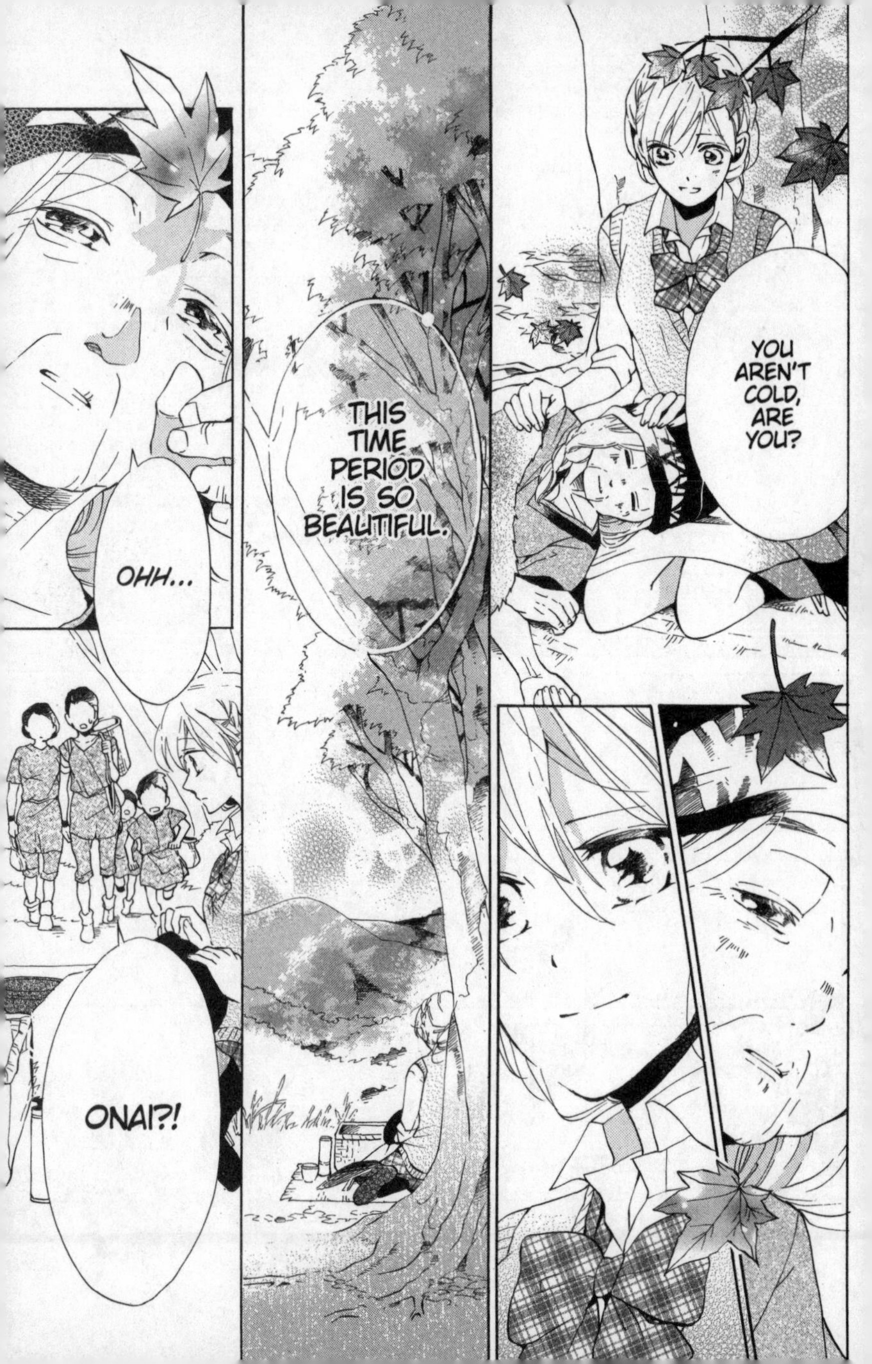
YOU AREN'T COLD, ARE YOU?
THIS TIME PERIOD IS SO BEAUTIFUL.
OHH...
ONAI?!

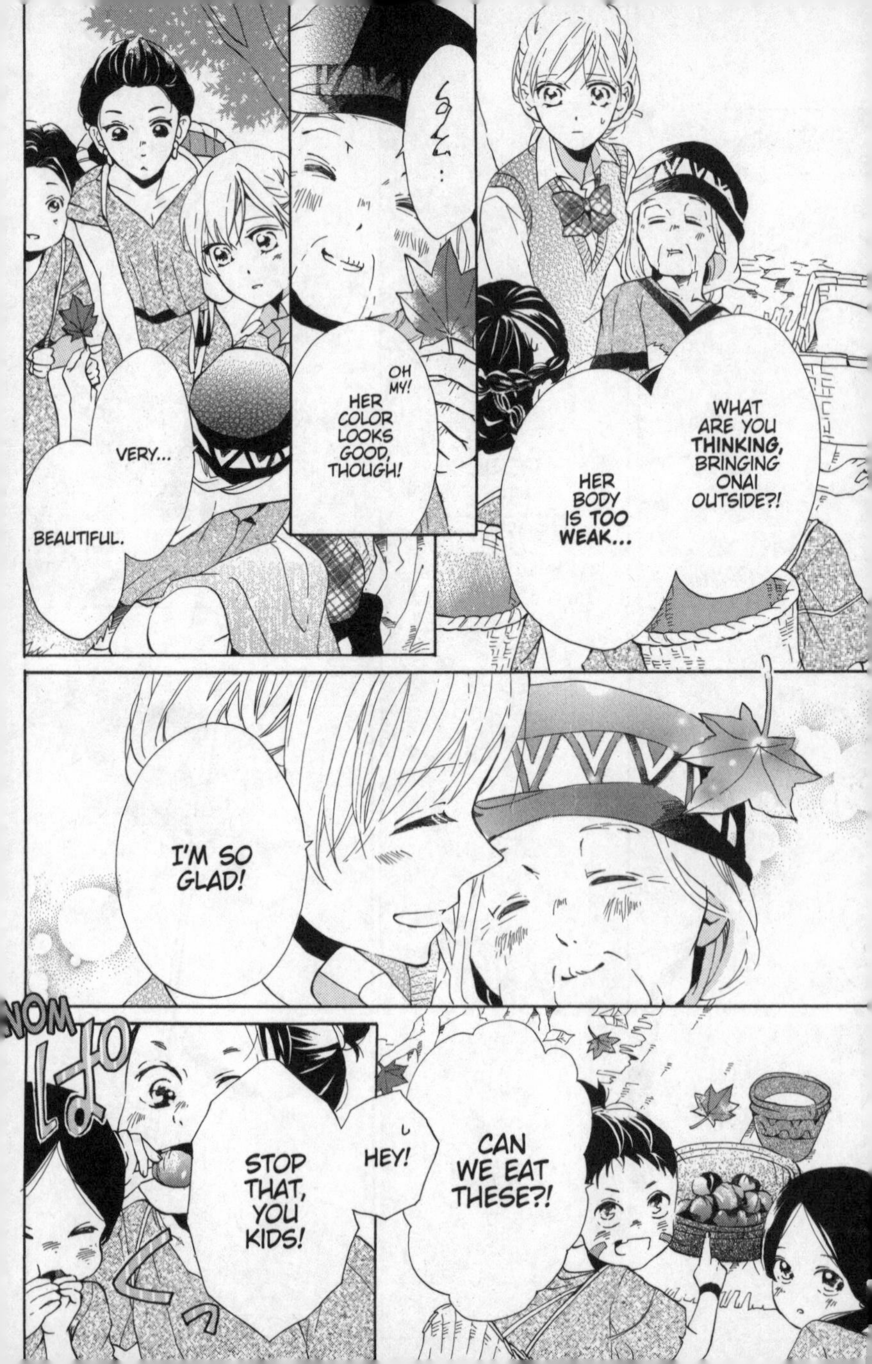
WHAT ARE YOU THINKING, BRINGING ONAI OUTSIDE?!
HER BODY IS TOO WEAK...
ふふ…
OH MY! HER COLOR LOOKS GOOD, THOUGH!
VERY...
BEAUTIFUL.
I'M SO GLAD!
CAN WE EAT THESE?!
HEY!
STOP THAT, YOU KIDS!
NOM

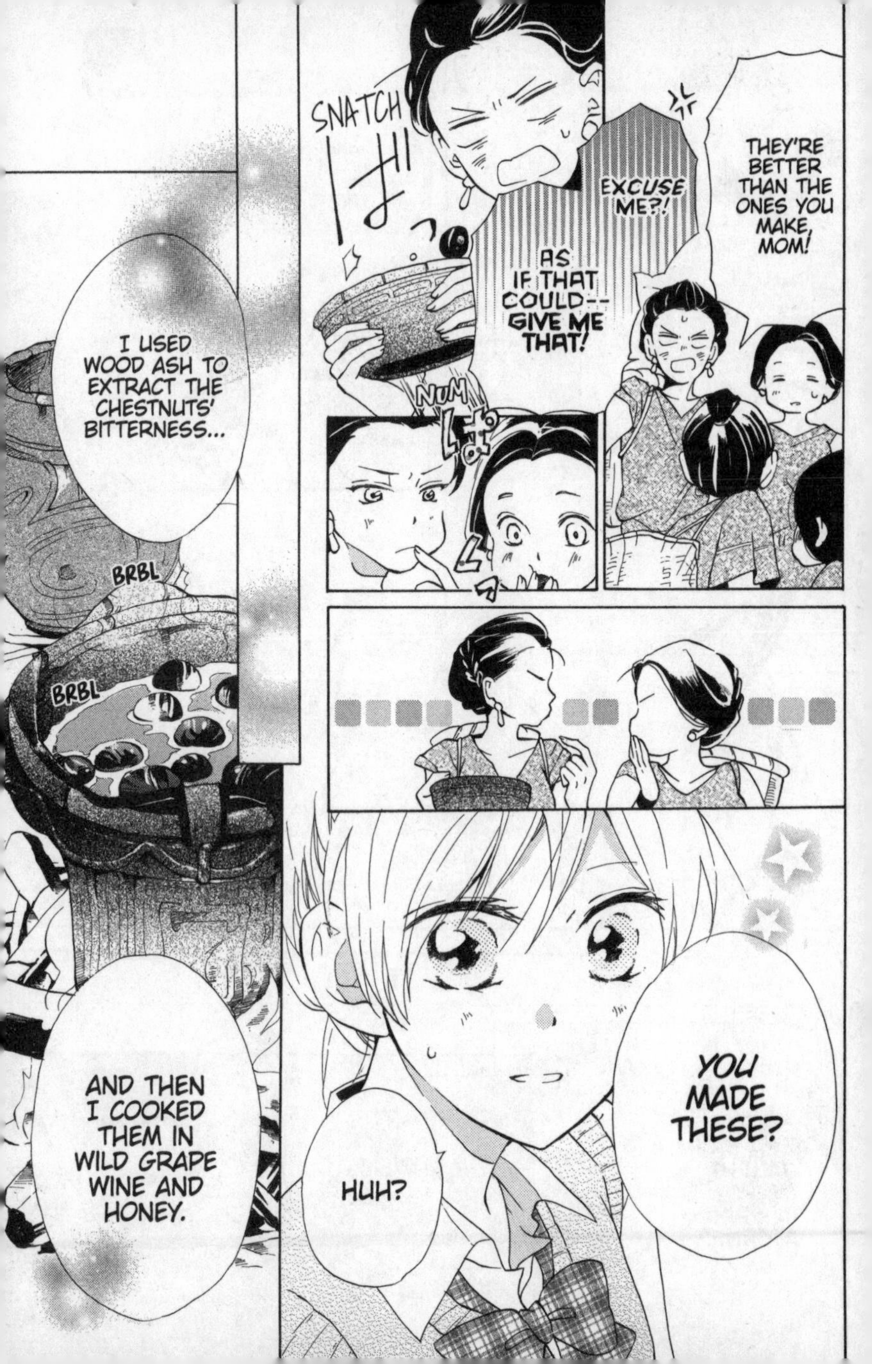
THEY'RE BETTER THAN THE ONES YOU MAKE, MOM!
EXCUSE ME?!
AS IF THAT COULD-- GIVE ME THAT!
SNATCH
NUM
YOU MADE THESE?
HUH?
I USED WOOD ASH TO EXTRACT THE CHESTNUTS' BITTERNESS...
BRBL
BRBL
AND THEN I COOKED THEM IN WILD GRAPE WINE AND HONEY.

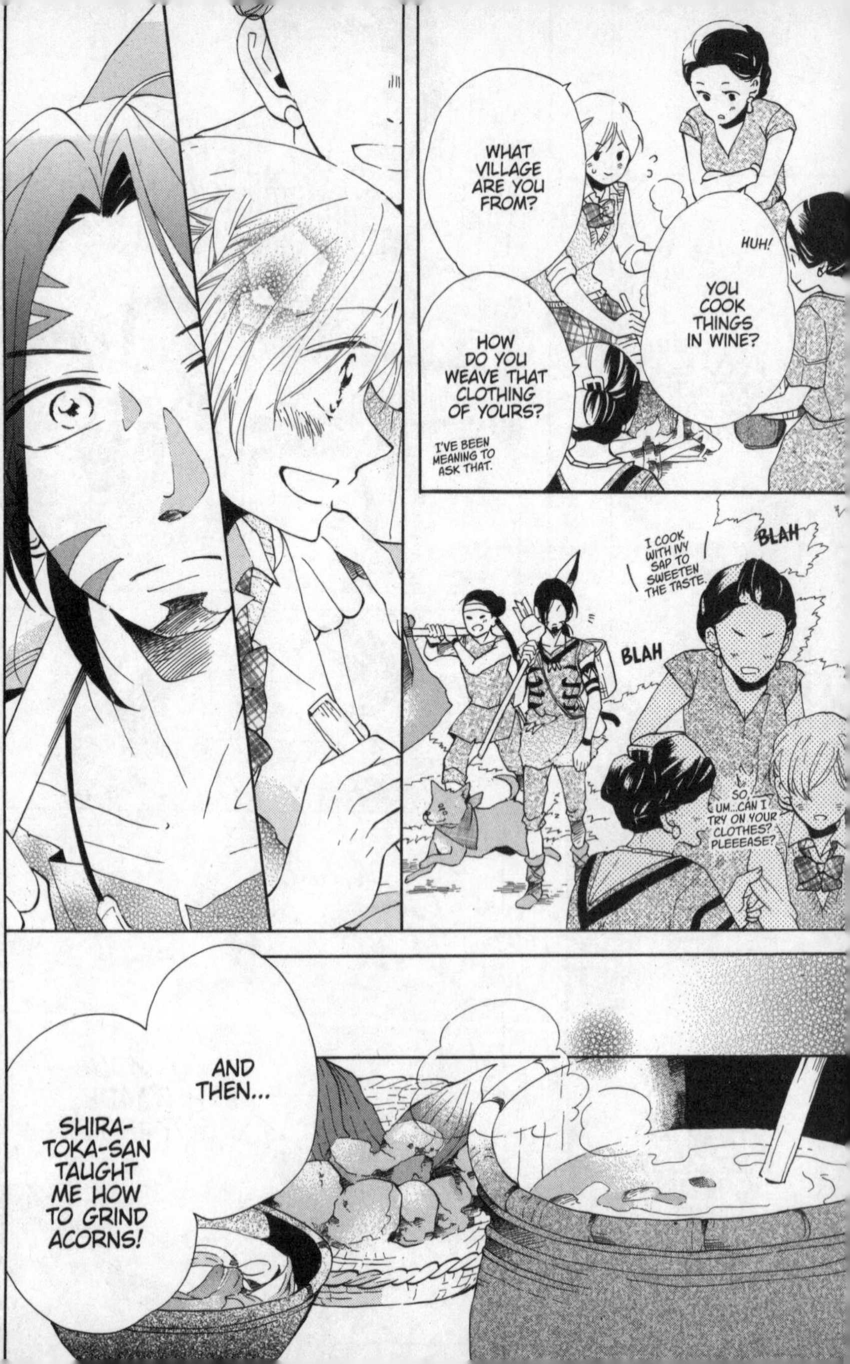
HUH!
YOU COOK THINGS IN WINE?
WHAT VILLAGE ARE YOU FROM?
HOW DO YOU WEAVE THAT CLOTHING OF YOURS?
I'VE BEEN MEANING TO ASK THAT.
BLAH
I COOK WITH IVY SAP TO SWEETEN THE TASTE.
BLAH
SO, UM...CAN I TRY ON YOUR CLOTHES? PLEEEASE?
AND THEN...
SHIRA-TOKA-SAN TAUGHT ME HOW TO GRIND ACORNS!

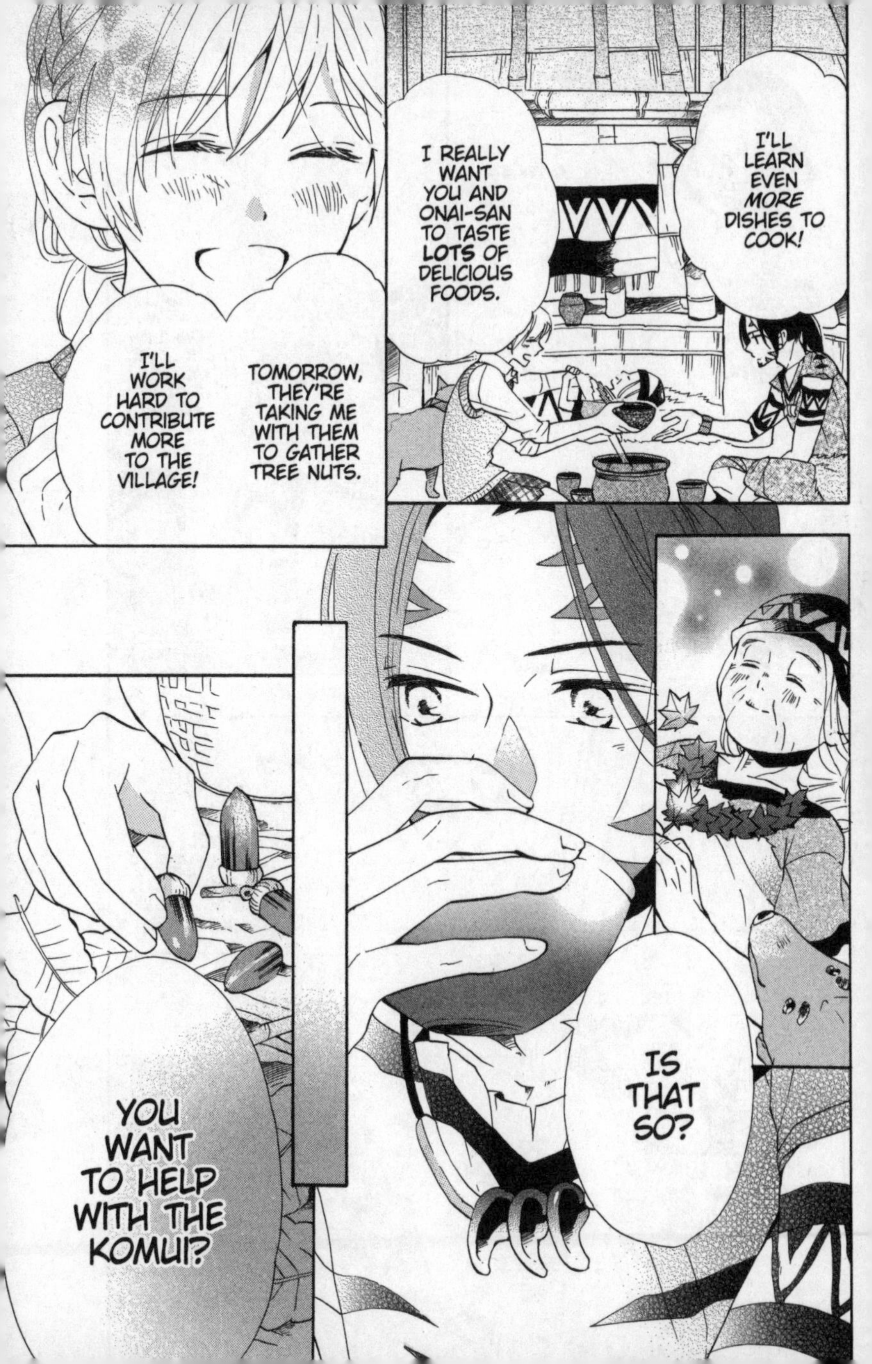
I'LL LEARN EVEN MORE DISHES TO COOK!
I REALLY WANT YOU AND ONAI-SAN TO TASTE LOTS OF DELICIOUS FOODS.
TOMORROW, THEY'RE TAKING ME WITH THEM TO GATHER TREE NUTS.
I'LL WORK HARD TO CONTRIBUTE MORE TO THE VILLAGE!
IS THAT SO?
YOU WANT TO HELP WITH THE KOMUI?

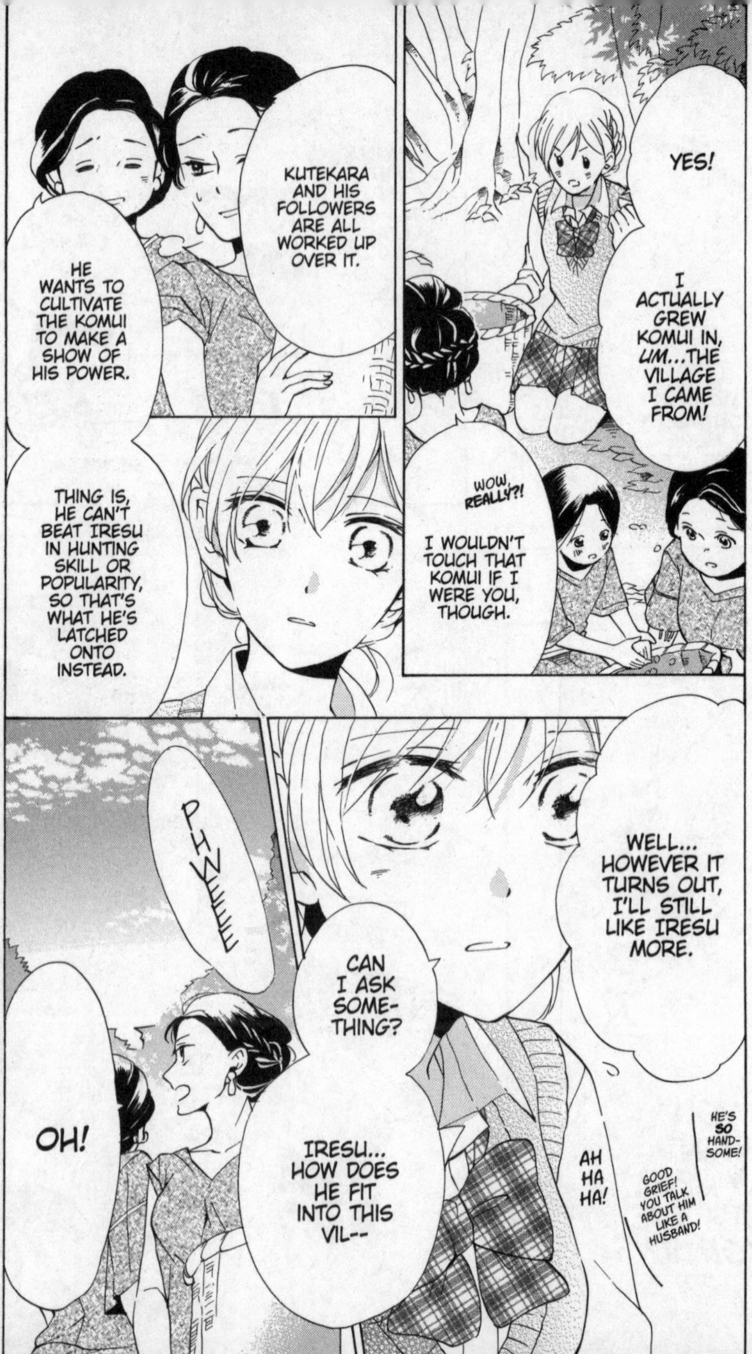
YES!
I ACTUALLY GREW KOMUI IN, UM...THE VILLAGE I CAME FROM!
WOW, REALLY?!
I WOULDN'T TOUCH THAT KOMUI IF I WERE YOU, THOUGH.
KUTEKARA AND HIS FOLLOWERS ARE ALL WORKED UP OVER IT.
HE WANTS TO CULTIVATE THE KOMUI TO MAKE A SHOW OF HIS POWER.
THING IS, HE CAN'T BEAT IRESU IN HUNTING SKILL OR POPULARITY, SO THAT'S WHAT HE'S LATCHED ONTO INSTEAD.
WELL... HOWEVER IT TURNS OUT, I'LL STILL LIKE IRESU MORE.
HE'S SO HANDSOME!
GOOD GRIEF! YOU TALK ABOUT HIM LIKE A HUSBAND!
AH HA HA!
CAN I ASK SOMETHING?
IRESU... HOW DOES HE FIT INTO THIS VIL--
PHWEEE
OH!

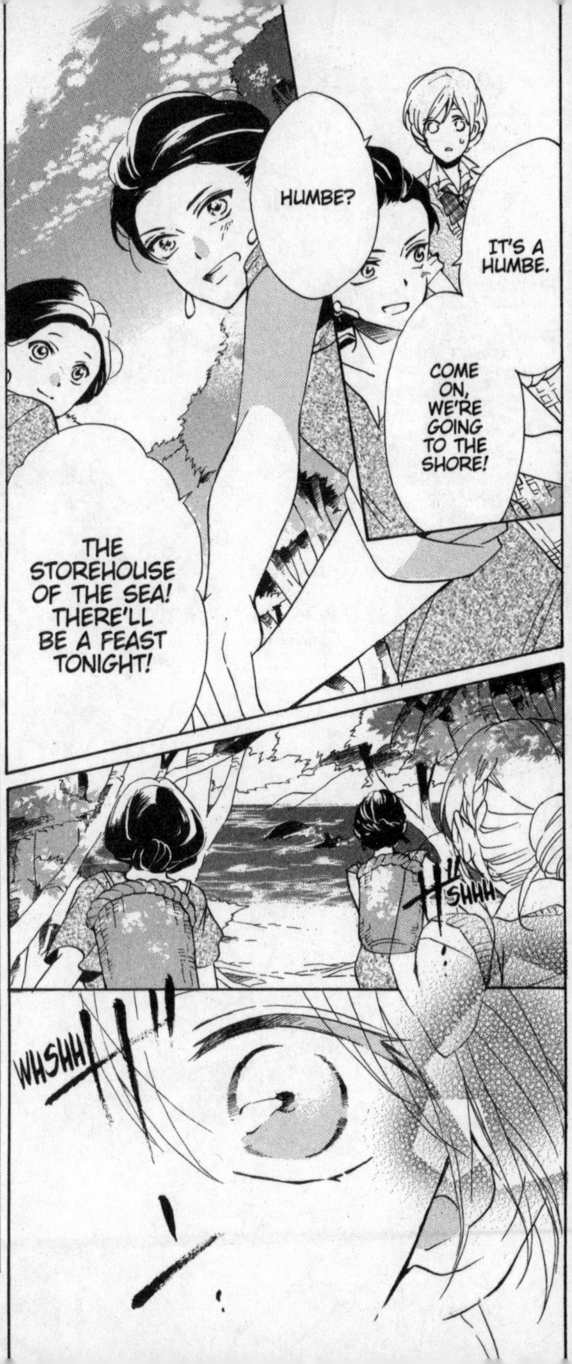
HUMBE?
IT'S A HUMBE.
COME ON, WE'RE GOING TO THE SHORE!
THE STOREHOUSE OF THE SEA! THERE'LL BE A FEAST TONIGHT!
SHHH
WHSHH

3

LIFE IN THE JOMON PERIOD

THROUGH SHEER EFFORT AND MOXIE, MITO ACTUALLY LEARNED TO CONVERSE WITH THOSE IN THE PAST. THIS WAS A NEW FEELING.

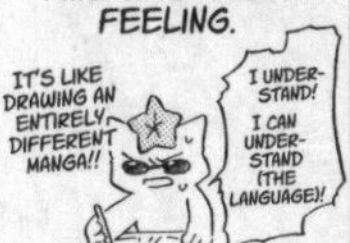
IT'S LIKE DRAWING AN ENTIRELY DIFFERENT MANGA!!
I UNDERSTAND! I CAN UNDERSTAND (THE LANGUAGE)!

ONE OF THE THINGS I DID FOR RESEARCH WAS GO TO THE OKAYAMA PREFECTURE TSUSHIMA HISTORICAL SITE TO STUDY PIT-DWELLING INTERIORS.

THE PIT HOUSES WERE RECONSTRUCTIONS, BUT YOU STILL HAVE TO BEND SLIGHTLY TO GO THROUGH THE ENTRANCES. THE DIM AND CHILL INSIDES, THE SMELLS OF EARTH AND GRASS... IT ALL FELT LIKE I WAS REALLY EXPERIENCING THE PERIOD. I HAD A GREAT TIME.

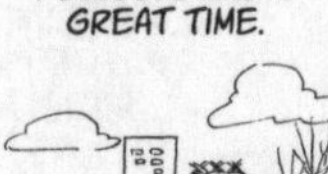

THE WAY THEY JUST...SAT IN THE CORNER OF THIS ATHLETIC FIELD IN A CITY FULL OF TALL BUILDINGS MADE ME EMOTIONAL.

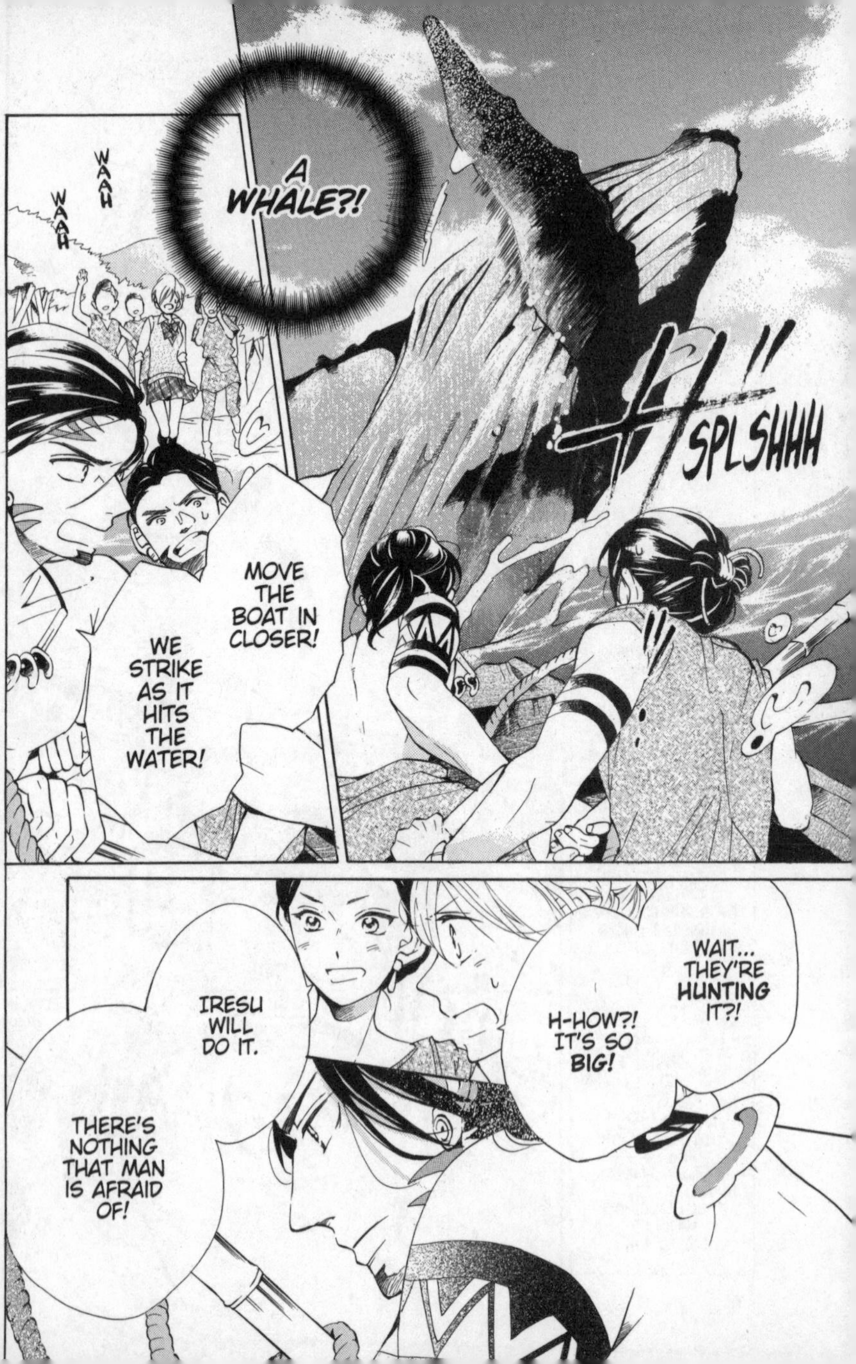
SPLSHHH
A WHALE?!
WAAH
WAAH
MOVE THE BOAT IN CLOSER!
WE STRIKE AS IT HITS THE WATER!
WAIT... THEY'RE HUNTING IT?!
H-HOW?! IT'S SO BIG!
IRESU WILL DO IT.
THERE'S NOTHING THAT MAN IS AFRAID OF!

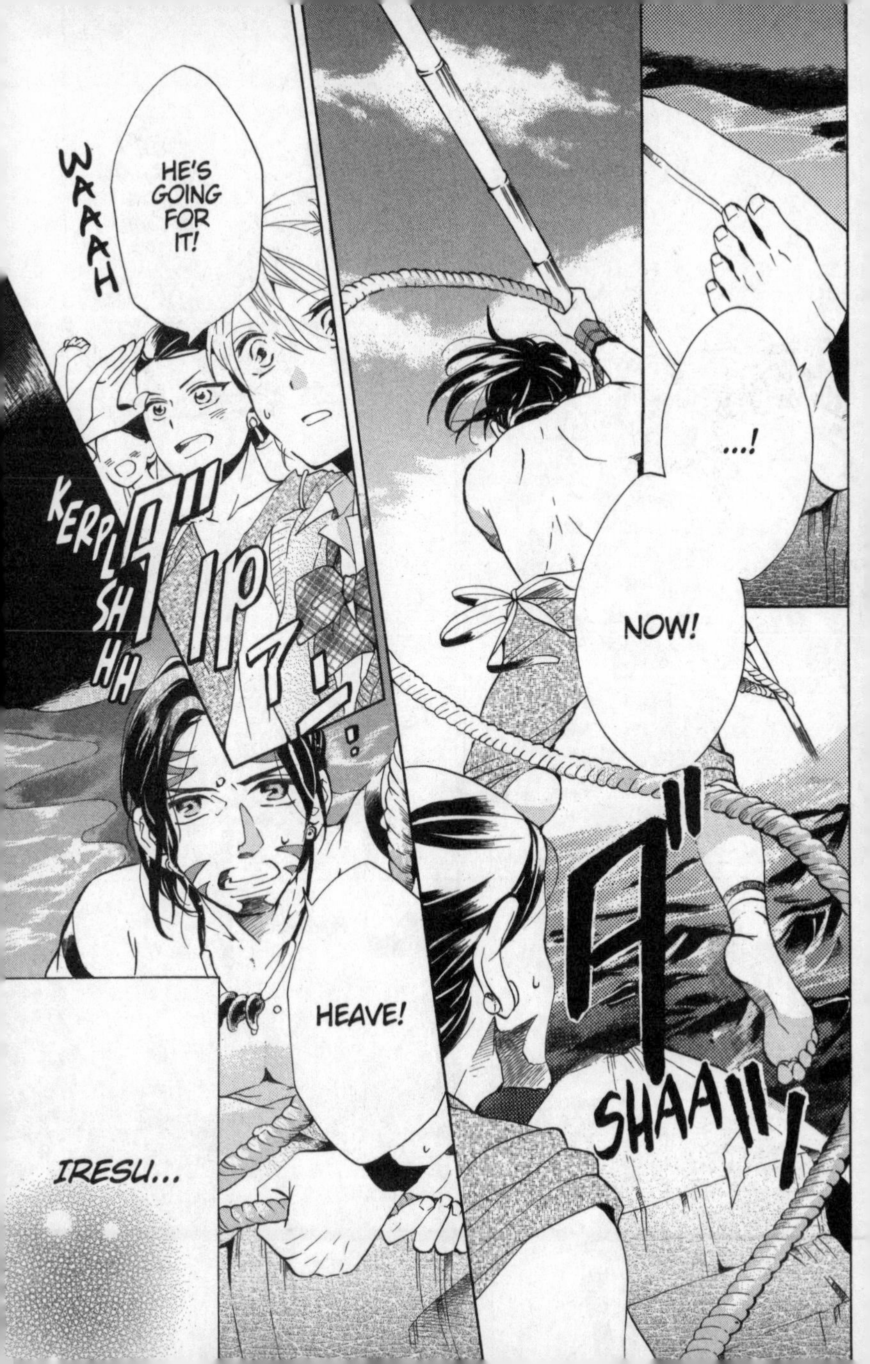
...!
NOW!
HE'S GOING FOR IT!
WAAAH
KERPLASHHH
SHAAIII
HEAVE!
IRESU...

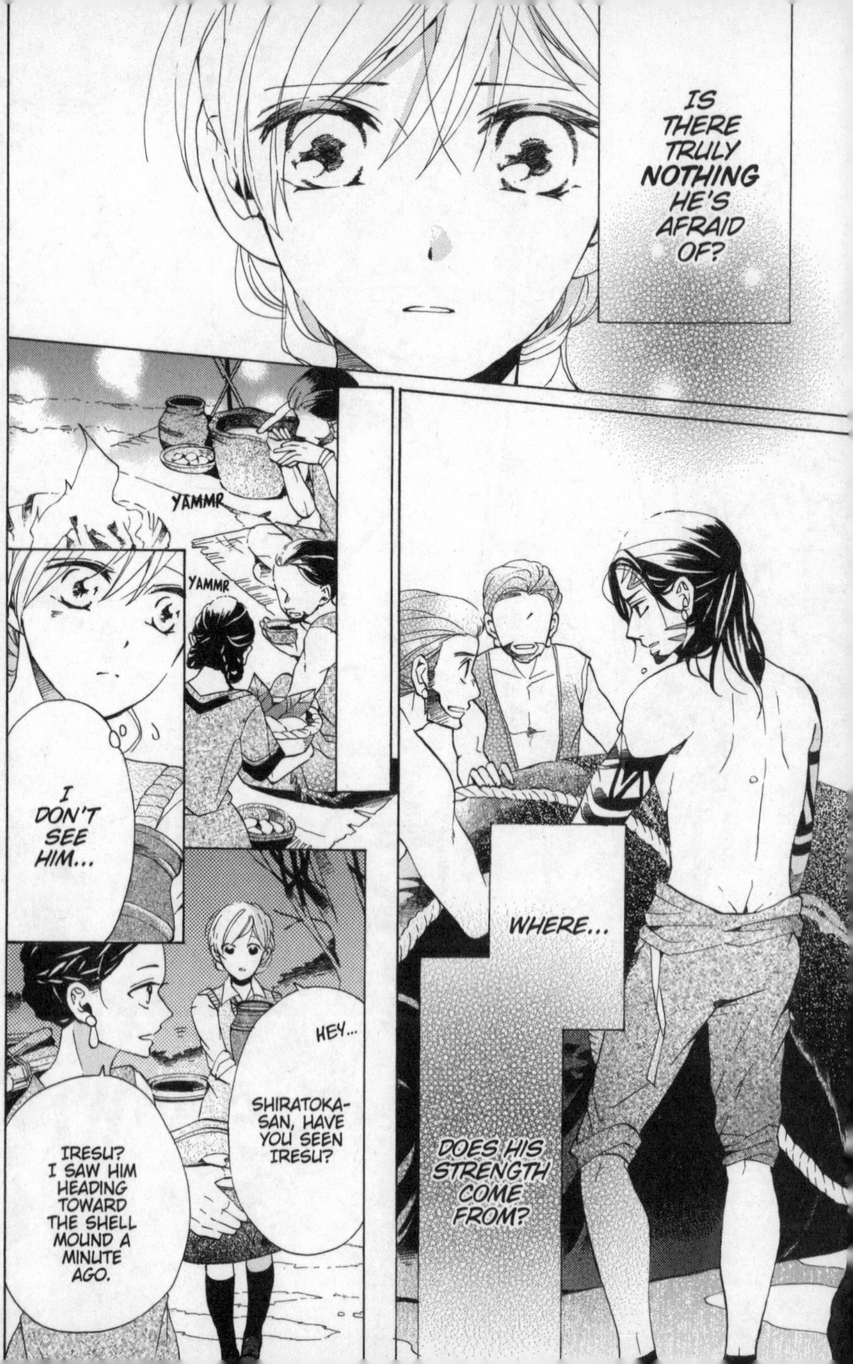
IS THERE TRULY NOTHING HE'S AFRAID OF?
WHERE...
DOES HIS STRENGTH COME FROM?
YAMMR
YAMMR
I DON'T SEE HIM...
HEY...
SHIRATOKA-SAN, HAVE YOU SEEN IRESU?
IRESU? I SAW HIM HEADING TOWARD THE SHELL MOUND A MINUTE AGO.

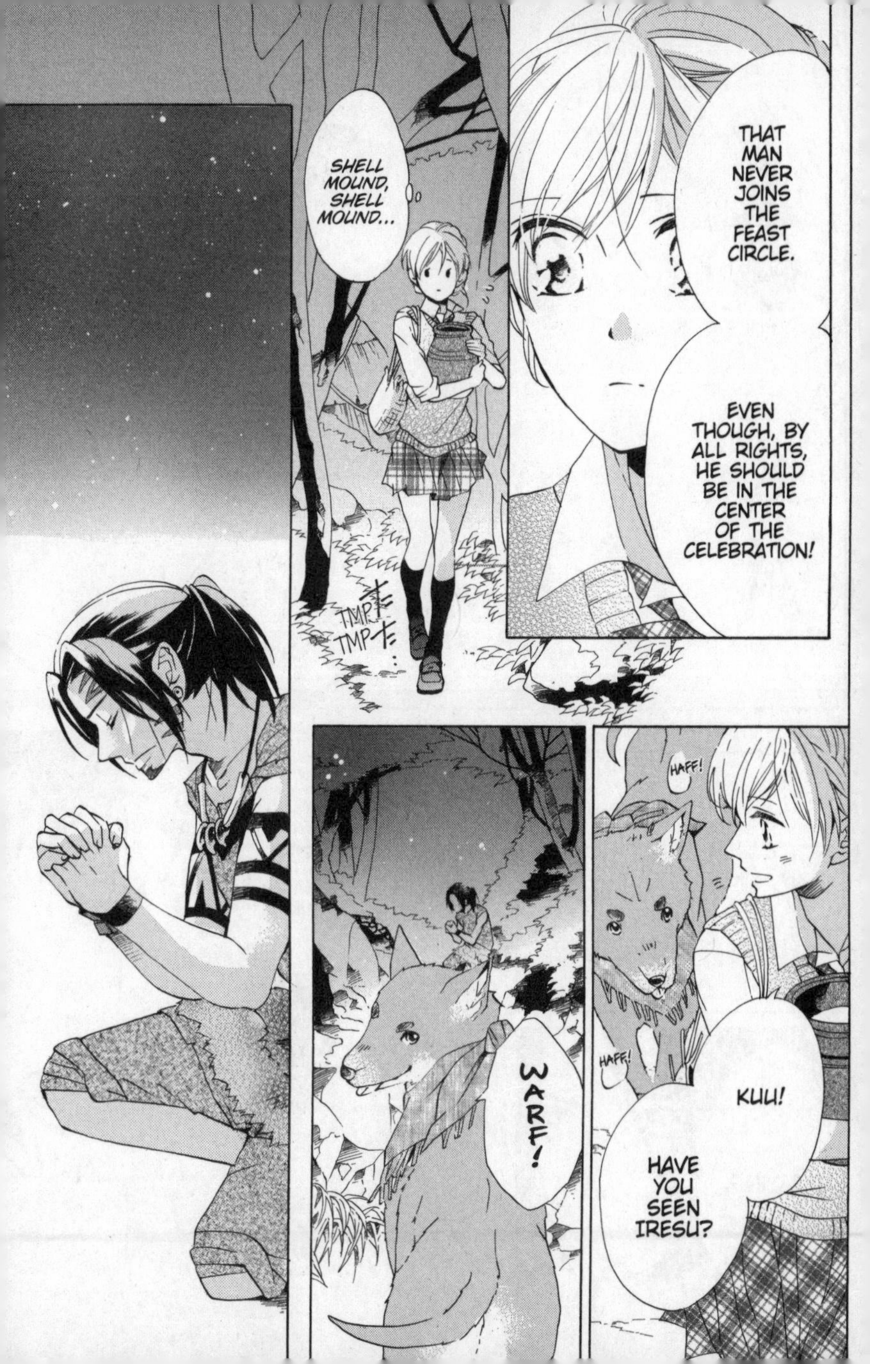
THAT MAN NEVER JOINS THE FEAST CIRCLE.
EVEN THOUGH, BY ALL RIGHTS, HE SHOULD BE IN THE CENTER OF THE CELEBRATION!
SHELL MOUND, SHELL MOUND...
TMP TMP
HAFF!
HAFF!
KUU!
HAVE YOU SEEN IRESU?
WARF!

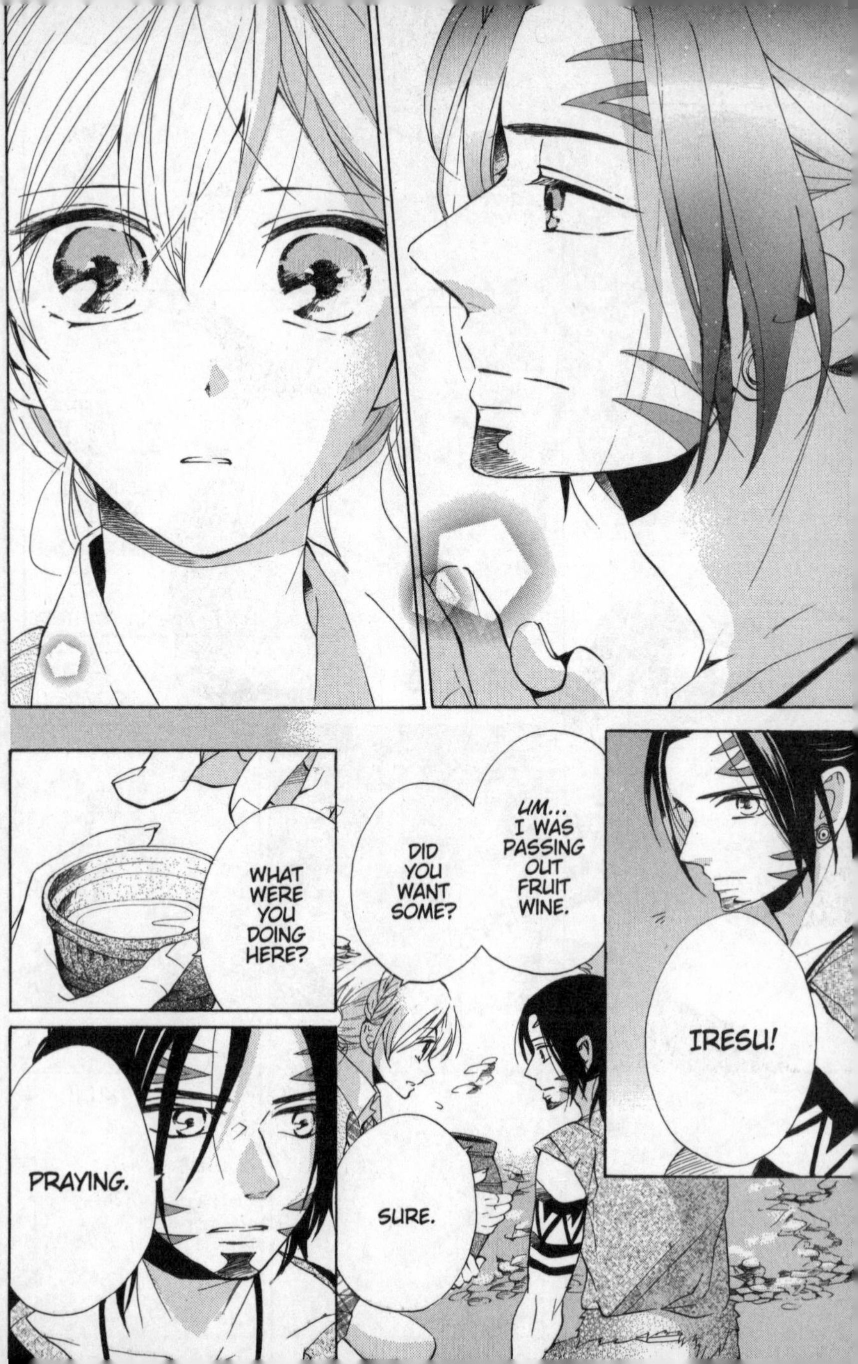
IRESU!
UM... I WAS PASSING OUT FRUIT WINE.
DID YOU WANT SOME?
WHAT WERE YOU DOING HERE?
SURE.
PRAYING.

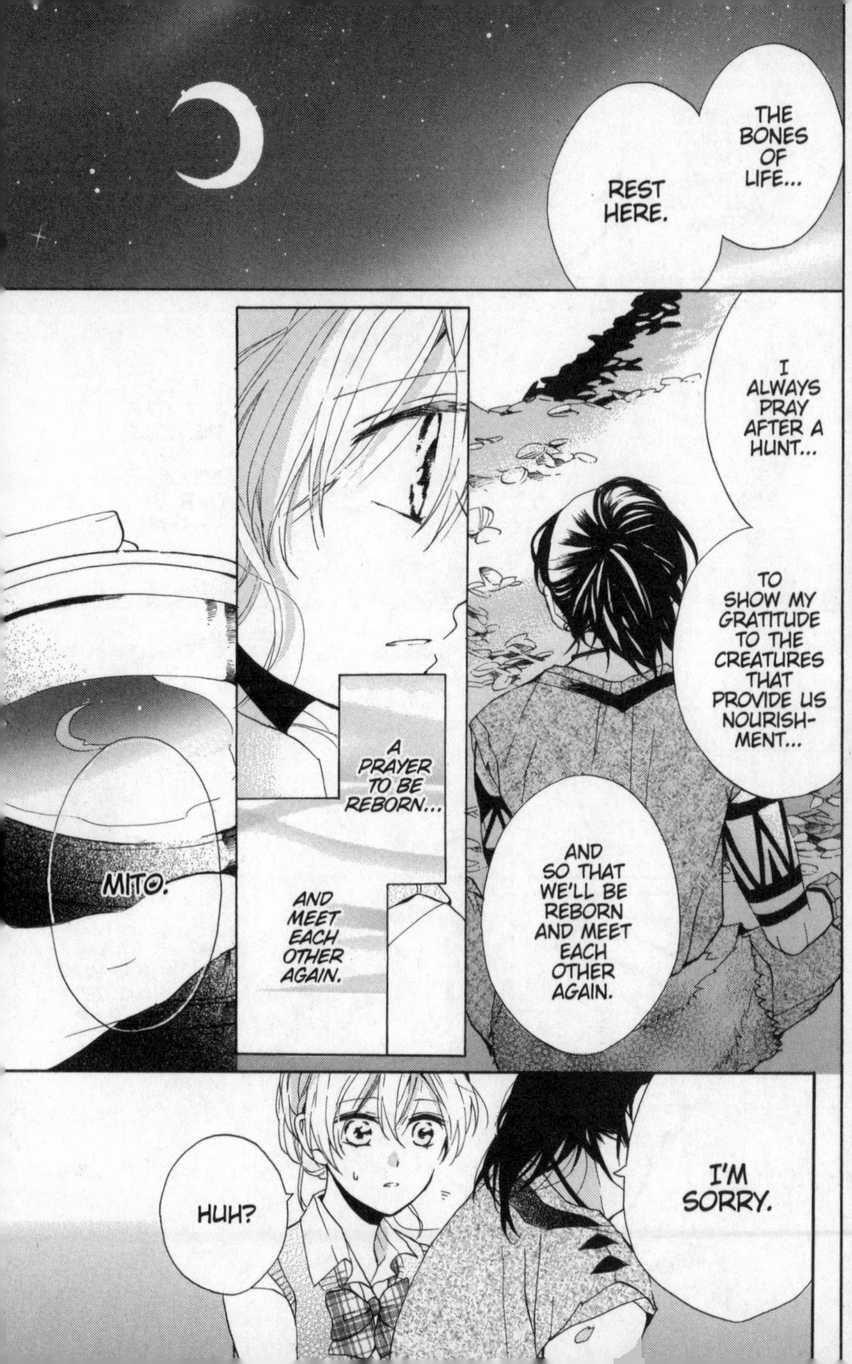
THE BONES OF LIFE...
REST HERE.
I ALWAYS PRAY AFTER A HUNT...
TO SHOW MY GRATITUDE TO THE CREATURES THAT PROVIDE US NOURISHMENT...
AND SO THAT WE'LL BE REBORN AND MEET EACH OTHER AGAIN.
A PRAYER TO BE REBORN...
AND MEET EACH OTHER AGAIN.
MITO.
I'M SORRY.
HUH?

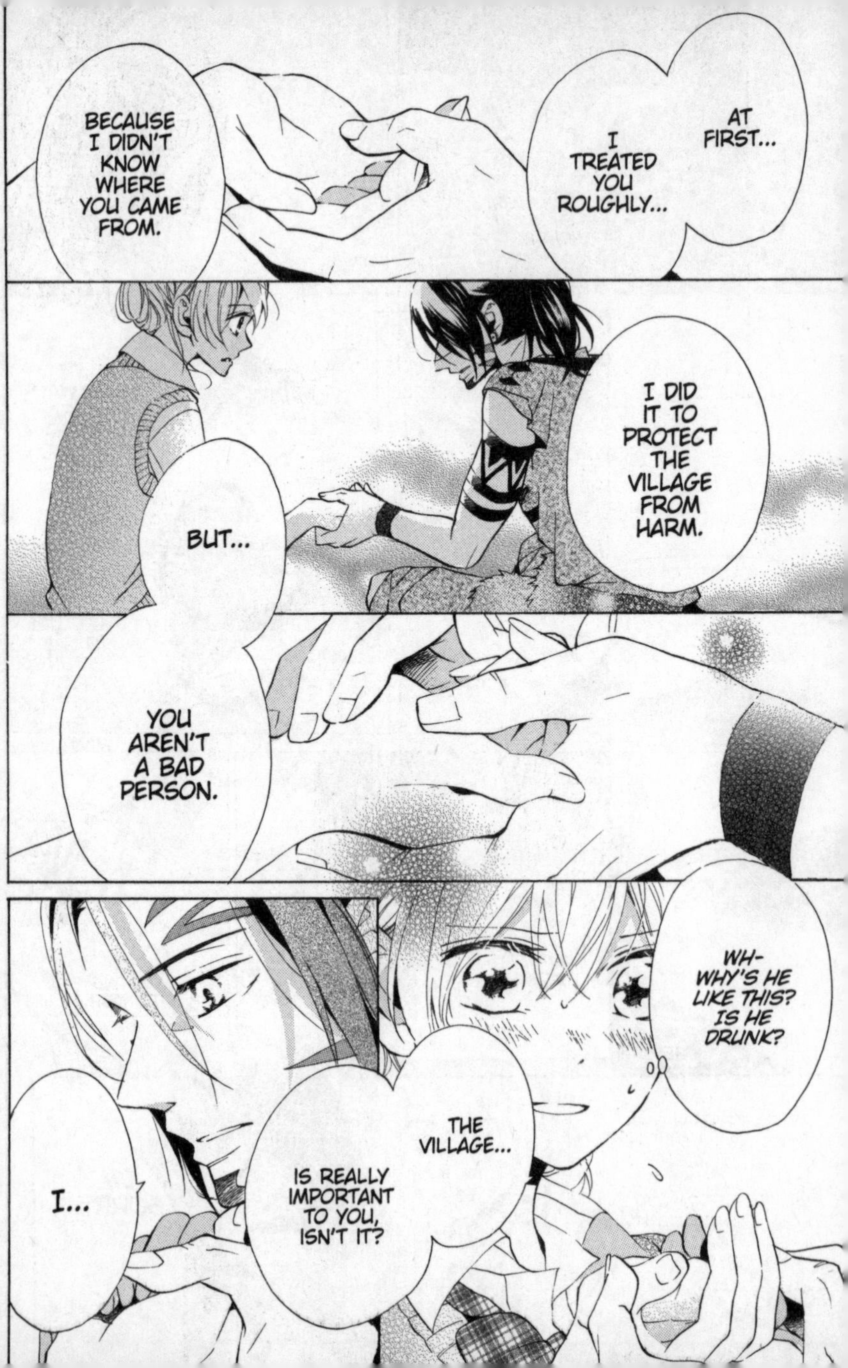
AT FIRST...
I TREATED YOU ROUGHLY...
BECAUSE I DIDN'T KNOW WHERE YOU CAME FROM.
I DID IT TO PROTECT THE VILLAGE FROM HARM.
BUT...
YOU AREN'T A BAD PERSON.
WH- WHY'S HE LIKE THIS? IS HE DRUNK?
THE VILLAGE...
IS REALLY IMPORTANT TO YOU, ISN'T IT?
I...

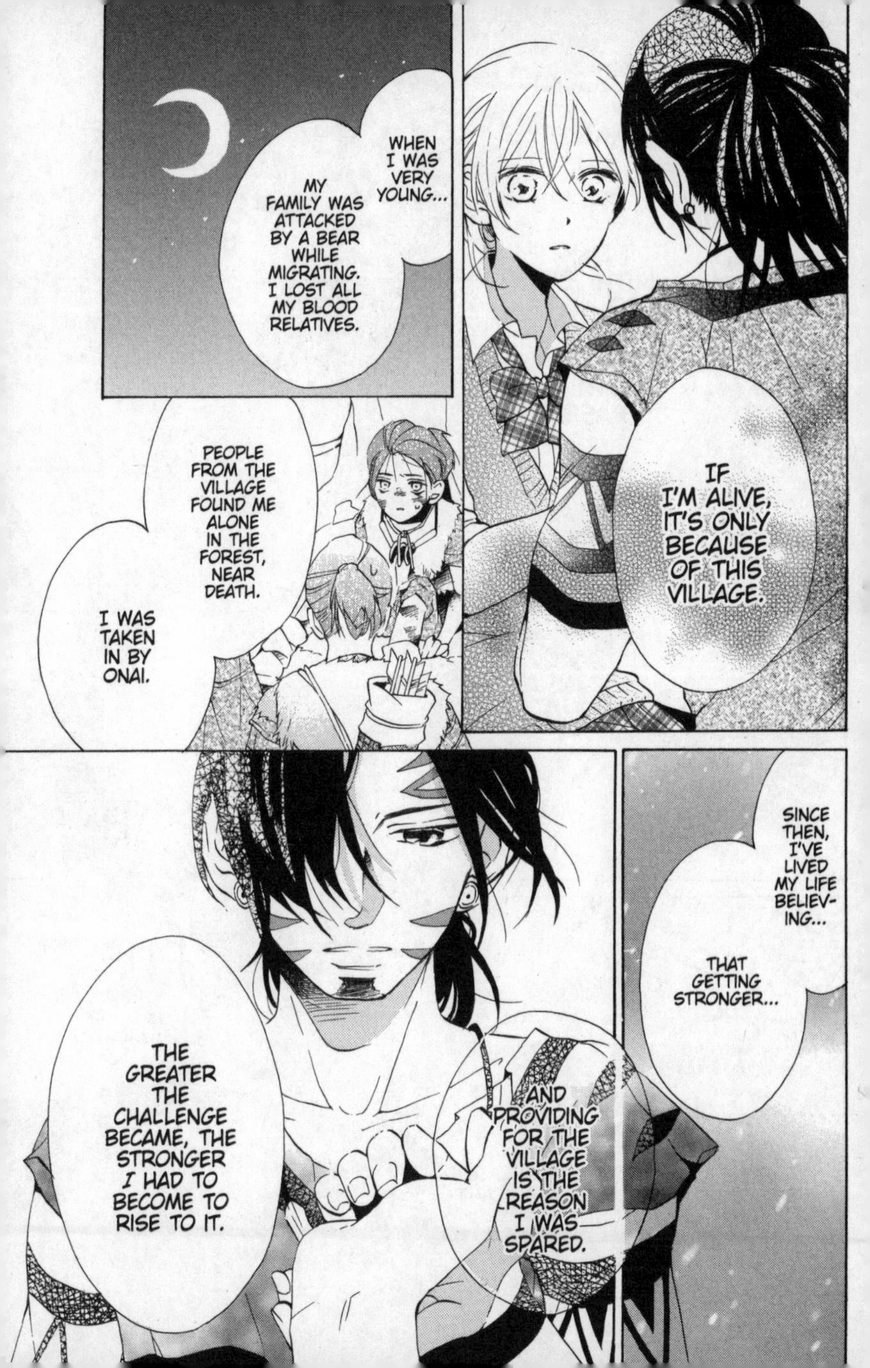
IF I'M ALIVE, IT'S ONLY BECAUSE OF THIS VILLAGE.
WHEN I WAS VERY YOUNG...
MY FAMILY WAS ATTACKED BY A BEAR WHILE MIGRATING. I LOST ALL MY BLOOD RELATIVES.
PEOPLE FROM THE VILLAGE FOUND ME ALONE IN THE FOREST, NEAR DEATH.
I WAS TAKEN IN BY ONAI.
SINCE THEN, I'VE LIVED MY LIFE BELIEV-ING...
THAT GETTING STRONGER...
AND PROVIDING FOR THE VILLAGE IS THE REASON I WAS SPARED.
THE GREATER THE CHALLENGE BECAME, THE STRONGER *I* HAD TO BECOME TO RISE TO IT.

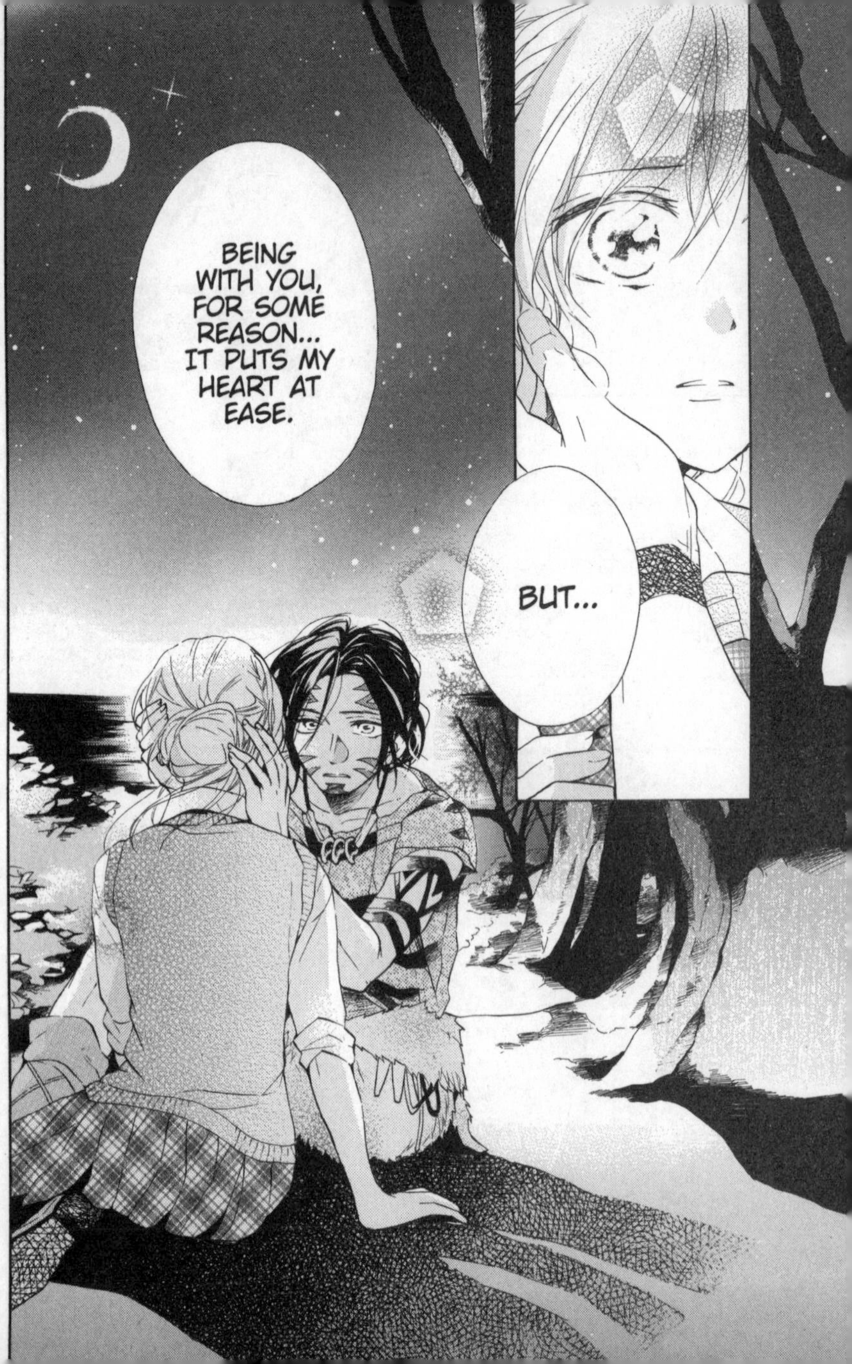
BEING WITH YOU, FOR SOME REASON... IT PUTS MY HEART AT EASE.
BUT...

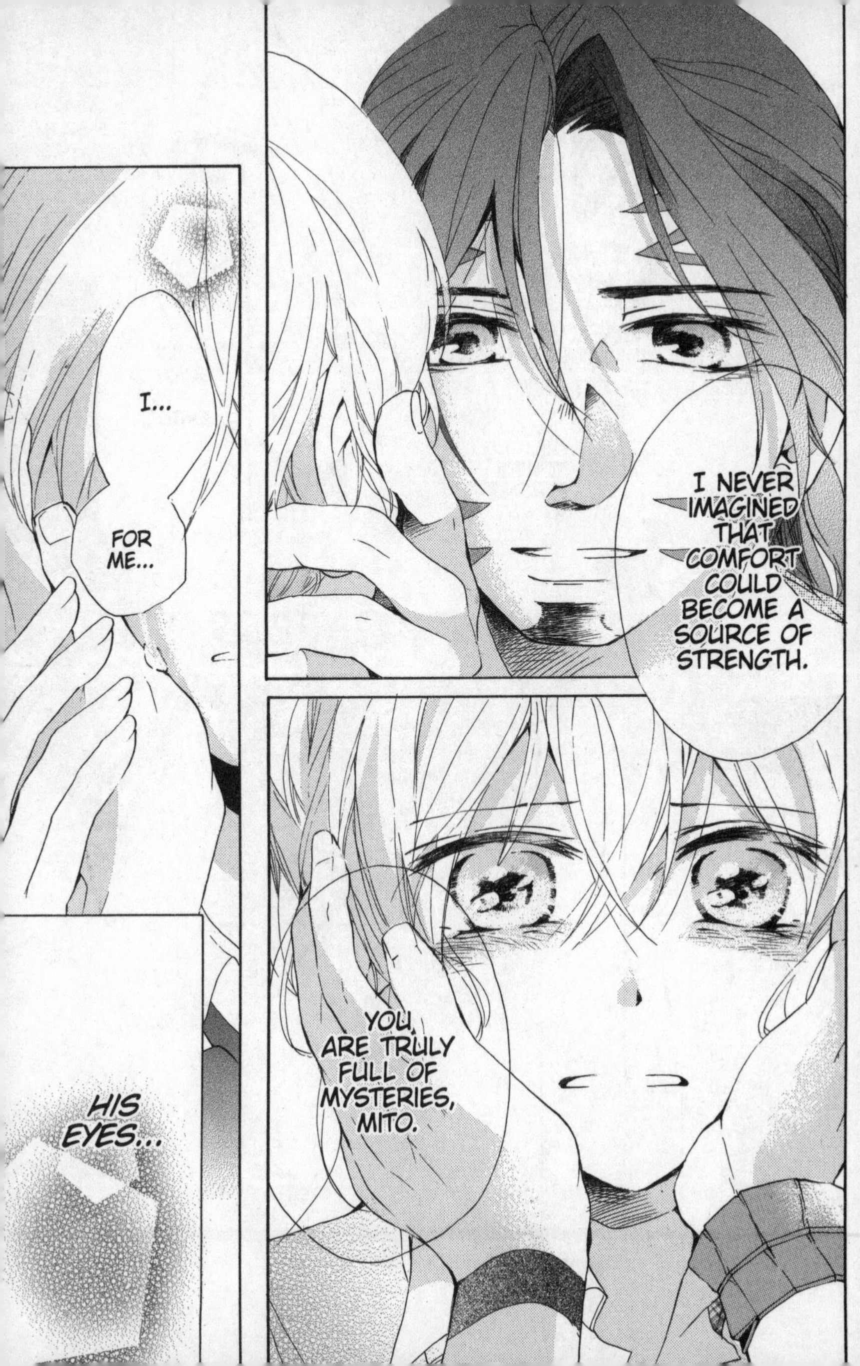
I NEVER IMAGINED THAT COMFORT COULD BECOME A SOURCE OF STRENGTH.
YOU, ARE TRULY FULL OF MYSTERIES, MITO.
I...
FOR ME...
HIS EYES...

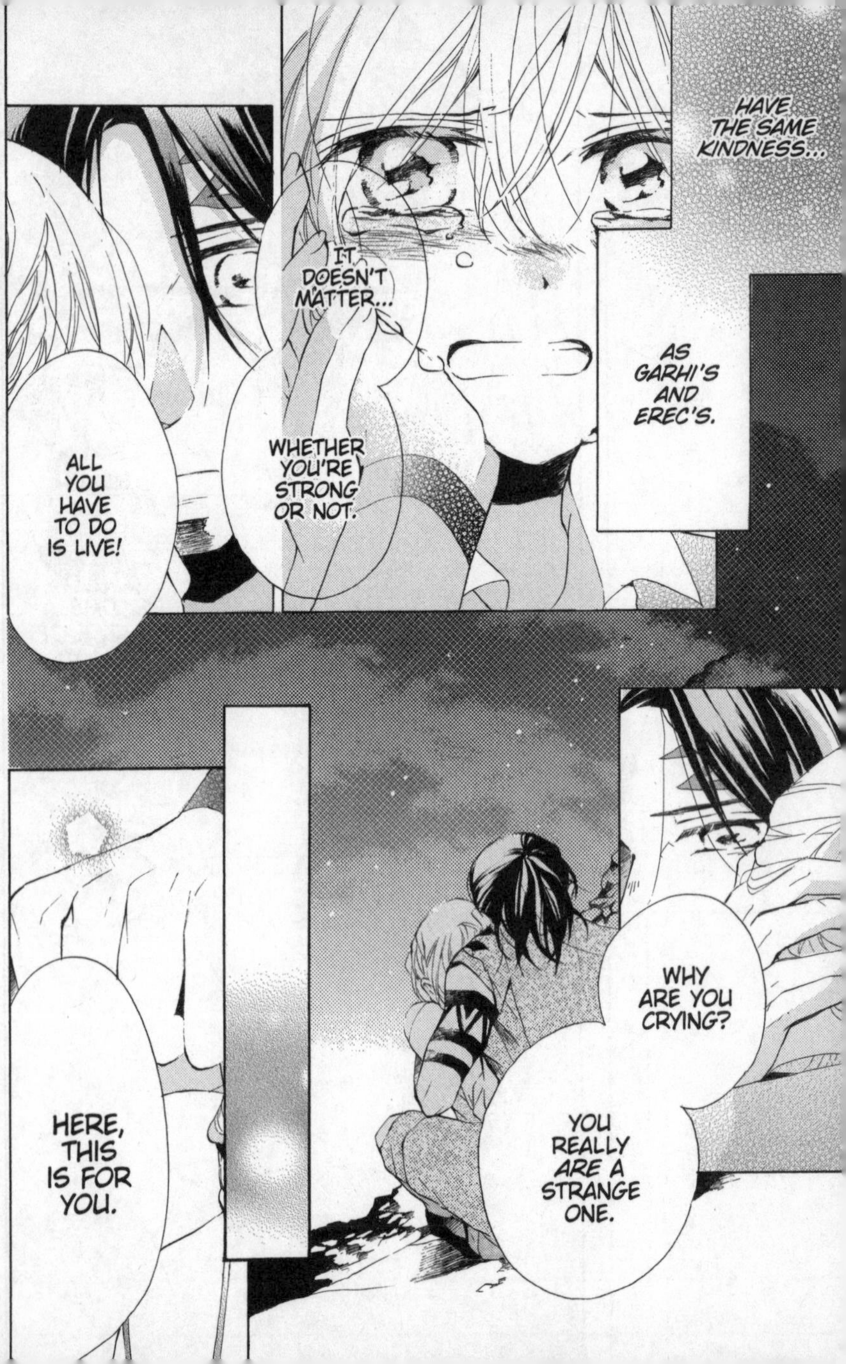
HAVE THE SAME KINDNESS...
AS GARHI'S AND EREC'S.
IT DOESN'T MATTER...
WHETHER YOU'RE STRONG OR NOT.
ALL YOU HAVE TO DO IS LIVE!
WHY ARE YOU CRYING?
YOU REALLY ARE A STRANGE ONE.
HERE, THIS IS FOR YOU.

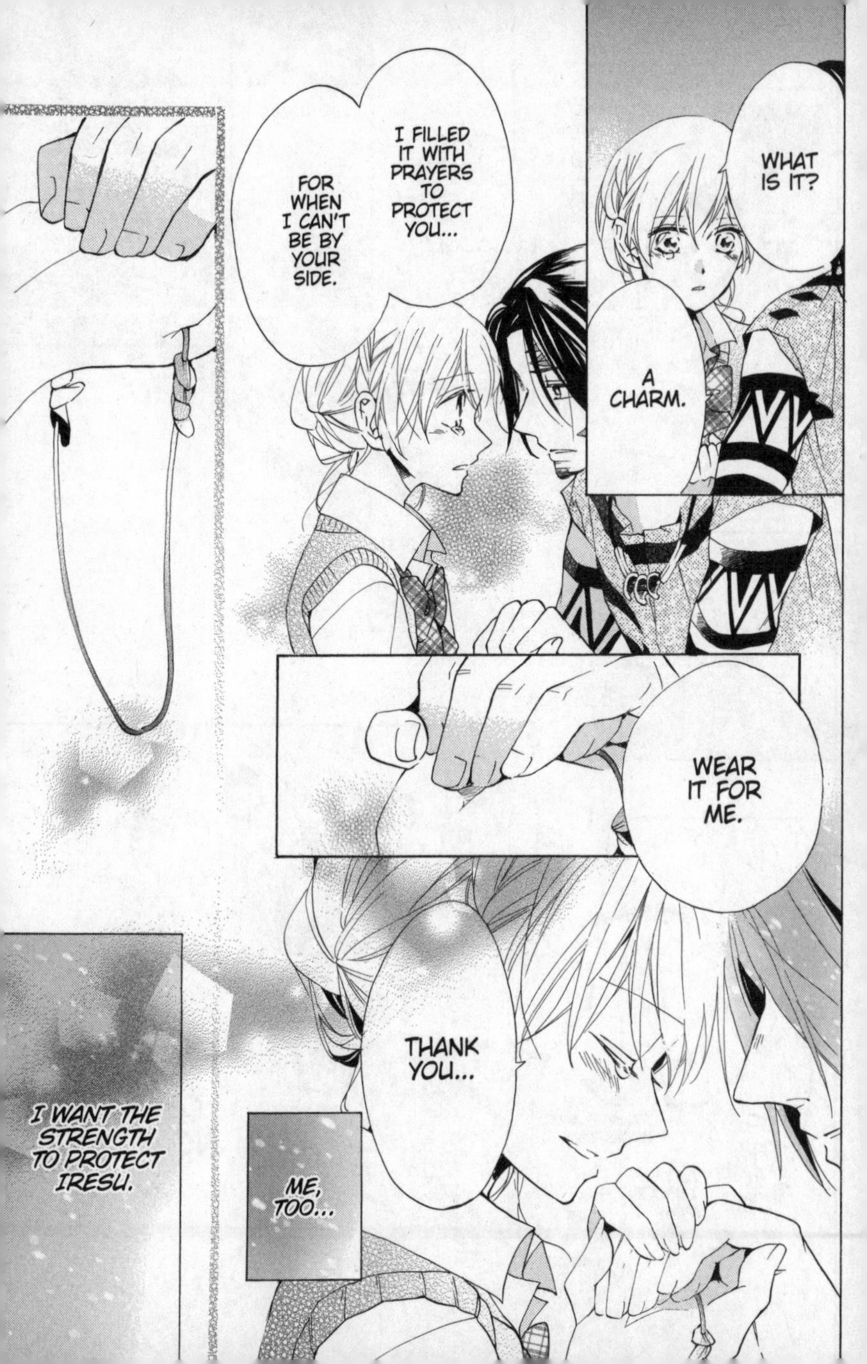
WHAT IS IT?
A CHARM.
I FILLED IT WITH PRAYERS TO PROTECT YOU...
FOR WHEN I CAN'T BE BY YOUR SIDE.
WEAR IT FOR ME.
THANK YOU...
ME, TOO...
I WANT THE STRENGTH TO PROTECT IRESU.

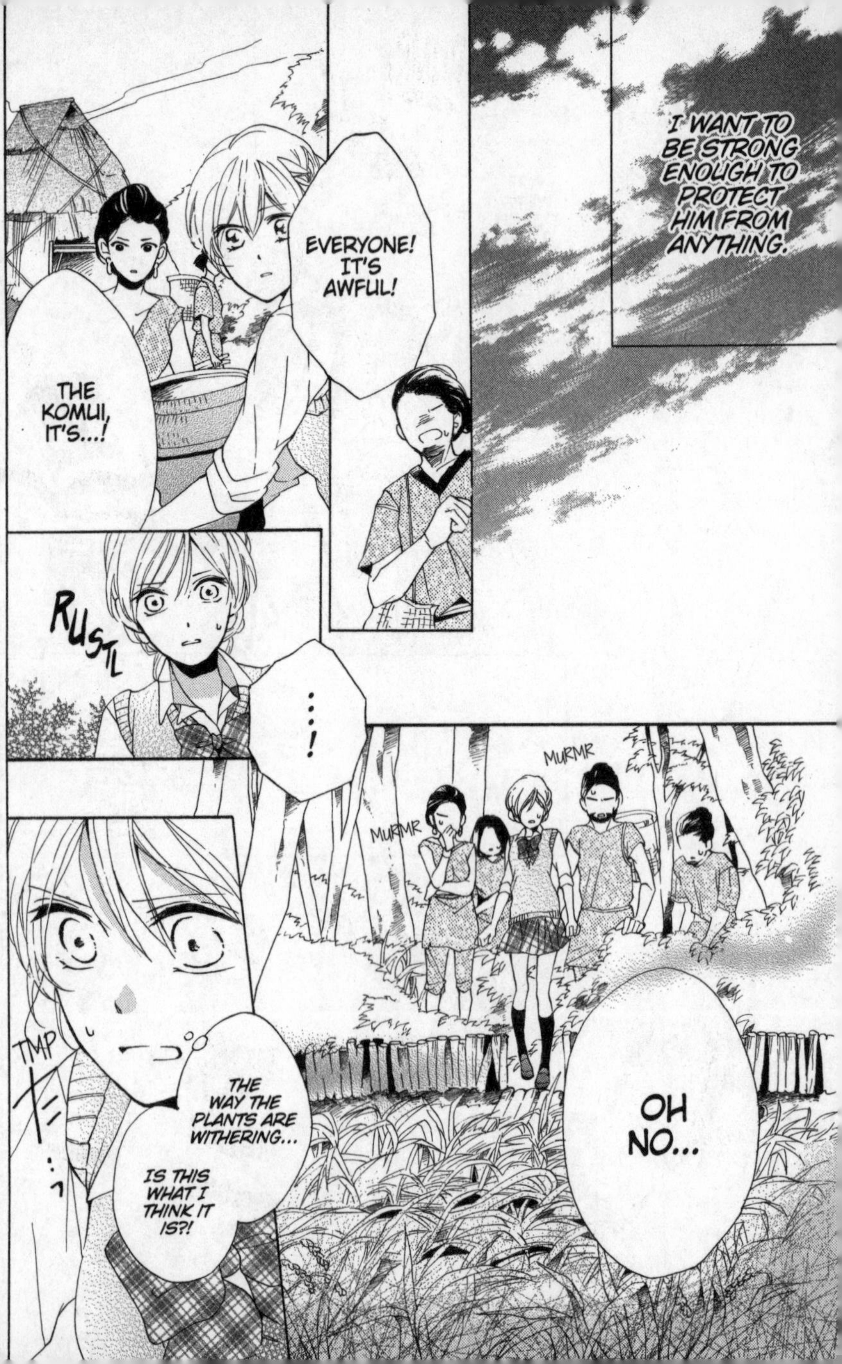

I WANT TO BE STRONG ENOUGH TO PROTECT HIM FROM ANYTHING.
EVERYONE! IT'S AWFUL!
THE KOMUII, IT'S...!
RUSTL
...!
MURMR
MURMR
OH NO...
THE WAY THE PLANTS ARE WITHERING...
IS THIS WHAT I THINK IT IS?!
TMP

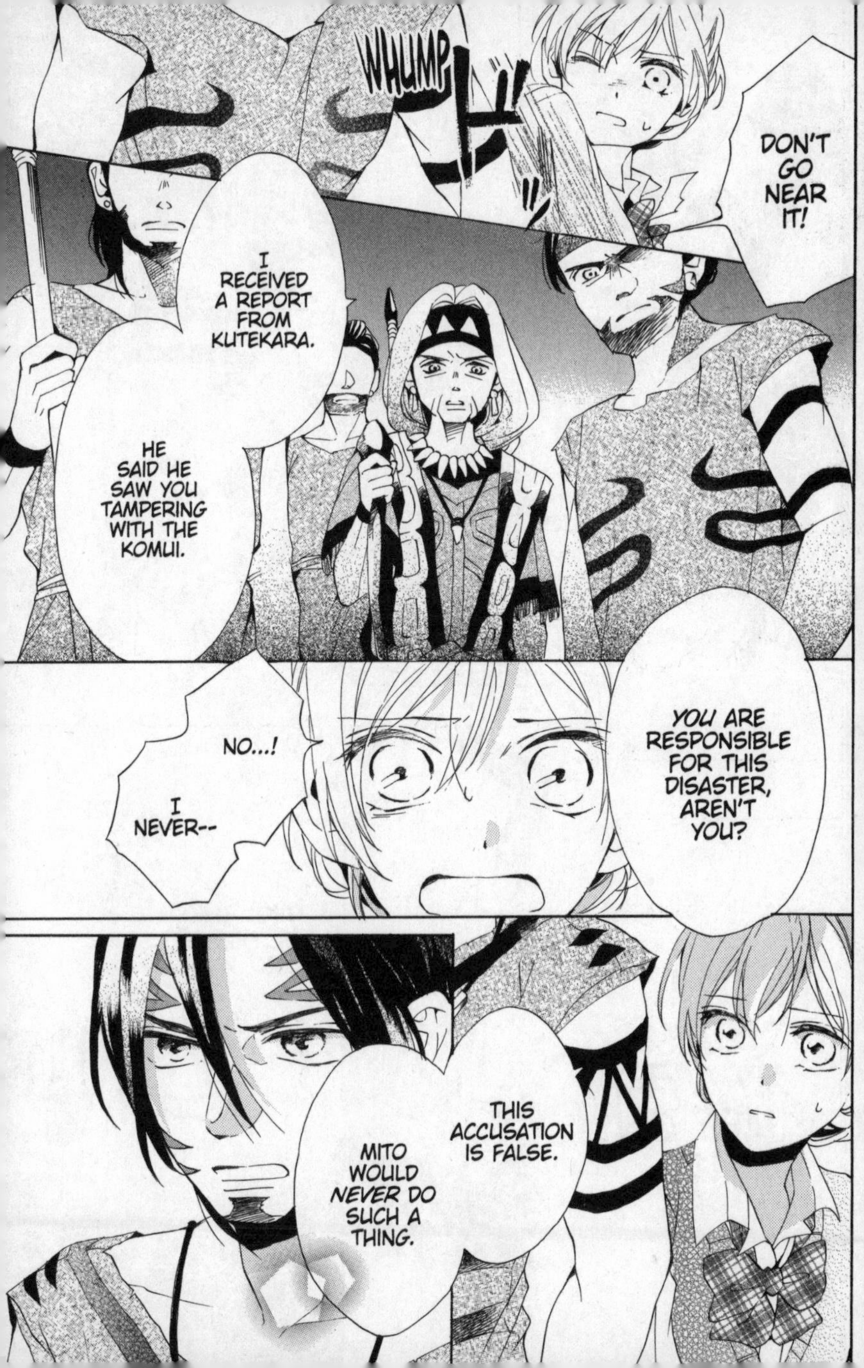
DON'T GO NEAR IT!
WHUMP
I RECEIVED A REPORT FROM KUTEKARA.
HE SAID HE SAW YOU TAMPERING WITH THE KOMUI.
YOU ARE RESPONSIBLE FOR THIS DISASTER, AREN'T YOU?
NO...!
I NEVER--
THIS ACCUSATION IS FALSE.
MITO WOULD *NEVER* DO SUCH A THING.

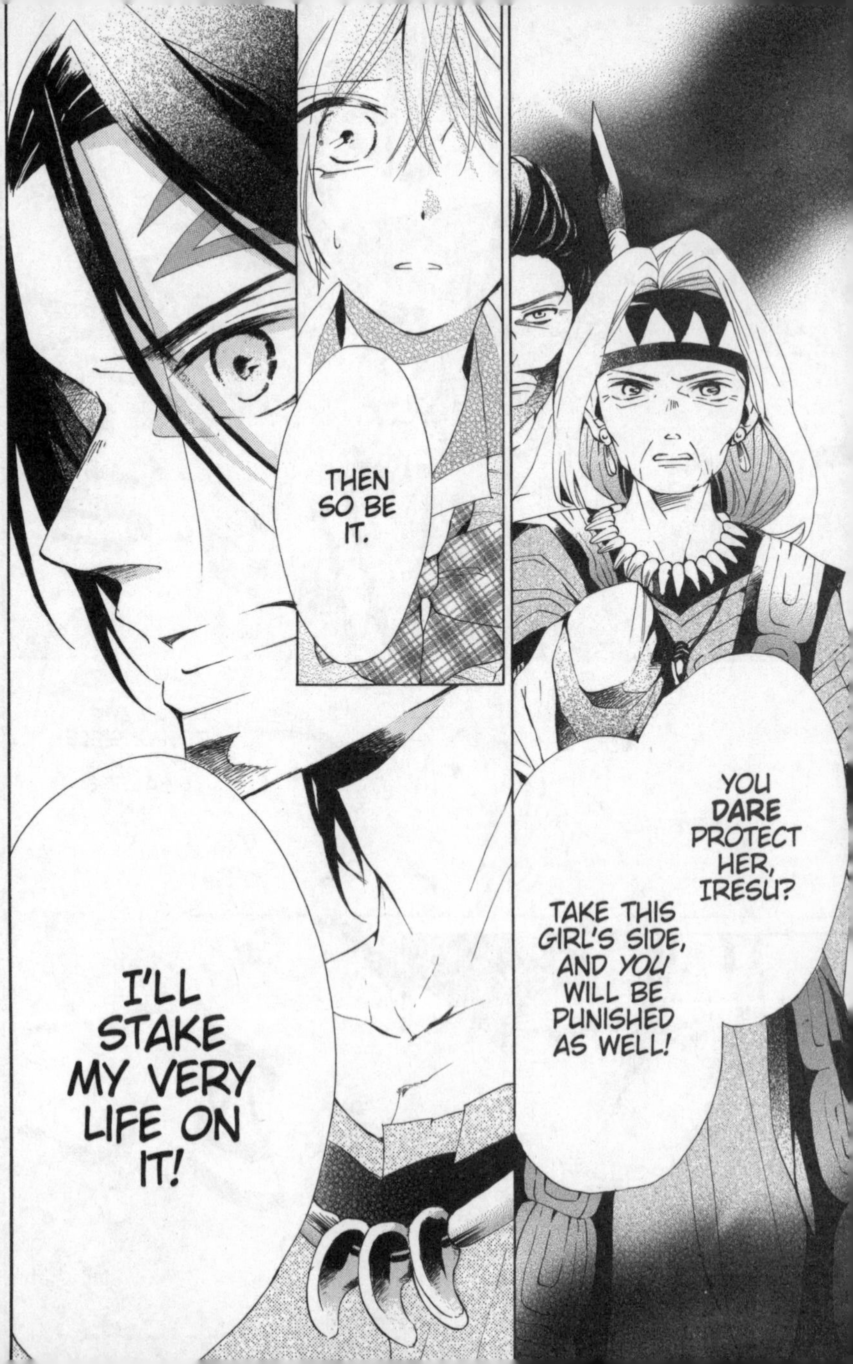
YOU DARE PROTECT HER, IRESU?
TAKE THIS GIRL'S SIDE, AND *YOU* WILL BE PUNISHED AS WELL!
THEN SO BE IT.
I'LL STAKE MY VERY LIFE ON IT!

CHAPTER 12

PRIMITIVE Boyfriend

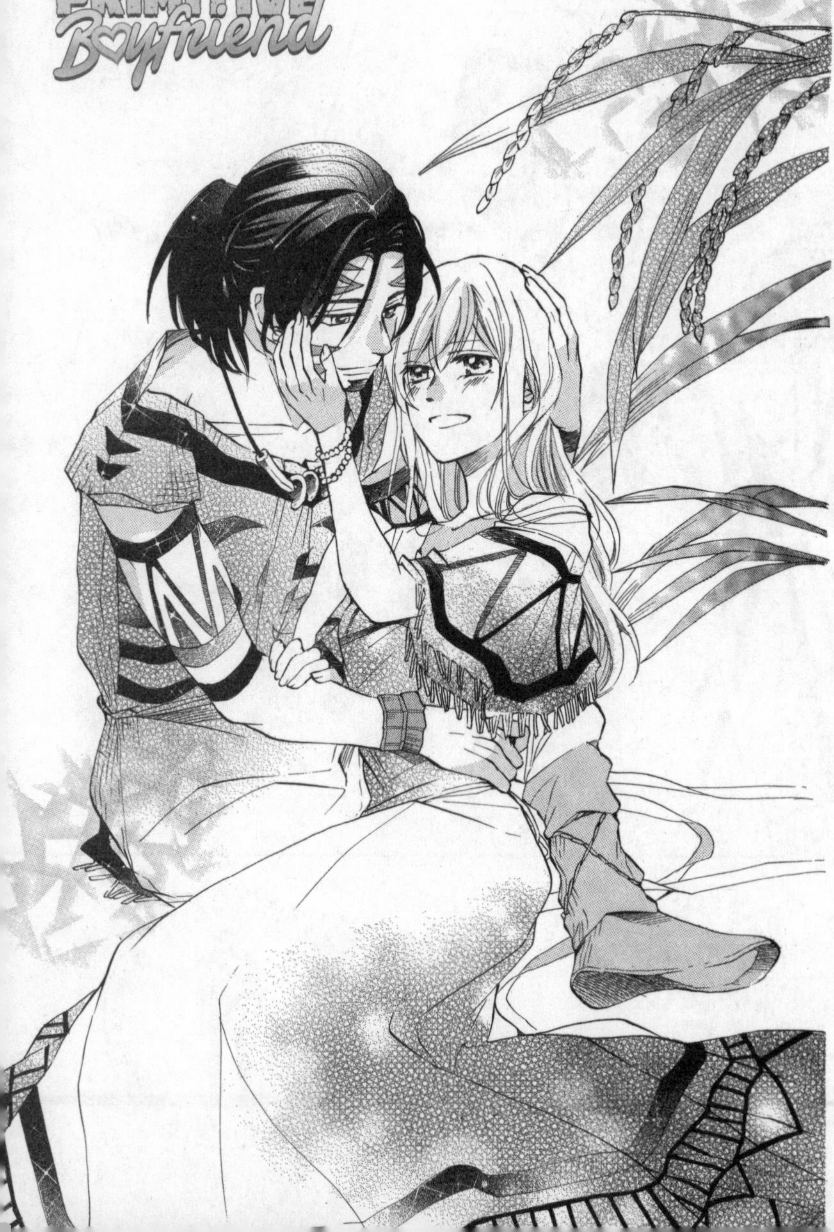

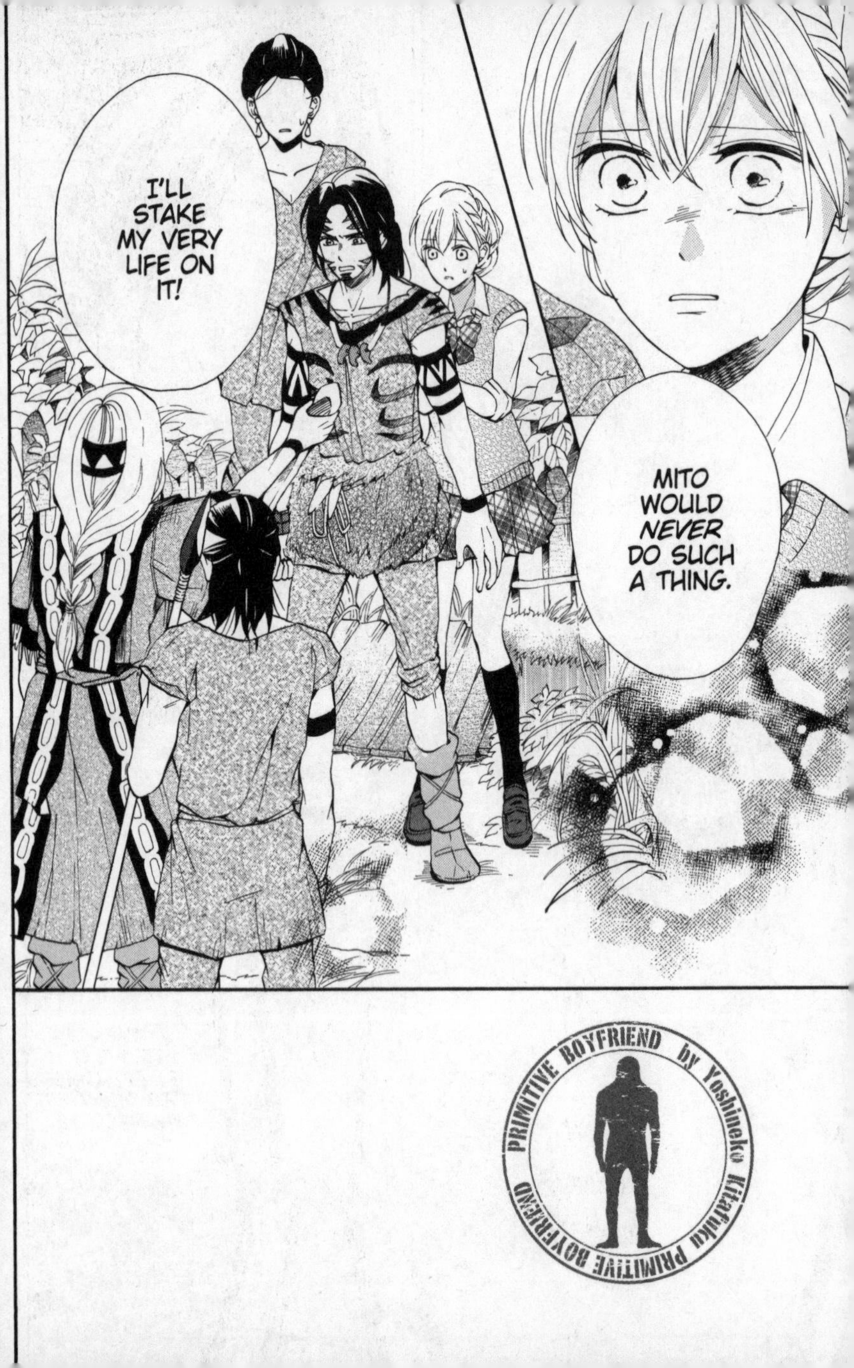
MITO WOULD NEVER DO SUCH A THING.
I'LL STAKE MY VERY LIFE ON IT!

PRIMITIVE BOYFRIEND by Yoshineko Kitafuku PRIMITIVE BOYFRIEND

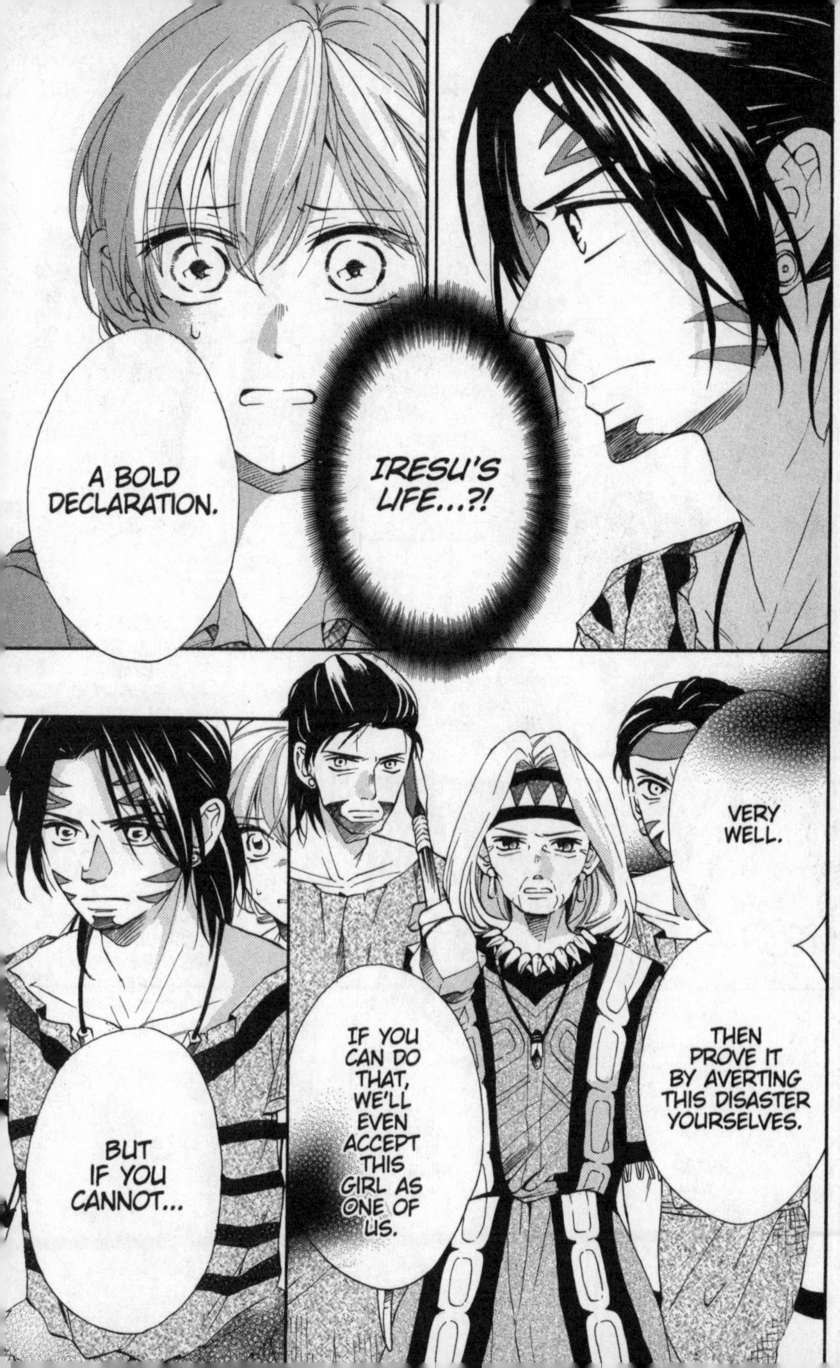
IRESU'S LIFE...?!
A BOLD DECLARATION.
VERY WELL.
THEN PROVE IT BY AVERTING THIS DISASTER YOURSELVES.
IF YOU CAN DO THAT, WE'LL EVEN ACCEPT THIS GIRL AS ONE OF US.
BUT IF YOU CANNOT...

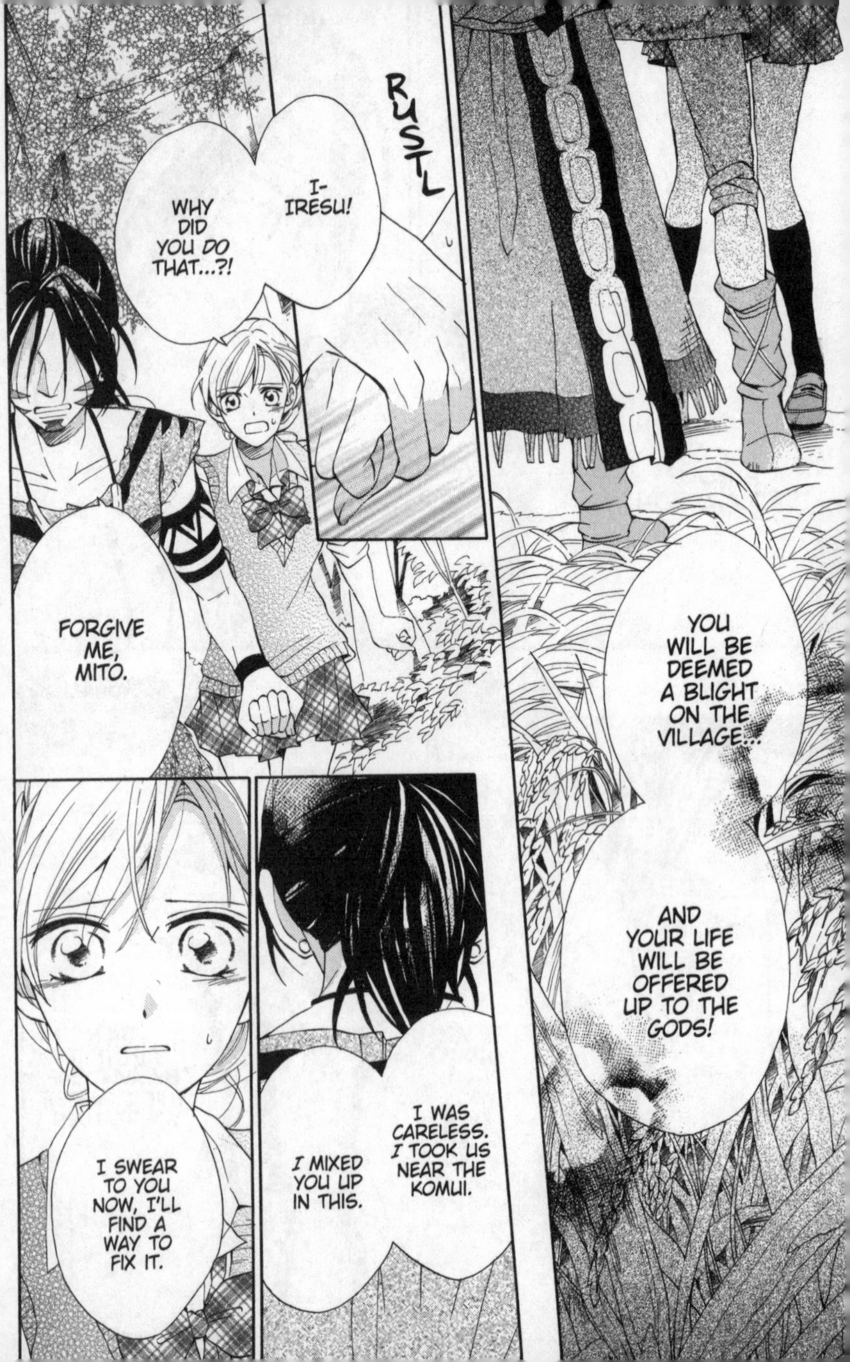
YOU WILL BE DEEMED A BLIGHT ON THE VILLAGE...
AND YOUR LIFE WILL BE OFFERED UP TO THE GODS!
RUSTL
I- IRESU!
WHY DID YOU *DO* THAT...?!
FORGIVE ME, MITO.
I WAS CARELESS. *I* TOOK US NEAR THE KOMUI.
I MIXED YOU UP IN THIS.
I SWEAR TO YOU NOW, I'LL FIND A WAY TO FIX IT.

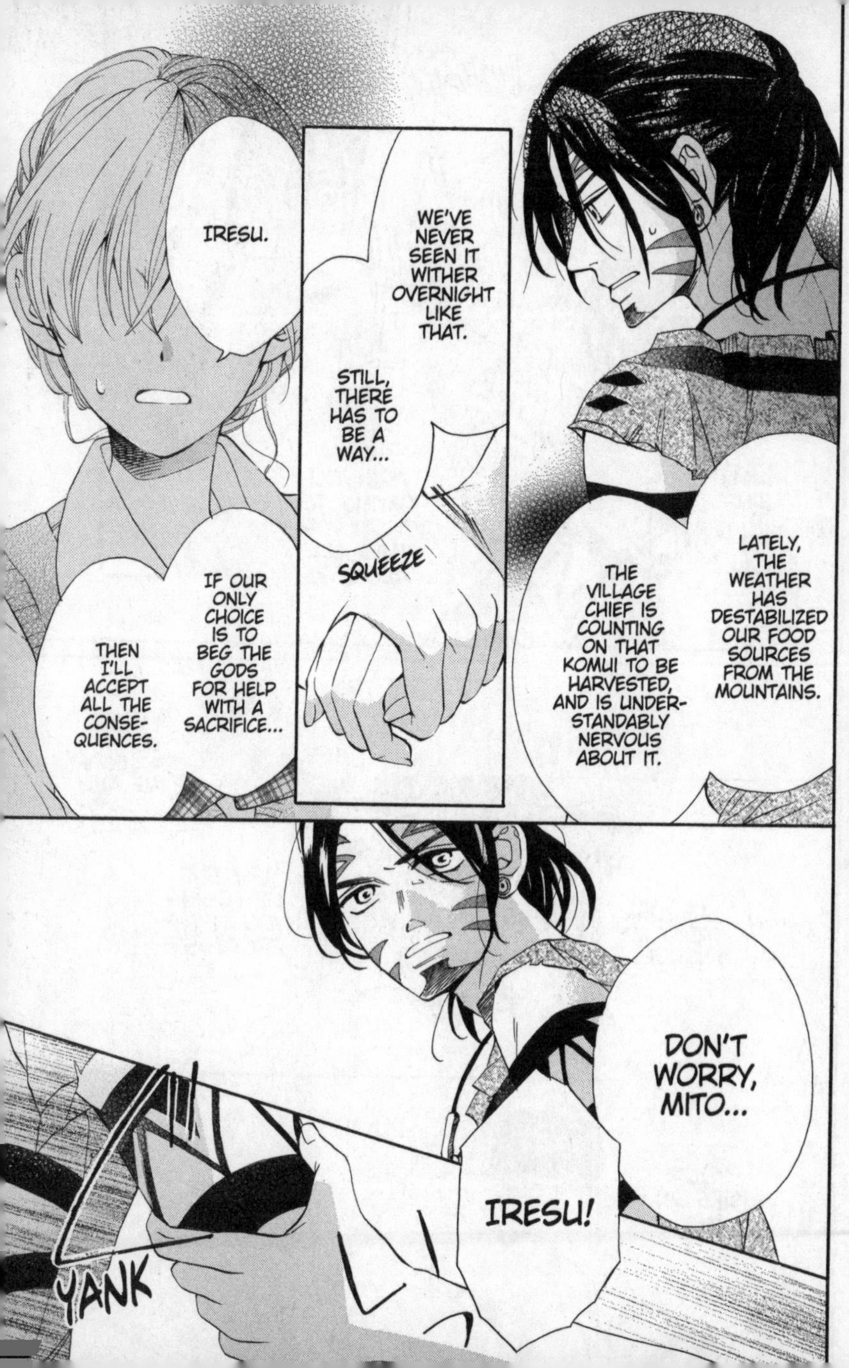
LATELY, THE WEATHER HAS DESTABILIZED OUR FOOD SOURCES FROM THE MOUNTAINS.
THE VILLAGE CHIEF IS COUNTING ON THAT KOMUI TO BE HARVESTED, AND IS UNDER-STANDABLY NERVOUS ABOUT IT.
WE'VE NEVER SEEN IT WITHER OVERNIGHT LIKE THAT.
STILL, THERE HAS TO BE A WAY...
SQUEEZE
IRESU.
IF OUR ONLY CHOICE IS TO BEG THE GODS FOR HELP WITH A SACRIFICE...
THEN I'LL ACCEPT ALL THE CONSE-QUENCES.
DON'T WORRY, MITO...
IRESU!
YANK

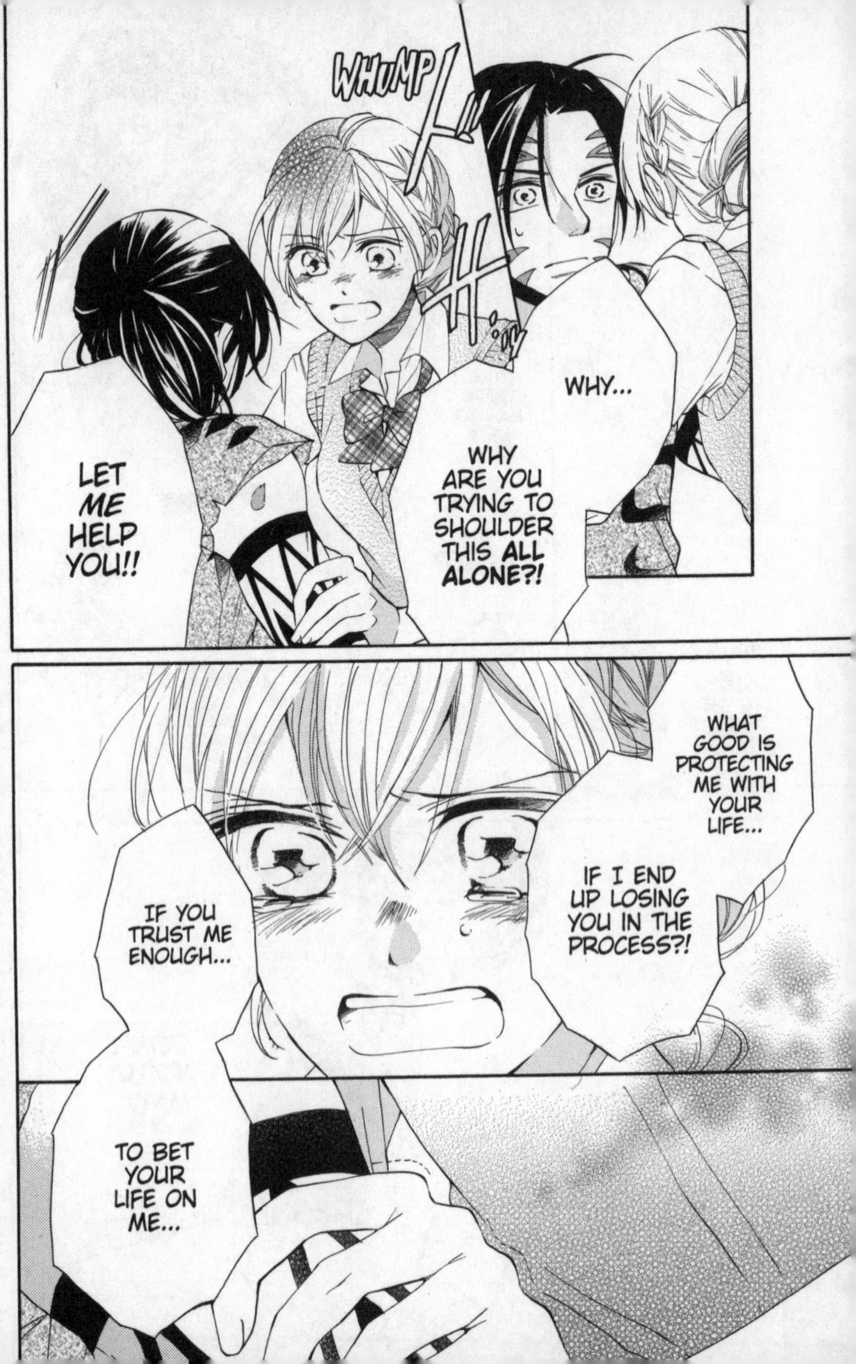
WHUMP
WHY...
WHY ARE YOU TRYING TO SHOULDER THIS ALL ALONE?!
LET ME HELP YOU!!
WHAT GOOD IS PROTECTING ME WITH YOUR LIFE...
IF I END UP LOSING YOU IN THE PROCESS?!
IF YOU TRUST ME ENOUGH...
TO BET YOUR LIFE ON ME...

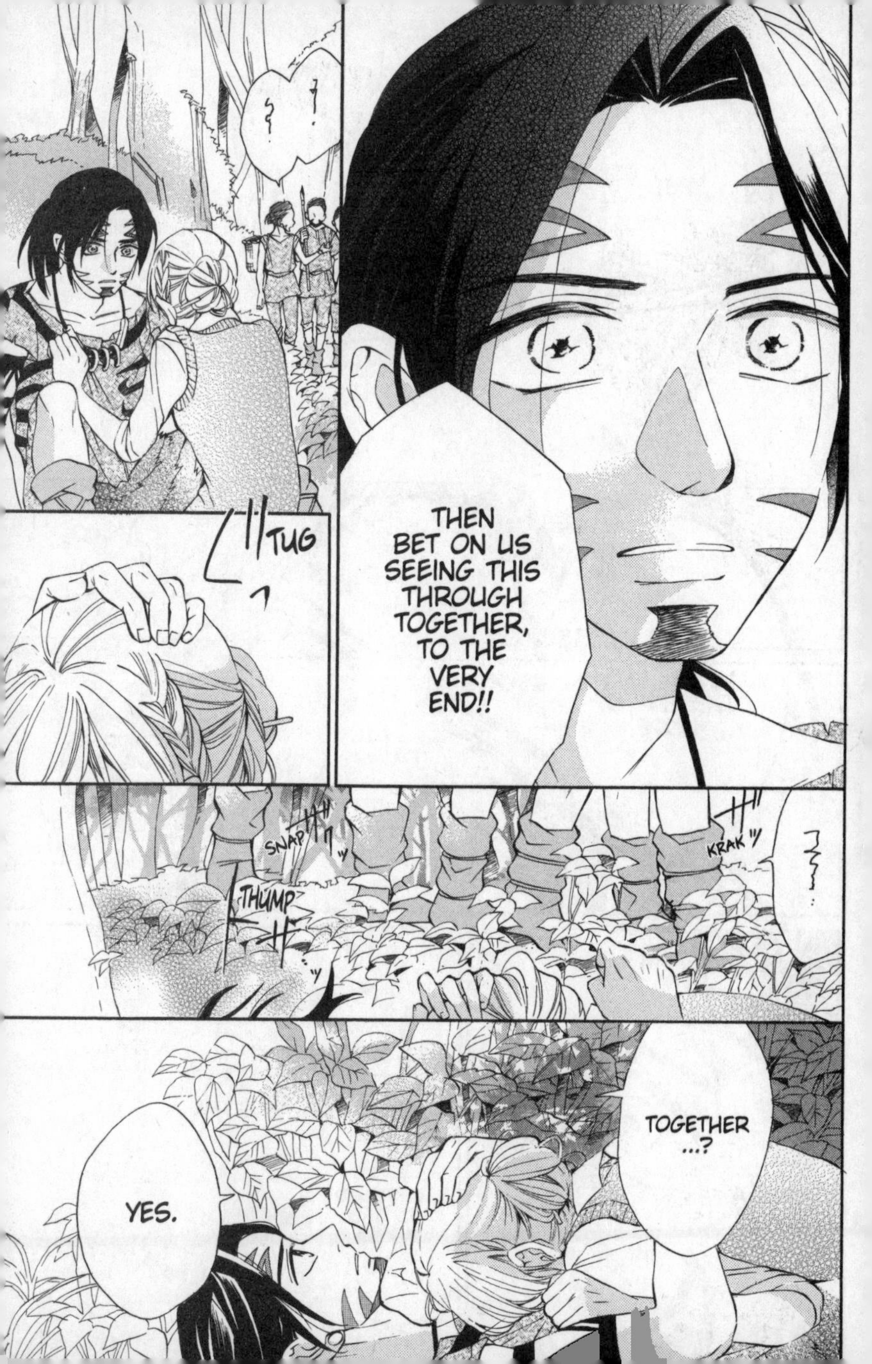
THEN BET ON US SEEING THIS THROUGH TOGETHER, TO THE VERY END!!
TUG
KRAK
SNAP
THUMP
TOGETHER ...?
YES.

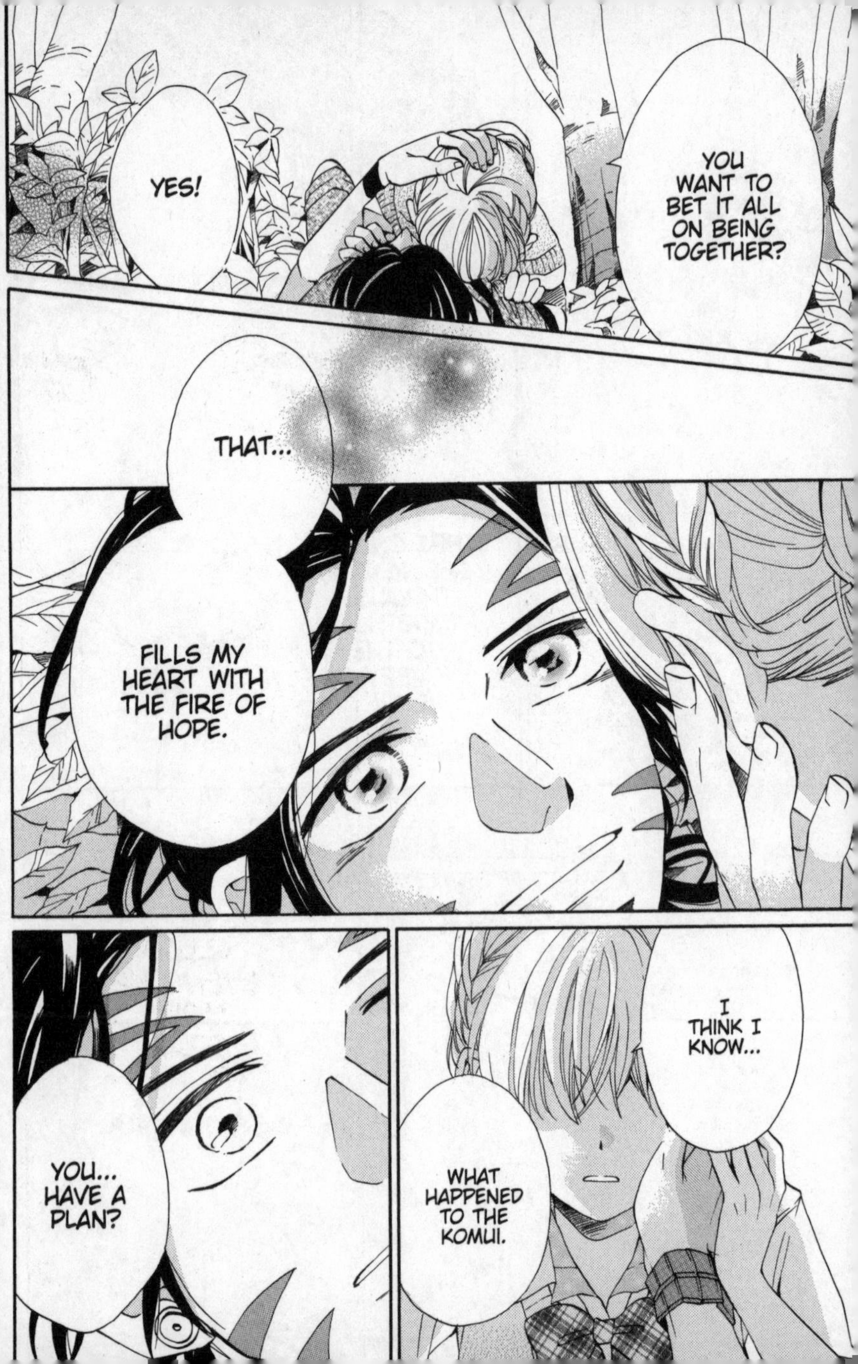
YOU WANT TO BET IT ALL ON BEING TOGETHER?
YES!
THAT...
FILLS MY HEART WITH THE FIRE OF HOPE.
I THINK I KNOW...
WHAT HAPPENED TO THE KOMUI.
YOU... HAVE A PLAN?

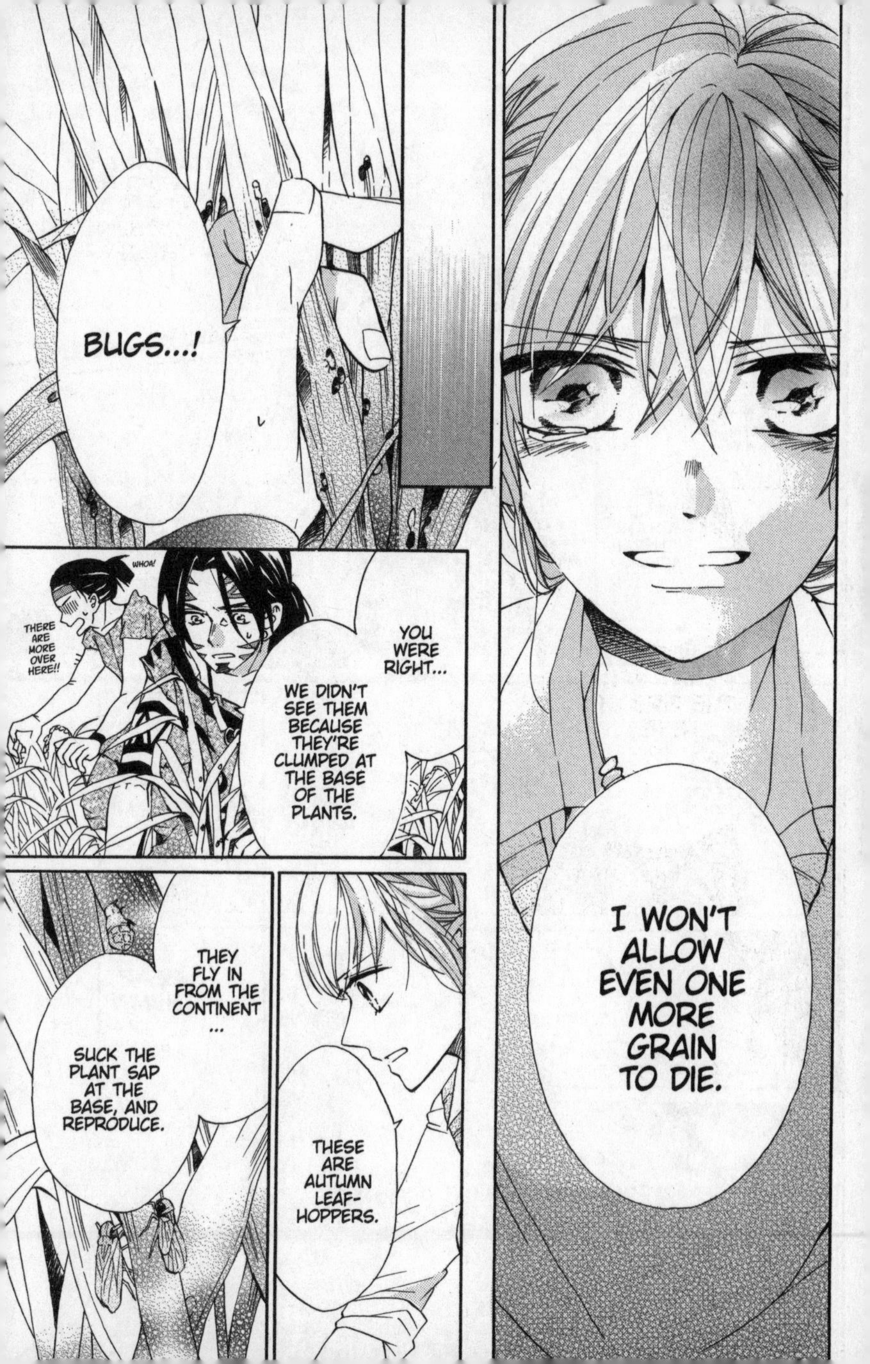
I WON'T ALLOW EVEN ONE MORE GRAIN TO DIE.
BUGS...!
YOU WERE RIGHT...
WE DIDN'T SEE THEM BECAUSE THEY'RE CLUMPED AT THE BASE OF THE PLANTS.
WHOA!
THERE ARE MORE OVER HERE!!
THESE ARE AUTUMN LEAF-HOPPERS.
THEY FLY IN FROM THE CONTINENT ...
SUCK THE PLANT SAP AT THE BASE, AND REPRODUCE.

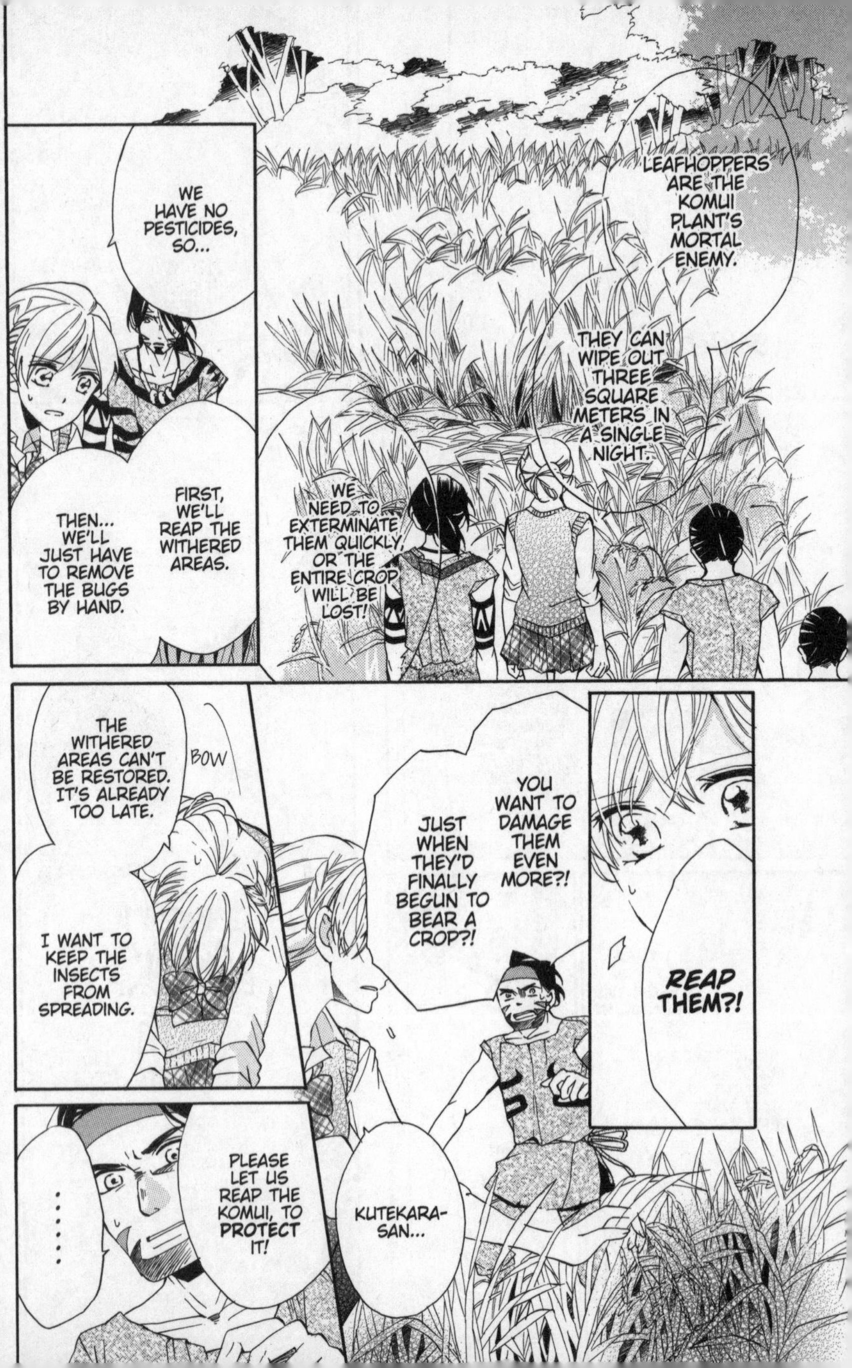
LEAFHOPPERS ARE THE KOMUI PLANT'S MORTAL ENEMY.
THEY CAN WIPE OUT THREE SQUARE METERS IN A SINGLE NIGHT.
WE NEED TO EXTERMINATE THEM QUICKLY, OR THE ENTIRE CROP WILL BE LOST!
WE HAVE NO PESTICIDES, SO...
FIRST, WE'LL REAP THE WITHERED AREAS.
THEN... WE'LL JUST HAVE TO REMOVE THE BUGS BY HAND.
REAP THEM?!
YOU WANT TO DAMAGE THEM EVEN MORE?!
JUST WHEN THEY'D FINALLY BEGUN TO BEAR A CROP?!
THE WITHERED AREAS CAN'T BE RESTORED. IT'S ALREADY TOO LATE.
BOW
I WANT TO KEEP THE INSECTS FROM SPREADING.
KUTEKARA-SAN...
PLEASE LET US REAP THE KOMUI, TO PROTECT IT!
......

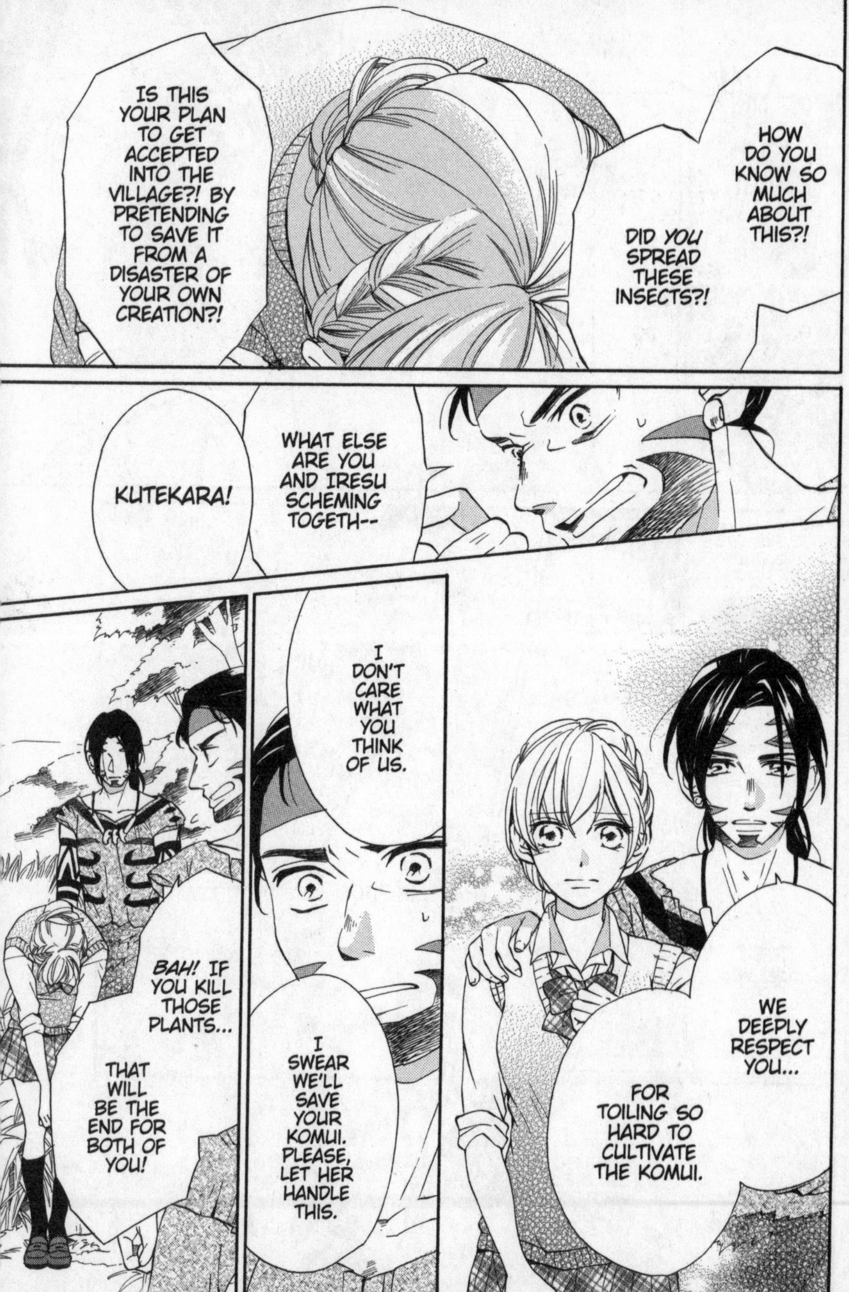
HOW DO YOU KNOW SO MUCH ABOUT THIS?!
DID YOU SPREAD THESE INSECTS?!
IS THIS YOUR PLAN TO GET ACCEPTED INTO THE VILLAGE?! BY PRETENDING TO SAVE IT FROM A DISASTER OF YOUR OWN CREATION?!
WHAT ELSE ARE YOU AND IRESU SCHEMING TOGETH--
KUTEKARA!
WE DEEPLY RESPECT YOU...
FOR TOILING SO HARD TO CULTIVATE THE KOMUI.
I DON'T CARE WHAT YOU THINK OF US.
I SWEAR WE'LL SAVE YOUR KOMUI. PLEASE, LET HER HANDLE THIS.
BAH! IF YOU KILL THOSE PLANTS...
THAT WILL BE THE END FOR BOTH OF YOU!

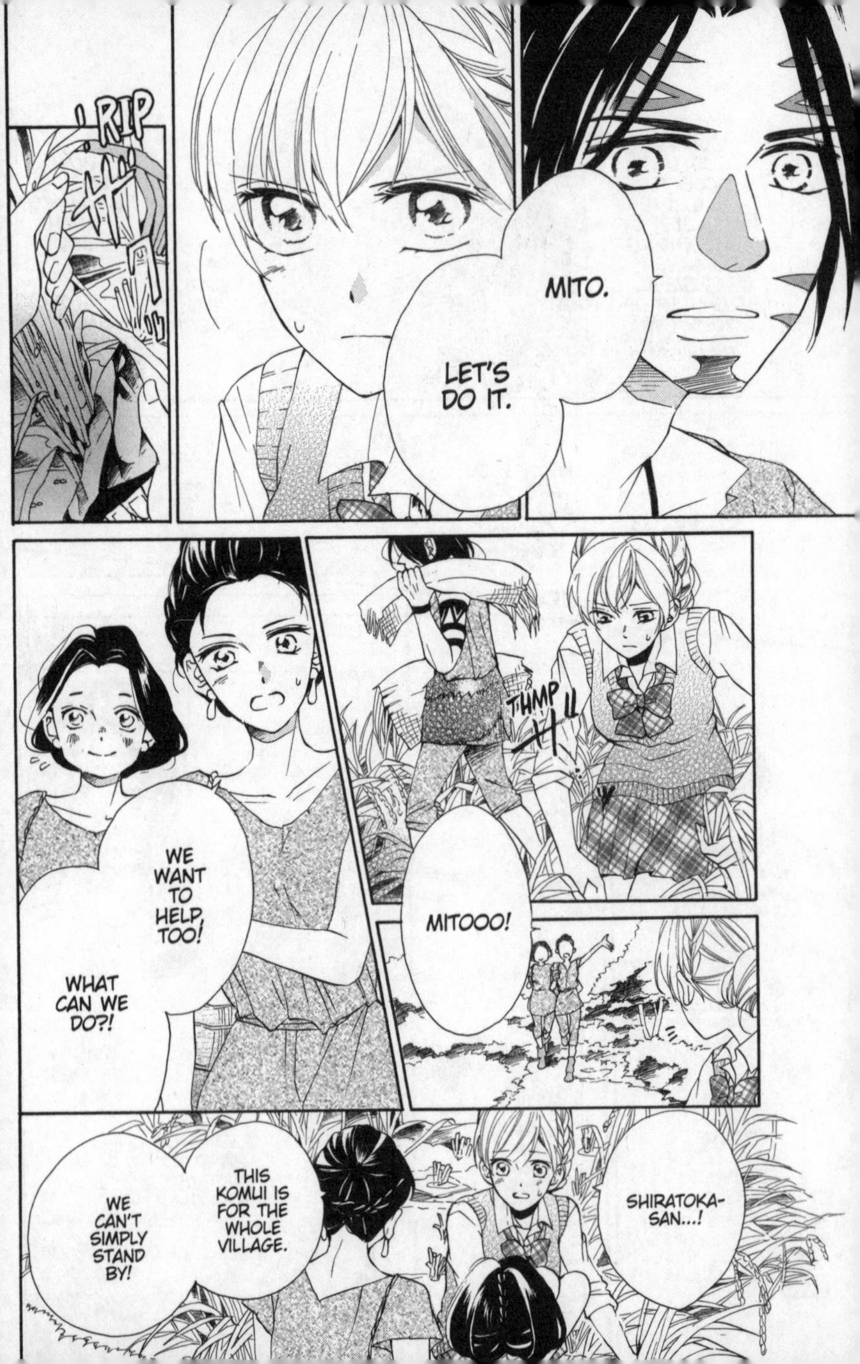

MITO.
LET'S DO IT.
RIP
THMP
MITOOO!
WE WANT TO HELP, TOO!
WHAT CAN WE DO?!
SHIRATOKA-SAN...!
THIS KOMUI IS FOR THE WHOLE VILLAGE.
WE CAN'T SIMPLY STAND BY!

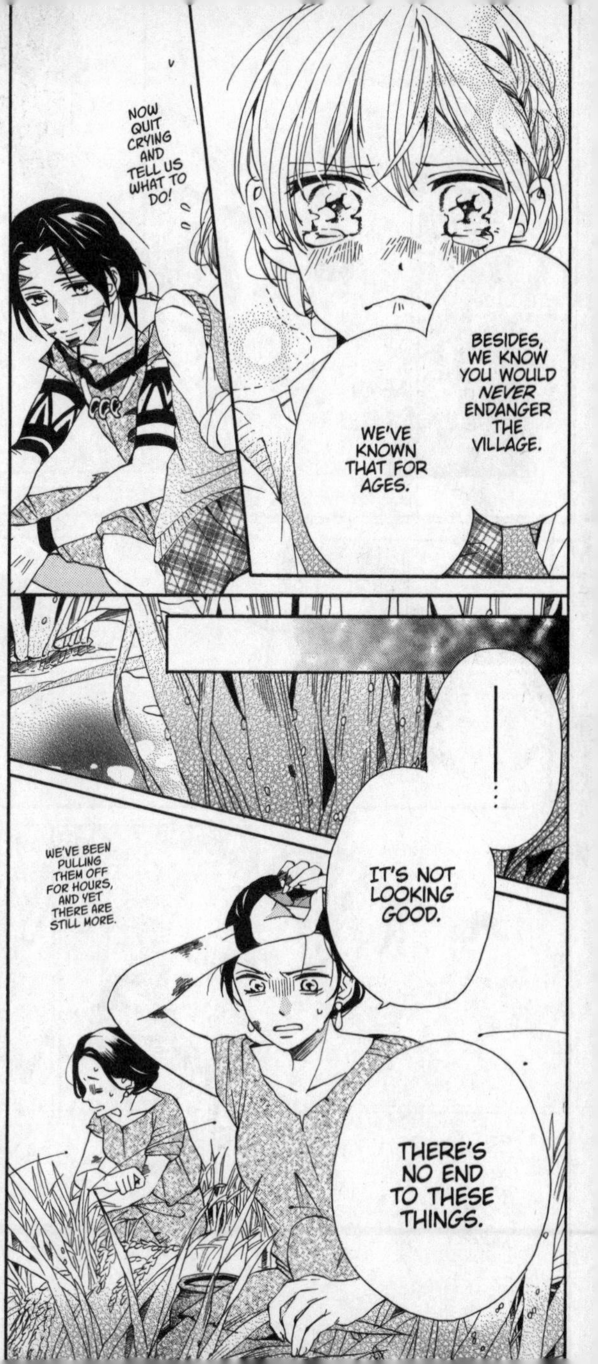
BESIDES, WE KNOW YOU WOULD *NEVER* ENDANGER THE VILLAGE.
WE'VE KNOWN THAT FOR AGES.
NOW QUIT CRYING AND TELL US WHAT TO DO!
...!
IT'S NOT LOOKING GOOD.
THERE'S NO END TO THESE THINGS.
WE'VE BEEN PULLING THEM OFF FOR HOURS, AND YET THERE ARE STILL MORE.

4

IT'S THE RICE CROP HELL CHAPTER. (LOL)

IRESU AND MITO ARE ALMOST THE SAME AGE. WHEN IRESU STOPPED FROWNING, HE SUDDENLY SEEMED MORE YOUTHFUL, AND I FELT LIKE A PARENT WHO'D WITNESSED THE MOMENT THEIR BLACK SHEEP OF A SON FELL IN LOVE.

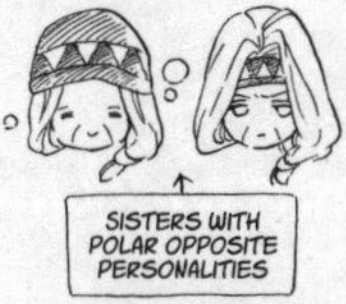
SISTERS WITH POLAR OPPOSITE PERSONALITIES

ONAI'S PEOPLE ARE A SOUTHERN TRIBE. IRESU'S WAS A NORTHERN TRIBE THAT MIGRATED SOUTH BECAUSE DECREASING TEMPERATURES CAUSED CROP FAILURES.

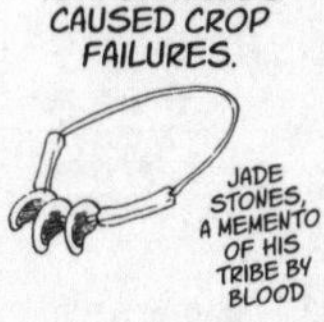
JADE STONES, A MEMENTO OF HIS TRIBE BY BLOOD

BY THE WAY, THESE TWO?

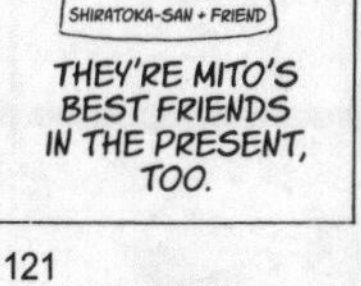
SHIRATOKA-SAN + FRIEND

THEY'RE MITO'S BEST FRIENDS IN THE PRESENT, TOO.

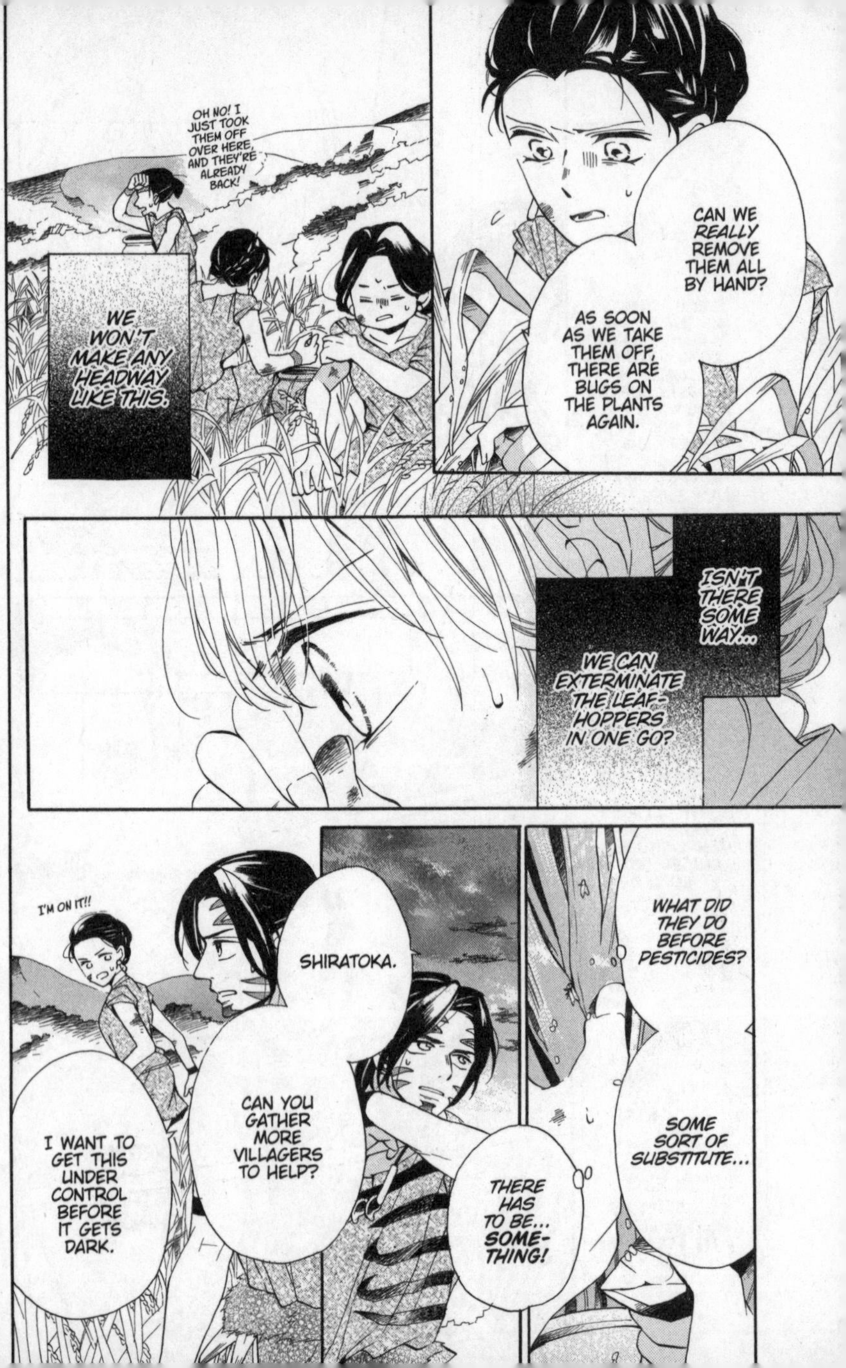
CAN WE REALLY REMOVE THEM ALL BY HAND?
AS SOON AS WE TAKE THEM OFF, THERE ARE BUGS ON THE PLANTS AGAIN.
OH NO! I JUST TOOK THEM OFF OVER HERE, AND THEY'RE ALREADY BACK!
WE WON'T MAKE ANY HEADWAY LIKE THIS.
ISN'T THERE SOME WAY...
WE CAN EXTERMINATE THE LEAF-HOPPERS IN ONE GO?
WHAT DID THEY DO BEFORE PESTICIDES?
SOME SORT OF SUBSTITUTE...
THERE HAS TO BE... SOMETHING!
SHIRATOKA.
CAN YOU GATHER MORE VILLAGERS TO HELP?
I WANT TO GET THIS UNDER CONTROL BEFORE IT GETS DARK.
I'M ON IT!!

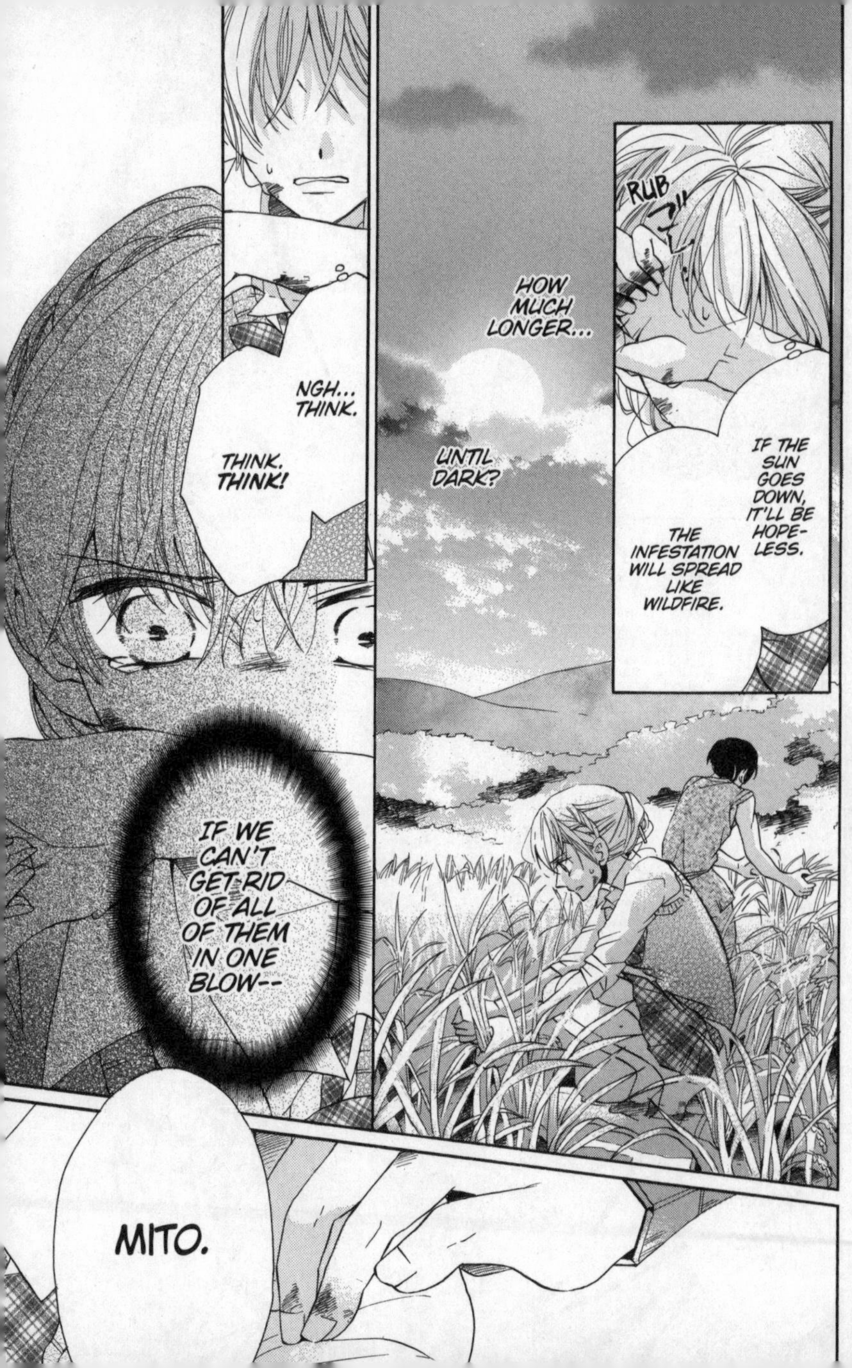
RUB
IF THE SUN GOES DOWN, IT'LL BE HOPELESS.
THE INFESTATION WILL SPREAD LIKE WILDFIRE.
HOW MUCH LONGER...
UNTIL DARK?
NGH... THINK.
THINK. THINK!
IF WE CAN'T GET RID OF ALL OF THEM IN ONE BLOW--
MITO.

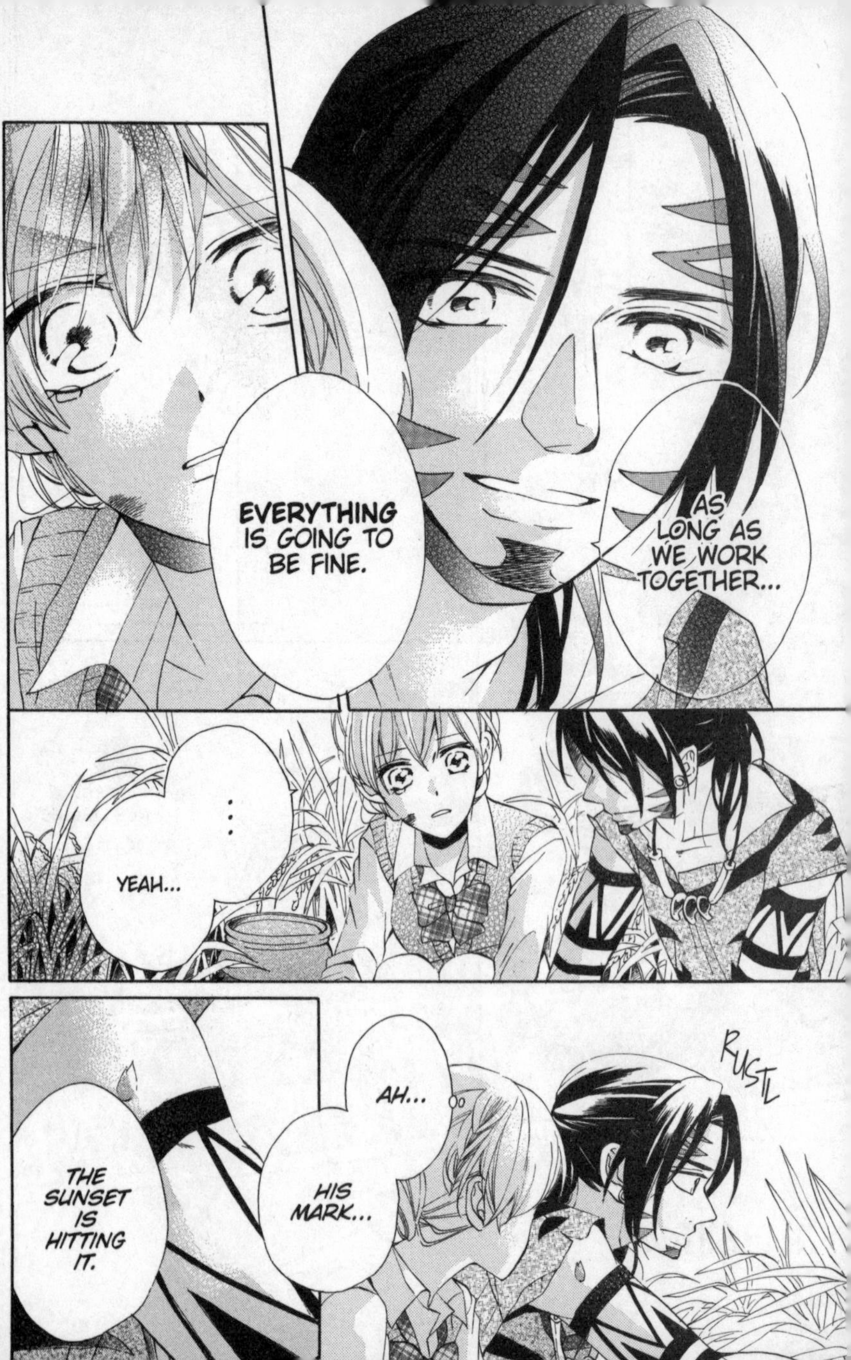
AS LONG AS WE WORK TOGETHER...
EVERYTHING IS GOING TO BE FINE.
... YEAH...
RUSTL
AH...
HIS MARK...
THE SUNSET IS HITTING IT.

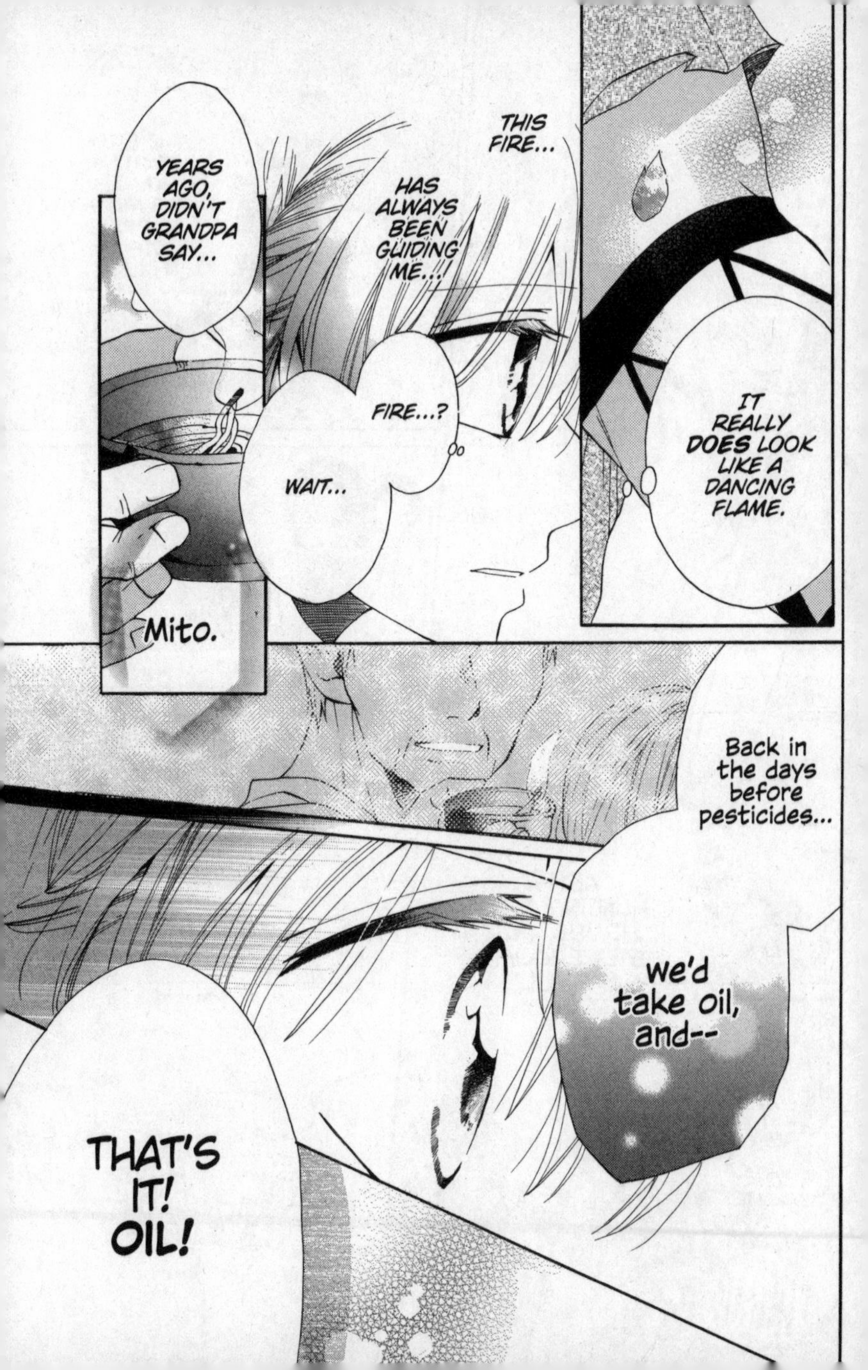
IT REALLY DOES LOOK LIKE A DANCING FLAME.
THIS FIRE...
HAS ALWAYS BEEN GUIDING ME...
FIRE...?
WAIT...
YEARS AGO, DIDN'T GRANDPA SAY...
Mito.
Back in the days before pesticides...
we'd take oil, and--
THAT'S IT! OIL!

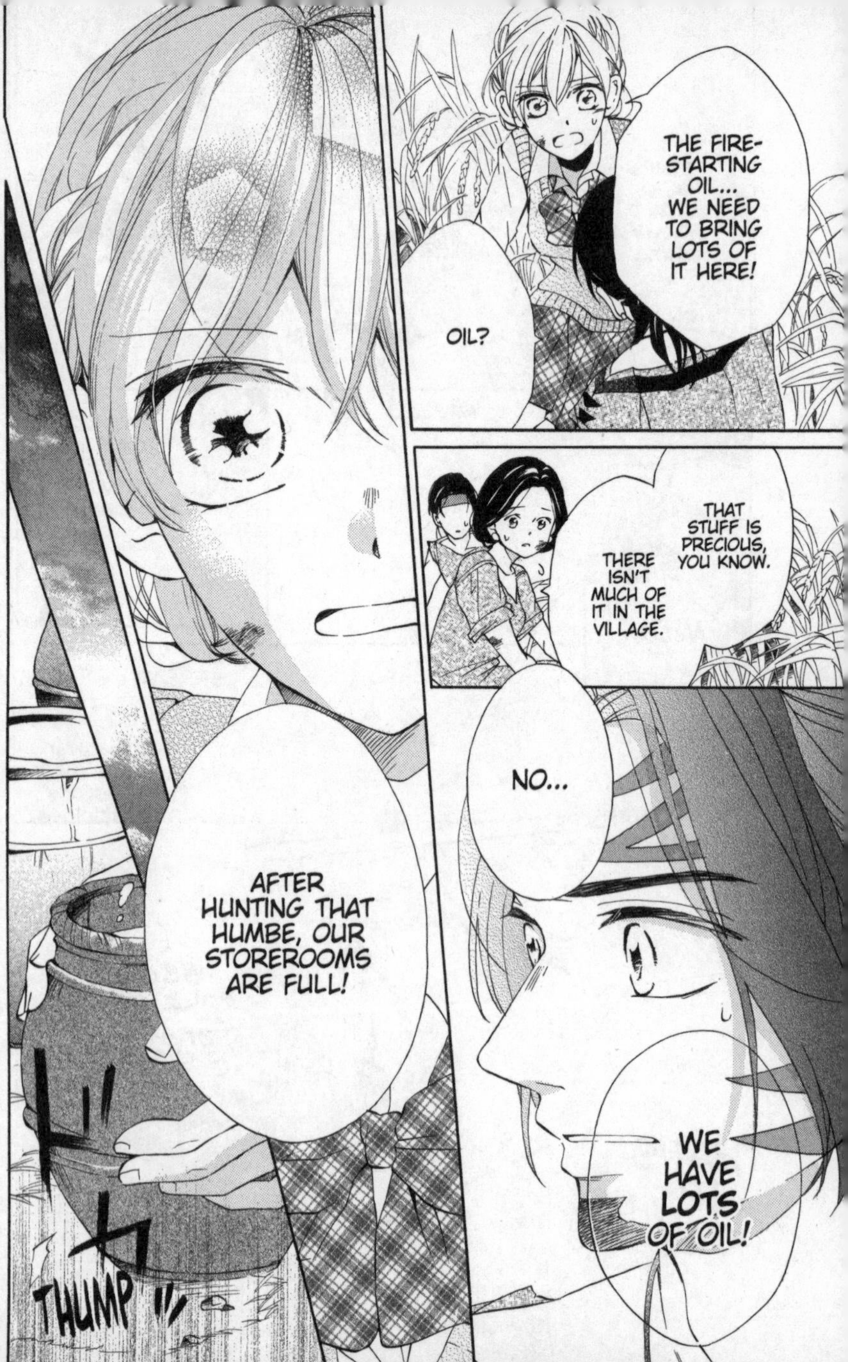
THE FIRE-STARTING OIL... WE NEED TO BRING LOTS OF IT HERE!
OIL?
THAT STUFF IS PRECIOUS, YOU KNOW.
THERE ISN'T MUCH OF IT IN THE VILLAGE.
NO...
WE HAVE LOTS OF OIL!
AFTER HUNTING THAT HUMBE, OUR STOREROOMS ARE FULL!
THUMP

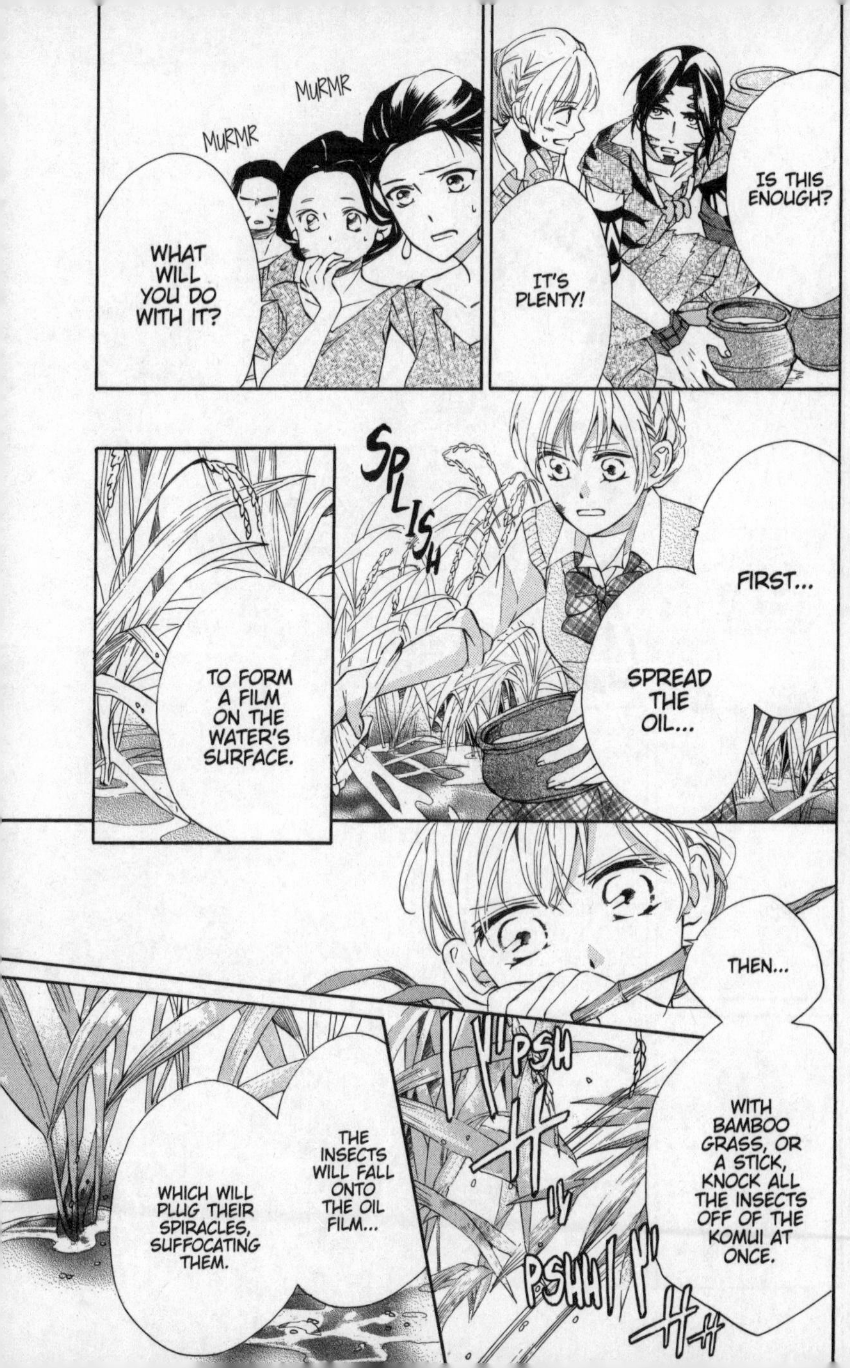
IS THIS ENOUGH?
IT'S PLENTY!
MURMR
MURMR
WHAT WILL YOU DO WITH IT?
SPLISH
FIRST...
SPREAD THE OIL...
TO FORM A FILM ON THE WATER'S SURFACE.
THEN...
WITH BAMBOO GRASS, OR A STICK, KNOCK ALL THE INSECTS OFF OF THE KOMUI AT ONCE.
THE INSECTS WILL FALL ONTO THE OIL FILM...
WHICH WILL PLUG THEIR SPIRACLES, SUFFOCATING THEM.

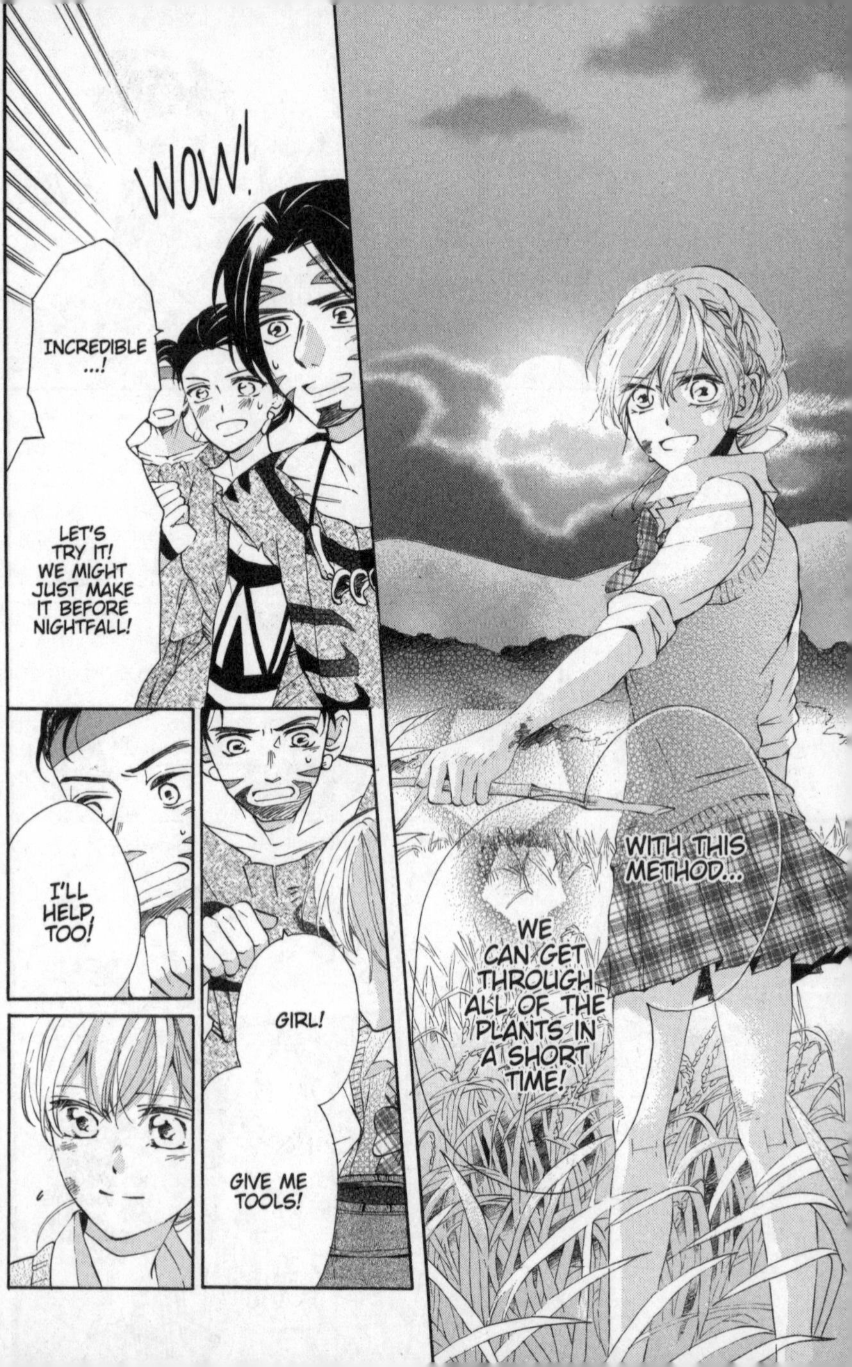
WITH THIS METHOD...
WE CAN GET THROUGH ALL OF THE PLANTS IN A SHORT TIME!
WOW!
INCREDIBLE ...!
LET'S TRY IT! WE MIGHT JUST MAKE IT BEFORE NIGHTFALL!
GIRL!
GIVE ME TOOLS!
I'LL HELP, TOO!

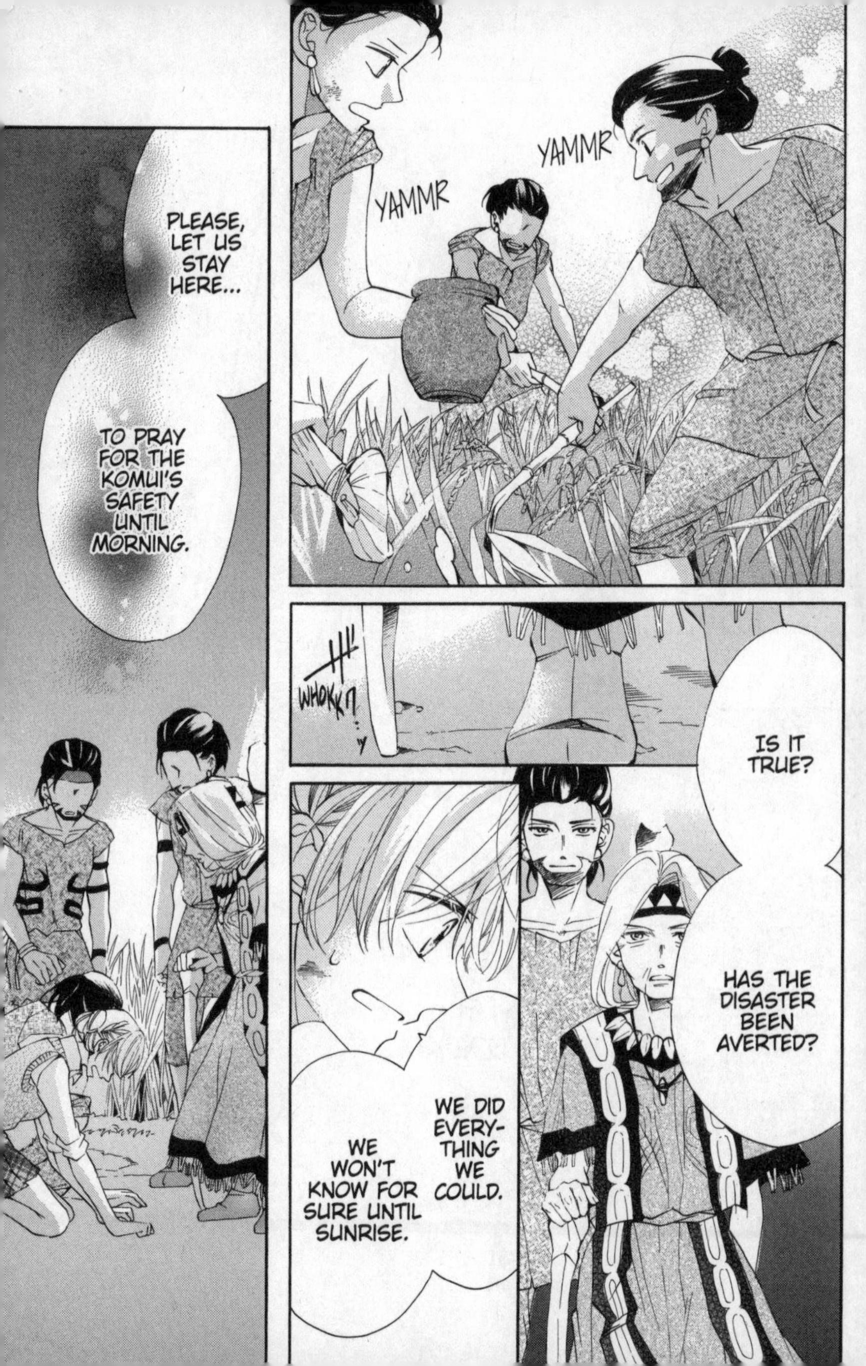
YAMMR
YAMMR
WHOKK
IS IT TRUE?
HAS THE DISASTER BEEN AVERTED?
WE DID EVERYTHING WE COULD.
WE WON'T KNOW FOR SURE UNTIL SUNRISE.
PLEASE, LET US STAY HERE...
TO PRAY FOR THE KOMUI'S SAFETY UNTIL MORNING.

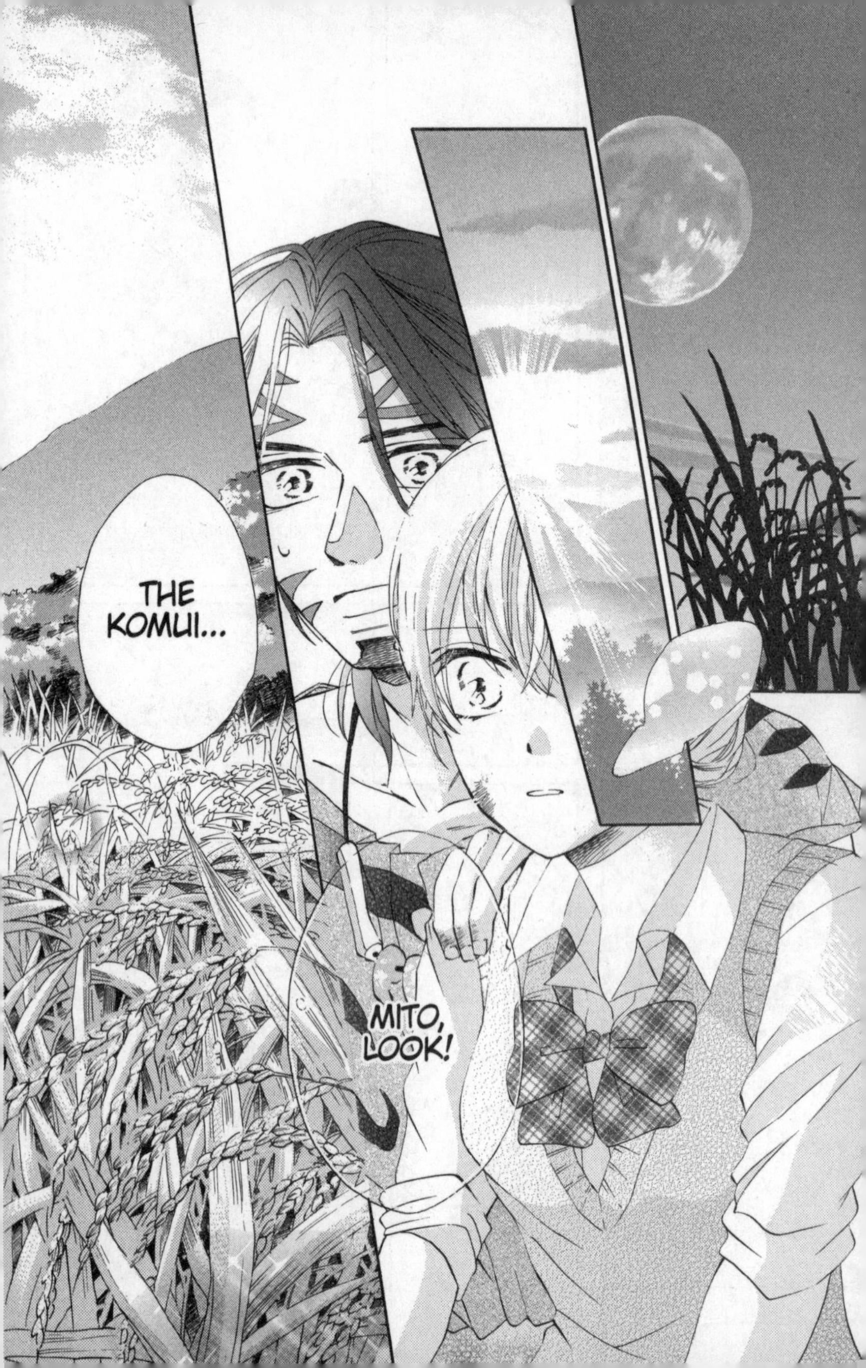
THE KOMUI...
MITO, LOOK!

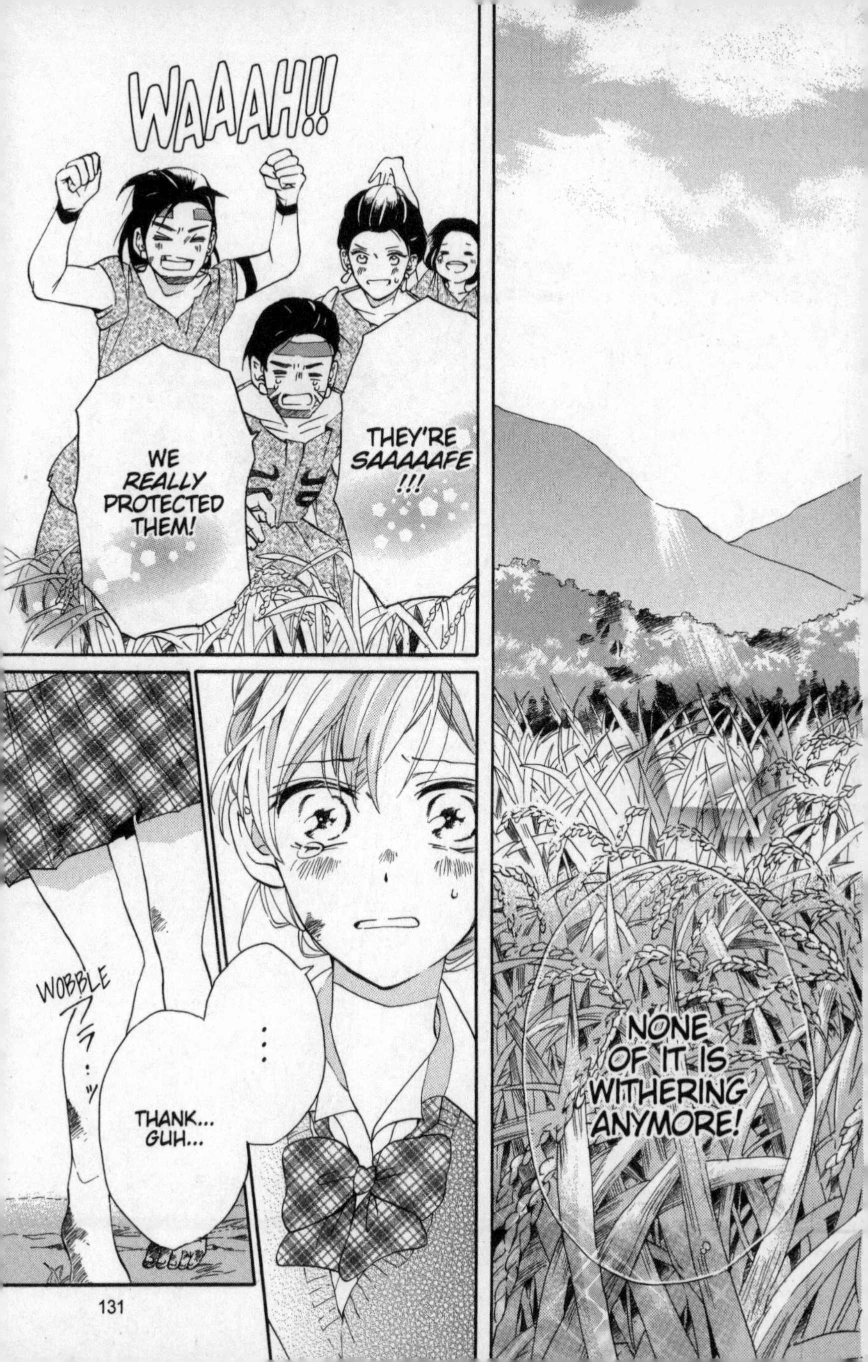
NONE OF IT IS WITHERING ANYMORE!
WAAAH!!
THEY'RE SAAAAAFE!!!
WE *REALLY* PROTECTED THEM!
...
THANK... GUH...
WOBBLE

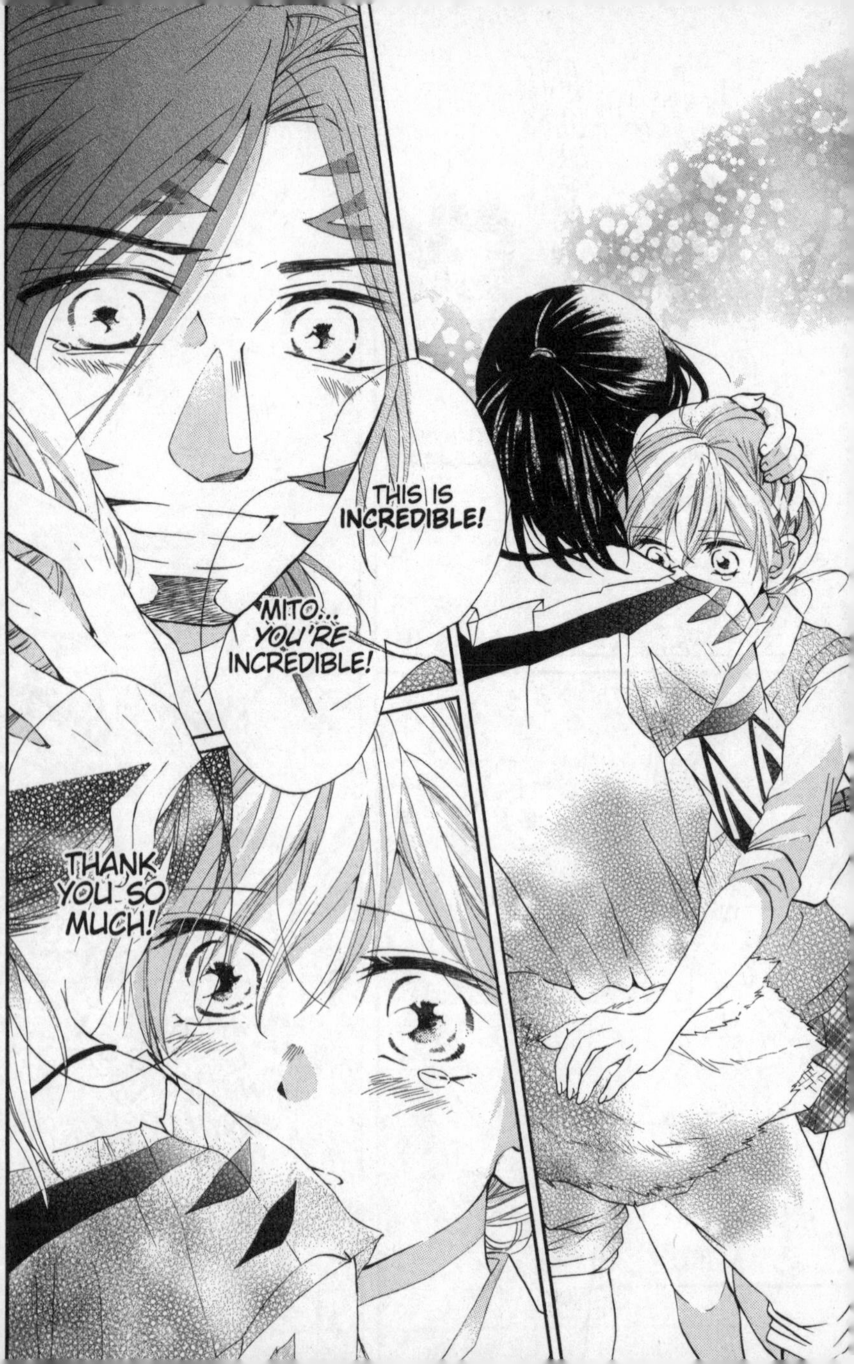
THIS IS INCREDIBLE!
MITO... YOU'RE INCREDIBLE!
THANK YOU SO MUCH!

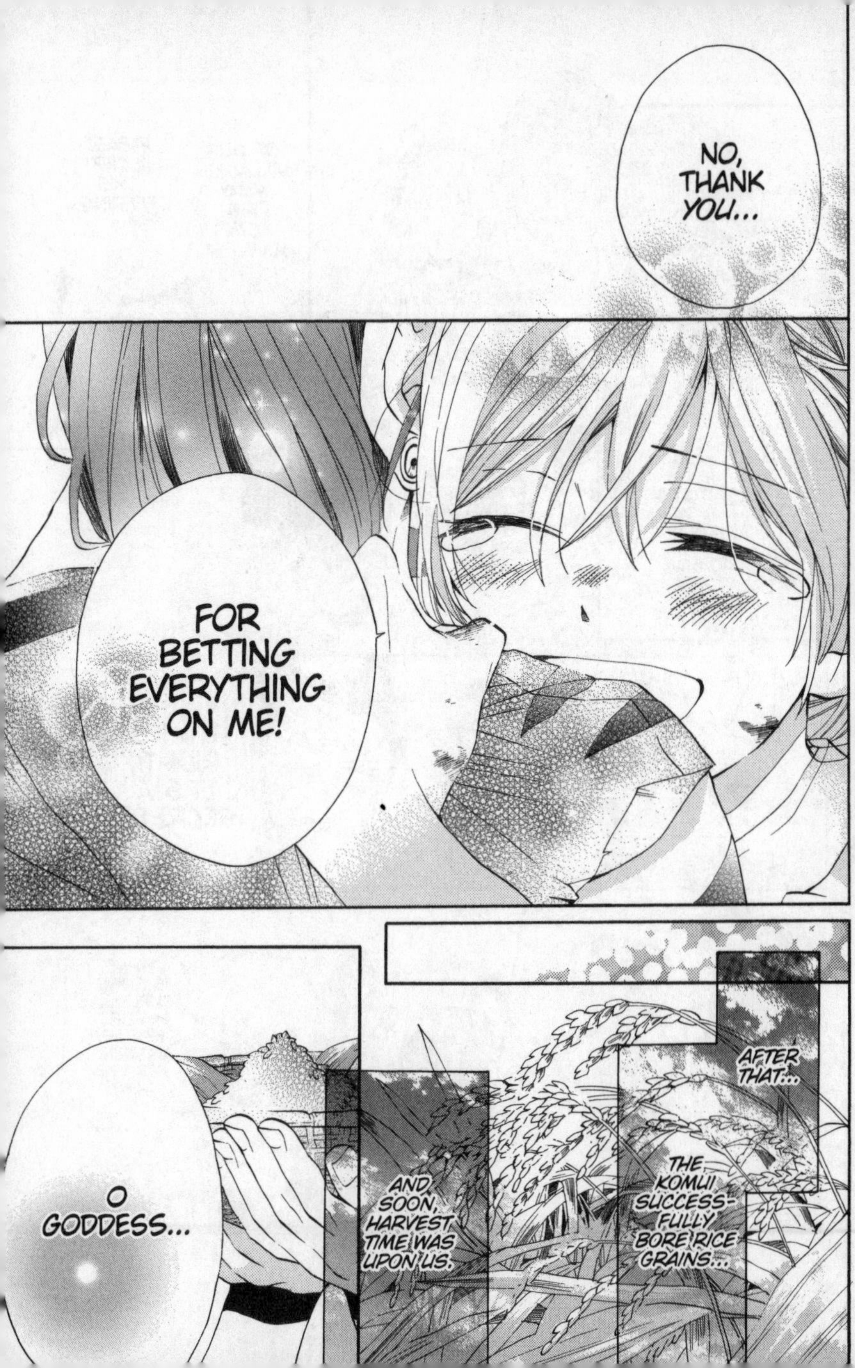
NO, THANK YOU...
FOR BETTING EVERYTHING ON ME!
AFTER THAT...
THE KOMUI SUCCESS-FULLY BORE RICE GRAINS...
AND SOON, HARVEST TIME WAS UPON US.
O GODDESS...

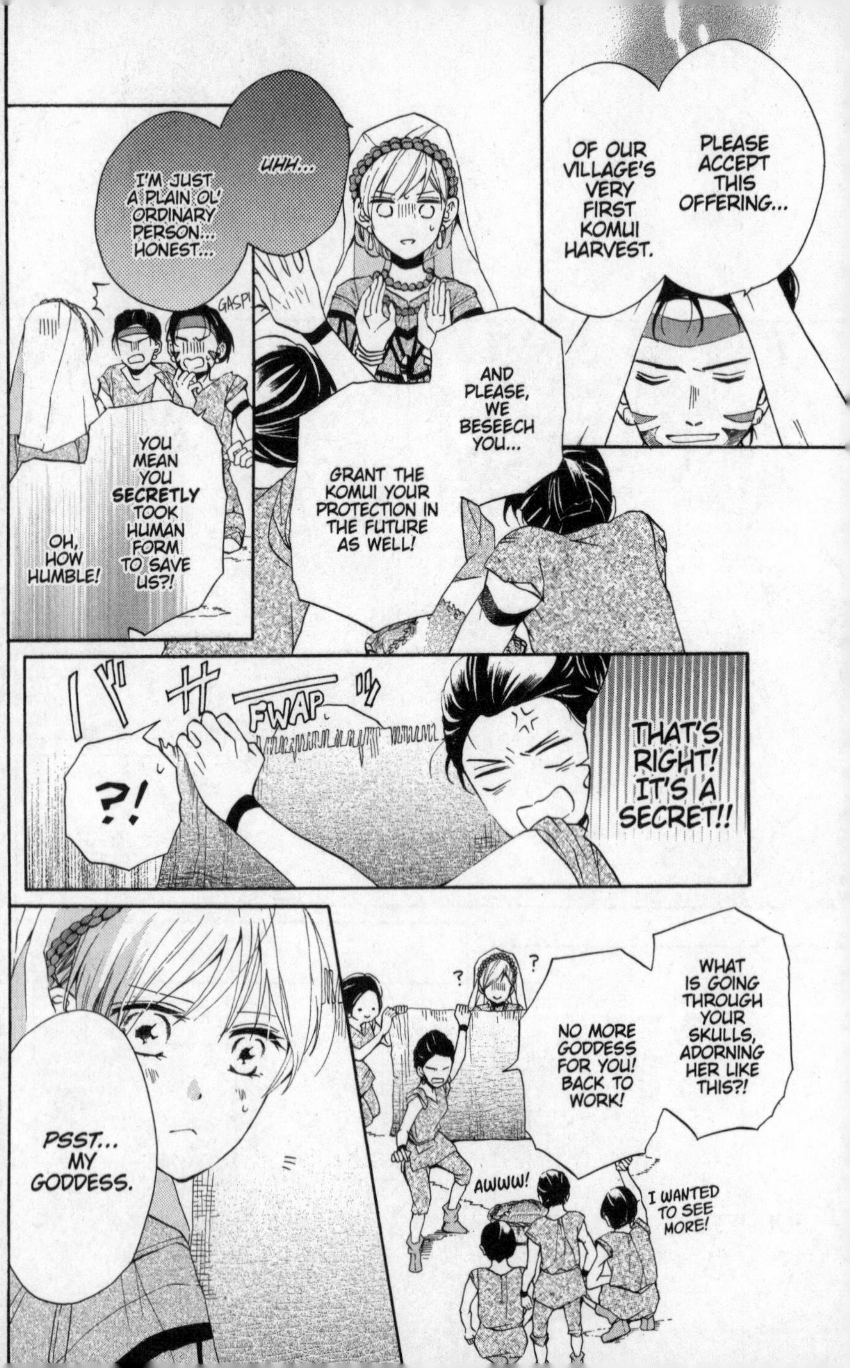
PLEASE ACCEPT THIS OFFERING...
OF OUR VILLAGE'S VERY FIRST KOMUI HARVEST.
UHH...
I'M JUST A PLAIN OL' ORDINARY PERSON... HONEST...
GASP!
YOU MEAN YOU SECRETLY TOOK HUMAN FORM TO SAVE US?!
OH, HOW HUMBLE!
AND PLEASE, WE BESEECH YOU...
GRANT THE KOMUI YOUR PROTECTION IN THE FUTURE AS WELL!
THAT'S RIGHT! IT'S A SECRET!!
FWAP
?!
WHAT IS GOING THROUGH YOUR SKULLS, ADORNING HER LIKE THIS?!
NO MORE GODDESS FOR YOU! BACK TO WORK!
I WANTED TO SEE MORE!
AWWW!
PSST... MY GODDESS.

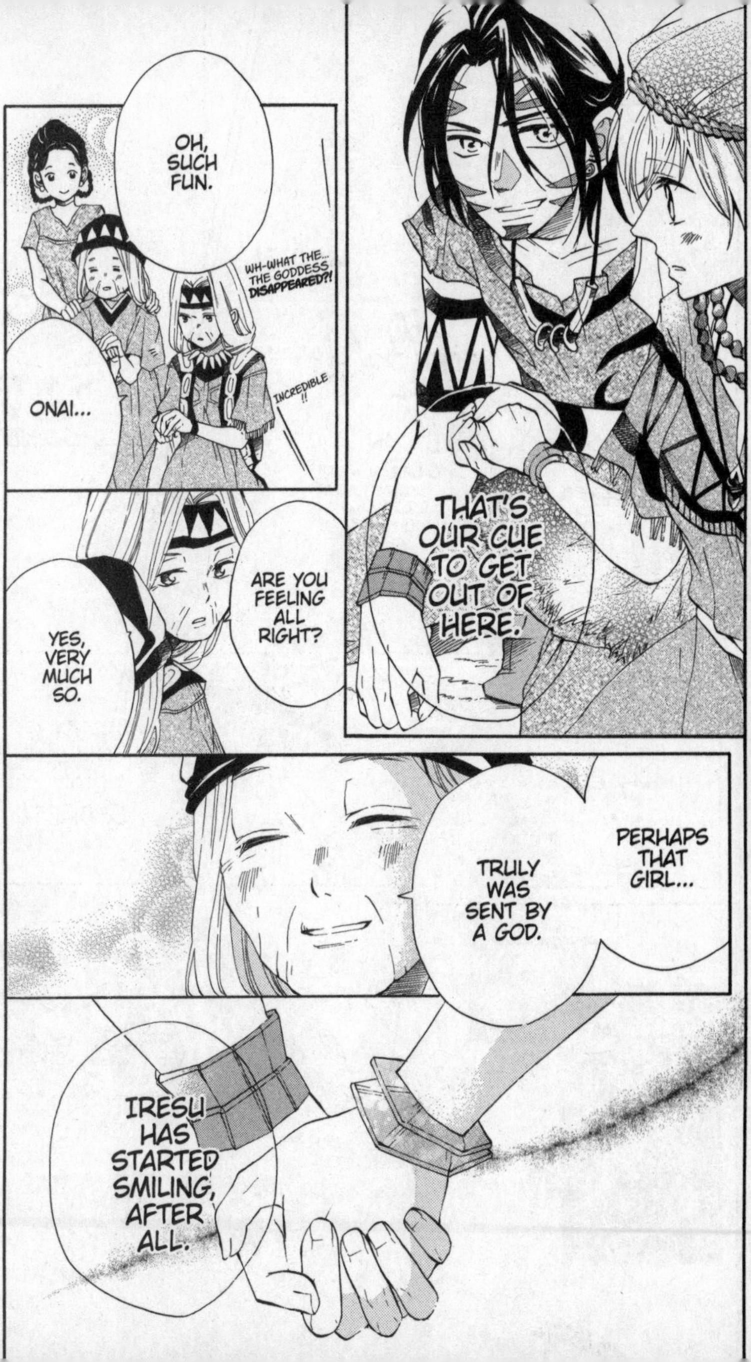
THAT'S OUR CUE TO GET OUT OF HERE.
OH, SUCH FUN.
WH-WHAT THE... THE GODDESS DISAPPEARED?!
INCREDIBLE!!
ONAI...
ARE YOU FEELING ALL RIGHT?
YES, VERY MUCH SO.
PERHAPS THAT GIRL...
TRULY WAS SENT BY A GOD.
IRESU HAS STARTED SMILING, AFTER ALL.

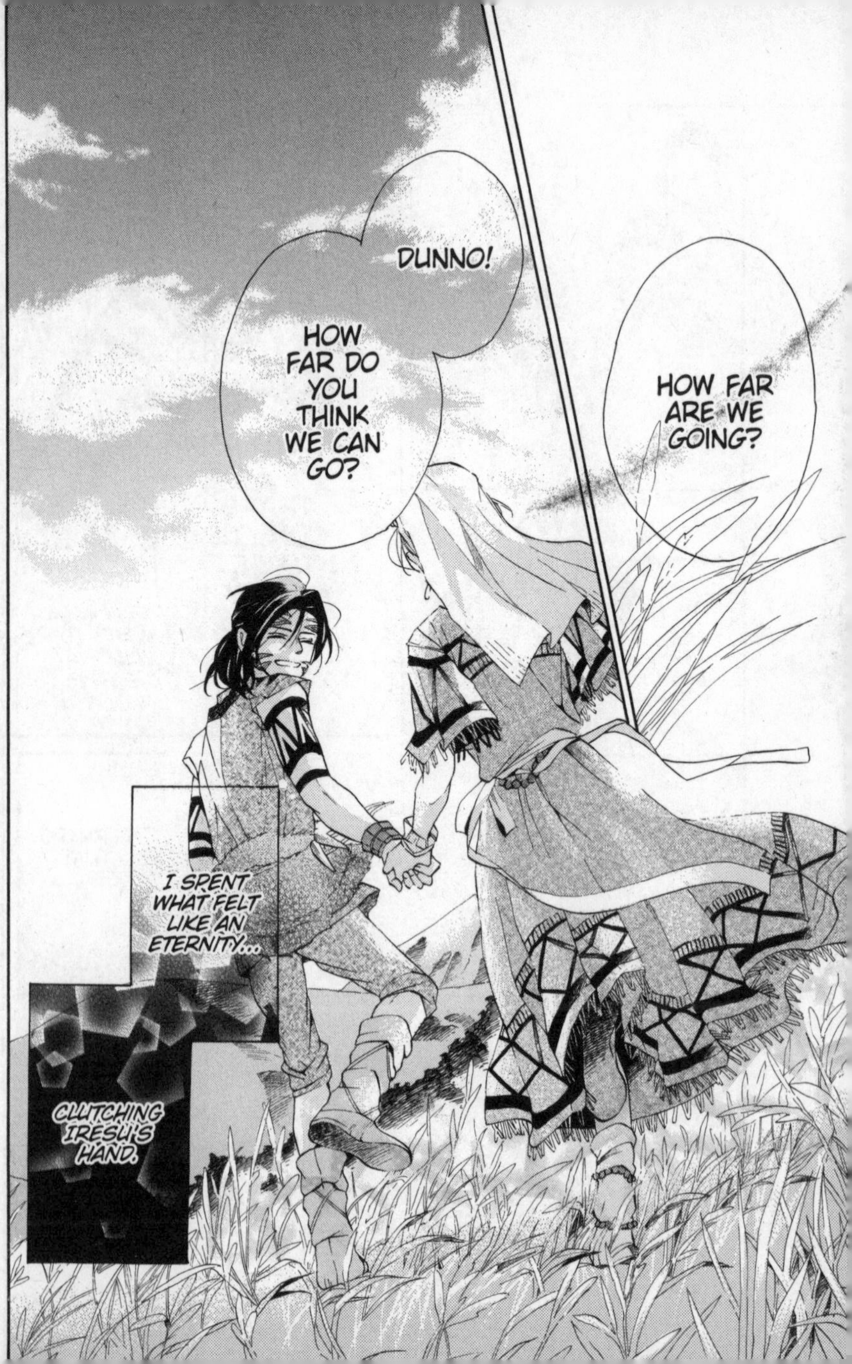
HOW FAR ARE WE GOING?
DUNNO!
HOW FAR DO YOU THINK WE CAN GO?
I SPENT WHAT FELT LIKE AN ETERNITY...
CLUTCHING IRESU'S HAND.

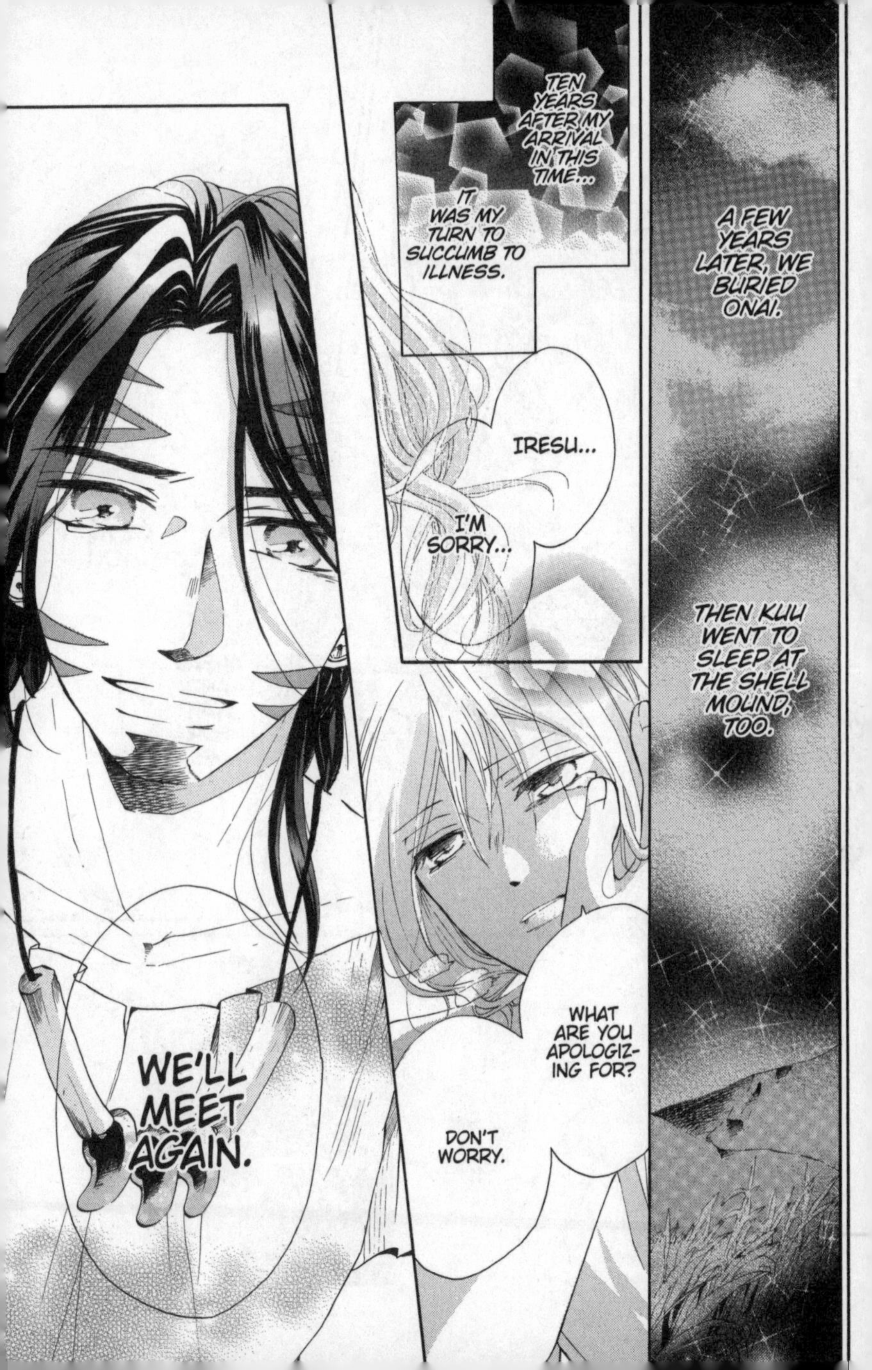
A FEW YEARS LATER, WE BURIED ONAI.
THEN KUU WENT TO SLEEP AT THE SHELL MOUND, TOO.
TEN YEARS AFTER MY ARRIVAL IN THIS TIME...
IT WAS MY TURN TO SUCCUMB TO ILLNESS.
IRESU...
I'M SORRY...
WHAT ARE YOU APOLOGIZING FOR?
DON'T WORRY.
WE'LL MEET AGAIN.

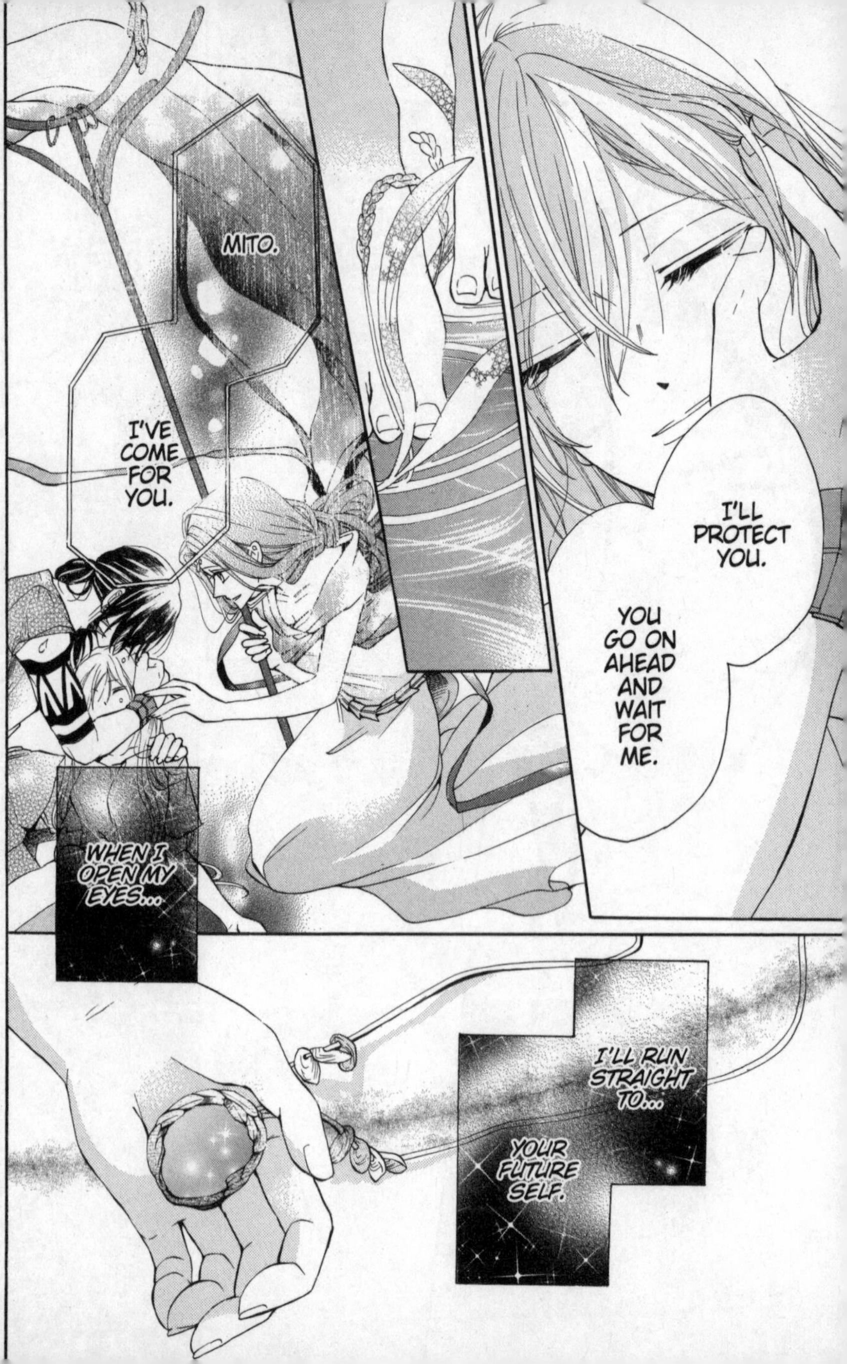
I'LL PROTECT YOU.
YOU GO ON AHEAD AND WAIT FOR ME.
MITO.
I'VE COME FOR YOU.
WHEN I OPEN MY EYES...
I'LL RUN STRAIGHT TO...
YOUR FUTURE SELF.

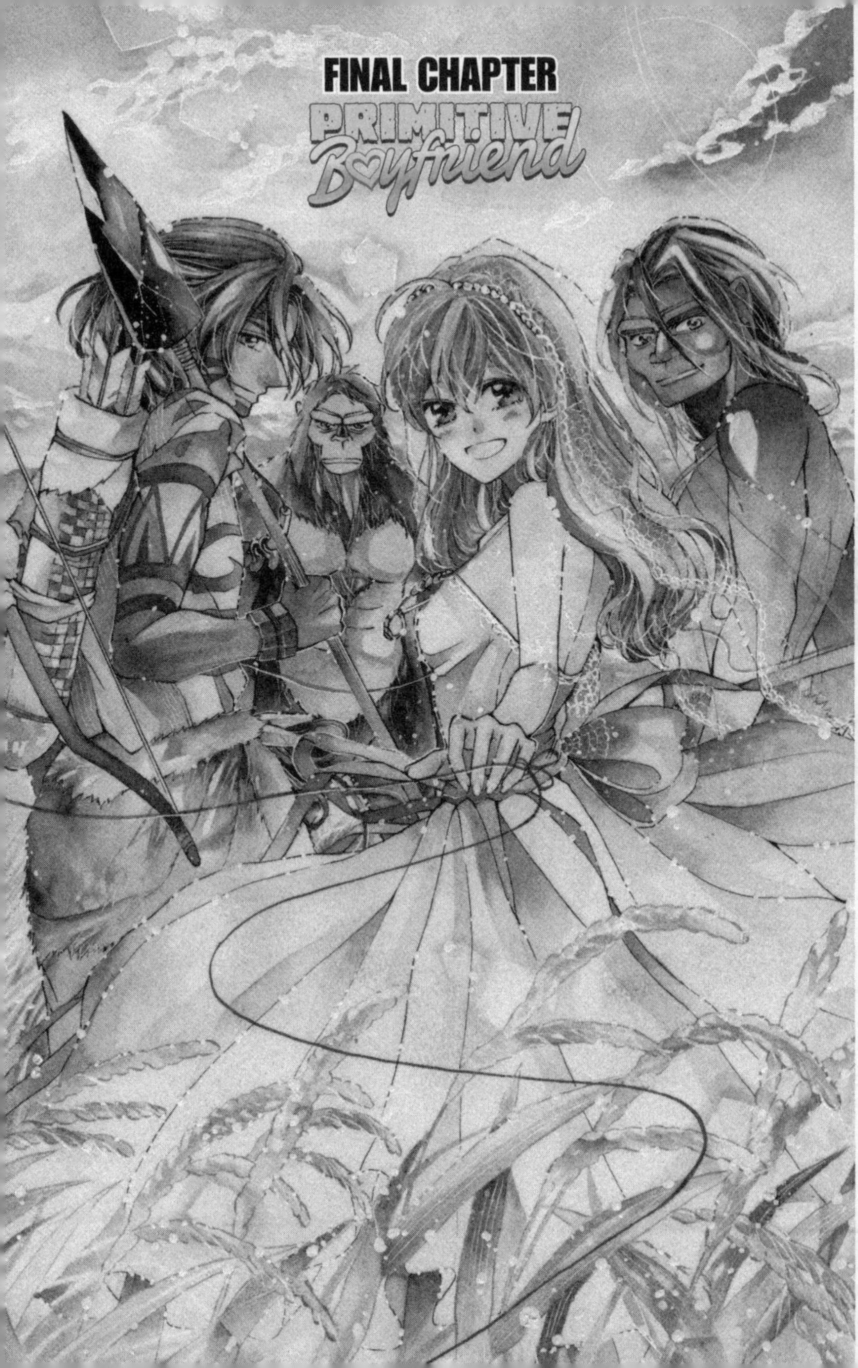
FINAL CHAPTER
PRIMITIVE
Boyfriend

PRIMITIVE BOYFRIEND by Yoshineko Kitafuku PRIMITIVE BOYFRIEND

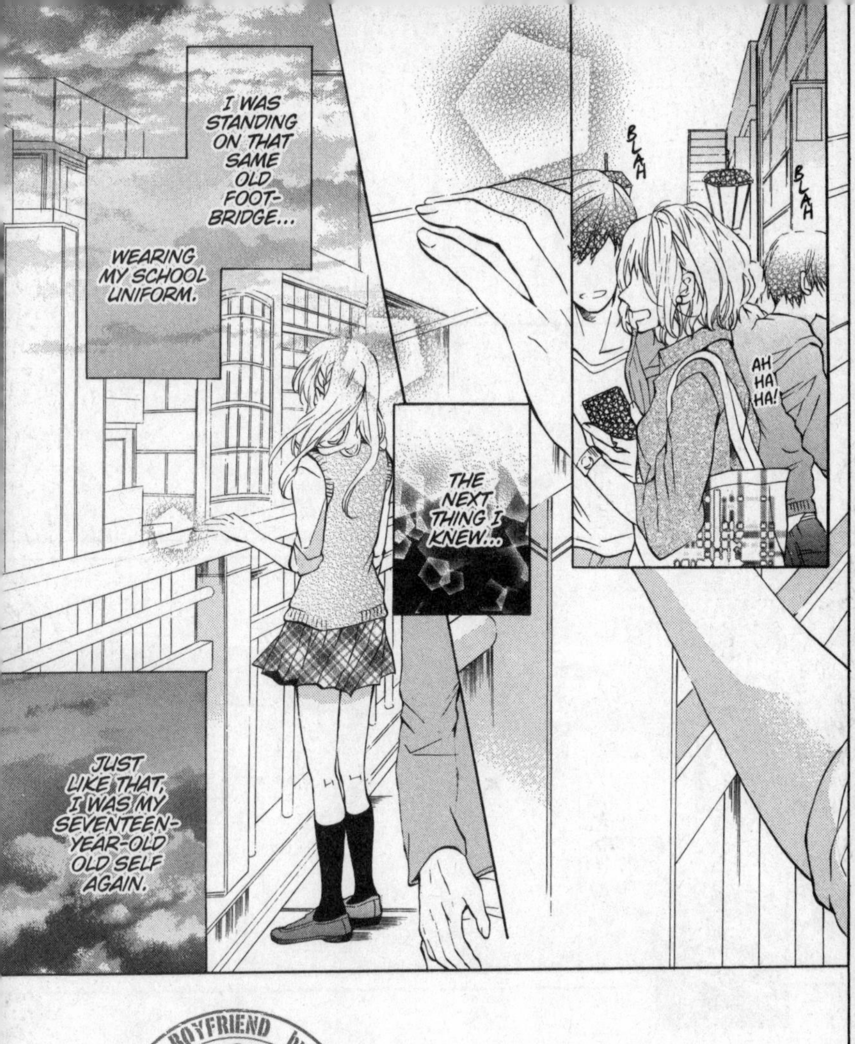
BLAH
BLAH
AH HA HA!
THE NEXT THING I KNEW...
I WAS STANDING ON THAT SAME OLD FOOT-BRIDGE...
WEARING MY SCHOOL UNIFORM.
JUST LIKE THAT, I WAS MY SEVENTEEN-YEAR-OLD OLD SELF AGAIN.

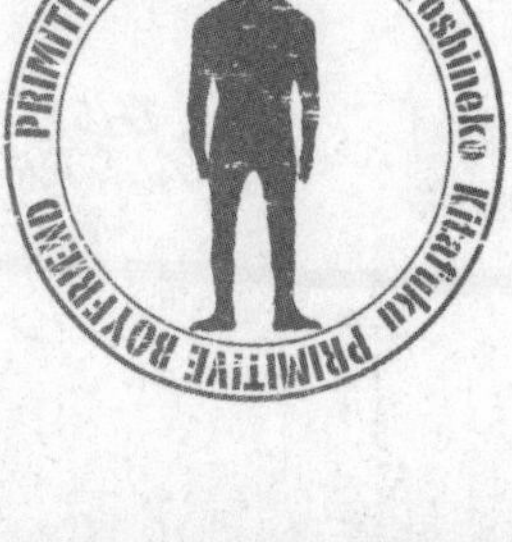
PRIMITIVE BOYFRIEND by Yoshineko Kitafuku PRIMITIVE BOYFRIEND

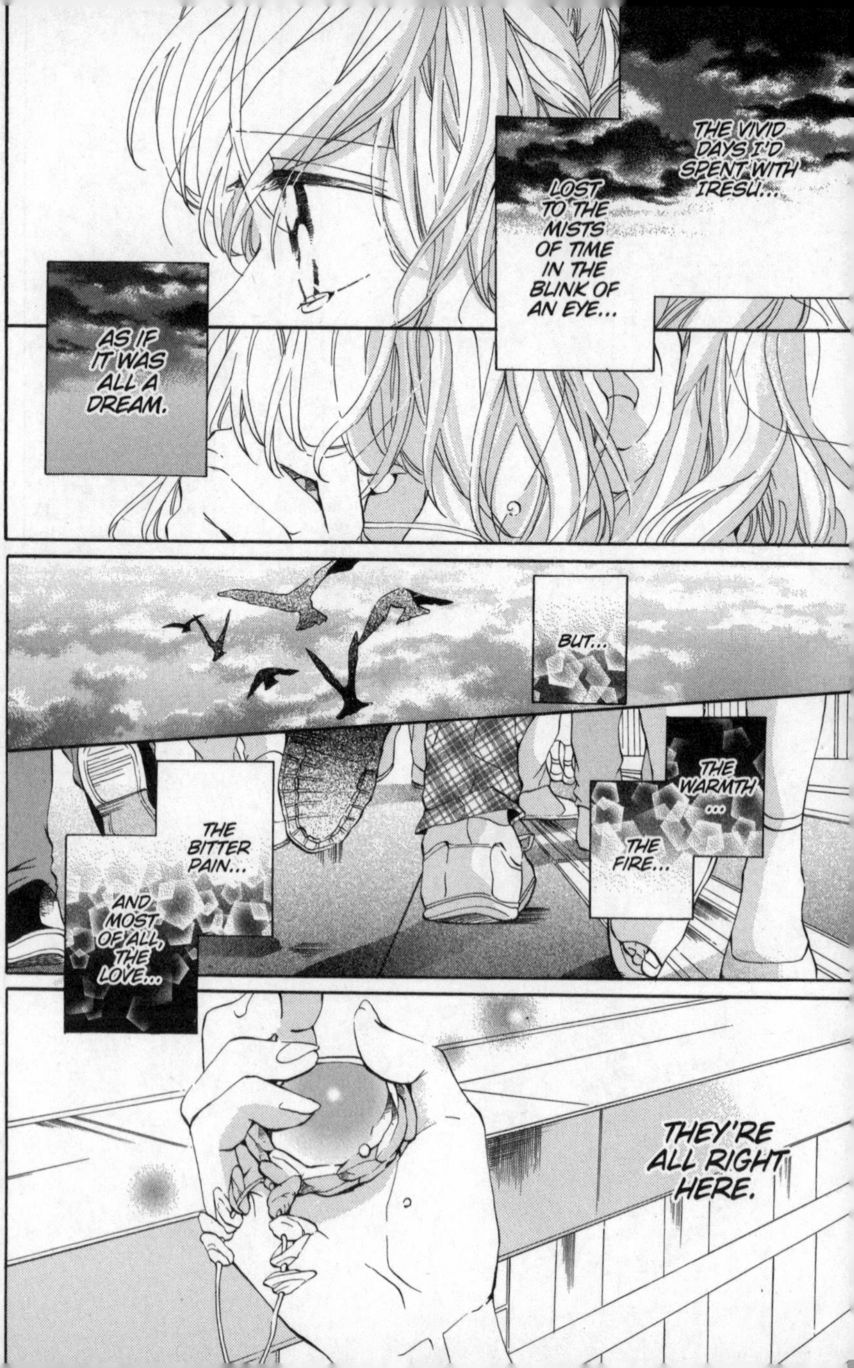
THE VIVID DAYS I'D SPENT WITH IRESU...
LOST TO THE MISTS OF TIME IN THE BLINK OF AN EYE...
AS IF IT WAS ALL A DREAM.
BUT...
THE WARMTH...
THE FIRE...
THE BITTER PAIN...
AND MOST OF ALL, THE LOVE...
THEY'RE ALL RIGHT HERE.

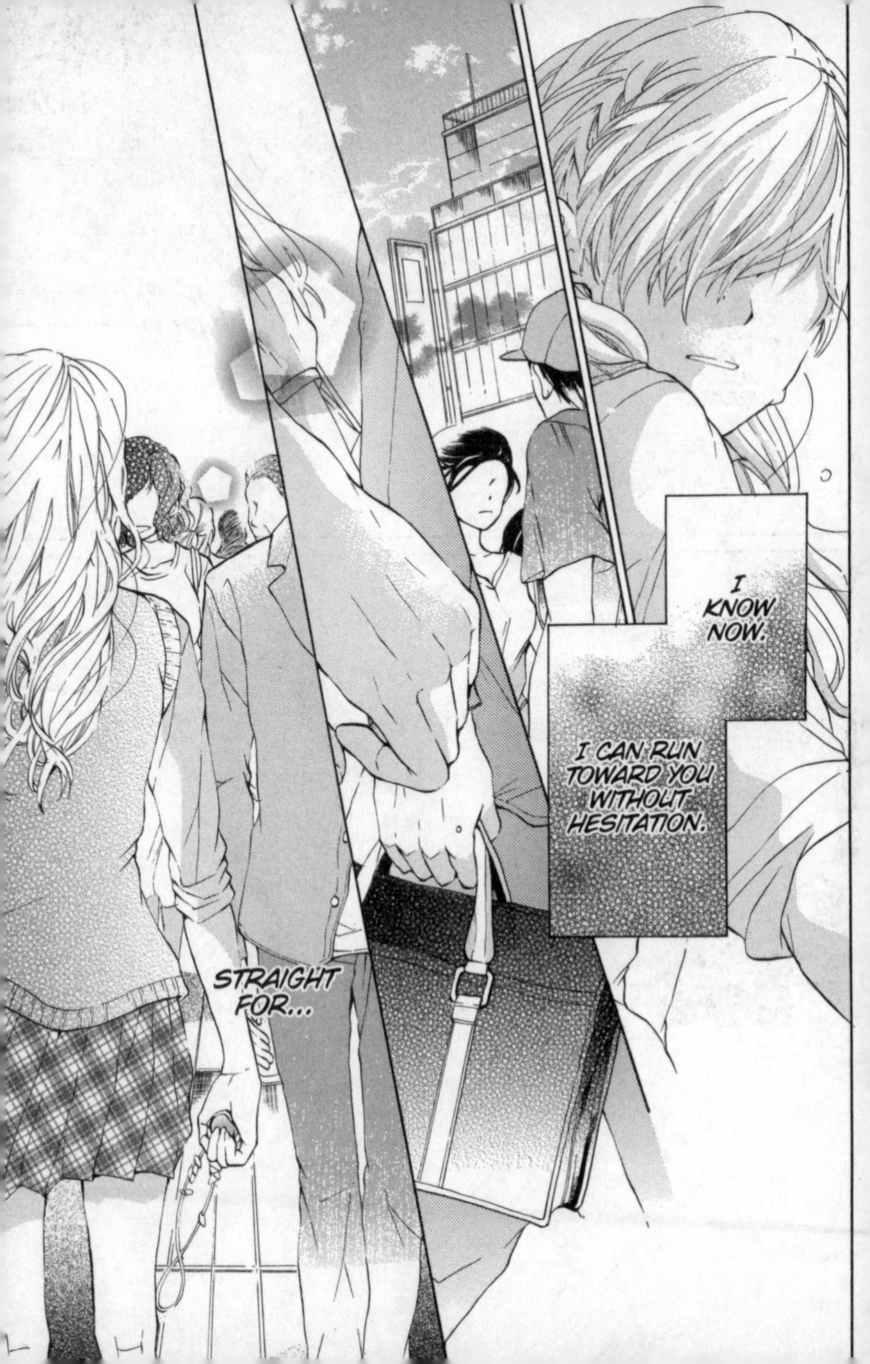
I KNOW NOW.
I CAN RUN TOWARD YOU WITHOUT HESITATION.
STRAIGHT FOR...

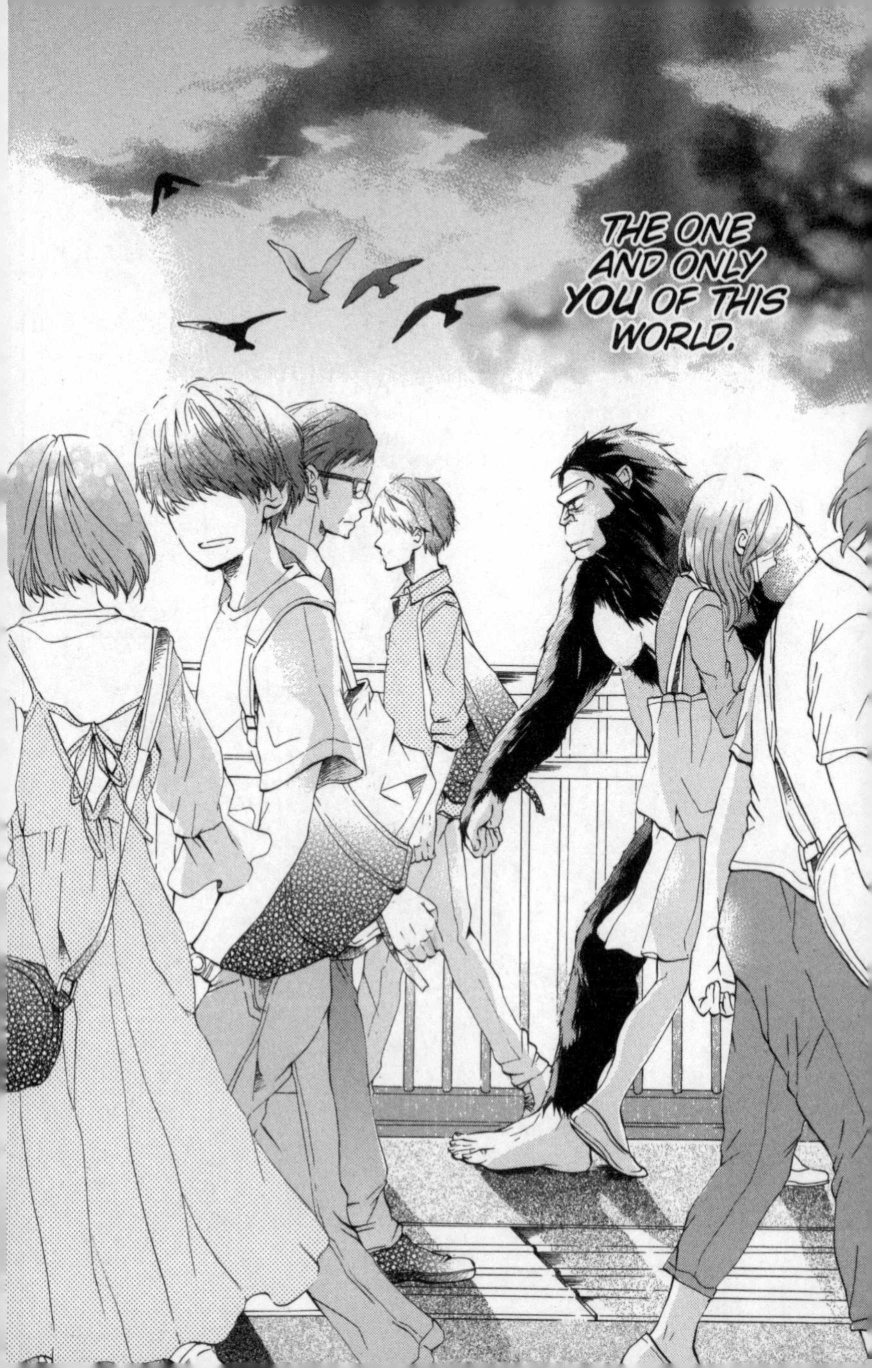
THE ONE AND ONLY YOU OF THIS WORLD.

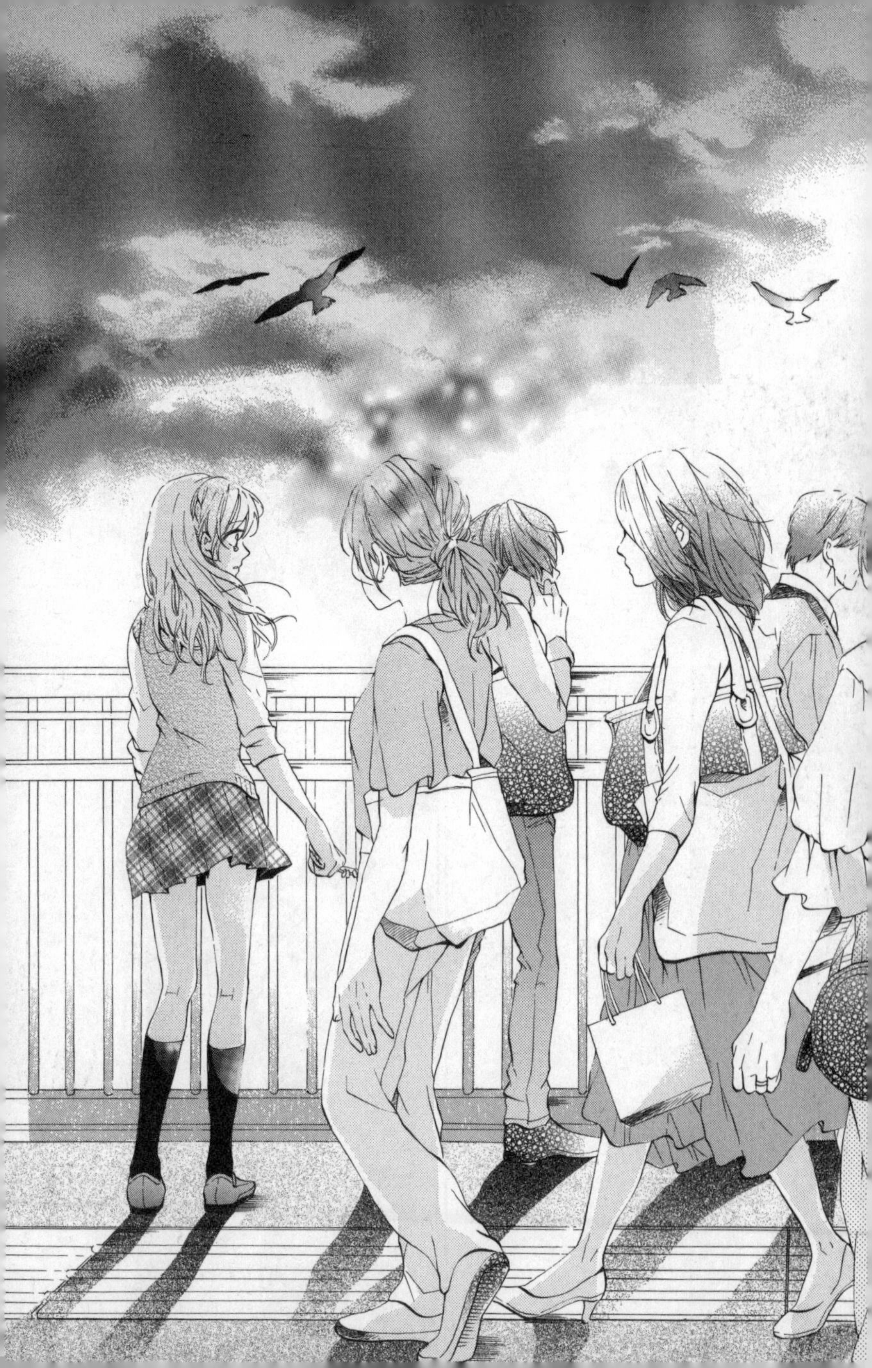

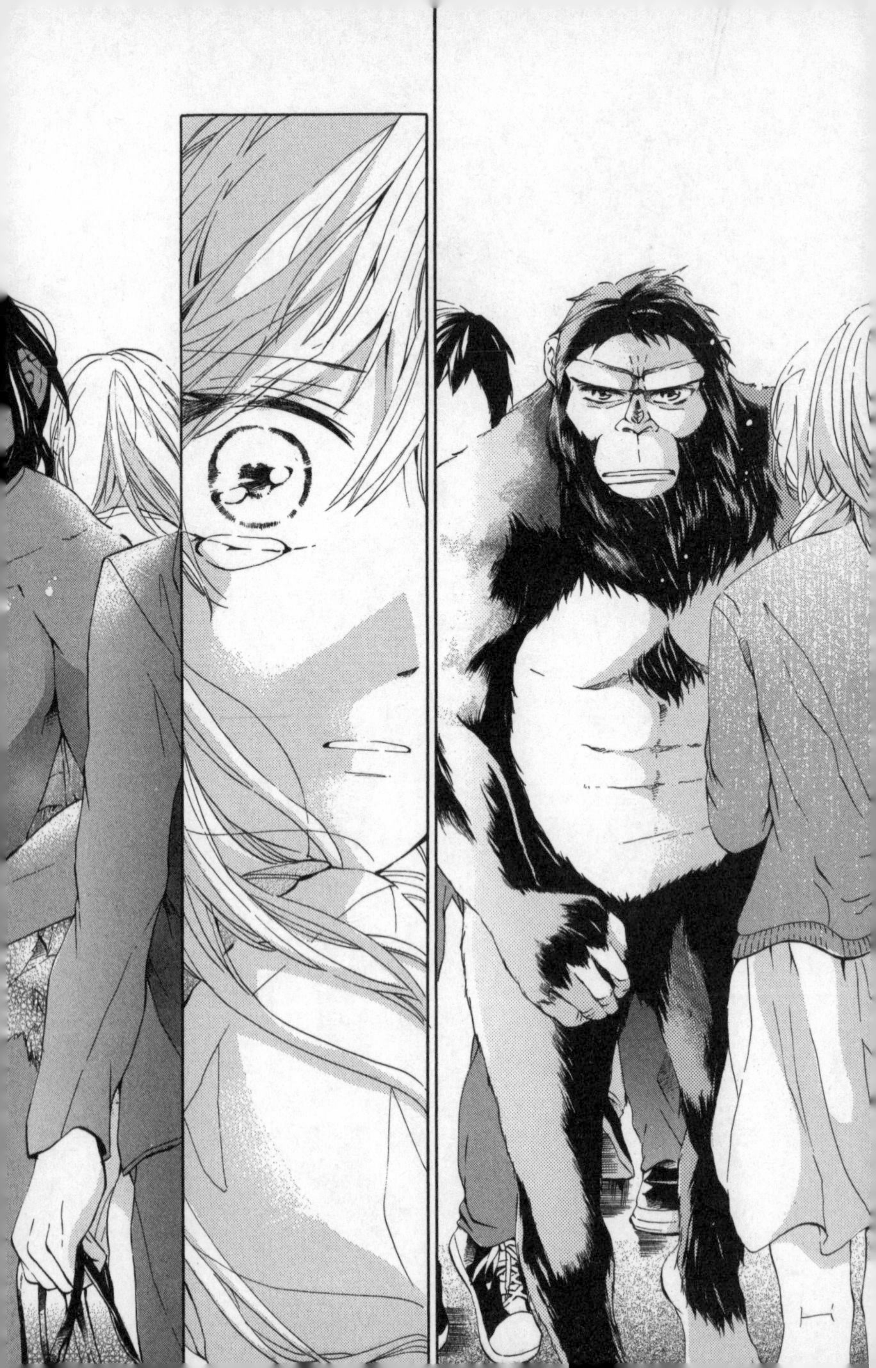

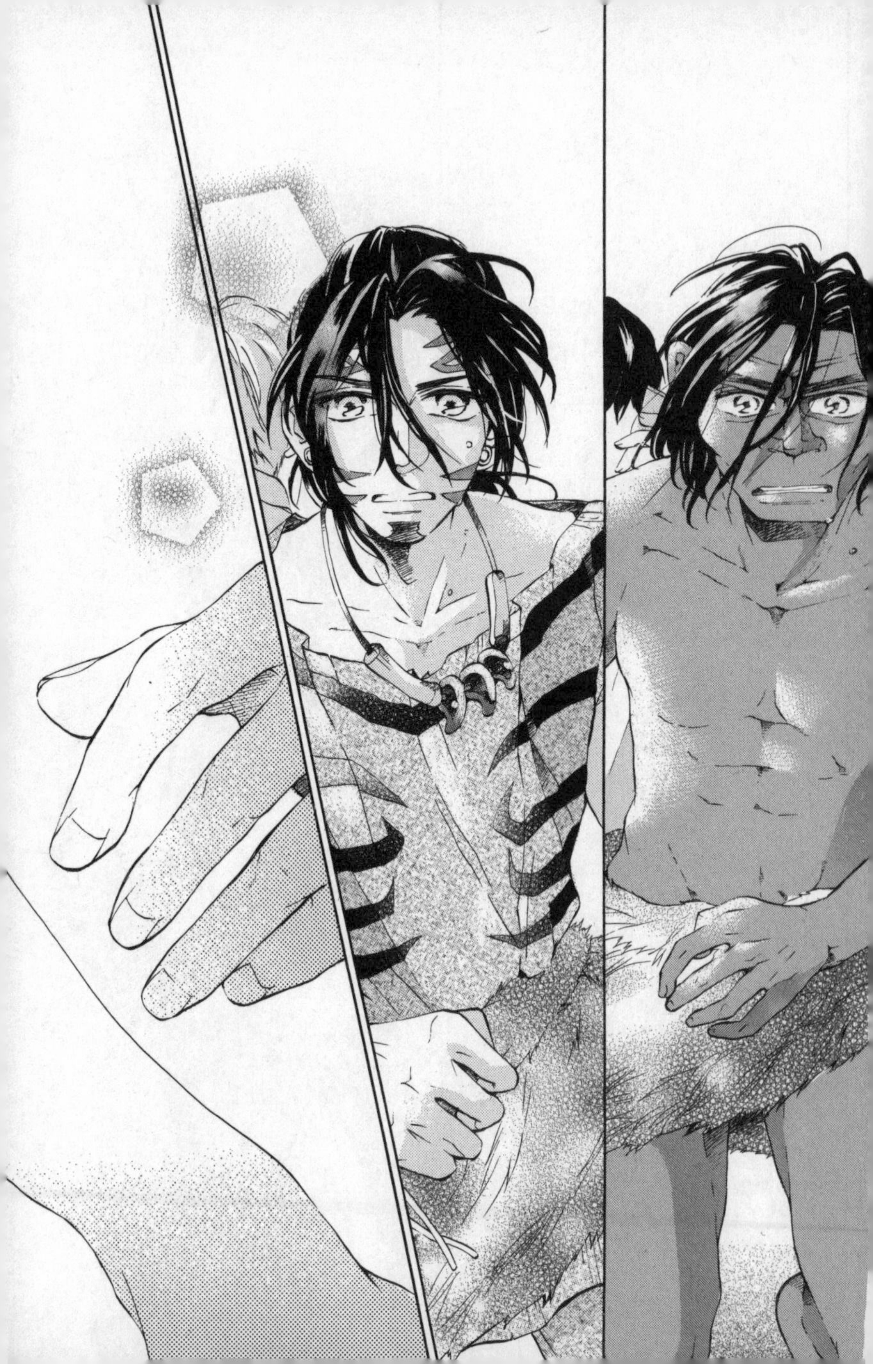

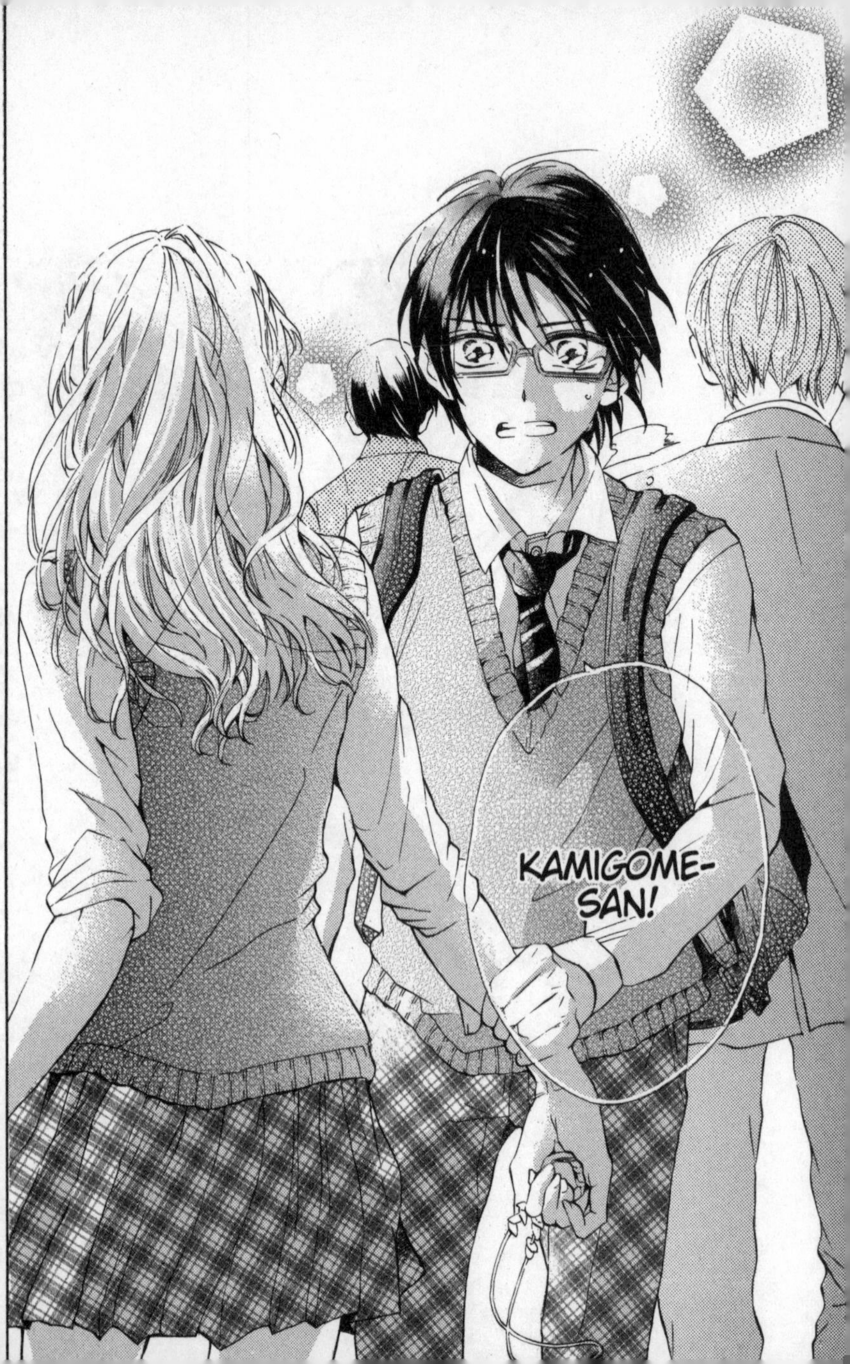
KAMIGOME-SAN!

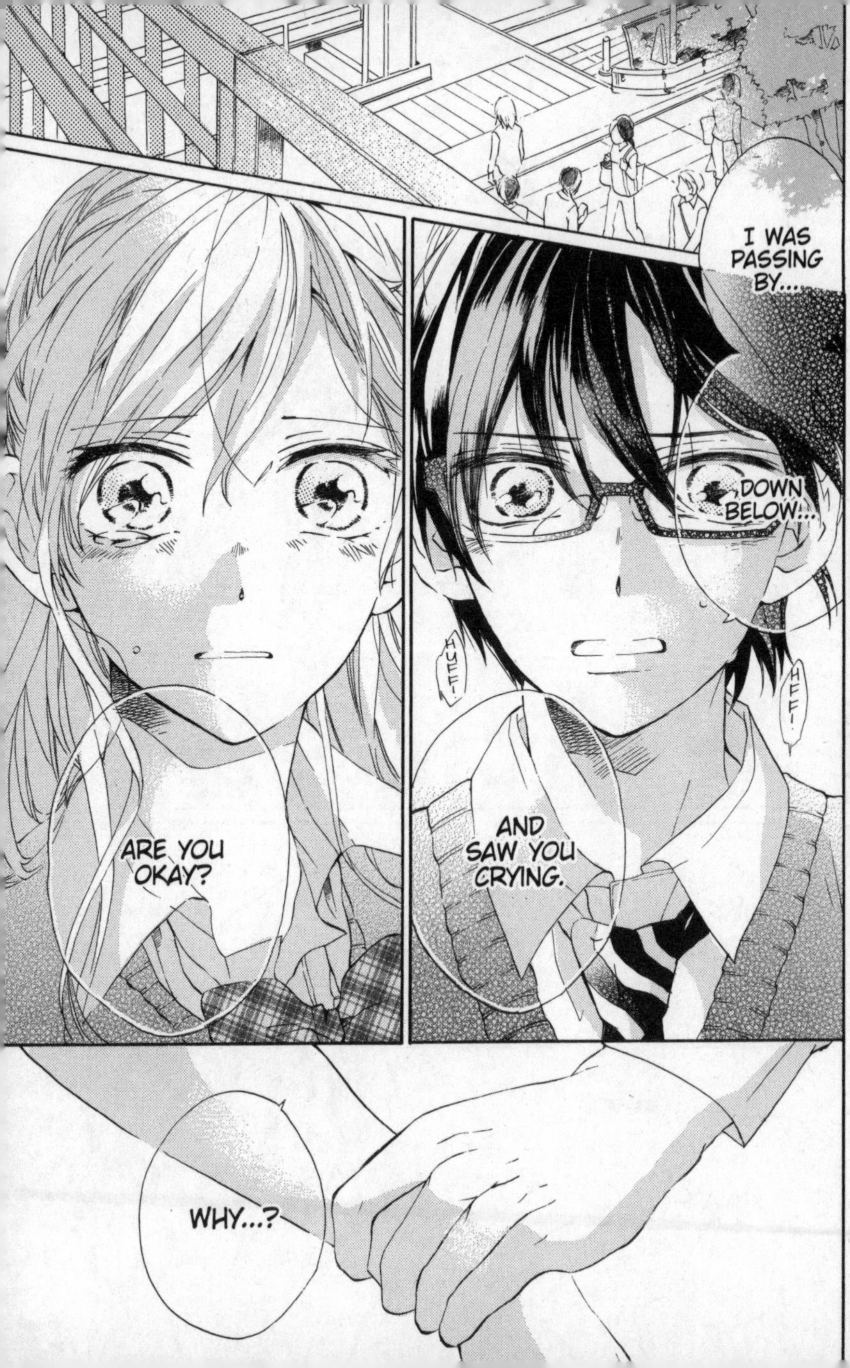
I WAS PASSING BY...
DOWN BELOW...
HUFF!
HFF!
AND SAW YOU CRYING.
ARE YOU OKAY?
WHY...?

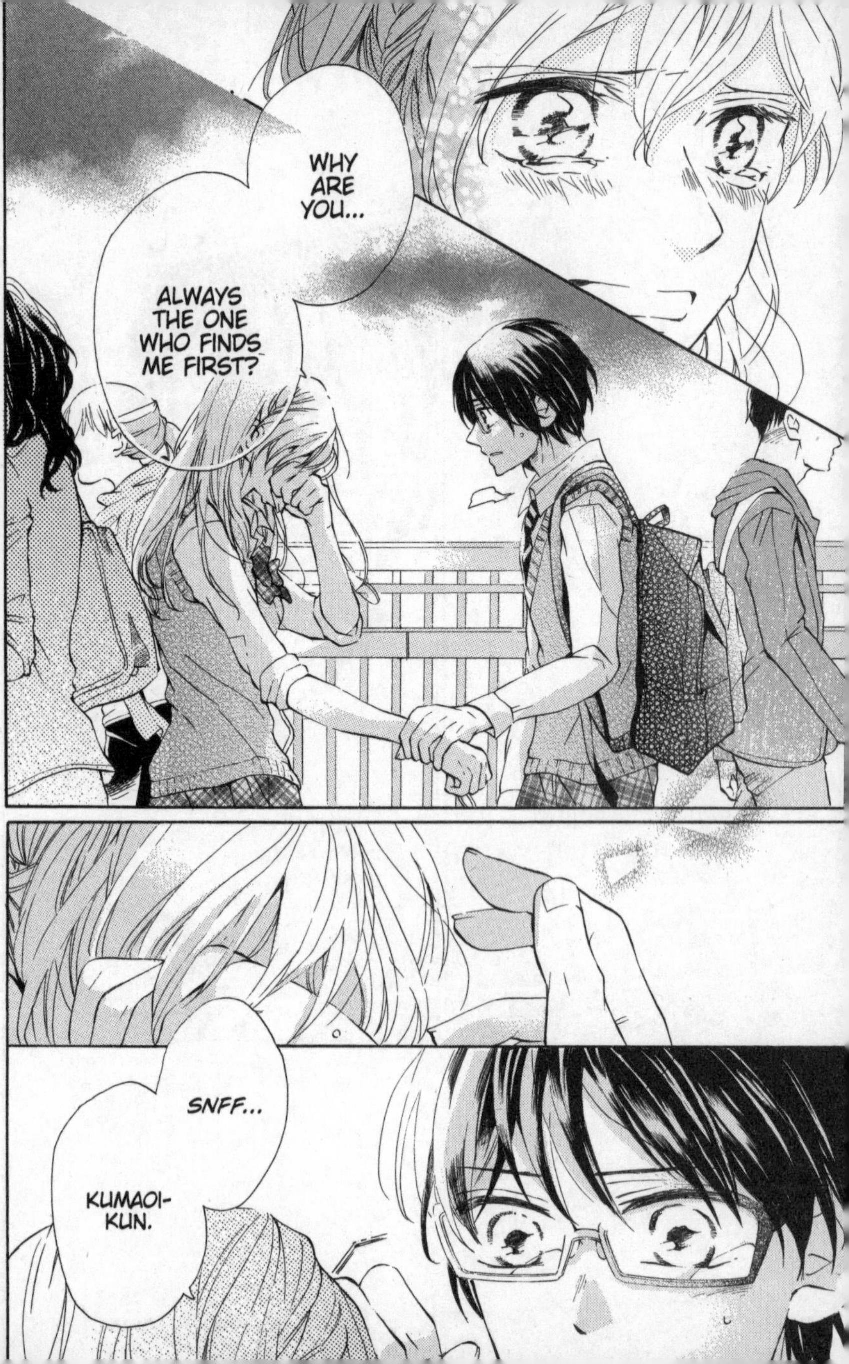
WHY ARE YOU...
ALWAYS THE ONE WHO FINDS ME FIRST?
SNFF...
KUMAOI-KUN.

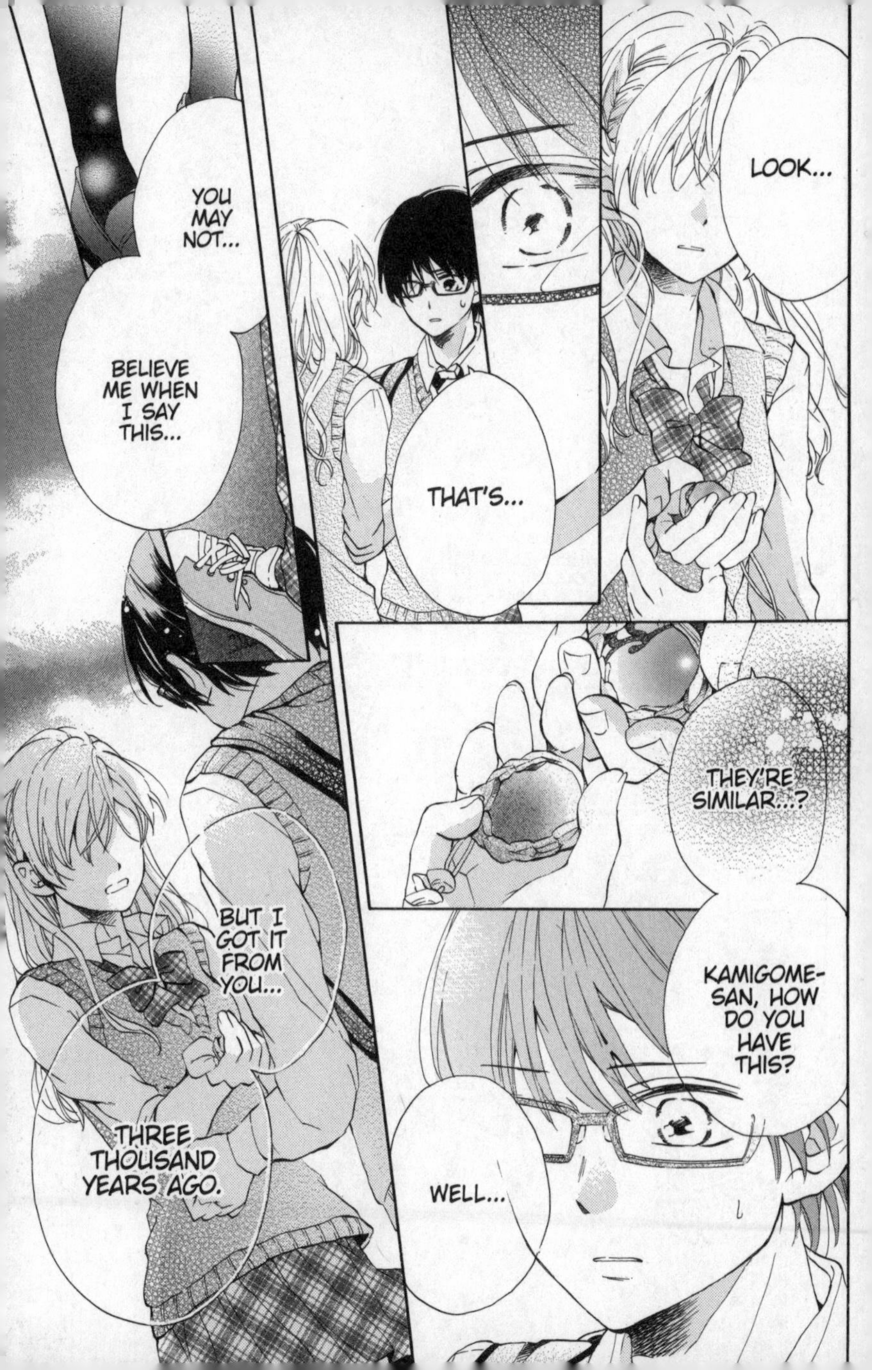
LOOK...
THAT'S...
THEY'RE SIMILAR...?
KAMIGOME-SAN, HOW DO YOU HAVE THIS?
WELL...
YOU MAY NOT...
BELIEVE ME WHEN I SAY THIS...
BUT I GOT IT FROM YOU...
THREE THOUSAND YEARS AGO.

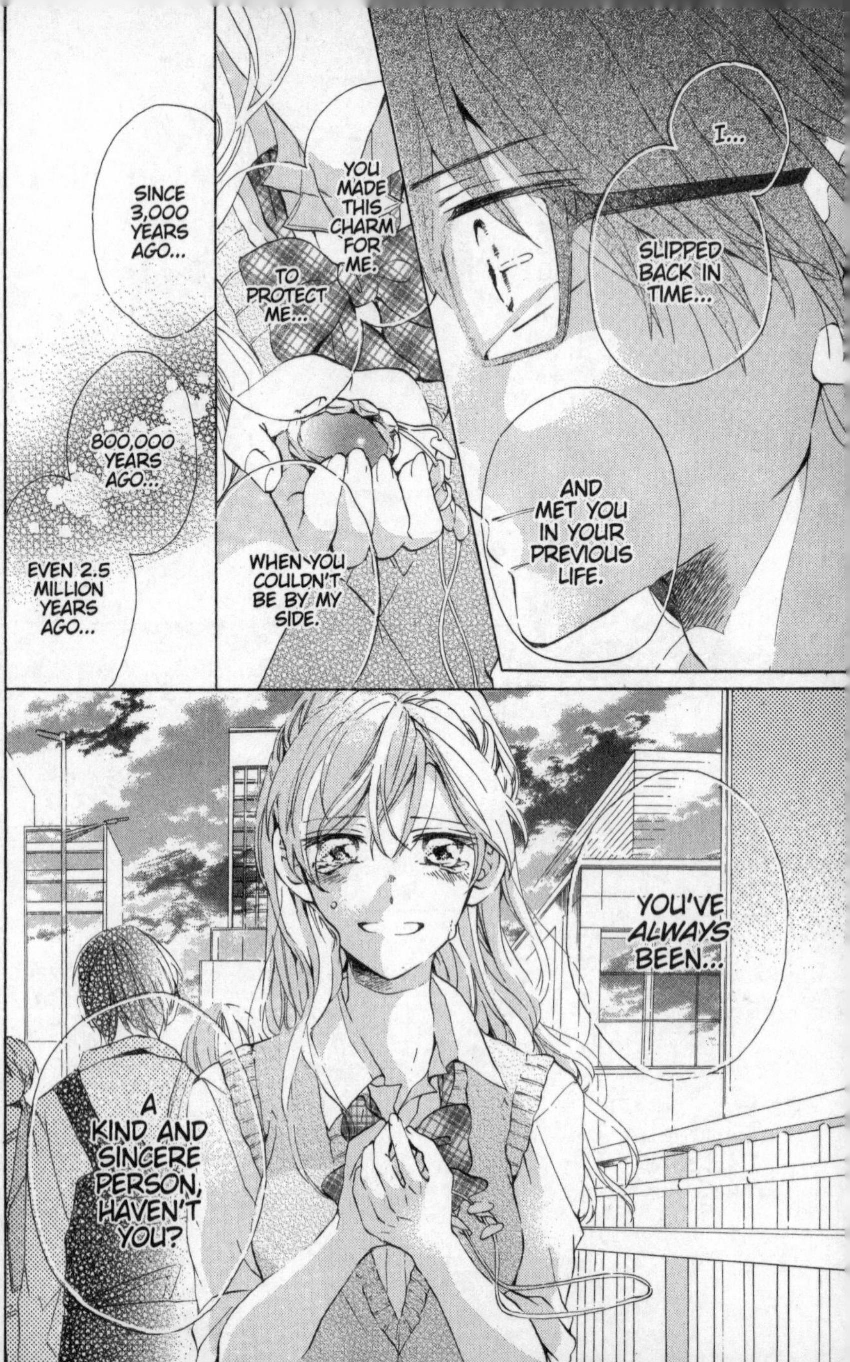
I...
SLIPPED BACK IN TIME...
AND MET YOU IN YOUR PREVIOUS LIFE.
YOU MADE THIS CHARM FOR ME.
TO PROTECT ME...
WHEN YOU COULDN'T BE BY MY SIDE.
SINCE 3,000 YEARS AGO...
800,000 YEARS AGO...
EVEN 2.5 MILLION YEARS AGO...
YOU'VE ALWAYS BEEN...
A KIND AND SINCERE PERSON, HAVEN'T YOU?

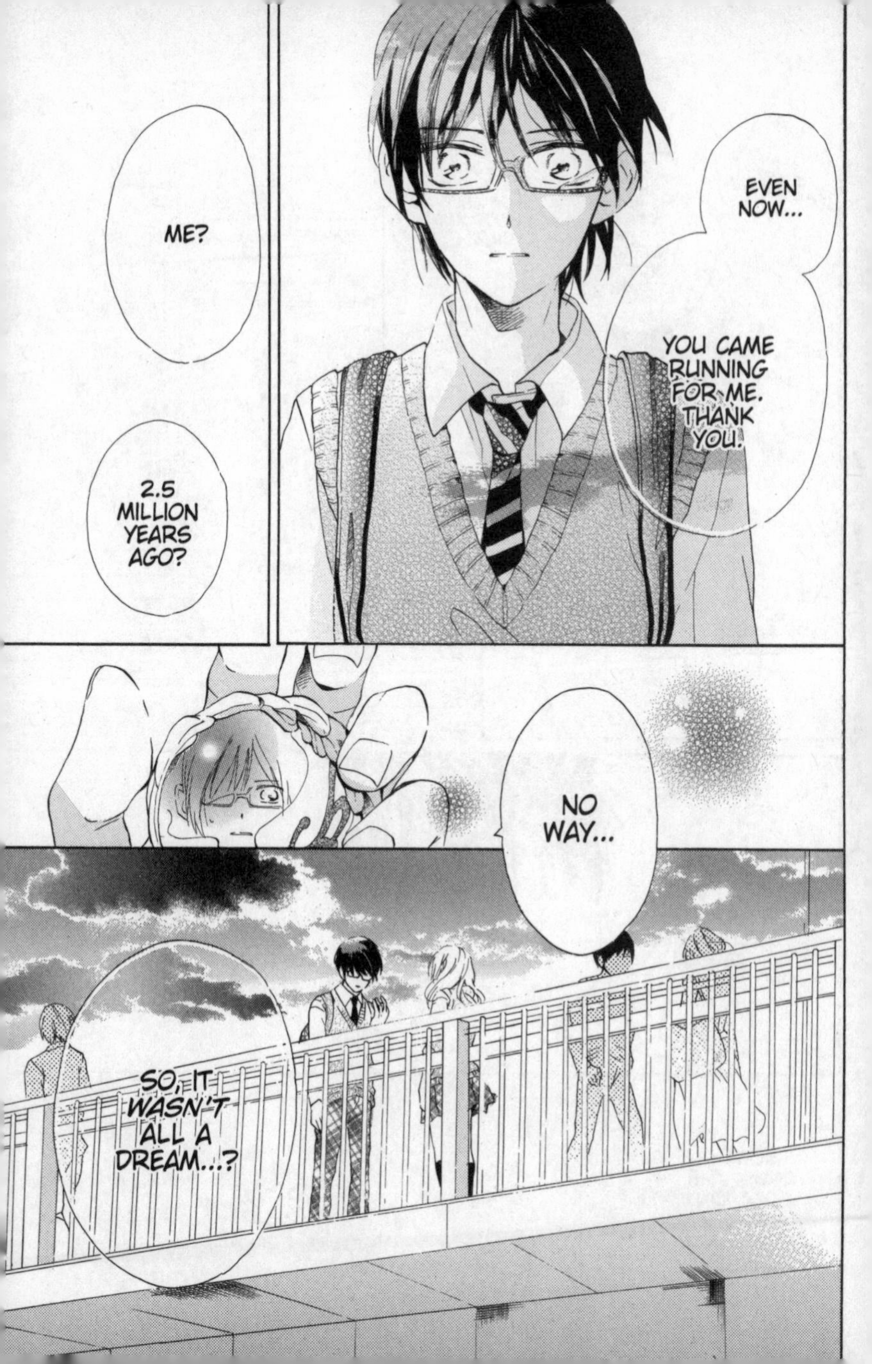
EVEN NOW...
YOU CAME RUNNING FOR ME. THANK YOU.
ME?
2.5 MILLION YEARS AGO?
NO WAY...
SO, IT WASN'T ALL A DREAM...?

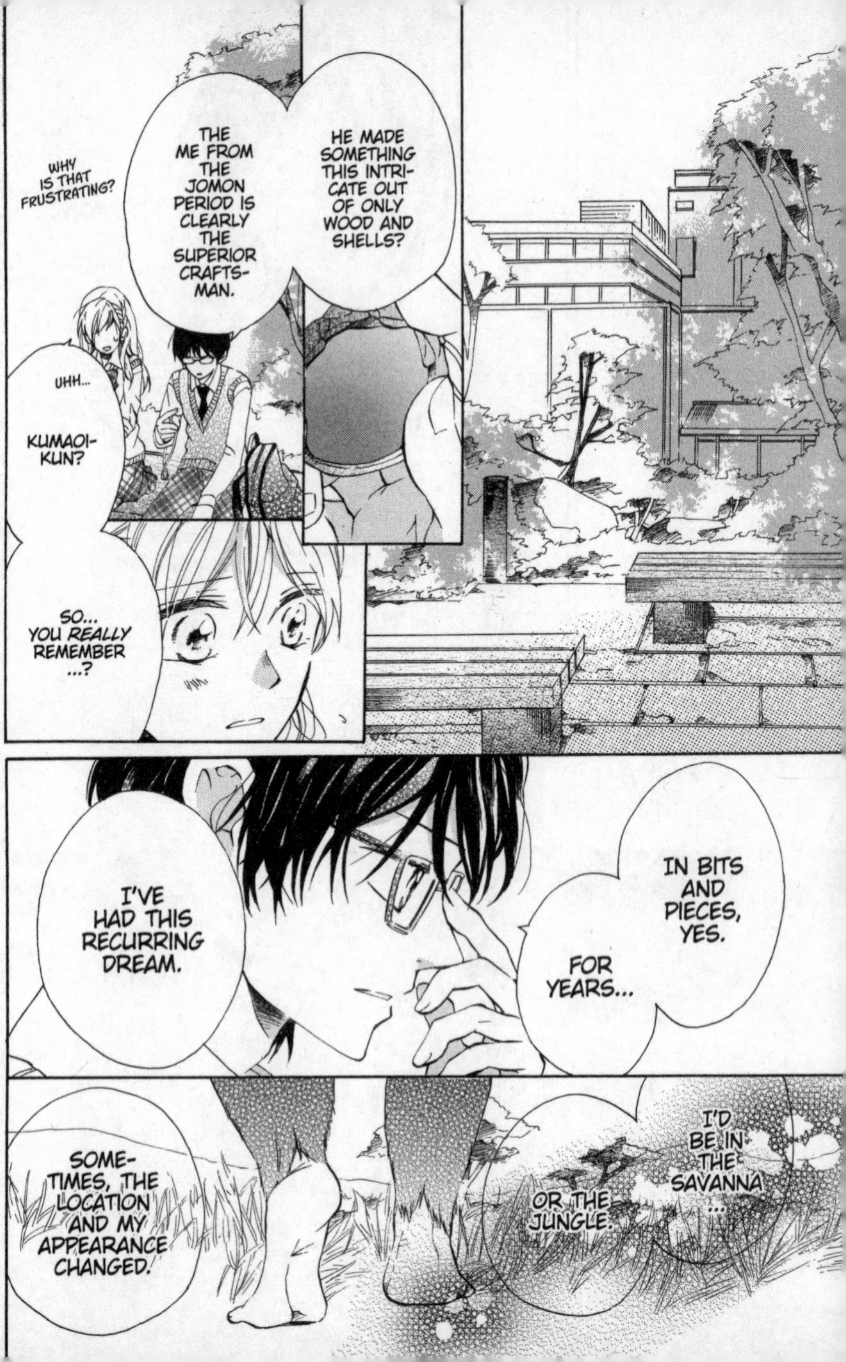
HE MADE SOMETHING THIS INTRICATE OUT OF ONLY WOOD AND SHELLS?
THE ME FROM THE JOMON PERIOD IS CLEARLY THE SUPERIOR CRAFTSMAN.
WHY IS THAT FRUSTRATING?
UHH...
KUMAOI-KUN?
SO... YOU *REALLY* REMEMBER ...?
IN BITS AND PIECES, YES.
FOR YEARS...
I'VE HAD THIS RECURRING DREAM.
I'D BE IN THE SAVANNA ...
OR THE JUNGLE.
SOMETIMES, THE LOCATION AND MY APPEARANCE CHANGED.

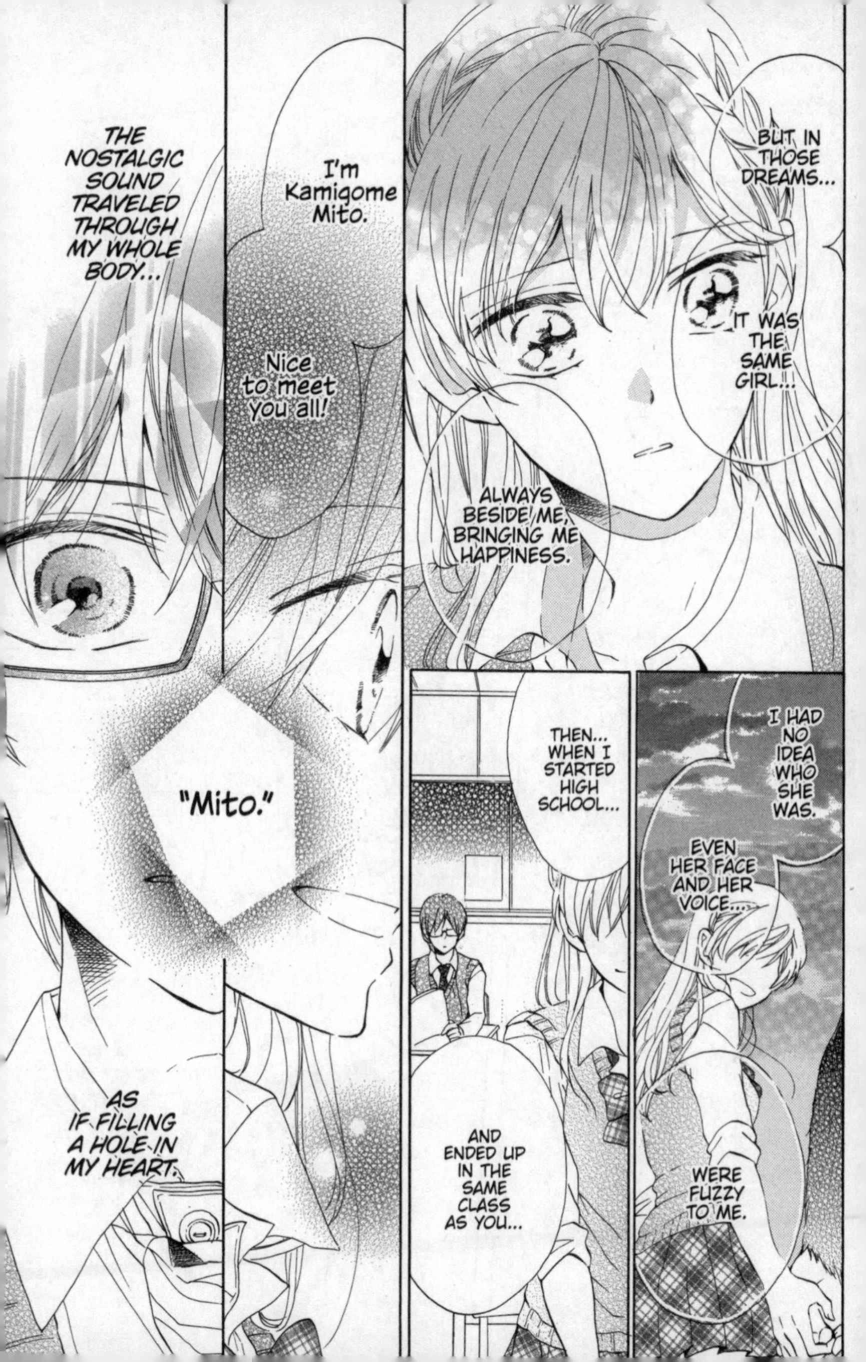
BUT IN THOSE DREAMS...
IT WAS THE SAME GIRL...
ALWAYS BESIDE ME, BRINGING ME HAPPINESS.
I HAD NO IDEA WHO SHE WAS.
EVEN HER FACE AND HER VOICE...
WERE FUZZY TO ME.
THEN... WHEN I STARTED HIGH SCHOOL...
AND ENDED UP IN THE SAME CLASS AS YOU...
I'm Kamigome Mito.
Nice to meet you all!
"Mito."
THE NOSTALGIC SOUND TRAVELED THROUGH MY WHOLE BODY...
AS IF FILLING A HOLE IN MY HEART.

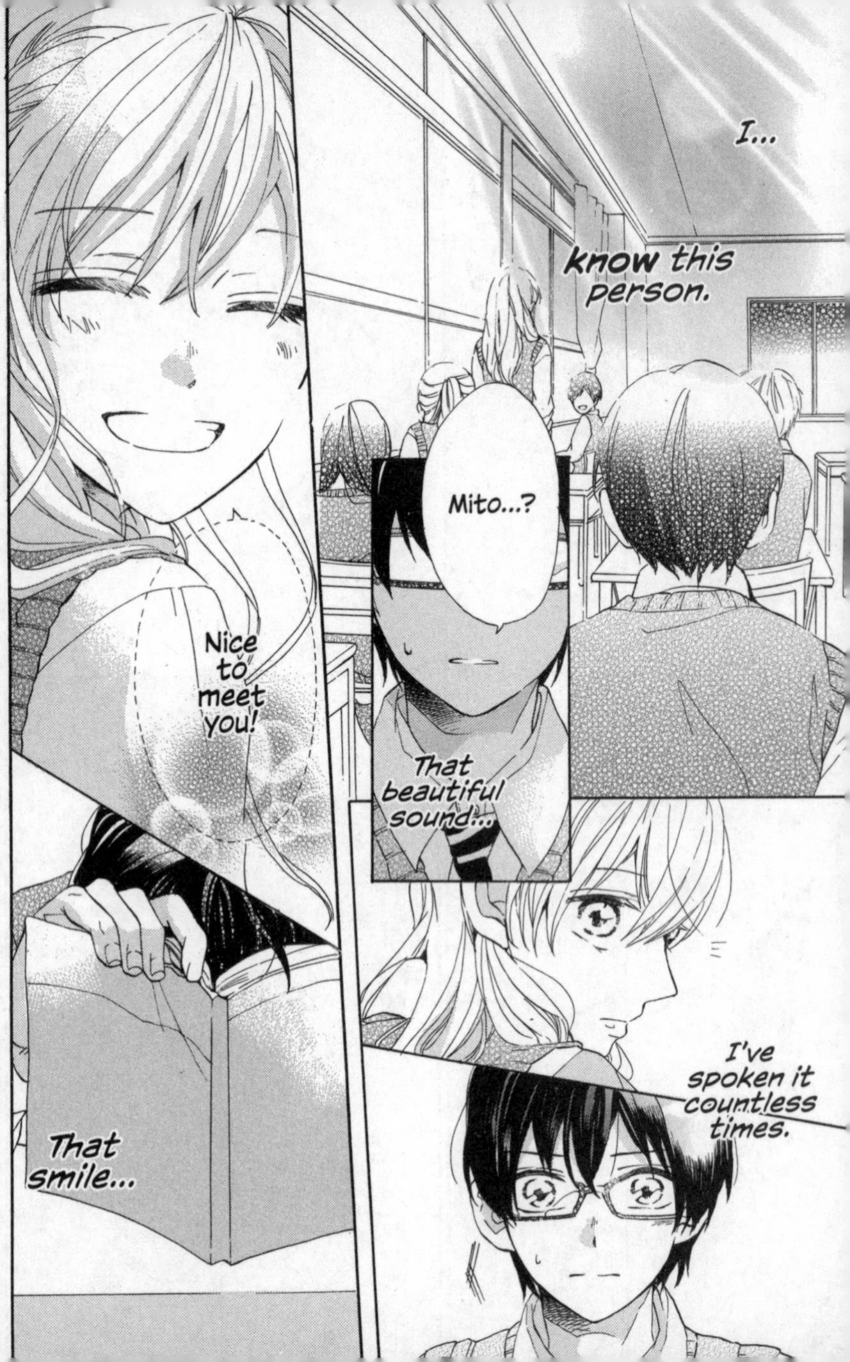
I...
know this person.
Mito...?
That beautiful sound...
I've spoken it countless times.
Nice to meet you!
That smile...

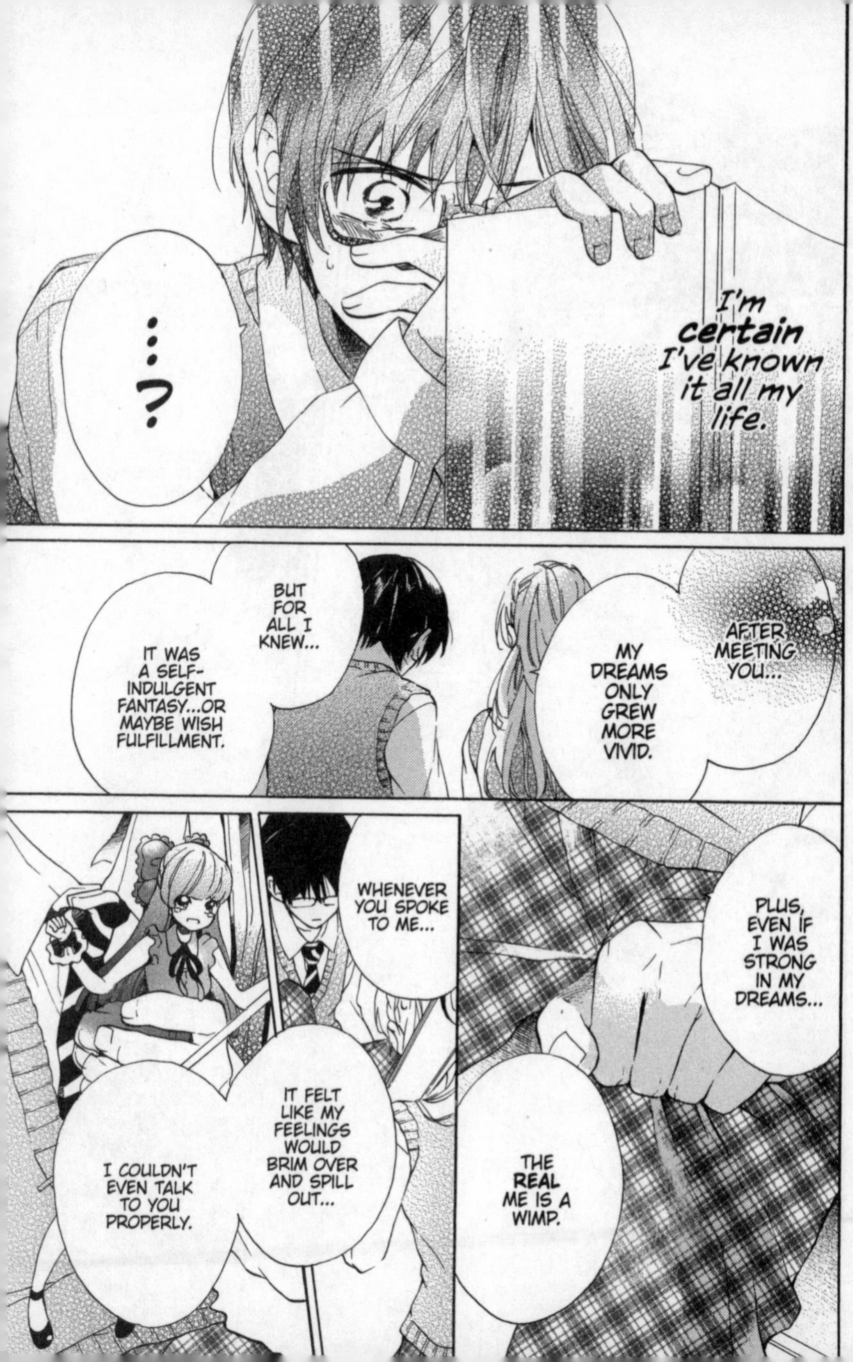
I'm certain I've known it all my life.
...?
AFTER MEETING YOU...
MY DREAMS ONLY GREW MORE VIVID.
BUT FOR ALL I KNEW...
IT WAS A SELF-INDULGENT FANTASY...OR MAYBE WISH FULFILLMENT.
PLUS, EVEN IF I WAS STRONG IN MY DREAMS...
THE REAL ME IS A WIMP.
WHENEVER YOU SPOKE TO ME...
IT FELT LIKE MY FEELINGS WOULD BRIM OVER AND SPILL OUT...
I COULDN'T EVEN TALK TO YOU PROPERLY.

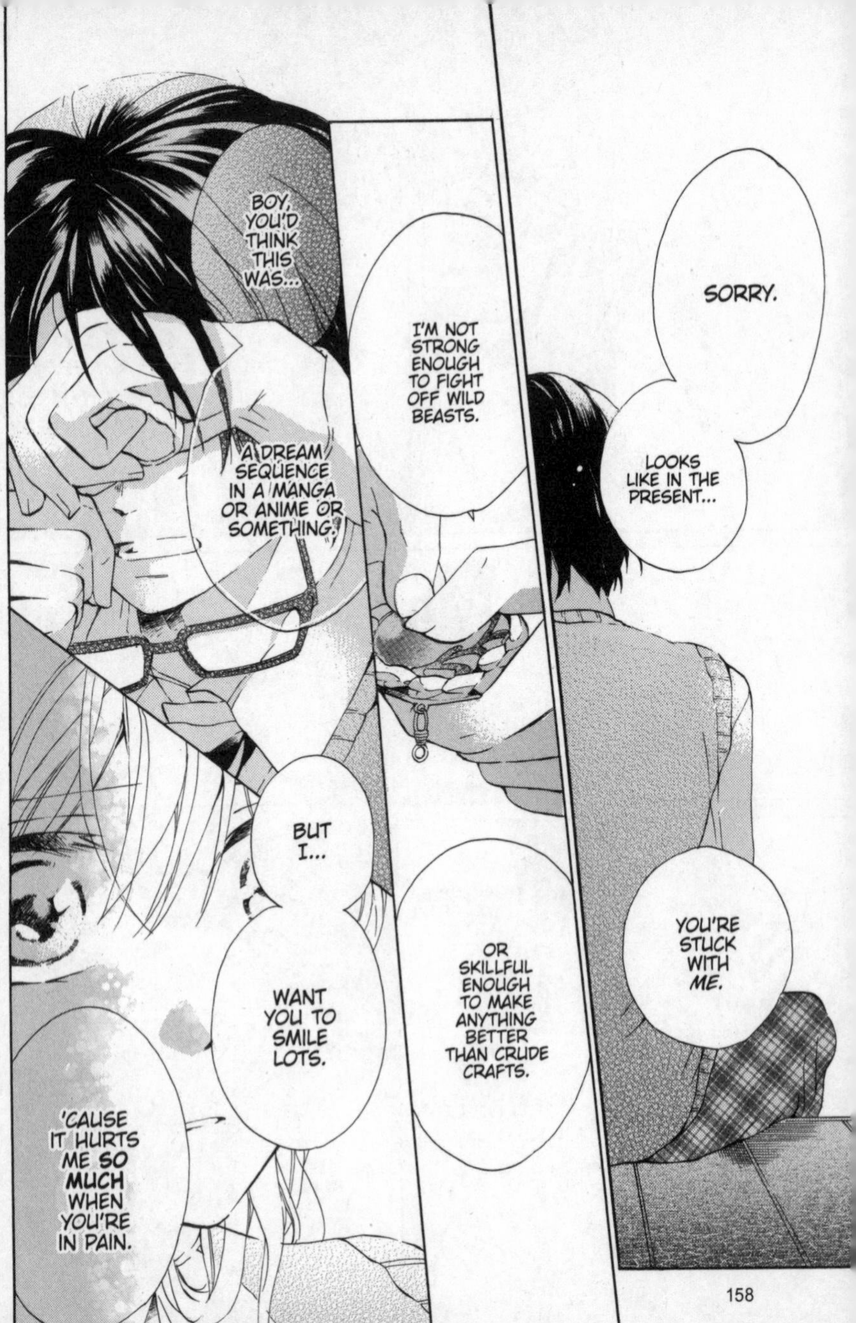
SORRY.
LOOKS LIKE IN THE PRESENT...
YOU'RE STUCK WITH ME.
I'M NOT STRONG ENOUGH TO FIGHT OFF WILD BEASTS.
OR SKILLFUL ENOUGH TO MAKE ANYTHING BETTER THAN CRUDE CRAFTS.
BOY, YOU'D THINK THIS WAS...
A DREAM SEQUENCE IN A MANGA OR ANIME OR SOMETHING.
BUT I...
WANT YOU TO SMILE LOTS.
'CAUSE IT HURTS ME SO MUCH WHEN YOU'RE IN PAIN.

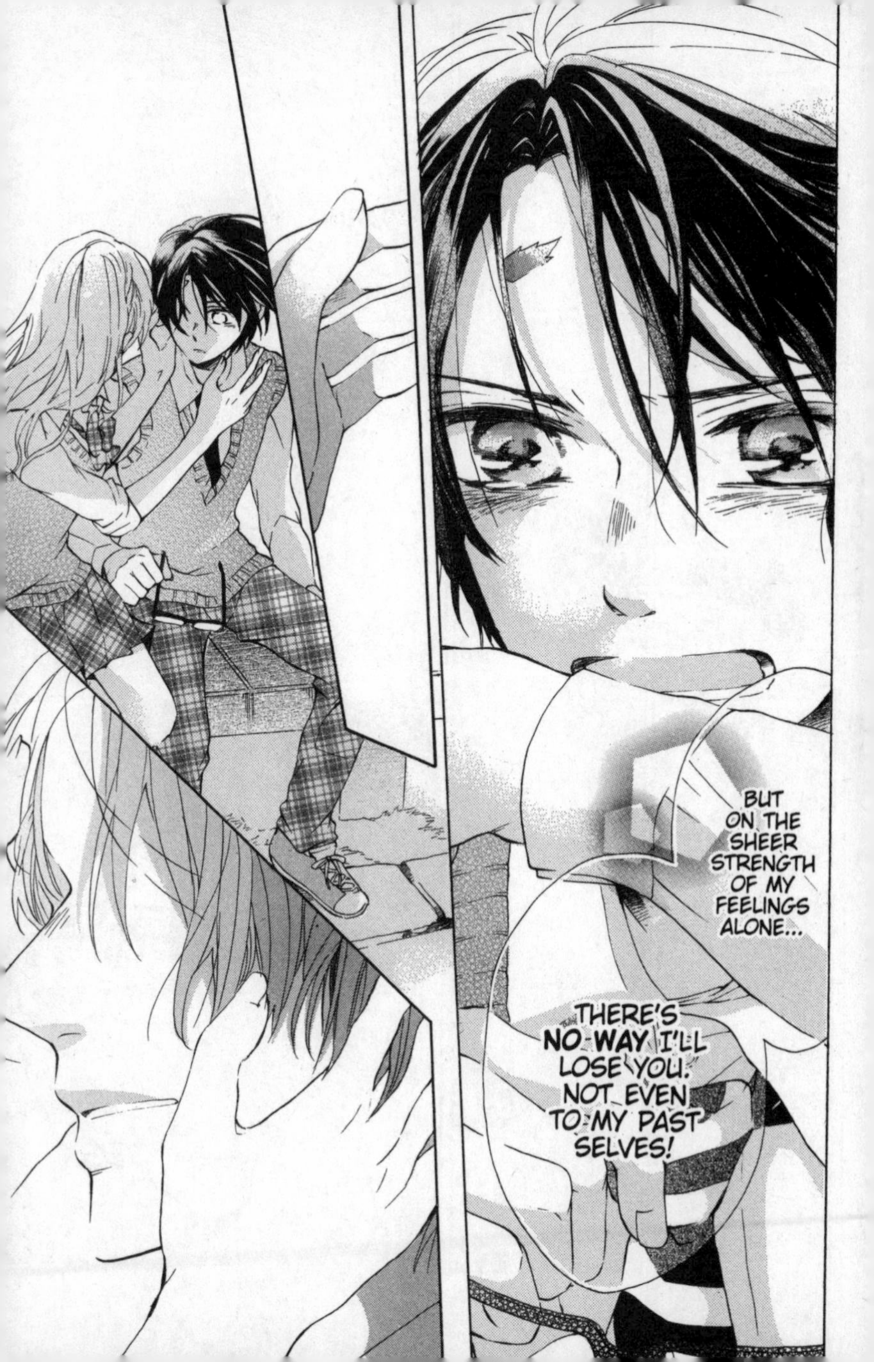
BUT ON THE SHEER STRENGTH OF MY FEELINGS ALONE...
THERE'S NO WAY I'LL LOSE YOU. NOT EVEN TO MY PAST SELVES!

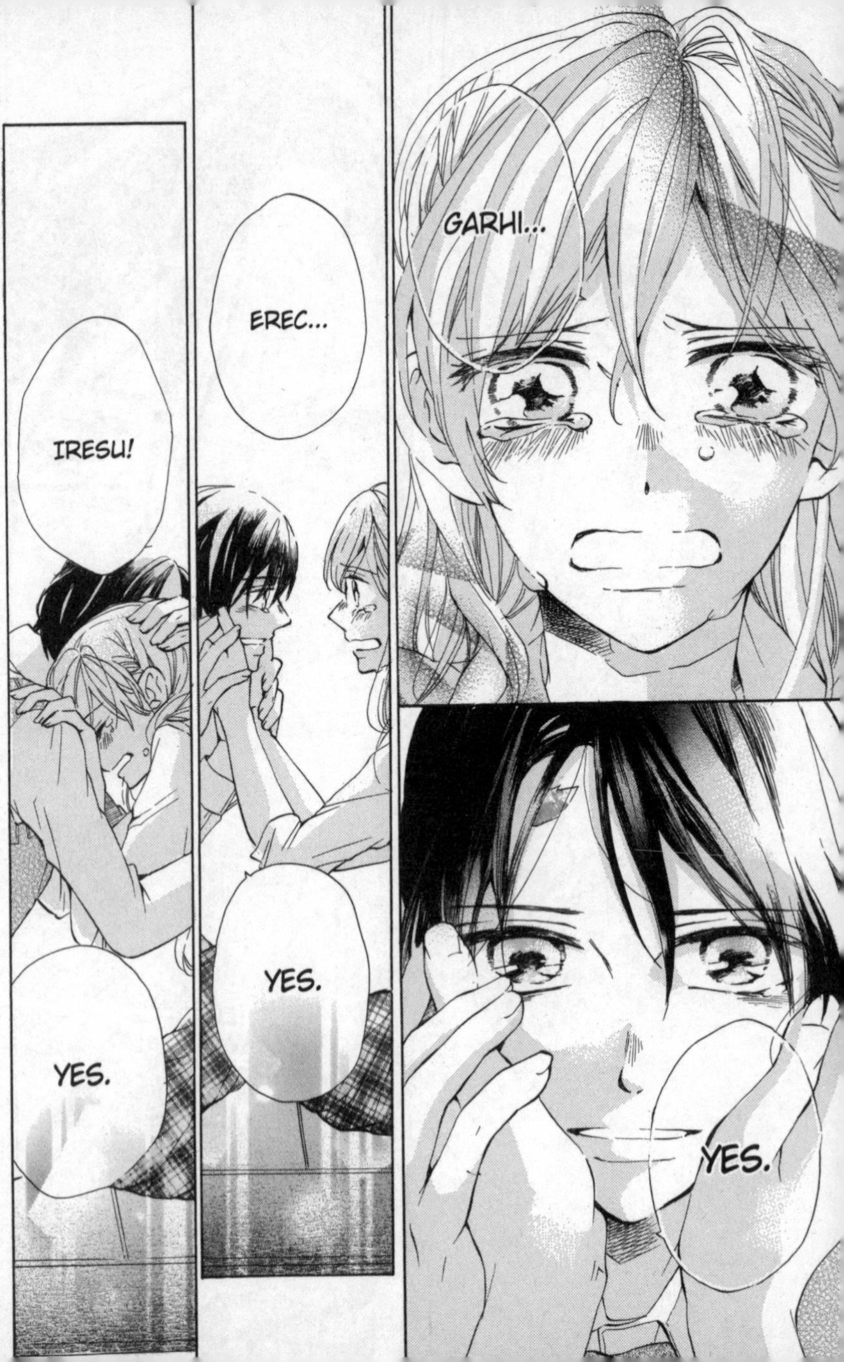

GARHI...
YES.
EREC...
YES.
IRESU!
YES.

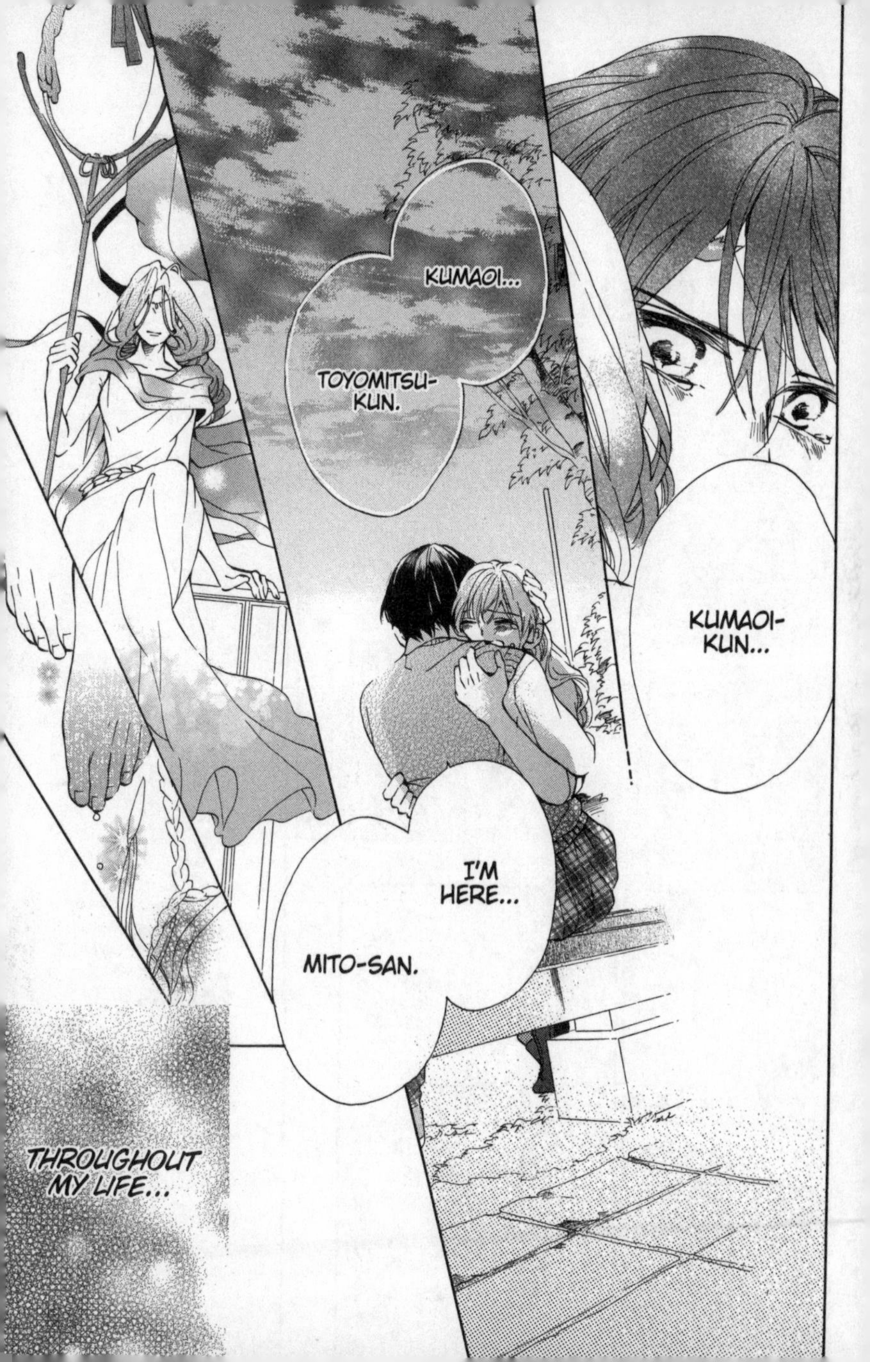
KUMAOI-KUN...
KUMAOI... TOYOMITSU-KUN.
I'M HERE... MITO-SAN.
THROUGHOUT MY LIFE...

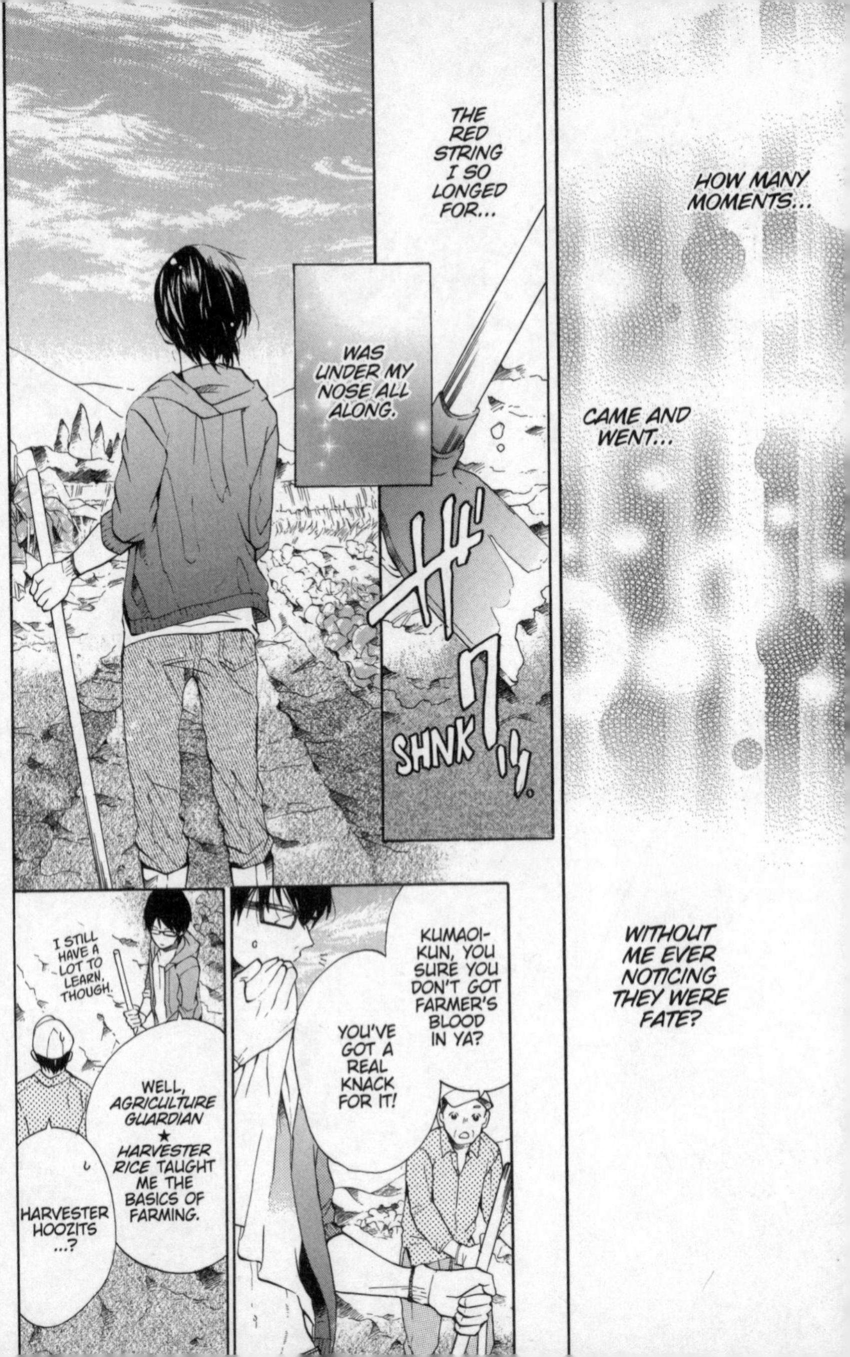
HOW MANY MOMENTS...
CAME AND WENT...
WITHOUT ME EVER NOTICING THEY WERE FATE?
THE RED STRING I SO LONGED FOR...
SHNK
WAS UNDER MY NOSE ALL ALONG.
KUMAOI-KUN, YOU SURE YOU DON'T GOT FARMER'S BLOOD IN YA?
YOU'VE GOT A REAL KNACK FOR IT!
WELL, AGRICULTURE GUARDIAN ★ HARVESTER RICE TAUGHT ME THE BASICS OF FARMING.
HARVESTER HOOZITS ...?
I STILL HAVE A LOT TO LEARN, THOUGH.

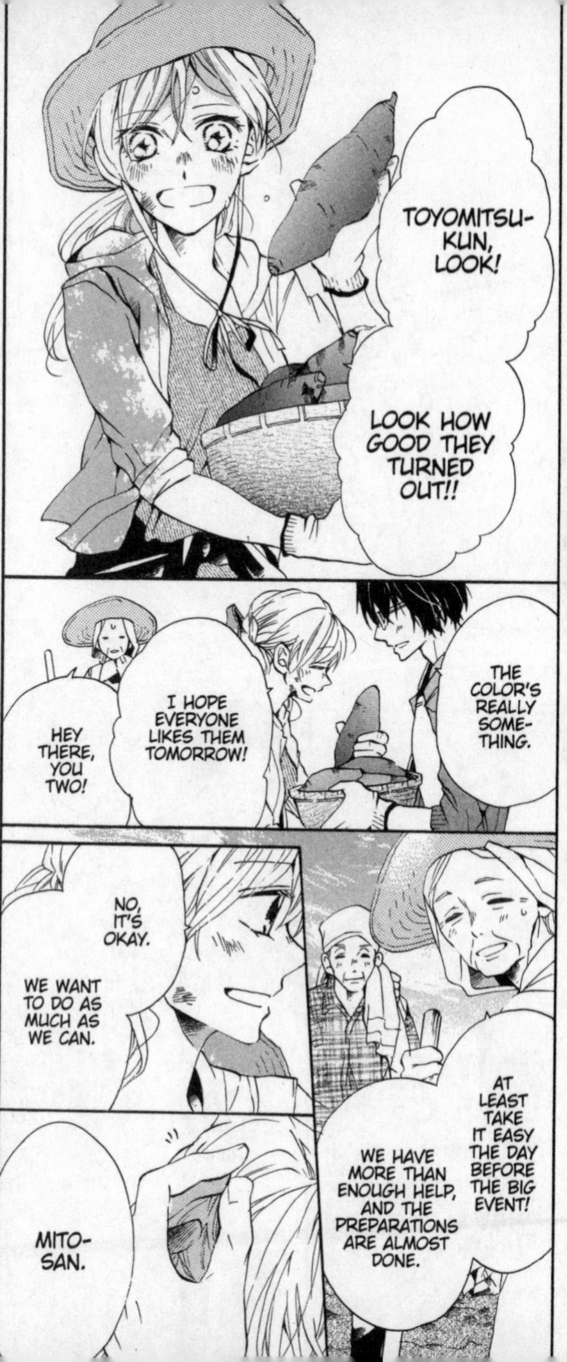
TOYOMITSU-KUN, LOOK!
LOOK HOW GOOD THEY TURNED OUT!!
THE COLOR'S REALLY SOME-THING.
I HOPE EVERYONE LIKES THEM TOMORROW!
HEY THERE, YOU TWO!
AT LEAST TAKE IT EASY THE DAY BEFORE THE BIG EVENT!
WE HAVE MORE THAN ENOUGH HELP, AND THE PREPARATIONS ARE ALMOST DONE.
NO, IT'S OKAY.
WE WANT TO DO AS MUCH AS WE CAN.
MITO-SAN.

5

IT'S THE FINAL CHAPTER.

AS I WORKED ON IT, THERE WAS A TORRENTIAL DOWNPOUR, AND MY WORKSPACE ENDED UP HALF FLOODED FROM LEAKS IN THE ROOF.

WHEN I TRIED TO GO TO THE CONVENIENCE STORE TO MAKE COPIES...

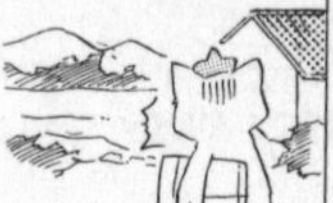

THE ROAD WAS JUST **GONE** UNDER THE RIVER. TALK ABOUT SCARY.

THANKFULLY OUR RESIDENCE WASN'T HEAVILY AFFECTED, BUT I PRAY THAT THOSE IN THE DISASTER AREA ARE ABLE TO RETURN TO THEIR NORMAL LIVES SOON.

WITH NO WAY TO GO OUT, AND MY FOOD RESERVES DWINDLING IN THE MIDDLE OF CRUNCH TIME, I SUSTAINED MYSELF WITH NUTRITIONAL JELLY DRINKS AND SNACKS MY EDITOR HAD KINDLY SENT ME. AND SO, I WAS ABLE TO FINISH THIS CHAPTER.

THANK YOU... THANK YOU SO MUCH!!

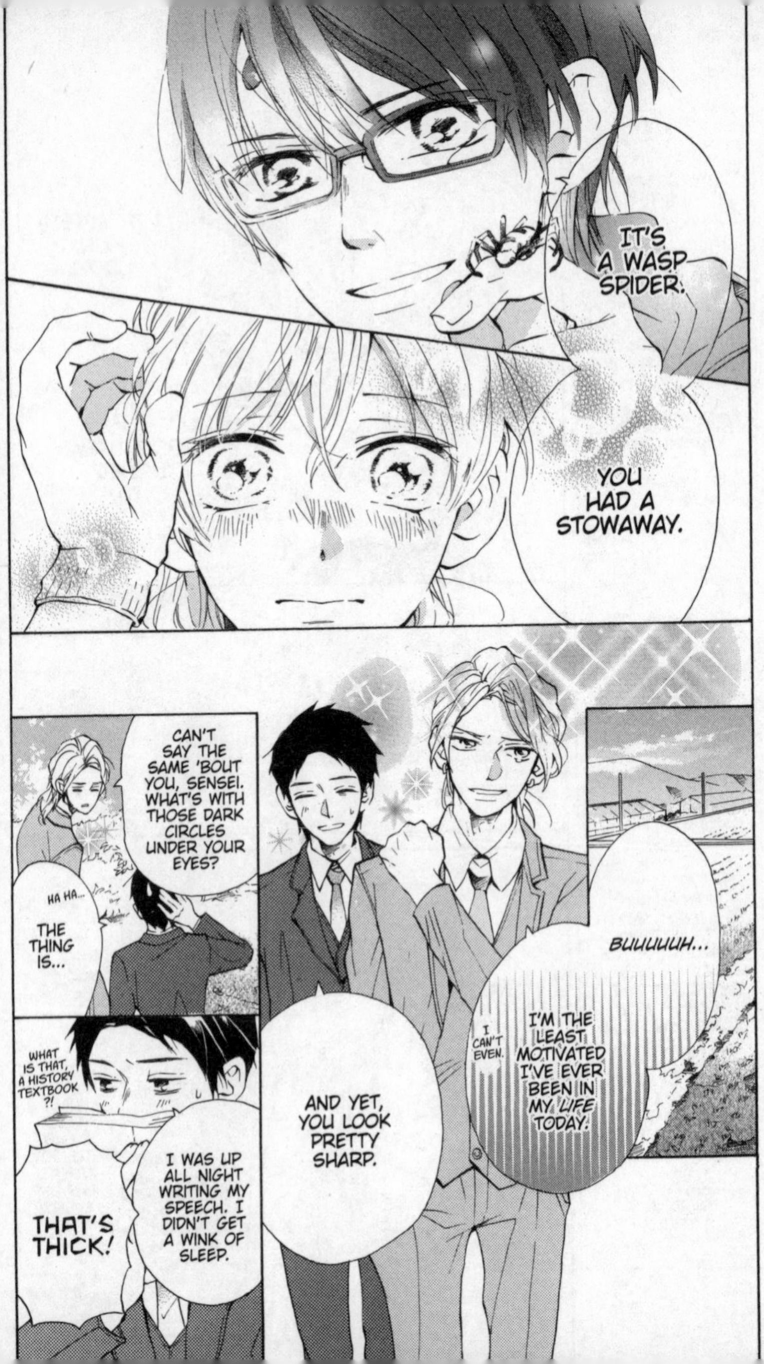
IT'S A WASP SPIDER.
YOU HAD A STOWAWAY.
BUUUUUH...
I'M THE LEAST MOTIVATED I'VE EVER BEEN IN MY *LIFE* TODAY.
I CAN'T EVEN.
AND YET, YOU LOOK PRETTY SHARP.
CAN'T SAY THE SAME 'BOUT YOU, SENSEI. WHAT'S WITH THOSE DARK CIRCLES UNDER YOUR EYES?
HA HA...
THE THING IS...
I WAS UP ALL NIGHT WRITING MY SPEECH. I DIDN'T GET A WINK OF SLEEP.
WHAT IS THAT, A HISTORY TEXTBOOK?!
THAT'S THICK!

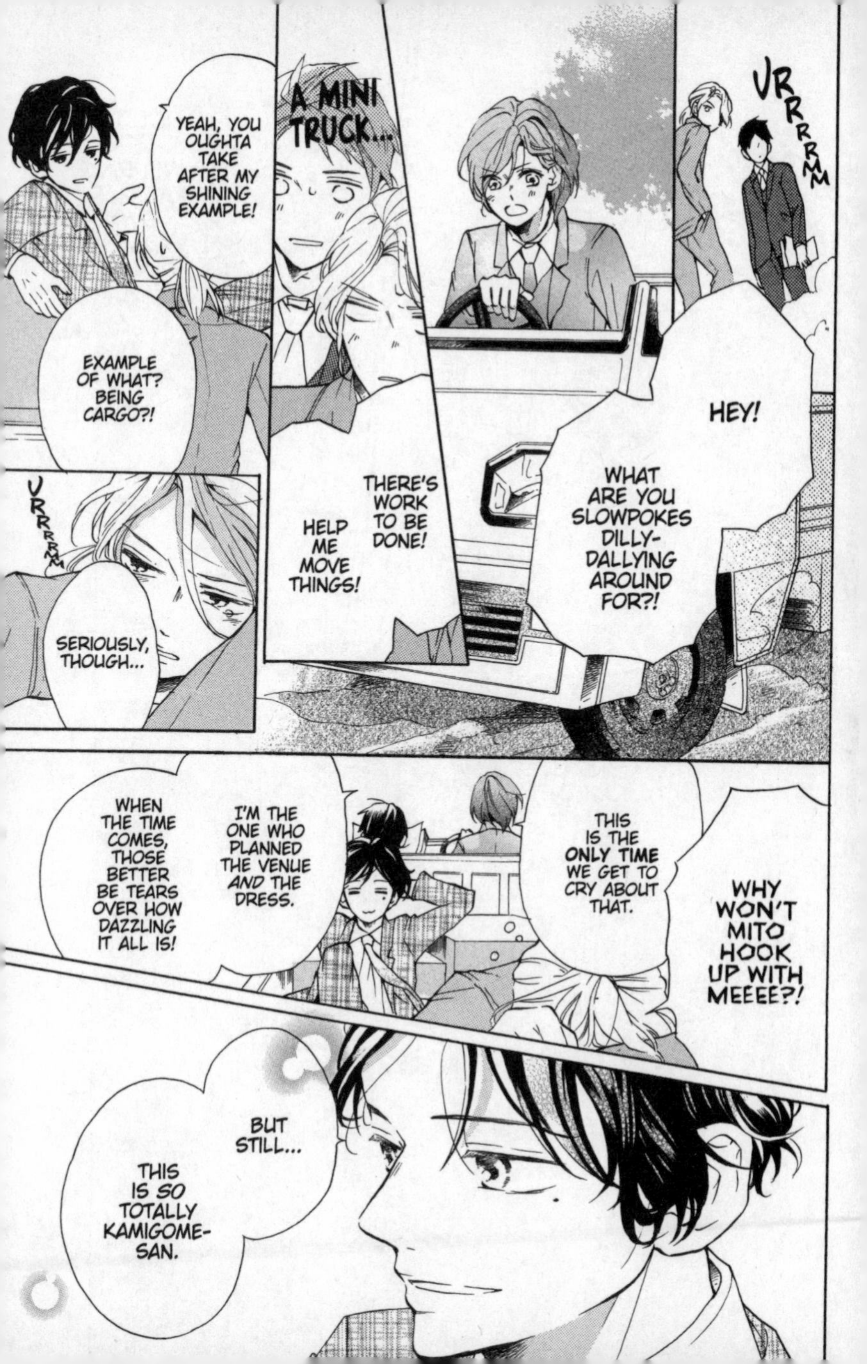
VRRRRRMM
HEY!
WHAT ARE YOU SLOWPOKES DILLY-DALLYING AROUND FOR?!
THERE'S WORK TO BE DONE!
HELP ME MOVE THINGS!
A MINI TRUCK...
YEAH, YOU OUGHTA TAKE AFTER MY SHINING EXAMPLE!
EXAMPLE OF WHAT? BEING CARGO?!
VRRRRMM
SERIOUSLY, THOUGH...
WHY WON'T MITO HOOK UP WITH MEEEE?!
THIS IS THE ONLY TIME WE GET TO CRY ABOUT THAT.
I'M THE ONE WHO PLANNED THE VENUE AND THE DRESS.
WHEN THE TIME COMES, THOSE BETTER BE TEARS OVER HOW DAZZLING IT ALL IS!
BUT STILL...
THIS IS SO TOTALLY KAMIGOME-SAN.

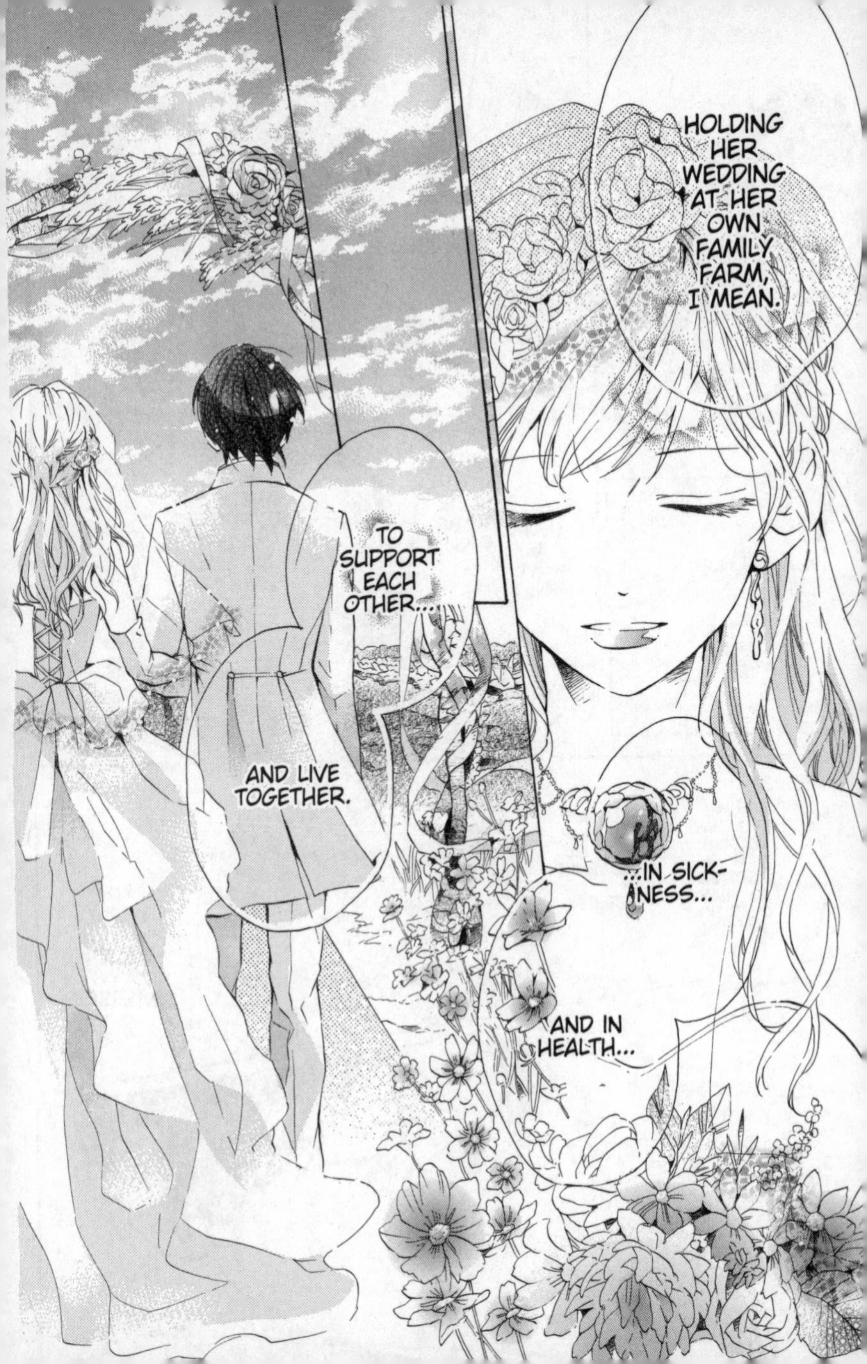
HOLDING HER WEDDING AT HER OWN FAMILY FARM, I MEAN.
...IN SICK-NESS...
AND IN HEALTH...
TO SUPPORT EACH OTHER...
AND LIVE TOGETHER.

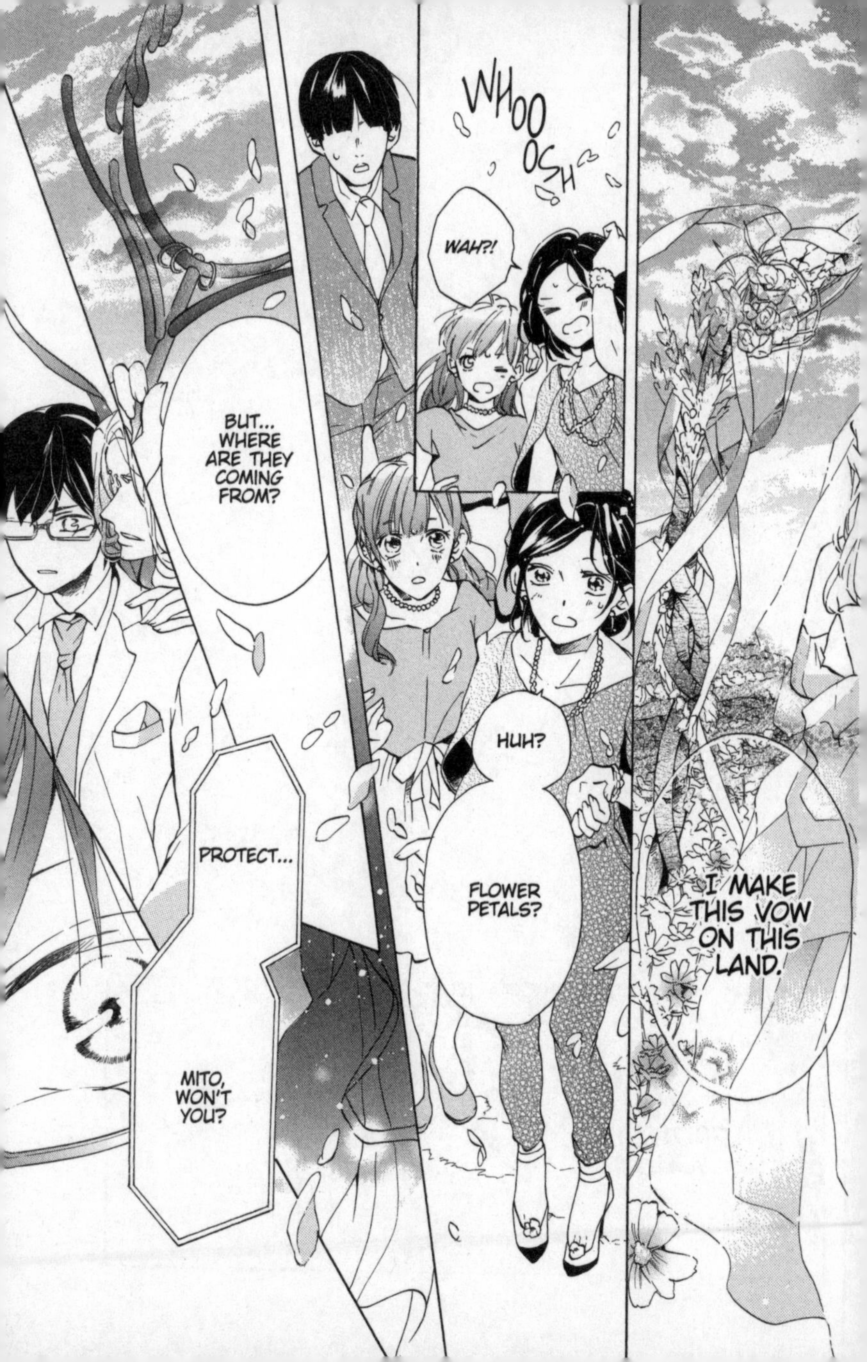
I MAKE THIS VOW ON THIS LAND.
WHOOOSH
WAH?!
HUH?
FLOWER PETALS?
BUT... WHERE ARE THEY COMING FROM?
PROTECT...
MITO, WON'T YOU?

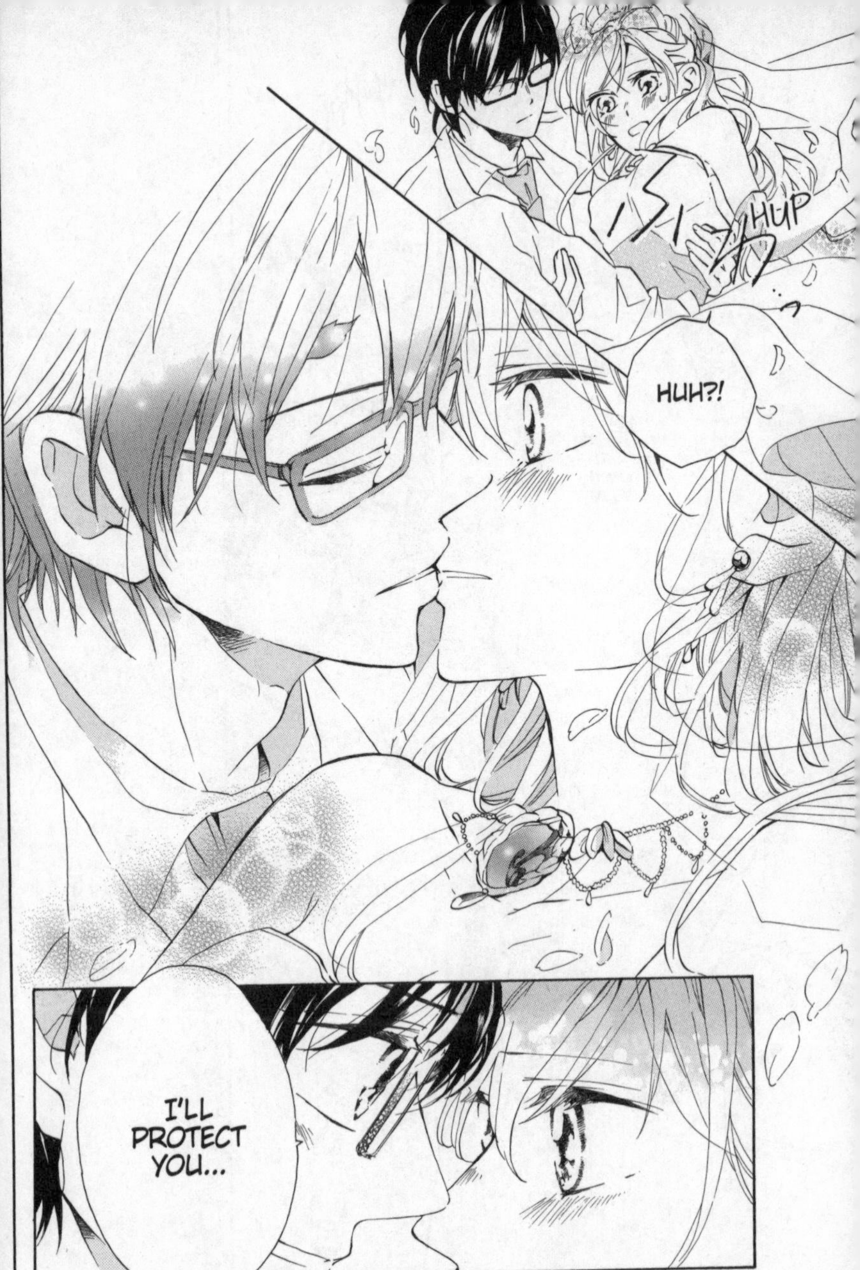
HUP
HUH?!
I'LL PROTECT YOU...

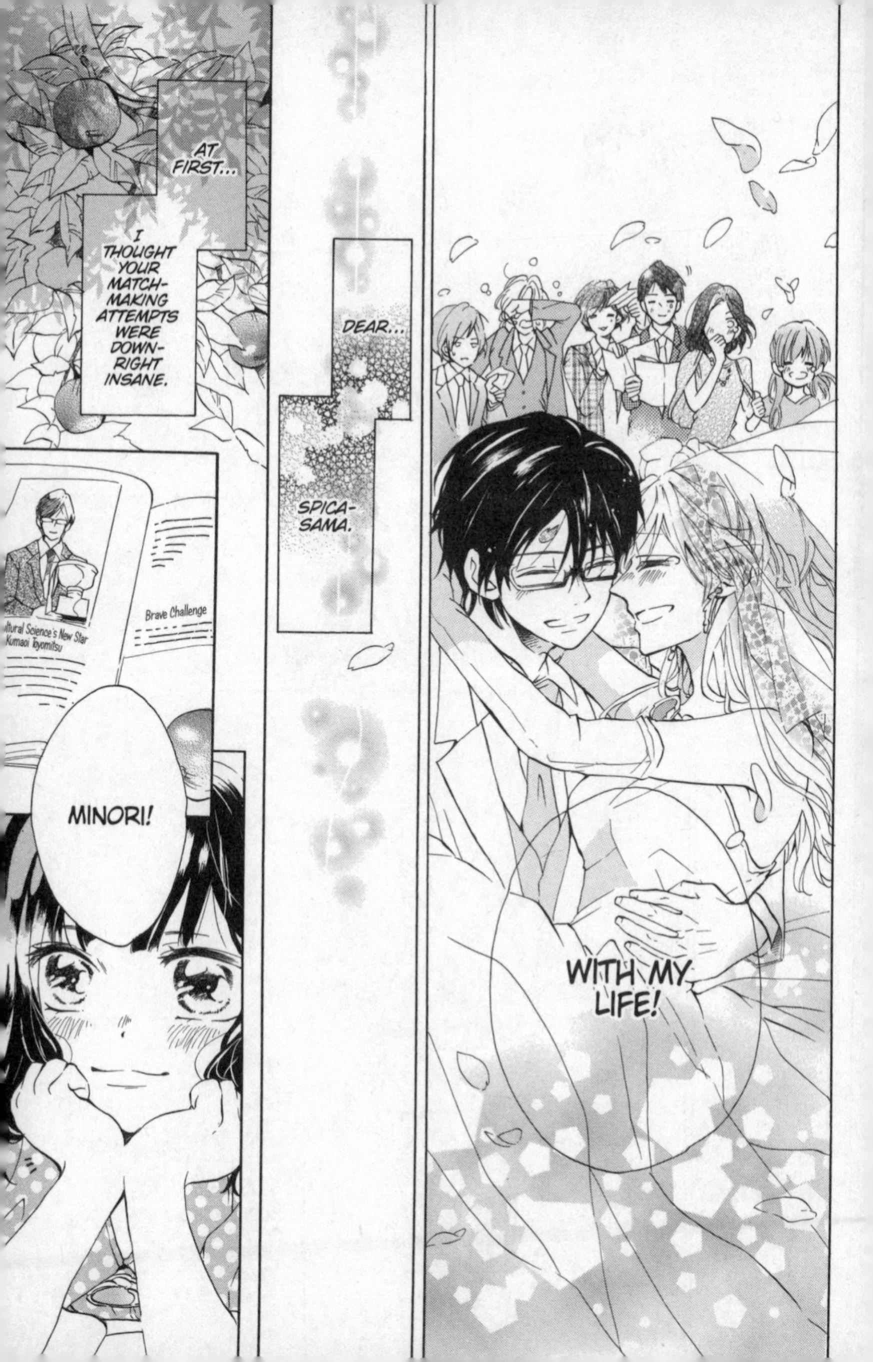
WITH MY LIFE!
DEAR...
SPICA-SAMA.
AT FIRST...
I THOUGHT YOUR MATCH-MAKING ATTEMPTS WERE DOWN-RIGHT INSANE.
ltural Science's New Star Kumaoi Toyomitsu
Brave Challenge
MINORI!

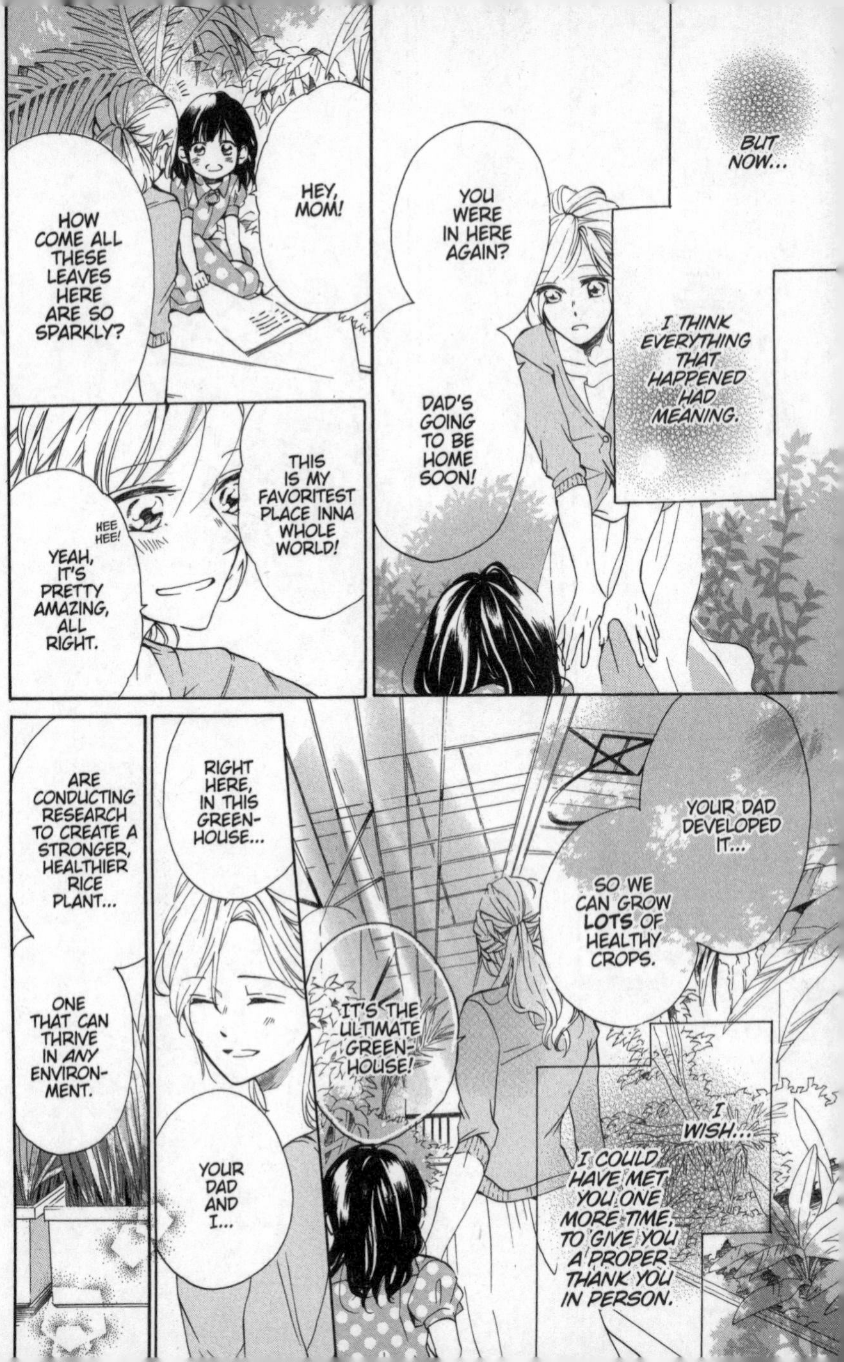
HEY, MOM!
HOW COME ALL THESE LEAVES HERE ARE SO SPARKLY?
THIS IS MY FAVORITEST PLACE INNA WHOLE WORLD!
HEE HEE!
YEAH, IT'S PRETTY AMAZING, ALL RIGHT.
YOU WERE IN HERE AGAIN?
DAD'S GOING TO BE HOME SOON!
I THINK EVERYTHING THAT HAPPENED HAD MEANING.
BUT NOW...
RIGHT HERE, IN THIS GREEN-HOUSE...
YOUR DAD AND I...
ARE CONDUCTING RESEARCH TO CREATE A STRONGER, HEALTHIER RICE PLANT...
ONE THAT CAN THRIVE IN *ANY* ENVIRONMENT.
YOUR DAD DEVELOPED IT...
SO WE CAN GROW **LOTS** OF HEALTHY CROPS.
IT'S THE ULTIMATE GREEN-HOUSE!
I WISH...
I COULD HAVE MET YOU ONE MORE TIME, TO GIVE YOU A PROPER THANK YOU IN PERSON.

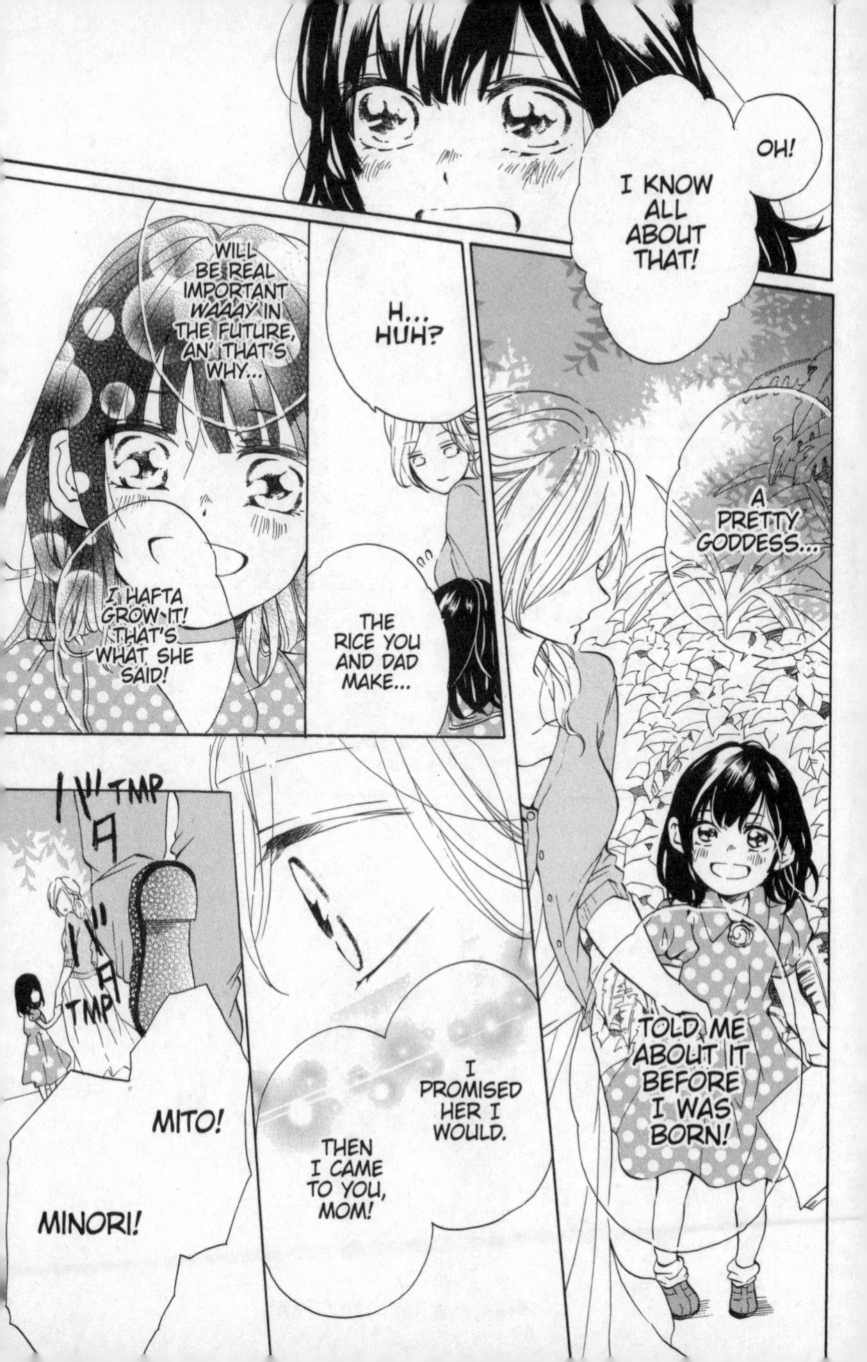
OH!
I KNOW ALL ABOUT THAT!
A PRETTY GODDESS...
TOLD ME ABOUT IT BEFORE I WAS BORN!
H... HUH?
THE RICE YOU AND DAD MAKE...
WILL BE REAL IMPORTANT WAAAY IN THE FUTURE, AN' THAT'S WHY...
I HAFTA GROW IT! THAT'S WHAT SHE SAID!
I PROMISED HER I WOULD.
THEN I CAME TO YOU, MOM!
TMP
TMP
MITO!
MINORI!

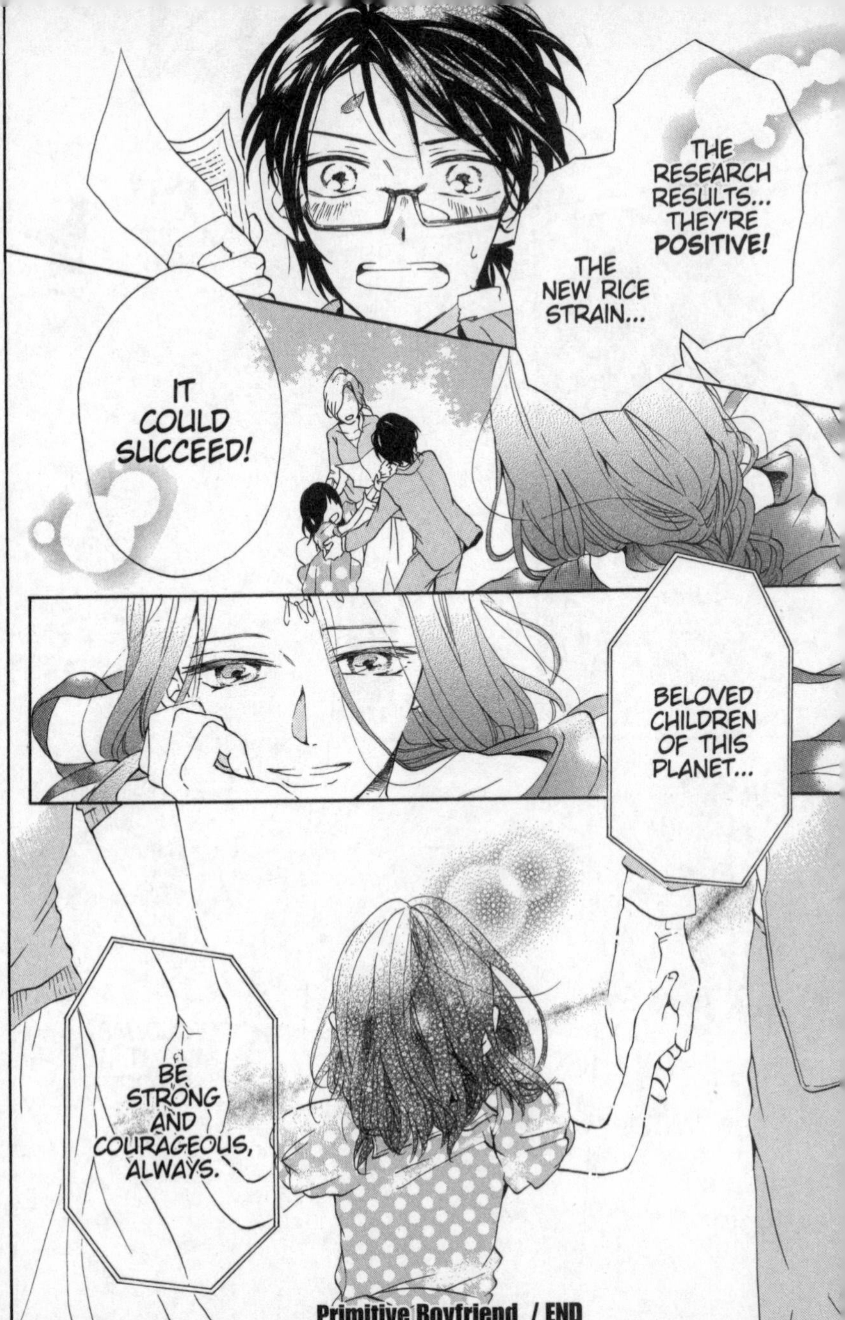
THE RESEARCH RESULTS... THEY'RE POSITIVE!
THE NEW RICE STRAIN...
IT COULD SUCCEED!
BELOVED CHILDREN OF THIS PLANET...
BE STRONG AND COURAGEOUS, ALWAYS.

Primitive Boyfriend / END

PRIMITIVE BOYFRIEND by Yoshiko

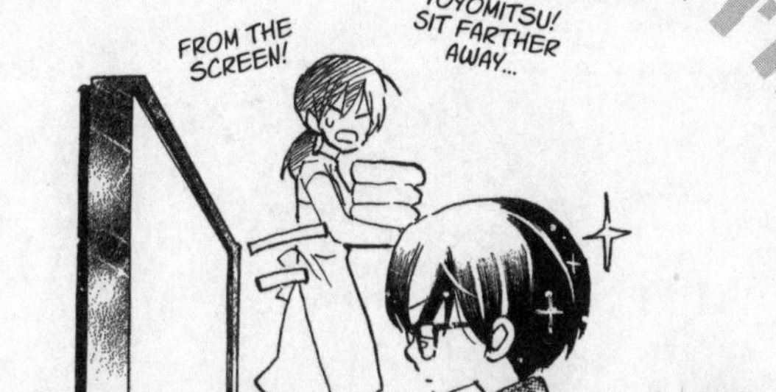
TOYOMITSU! SIT FARTHER AWAY...
FROM THE SCREEN!
Anime Notes
SUPER SERIOUS

KUMAOI TOYOMITSU AS A SMALL CHILD

THE FOLLOWING STORY IS ABOUT MITO'S FIRST DATE WITH KUMAOI-KUN. PLEASE WATCH OVER THEM...

Bonus Chapter: Service Track

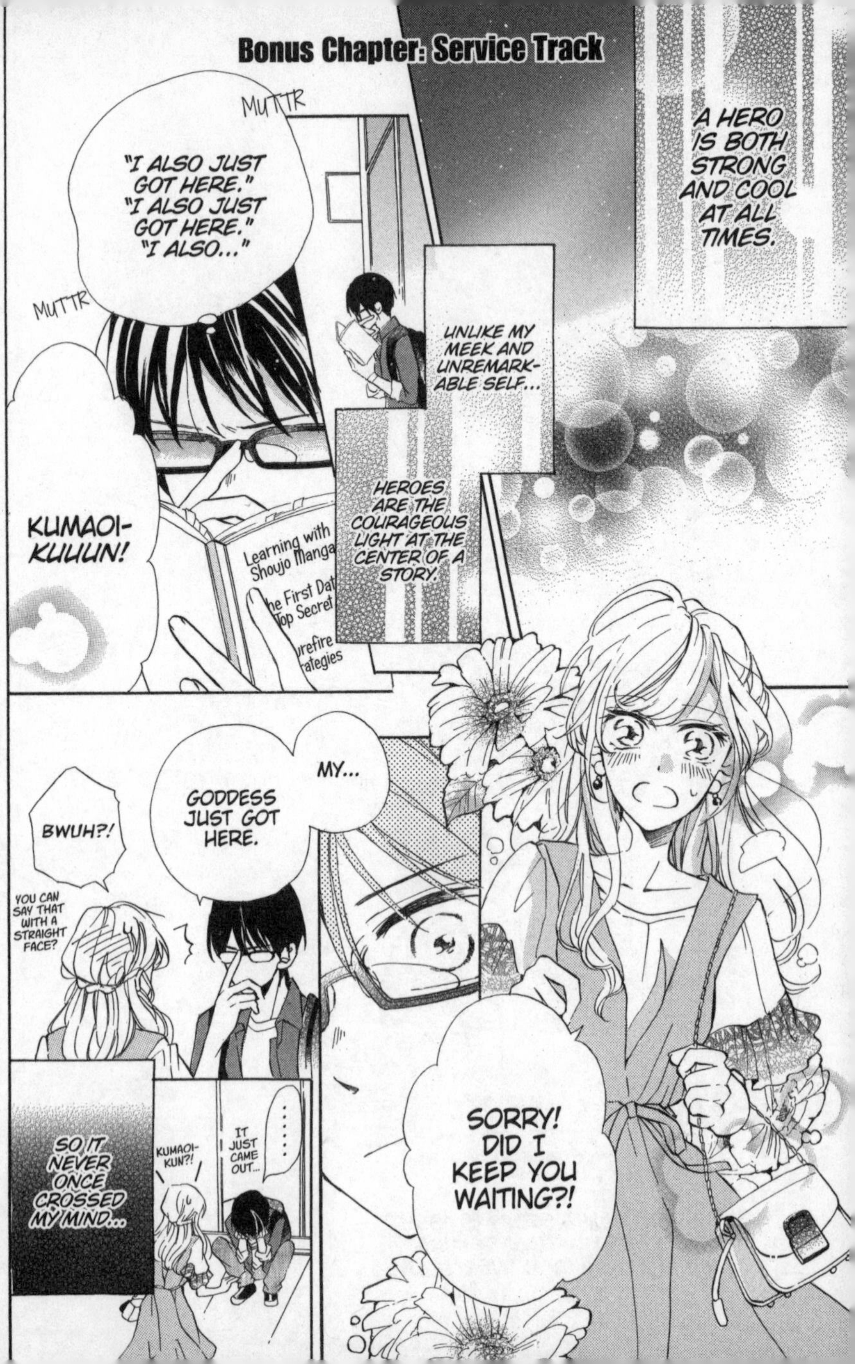

A HERO IS BOTH STRONG AND COOL AT ALL TIMES.
UNLIKE MY MEEK AND UNREMARKABLE SELF...
HEROES ARE THE COURAGEOUS LIGHT AT THE CENTER OF A STORY.
MUTTR
"I ALSO JUST GOT HERE." "I ALSO JUST GOT HERE." "I ALSO..."
MUTTR
Learning with Shoujo Manga
KUMAOI-KUUUN!
SORRY! DID I KEEP YOU WAITING?!
MY...
GODDESS JUST GOT HERE.
BWUH?!
YOU CAN SAY THAT WITH A STRAIGHT FACE?
SO IT NEVER ONCE CROSSED MY MIND...
......
IT JUST CAME OUT...
KUMAOI-KUN?!

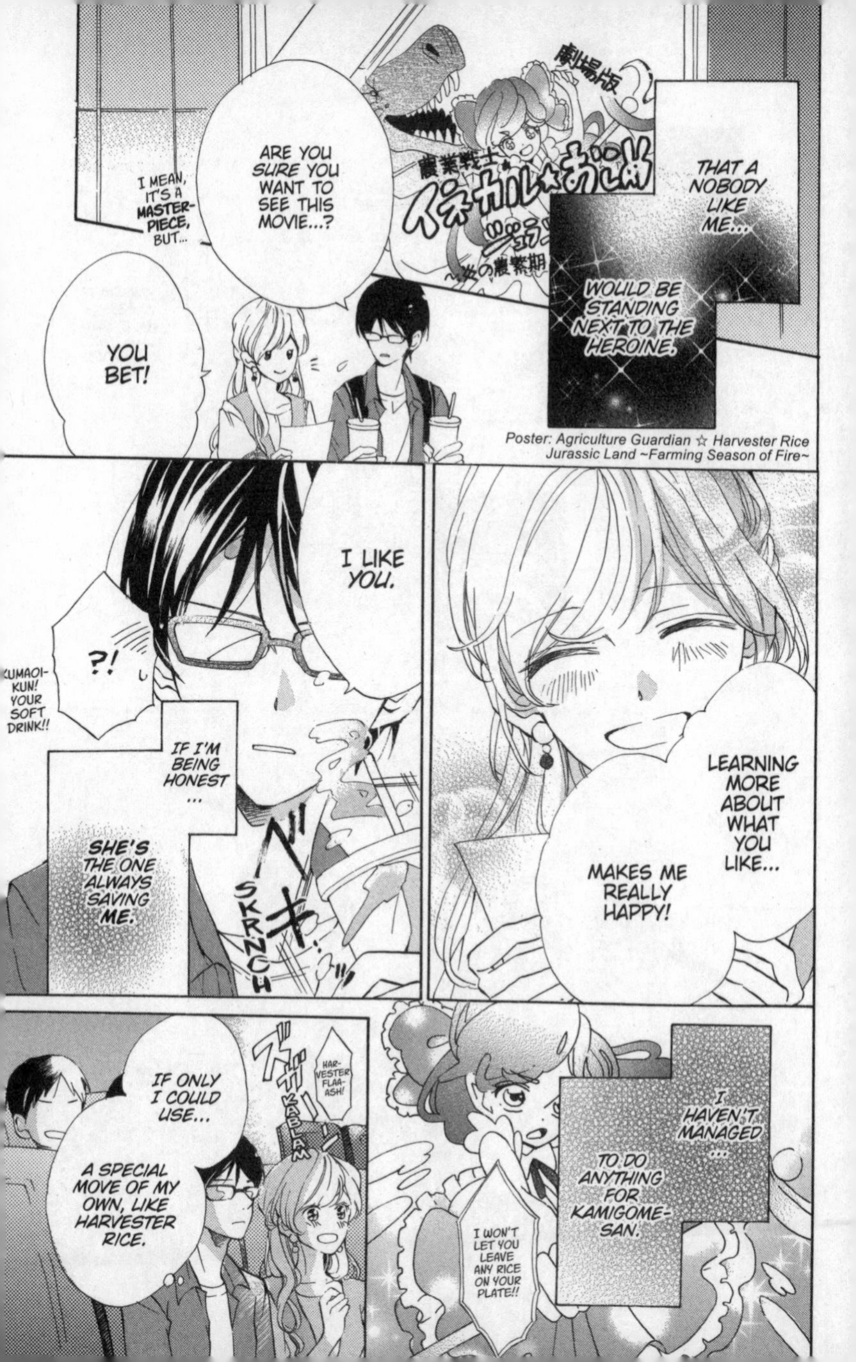
THAT A NOBODY LIKE ME...
WOULD BE STANDING NEXT TO THE HEROINE.
劇場版
農業戦士
ARE YOU SURE YOU WANT TO SEE THIS MOVIE...?
I MEAN, IT'S A MASTER-PIECE, BUT...
YOU BET!
Poster: Agriculture Guardian ☆ Harvester Rice
Jurassic Land ~Farming Season of Fire~
LEARNING MORE ABOUT WHAT YOU LIKE...
MAKES ME REALLY HAPPY!
I LIKE YOU.
?!
KUMAOI-KUN! YOUR SOFT DRINK!!
IF I'M BEING HONEST...
SHE'S THE ONE ALWAYS SAVING ME.
SKRNCH
I HAVEN'T MANAGED...
TO DO ANYTHING FOR KAMIGOME-SAN.
I WON'T LET YOU LEAVE ANY RICE ON YOUR PLATE!!
HARVESTER FLAASH!
KABLAM
IF ONLY I COULD USE...
A SPECIAL MOVE OF MY OWN, LIKE HARVESTER RICE.

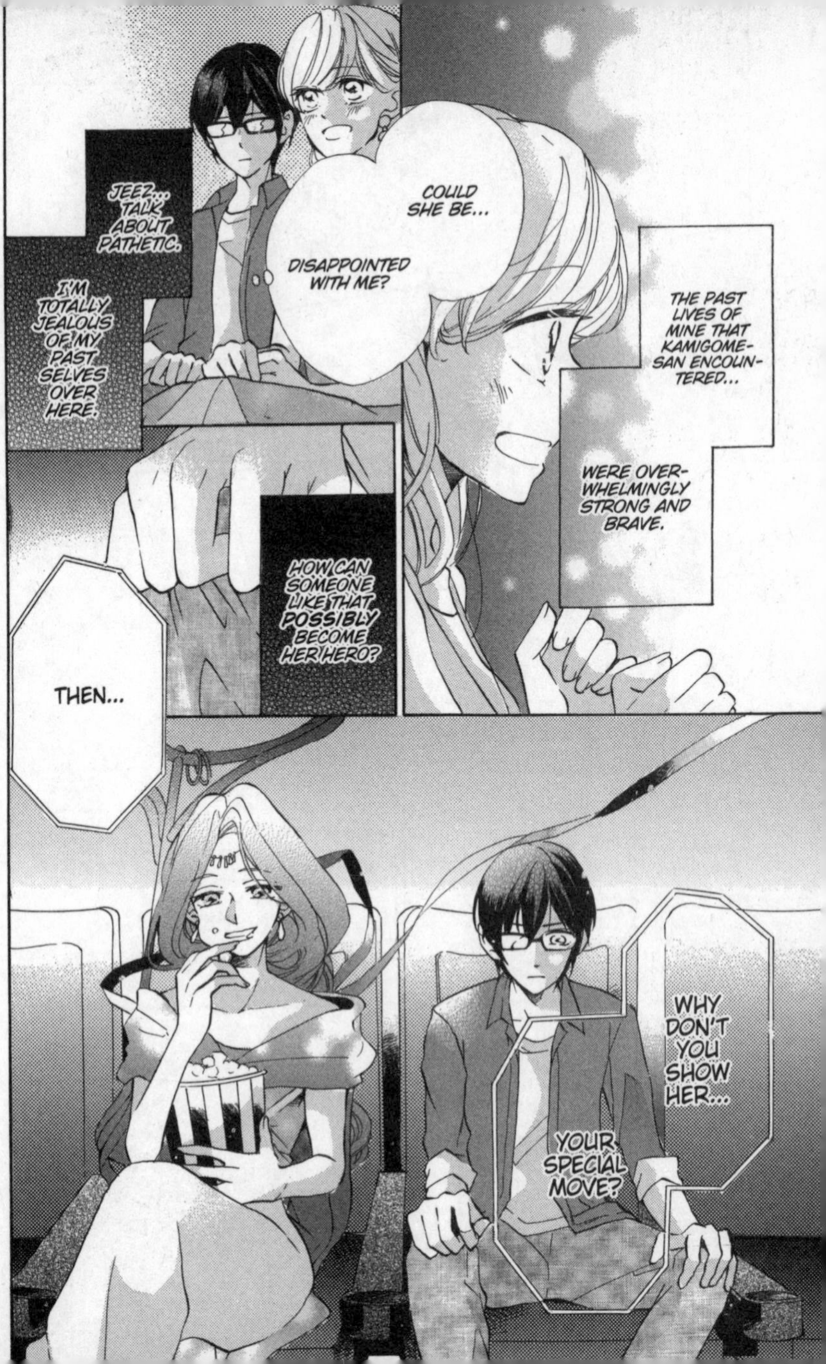
COULD SHE BE...
DISAPPOINTED WITH ME?
THE PAST LIVES OF MINE THAT KAMIGOME-SAN ENCOUNTERED...
WERE OVERWHELMINGLY STRONG AND BRAVE.
JEEZ... TALK ABOUT PATHETIC.
I'M TOTALLY JEALOUS OF MY PAST SELVES OVER HERE.
HOW CAN SOMEONE LIKE THAT POSSIBLY BECOME HER HERO?
THEN...
WHY DON'T YOU SHOW HER...
YOUR SPECIAL MOVE?

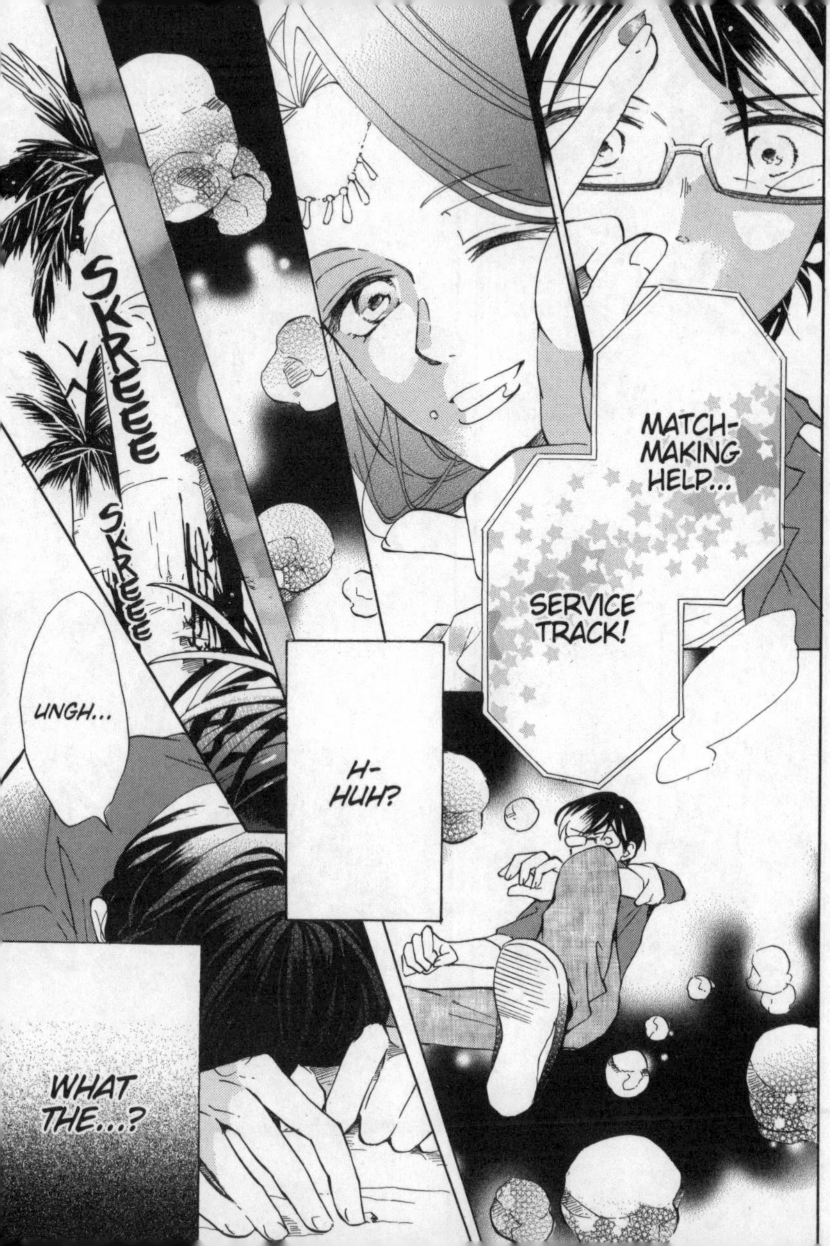
MATCH-MAKING HELP...
SERVICE TRACK!
SKREEEE
SKREEE
H-HUH?
UNGH...
WHAT THE...?

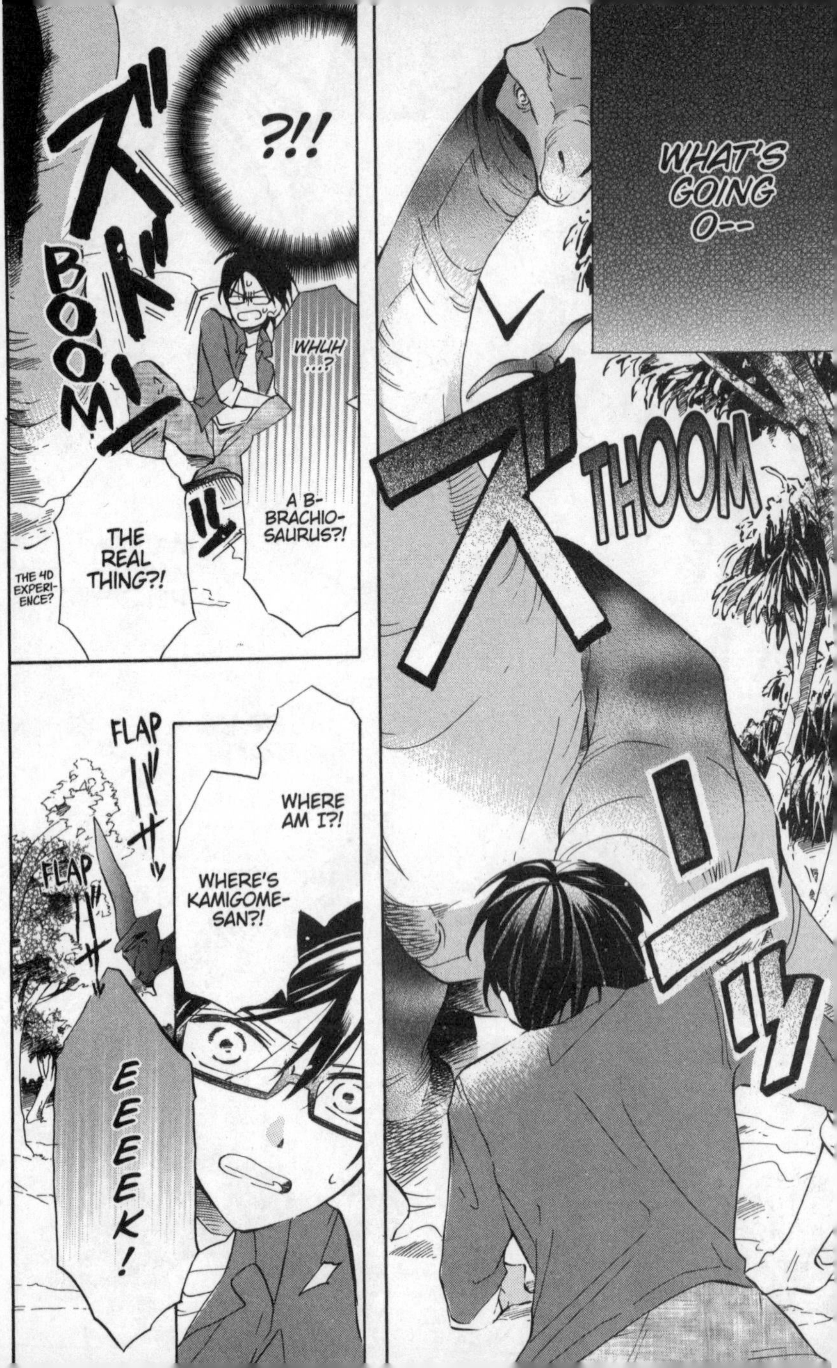
WHAT'S GOING O--
THOOM
?!!
BOOM!
WHUH ...?
A B-BRACHIO-SAURUS?!
THE REAL THING?!
THE 4D EXPERI-ENCE?
WHERE AM I?!
WHERE'S KAMIGOME-SAN?!
FLAP
FLAP
EEEEEK!

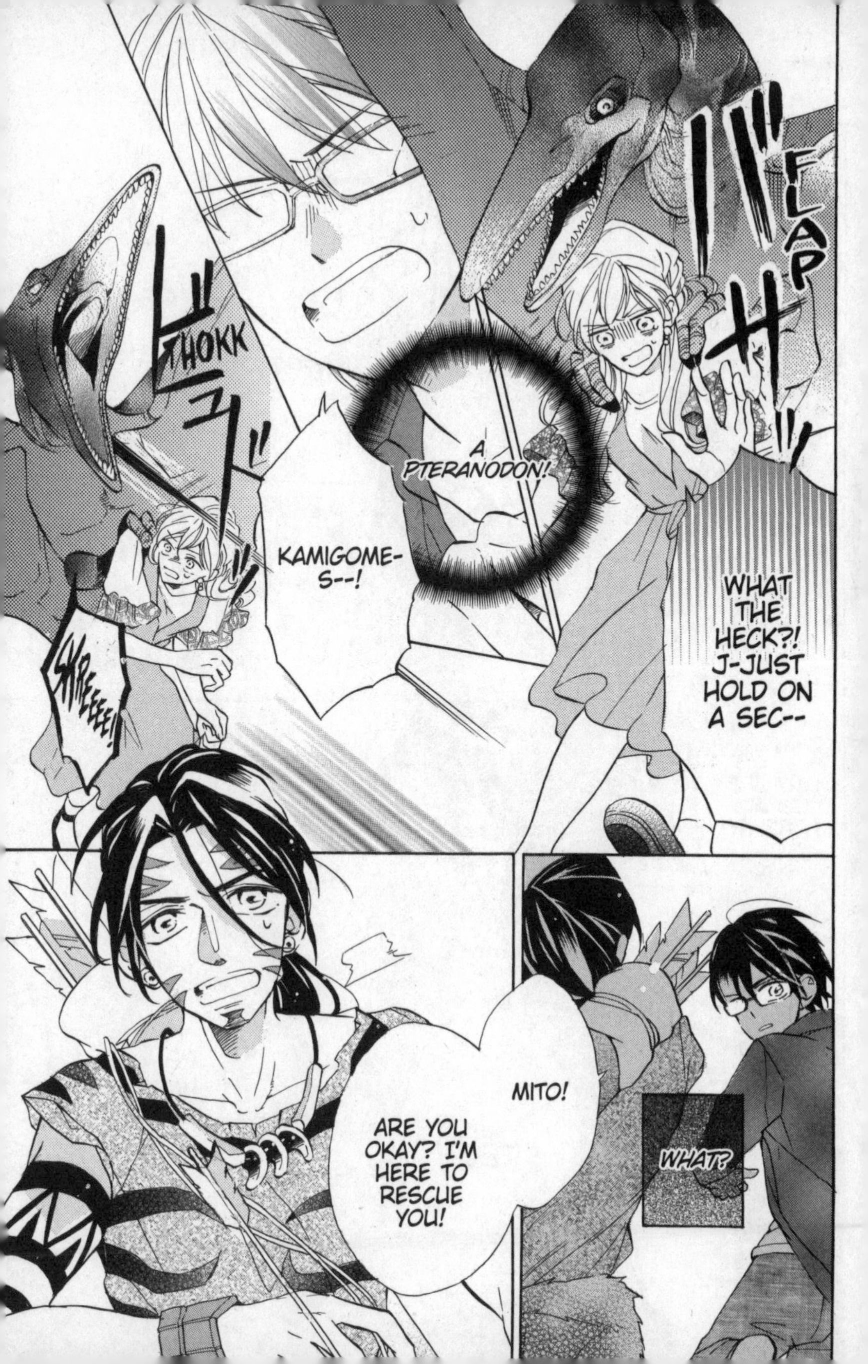
FLAP
A PTERANODON!
WHAT THE HECK?! J-JUST HOLD ON A SEC--
THOKK
KAMIGOMES--!
SHREEEE!
MITO!
ARE YOU OKAY? I'M HERE TO RESCUE YOU!
WHAT?

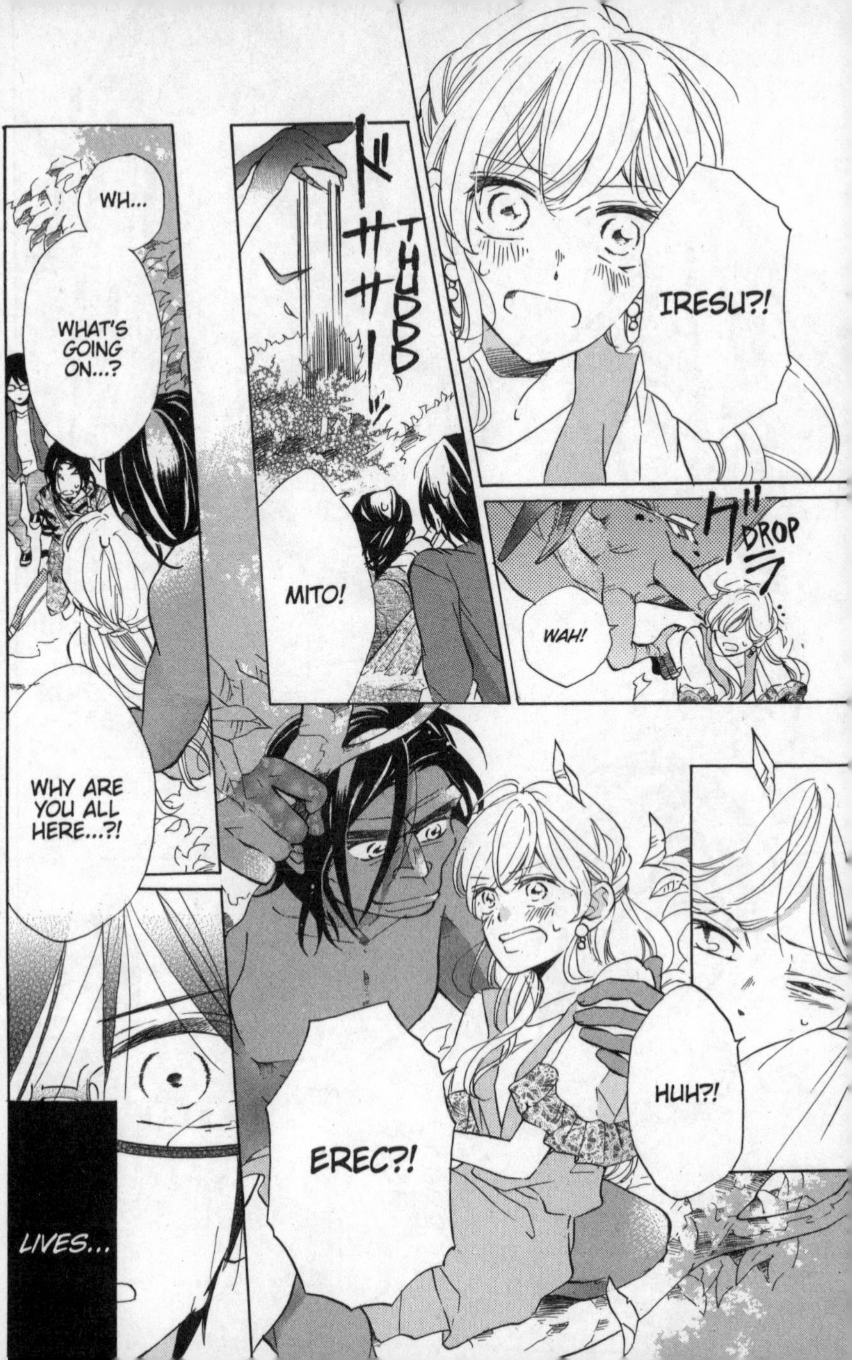
IRESU?!
DROP
WAH!
THUDD
MITO!
WH...
WHAT'S GOING ON...?
WHY ARE YOU ALL HERE...?!
HUH?!
EREC?!
LIVES...

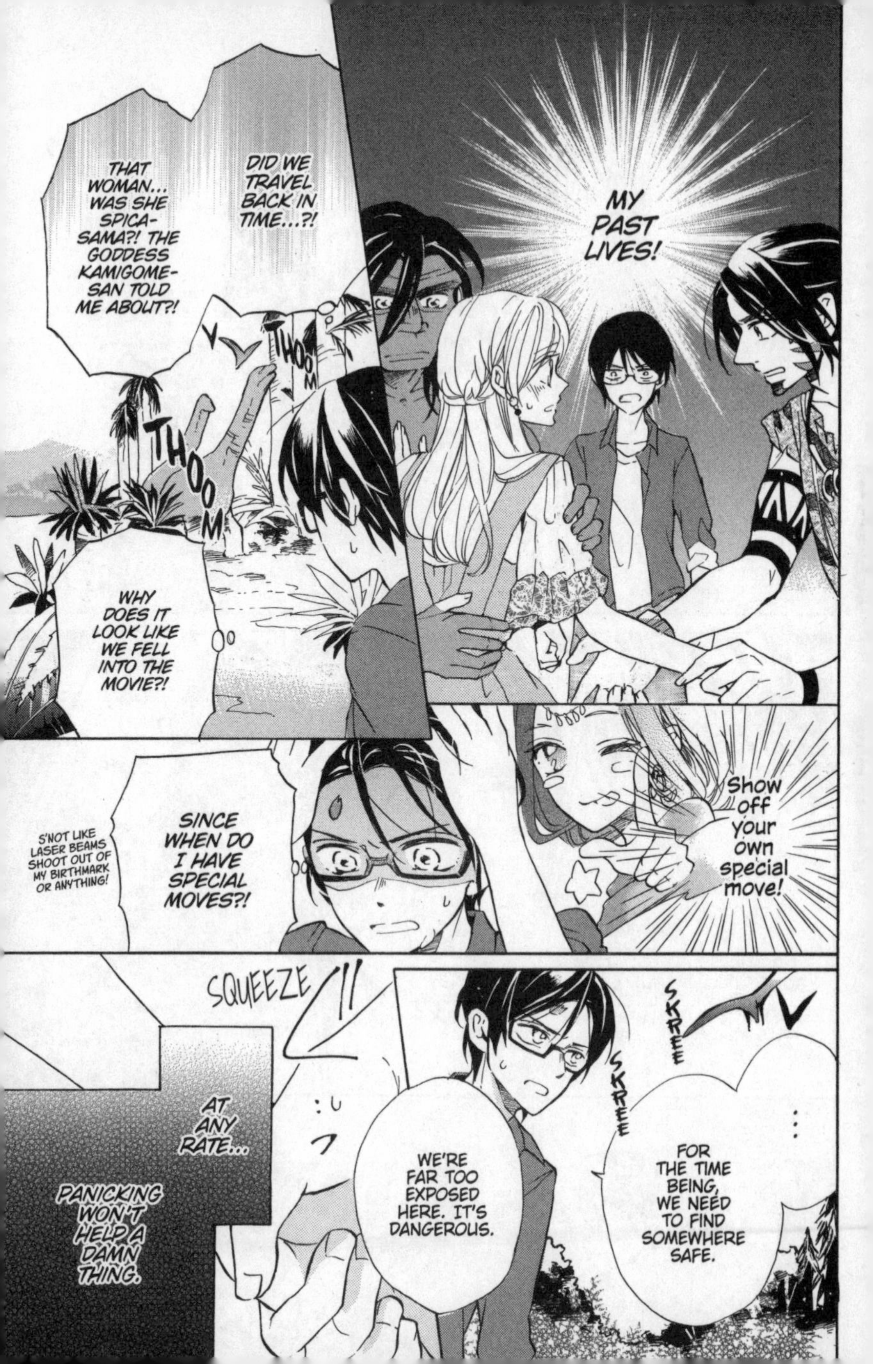
MY PAST LIVES!
DID WE TRAVEL BACK IN TIME...?!
THAT WOMAN... WAS SHE SPICA-SAMA?! THE GODDESS KAMIGOME-SAN TOLD ME ABOUT?!
THOOM
THOOM
WHY DOES IT LOOK LIKE WE FELL INTO THE MOVIE?!
Show off your own special move!
SINCE WHEN DO I HAVE SPECIAL MOVES?!
S'NOT LIKE LASER BEAMS SHOOT OUT OF MY BIRTHMARK OR ANYTHING!
SKRE
SKRE
SQUEEZE
FOR THE TIME BEING, WE NEED TO FIND SOMEWHERE SAFE.
WE'RE FAR TOO EXPOSED HERE. IT'S DANGEROUS.
AT ANY RATE...
PANICKING WON'T HELP A DAMN THING.

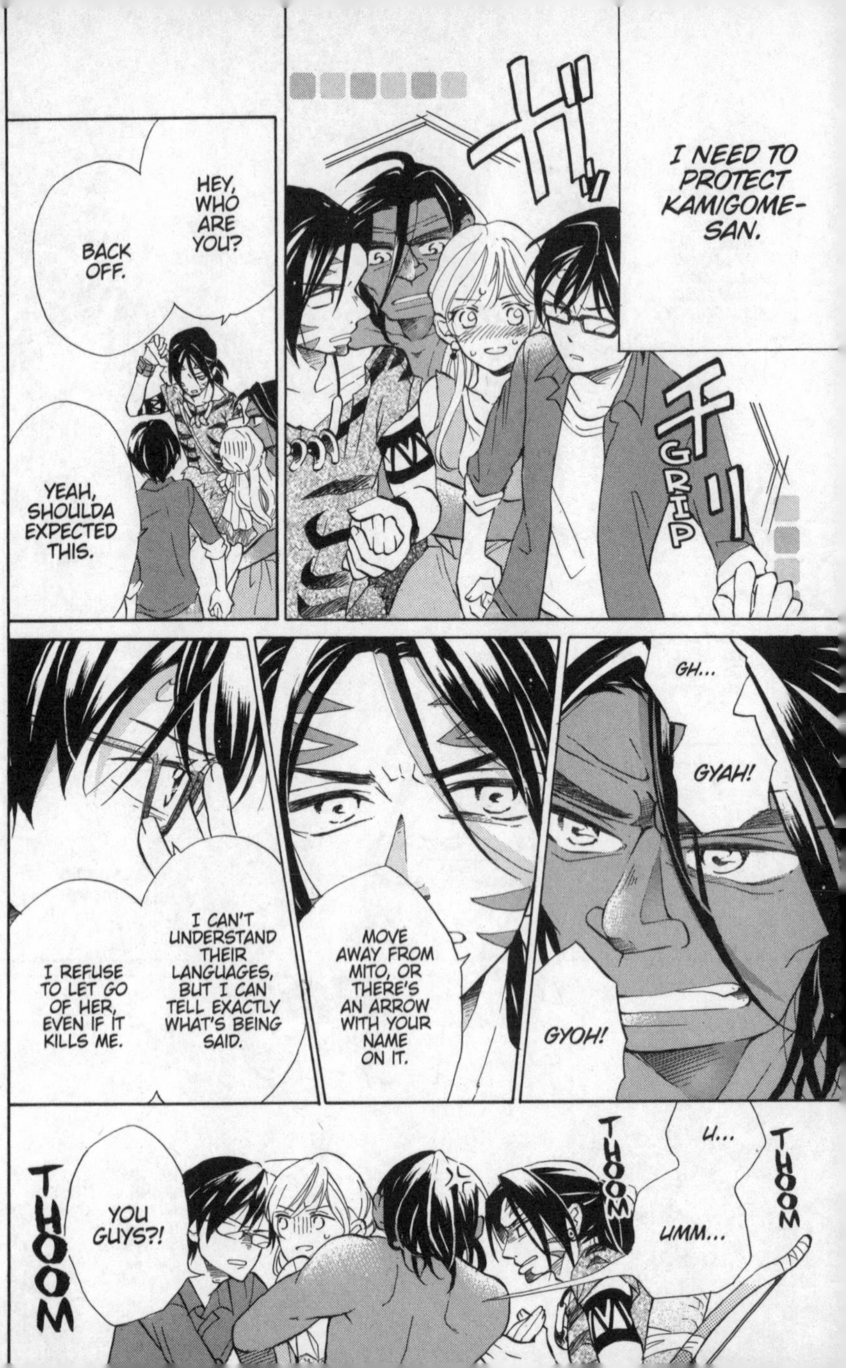
I NEED TO PROTECT KAMIGOME-SAN.
GRIP
HEY, WHO ARE YOU?
BACK OFF.
YEAH, SHOULDA EXPECTED THIS.
GH...
GYAH!
GYOH!
MOVE AWAY FROM MITO, OR THERE'S AN ARROW WITH YOUR NAME ON IT.
I CAN'T UNDERSTAND THEIR LANGUAGES, BUT I CAN TELL EXACTLY WHAT'S BEING SAID.
I REFUSE TO LET GO OF HER, EVEN IF IT KILLS ME.
THOOM
U...
UMM...
THOOM
YOU GUYS?!
THOOM

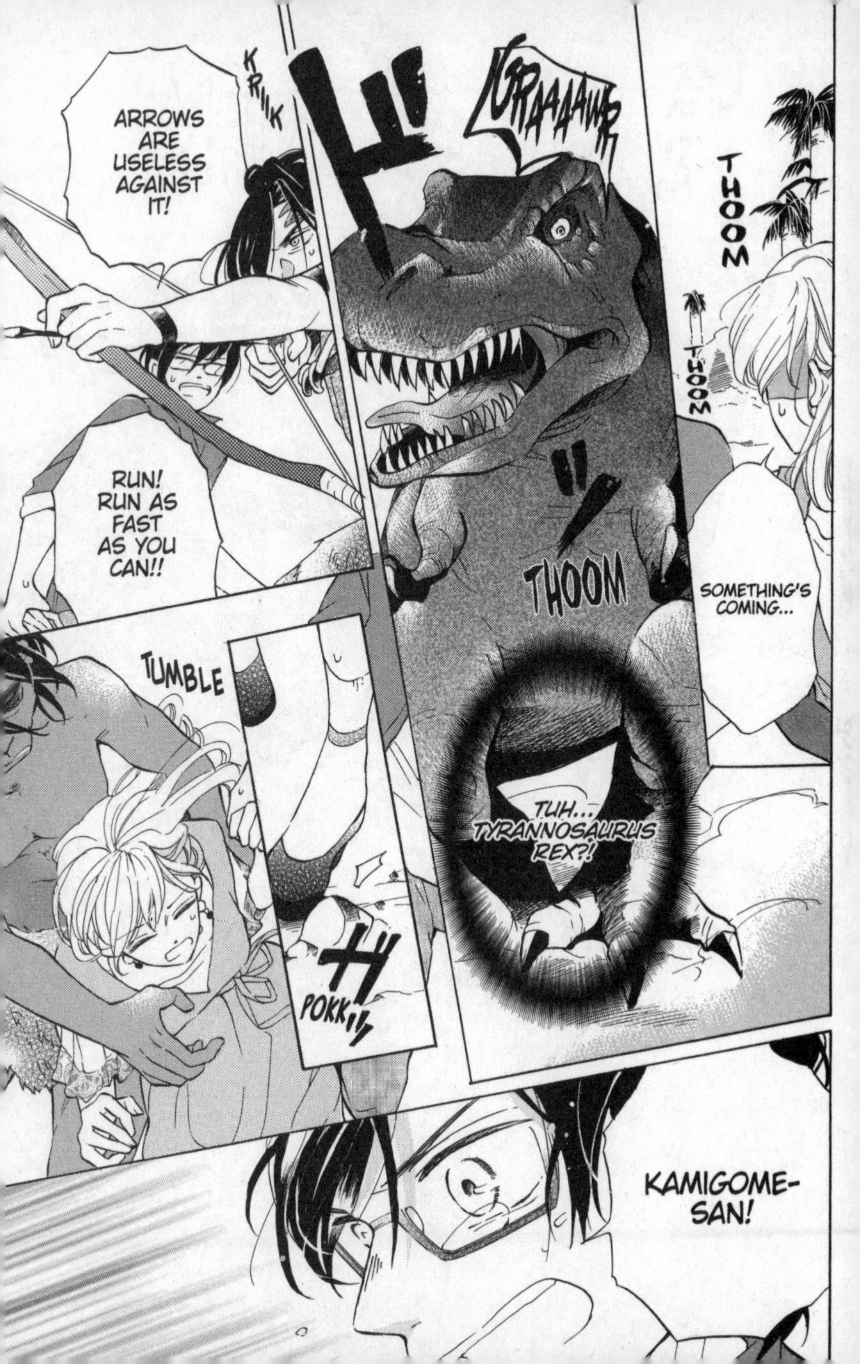
THOOM
THOOM
SOMETHING'S COMING...
GRAAAAWR
THOOM
TUH... TYRANNOSAURUS REX?!
KRIIK
ARROWS ARE USELESS AGAINST IT!
RUN! RUN AS FAST AS YOU CAN!!
POKK
TUMBLE
KAMIGOME-SAN!

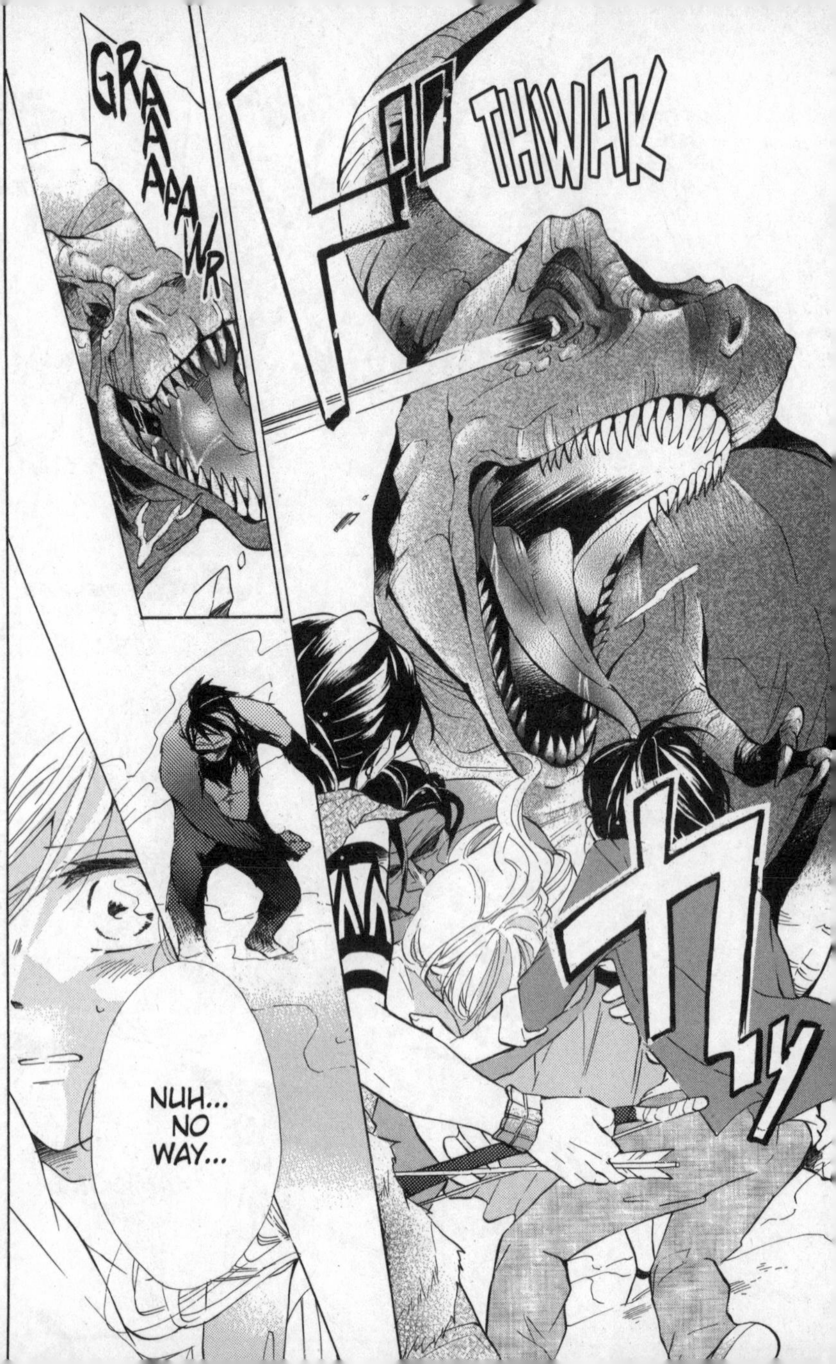
THWAK
GRAAAPAWR
NUH... NO WAY...

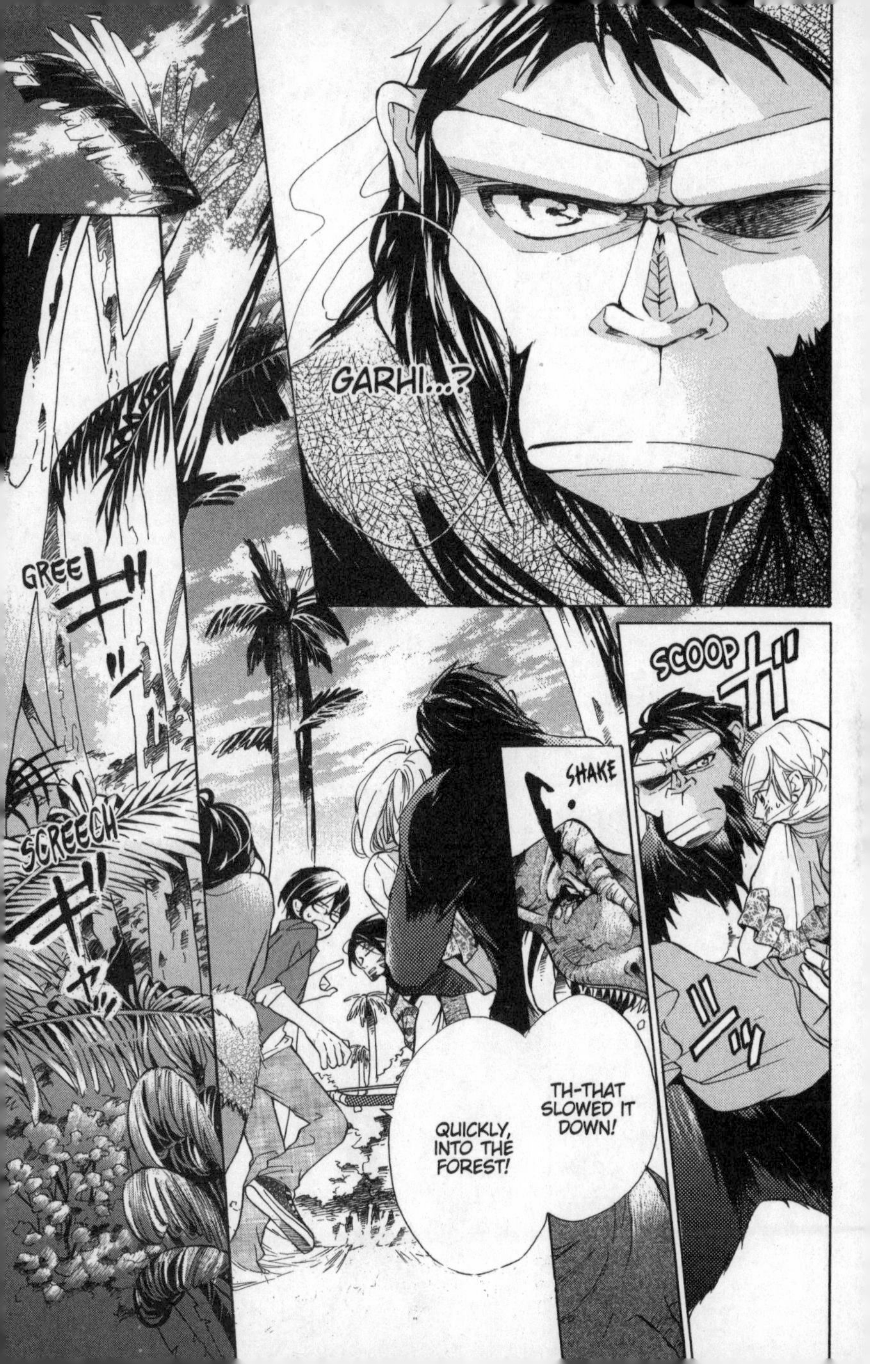
GARHI...?
SCOOP
SHAKE
TH-THAT SLOWED IT DOWN!
QUICKLY, INTO THE FOREST!
GREE
SCREECH

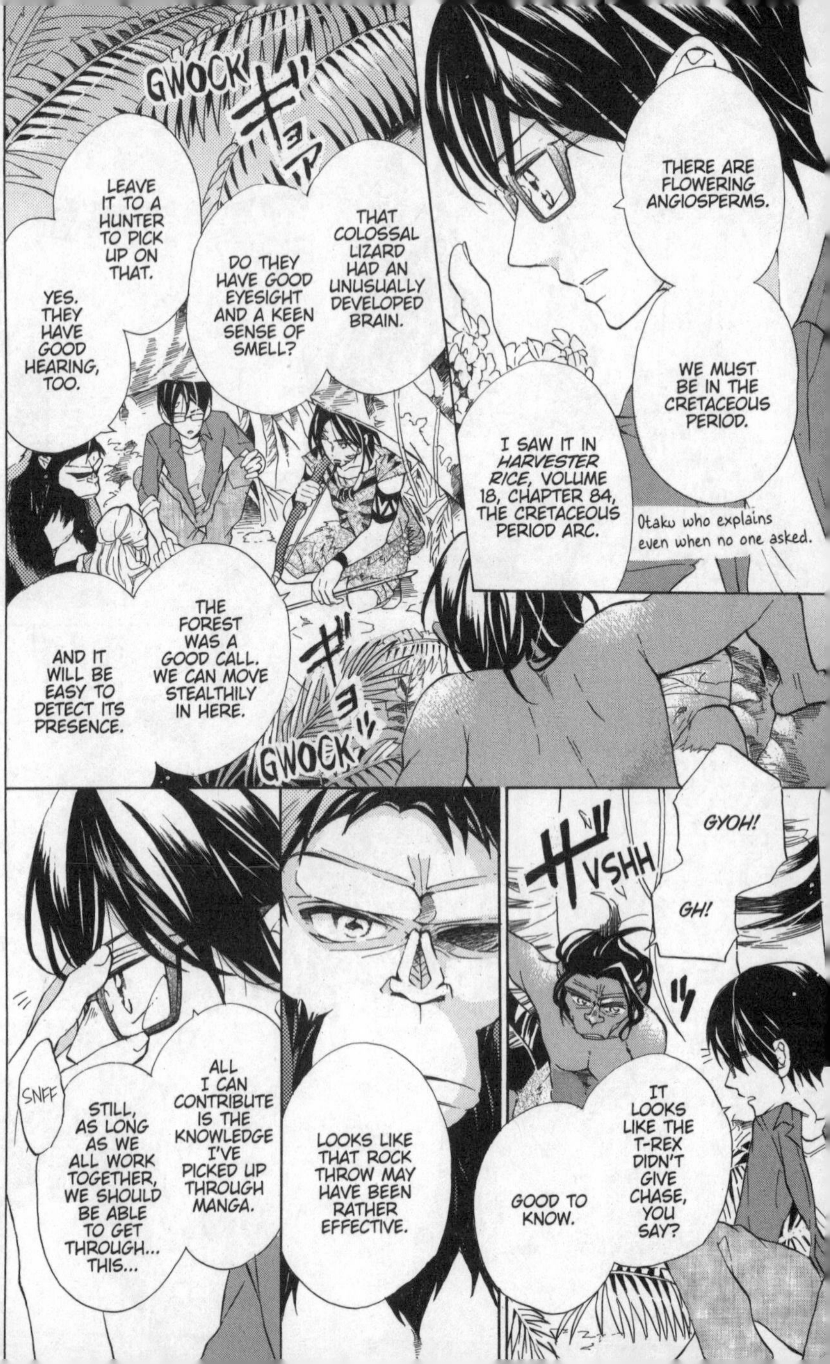
THERE ARE FLOWERING ANGIOSPERMS.
WE MUST BE IN THE CRETACEOUS PERIOD.
I SAW IT IN *HARVESTER RICE*, VOLUME 18, CHAPTER 84, THE CRETACEOUS PERIOD ARC.
Otaku who explains even when no one asked.
GWOCK
THAT COLOSSAL LIZARD HAD AN UNUSUALLY DEVELOPED BRAIN.
DO THEY HAVE GOOD EYESIGHT AND A KEEN SENSE OF SMELL?
LEAVE IT TO A HUNTER TO PICK UP ON THAT.
YES. THEY HAVE GOOD HEARING, TOO.
GWOCK
THE FOREST WAS A GOOD CALL. WE CAN MOVE STEALTHILY IN HERE.
AND IT WILL BE EASY TO DETECT ITS PRESENCE.
VSHH
GYOH!
GH!
IT LOOKS LIKE THE T-REX DIDN'T GIVE CHASE, YOU SAY?
GOOD TO KNOW.
LOOKS LIKE THAT ROCK THROW MAY HAVE BEEN RATHER EFFECTIVE.
ALL I CAN CONTRIBUTE IS THE KNOWLEDGE I'VE PICKED UP THROUGH MANGA.
SNFF
STILL, AS LONG AS WE ALL WORK TOGETHER, WE SHOULD BE ABLE TO GET THROUGH... THIS...

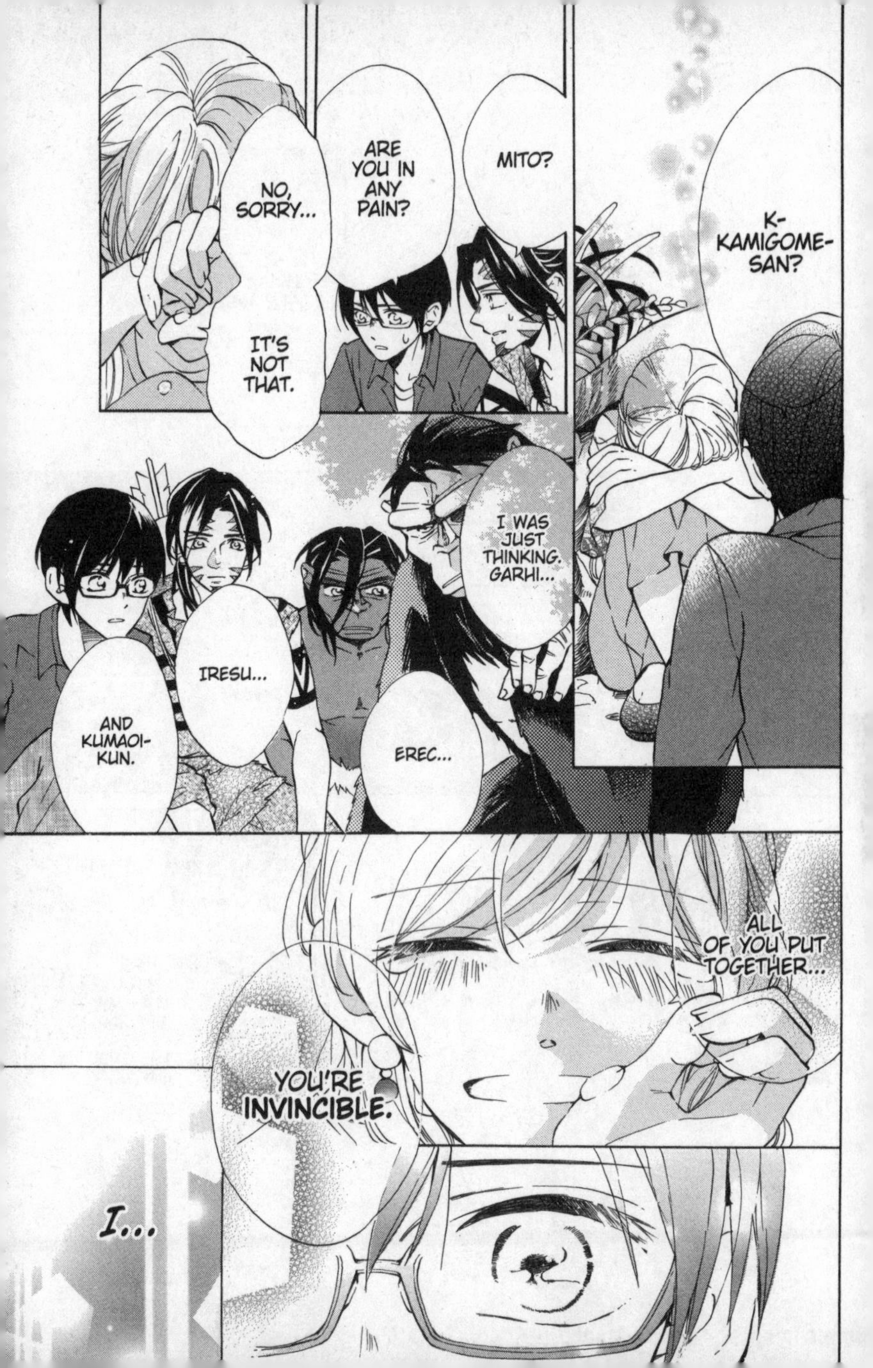
K-KAMIGOME-SAN?
MITO?
ARE YOU IN ANY PAIN?
NO, SORRY...
IT'S NOT THAT.
I WAS JUST THINKING. GARHI...
EREC...
IRESU...
AND KUMAOI-KUN.
ALL OF YOU PUT TOGETHER...
YOU'RE INVINCIBLE.
I...

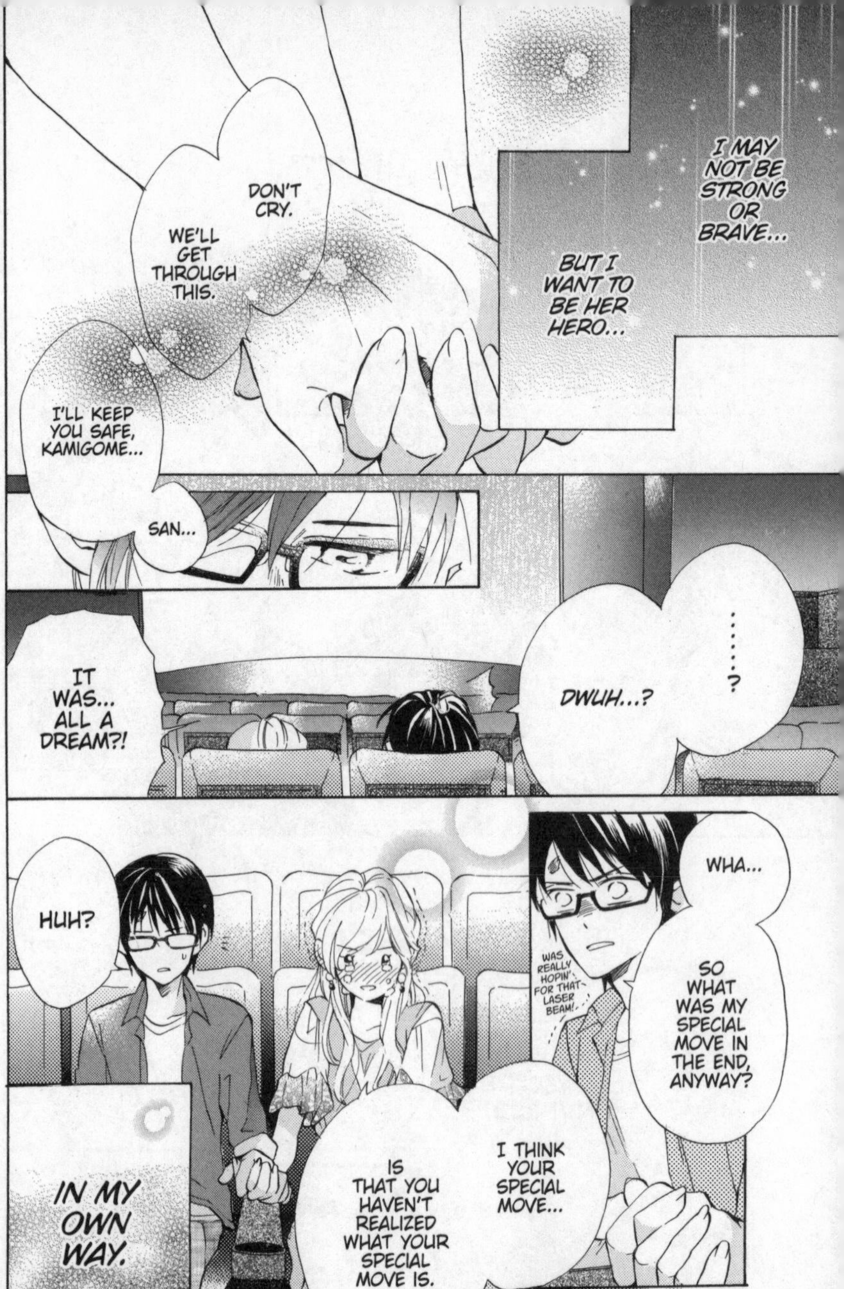
I MAY NOT BE STRONG OR BRAVE...
BUT I WANT TO BE HER HERO...
DON'T CRY.
WE'LL GET THROUGH THIS.
I'LL KEEP YOU SAFE, KAMIGOME...
SAN...
......?
DWUH...?
IT WAS... ALL A DREAM?!
WHA...
SO WHAT WAS MY SPECIAL MOVE IN THE END, ANYWAY?
WAS REALLY HOPIN' FOR THAT LASER BEAM!
HUH?
I THINK YOUR SPECIAL MOVE...
IS THAT YOU HAVEN'T REALIZED WHAT YOUR SPECIAL MOVE IS.
IN MY OWN WAY.

Bonus Chapter: Service Track / End

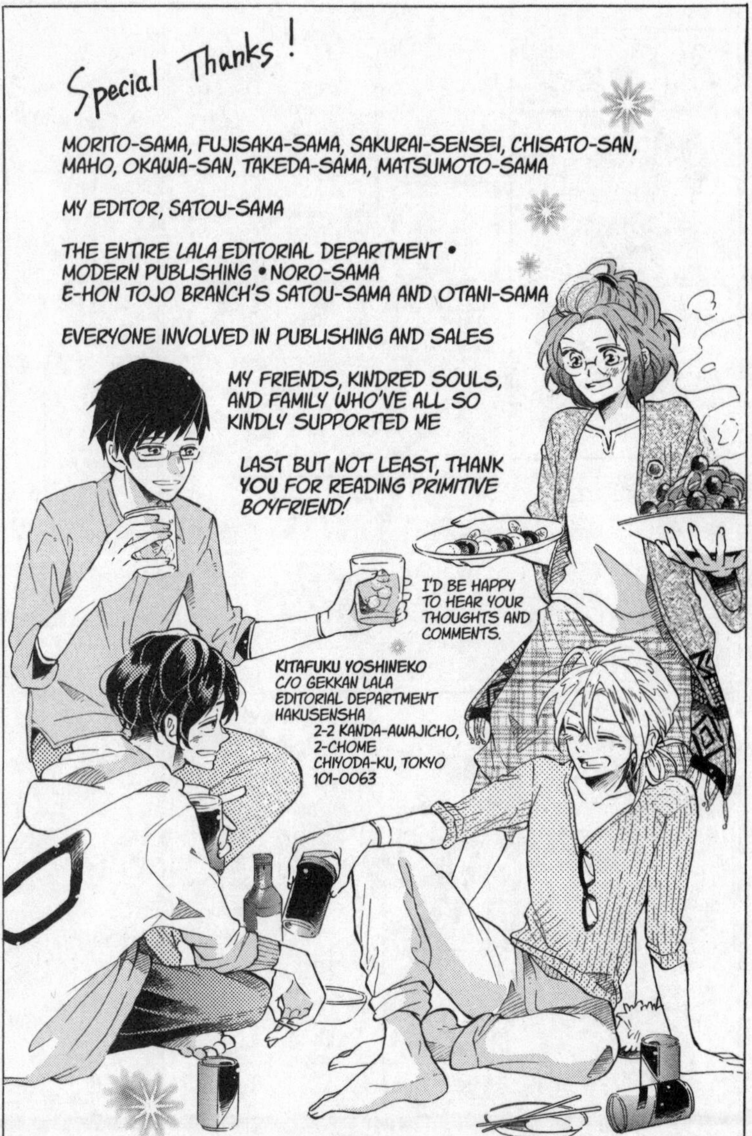
Special Thanks!
MORITO-SAMA, FUJISAKA-SAMA, SAKURAI-SENSEI, CHISATO-SAN, MAHO, OKAWA-SAN, TAKEDA-SAMA, MATSUMOTO-SAMA
MY EDITOR, SATOU-SAMA
THE ENTIRE LALA EDITORIAL DEPARTMENT • MODERN PUBLISHING • NORO-SAMA
E-HON TOJO BRANCH'S SATOU-SAMA AND OTANI-SAMA
EVERYONE INVOLVED IN PUBLISHING AND SALES
MY FRIENDS, KINDRED SOULS, AND FAMILY WHO'VE ALL SO KINDLY SUPPORTED ME
LAST BUT NOT LEAST, THANK YOU FOR READING PRIMITIVE BOYFRIEND!
I'D BE HAPPY TO HEAR YOUR THOUGHTS AND COMMENTS.
KITAFUKU YOSHINEKO
C/O GEKKAN LALA
EDITORIAL DEPARTMENT
HAKUSENSHA
2-2 KANDA-AWAJICHO,
2-CHOME
CHIYODA-KU, TOKYO
101-0063

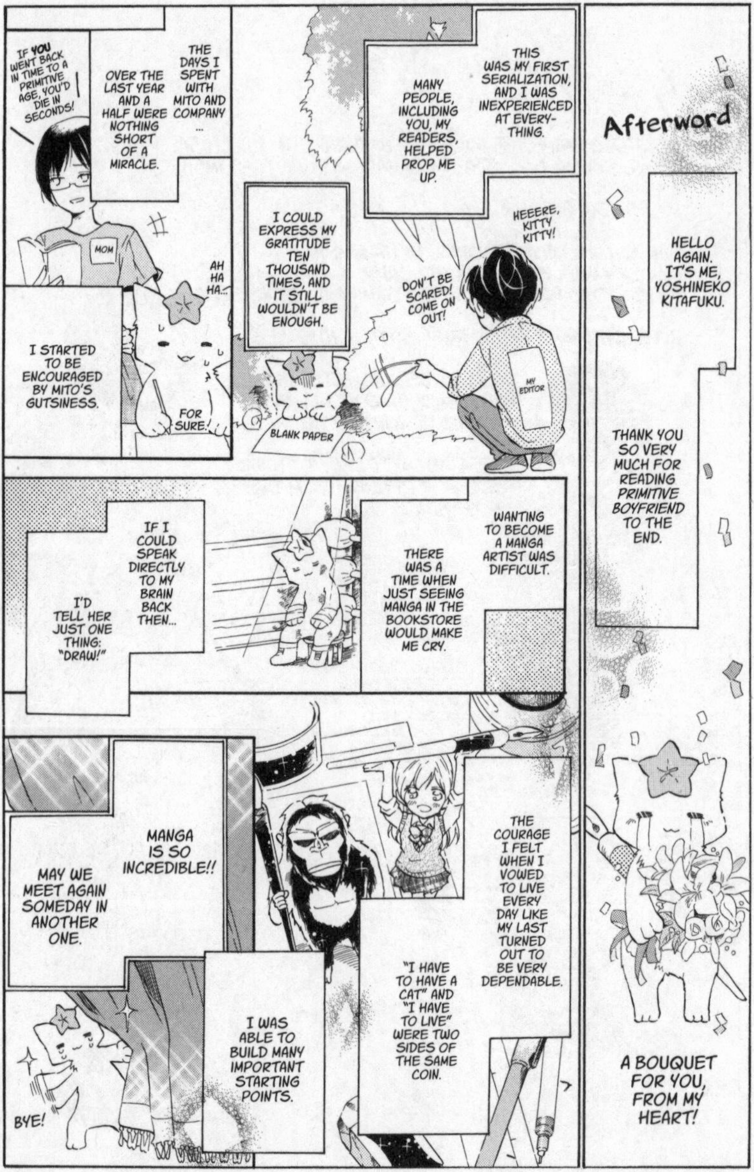

Afterword
HELLO AGAIN. IT'S ME, YOSHINEKO KITAFUKU.
THANK YOU SO VERY MUCH FOR READING PRIMITIVE BOYFRIEND TO THE END.
A BOUQUET FOR YOU, FROM MY HEART!
THIS WAS MY FIRST SERIALIZATION, AND I WAS INEXPERIENCED AT EVERY-THING.
MANY PEOPLE, INCLUDING YOU, MY READERS, HELPED PROP ME UP.
HEEERE, KITTY KITTY!
DON'T BE SCARED! COME ON OUT!
MY EDITOR
I COULD EXPRESS MY GRATITUDE TEN THOUSAND TIMES, AND IT STILL WOULDN'T BE ENOUGH.
BLANK PAPER
THE DAYS I SPENT WITH MITO AND COMPANY ...
OVER THE LAST YEAR AND A HALF WERE NOTHING SHORT OF A MIRACLE.
IF YOU WENT BACK IN TIME TO A PRIMITIVE AGE, YOU'D DIE IN SECONDS!
MOM
AH HA HA...
I STARTED TO BE ENCOURAGED BY MITO'S GUTSINESS.
FOR SURE.
WANTING TO BECOME A MANGA ARTIST WAS DIFFICULT.
THERE WAS A TIME WHEN JUST SEEING MANGA IN THE BOOKSTORE WOULD MAKE ME CRY.
IF I COULD SPEAK DIRECTLY TO MY BRAIN BACK THEN...
I'D TELL HER JUST ONE THING: "DRAW!"
THE COURAGE I FELT WHEN I VOWED TO LIVE EVERY DAY LIKE MY LAST TURNED OUT TO BE VERY DEPENDABLE.
"I HAVE TO HAVE A CAT" AND "I HAVE TO LIVE" WERE TWO SIDES OF THE SAME COIN.
I WAS ABLE TO BUILD MANY IMPORTANT STARTING POINTS.
MANGA IS SO INCREDIBLE!!
MAY WE MEET AGAIN SOMEDAY IN ANOTHER ONE.
BYE!

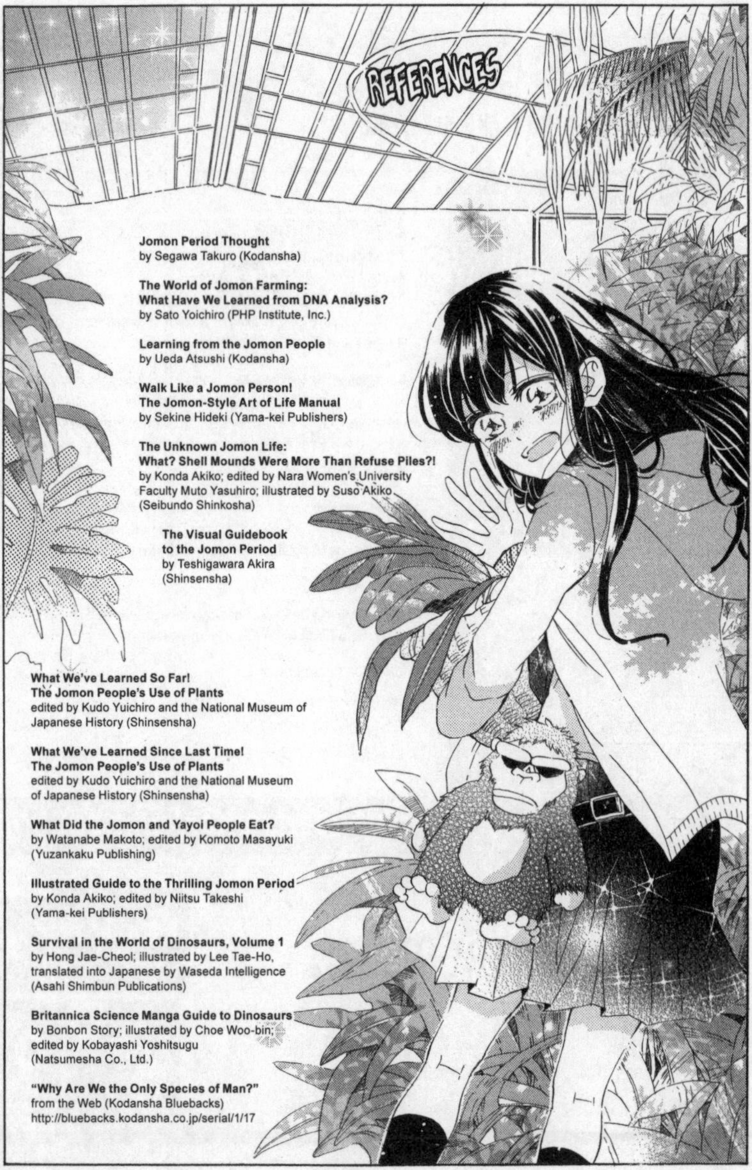

REFERENCES

Jomon Period Thought
by Segawa Takuro (Kodansha)

The World of Jomon Farming: What Have We Learned from DNA Analysis?
by Sato Yoichiro (PHP Institute, Inc.)

Learning from the Jomon People
by Ueda Atsushi (Kodansha)

Walk Like a Jomon Person! The Jomon-Style Art of Life Manual
by Sekine Hideki (Yama-kei Publishers)

The Unknown Jomon Life: What? Shell Mounds Were More Than Refuse Piles?!
by Konda Akiko; edited by Nara Women's University Faculty Muto Yasuhiro; illustrated by Suso Akiko (Seibundo Shinkosha)

The Visual Guidebook to the Jomon Period
by Teshigawara Akira (Shinsensha)

What We've Learned So Far! The Jomon People's Use of Plants
edited by Kudo Yuichiro and the National Museum of Japanese History (Shinsensha)

What We've Learned Since Last Time! The Jomon People's Use of Plants
edited by Kudo Yuichiro and the National Museum of Japanese History (Shinsensha)

What Did the Jomon and Yayoi People Eat?
by Watanabe Makoto; edited by Komoto Masayuki (Yuzankaku Publishing)

Illustrated Guide to the Thrilling Jomon Period
by Konda Akiko; edited by Niitsu Takeshi (Yama-kei Publishers)

Survival in the World of Dinosaurs, Volume 1
by Hong Jae-Cheol; illustrated by Lee Tae-Ho, translated into Japanese by Waseda Intelligence (Asahi Shimbun Publications)

Britannica Science Manga Guide to Dinosaurs
by Bonbon Story; illustrated by Choe Woo-bin; edited by Kobayashi Yoshitsugu (Natsumesha Co., Ltd.)

"Why Are We the Only Species of Man?"
from the Web (Kodansha Bluebacks)
http://bluebacks.kodansha.co.jp/serial/1/17

SEVEN SEAS ENTERTAINMENT PRESENTS

PRIMITIVE Boyfriend

story and art by YOSHINEKO KITAFUKU   VOLUME 3

TRANSLATION
Amanda Haley

ADAPTATION
David Lumsdon

LETTERING AND RETOUCH
Brandon Bovia

COVER DESIGN
Nicky Lim
George Panella (LOGO)

PROOFREADER
Kurestin Armada

EDITOR
Peter Adrian Behravesh

PREPRESS TECHNICIAN
Rhiannon Rasmussen-Silverstein

PRODUCTION MANAGER
Lissa Pattillo

MANAGING EDITOR
Julie Davis

ASSOCIATE PUBLISHER
Adam Arnold

PUBLISHER
Jason DeAngelis

GENSHIJIN KARESHI
by YOSHINEKO KITAFUKU
© Yoshineko Kitafuku 2018
All rights reserved.
First published in Japan in 2018 by HAKUSENSHA, INC., Tokyo.
English language translation rights in U.S.A. arranged with HAKUSENSHA, INC.,
Tokyo through TOHAN CORPORATION, Tokyo.

Seven Seas press and purchase enquiries can be sent to Marketing Manager
Lianne Sentar at press@gomanga.com. Information regarding the distribution
and purchase of digital editions is available from Digital Manager CK Russell
at digital@gomanga.com.

Seven Seas and the Seven Seas logo are trademarks of
Seven Seas Entertainment. All rights reserved.

ISBN: 978-1-64505-780-2

Printed in Canada

First Printing: November 2020

10 9 8 7 6 5 4 3 2 1

FOLLOW US ONLINE: www.sevenseasentertainment.com

READING DIRECTIONS

This book reads from *right to left*, Japanese style.
If this is your first time reading manga, you start
reading from the top right panel on each page and
take it from there. If you get lost, just follow the
numbered diagram here. It may seem backwards at
first, but you'll get the hang of it! Have fun!!

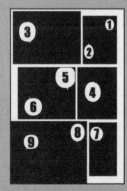